HISTORY OF EUROPE
1450–1660

HISTORY OF EUROPE
1450—1660

P. J. HELM

FREDERICK UNGAR PUBLISHING CO.
NEW YORK

Copyright © 1961 by
G. Bell and Sons Ltd

First published 1961
Reprinted 1963
First American edition 1964
by arrangement with the original publishers

Printed in Great Britain

CONTENTS

v

LIST OF MAPS

PREFACE

'And freely men confess that this world's spent,
When in the Planets, and the Firmament
They seek so many new; . . .'

John Donne, 1610

THE period covered by this book was one in which the whole social, political, and intellectual structure of western Europe changed. It is this that gives to the age its fascination and its importance. The rate of change was far greater than it had ever been in the past. It is arguable that the revolutions that occurred were also greater in character – though not, of course, in degree – than those of later centuries. Europe, still essentially medieval in the fifteenth century, was standing by 1660 on the threshold of modern times. 'We may take the line,' Professor Butterfield has written, 'that here, for practical purposes, our modern civilization is coming out in a perceptible manner into the daylight.'

No other period seems to me to bear such a strong resemblance to the present day as that of the sixteenth and seventeenth centuries. Its problems are our problems. A conflict of ideologies cutting across national loyalties; the faint beginnings of that scientific revolution which now envelops us all; a sudden recession of old horizons as new worlds become accessible – those are only some of the ways in which one age echoes the other. Calvinist and Communist; *Santa Maria* and *Sputnik*; Galileo's telescope and the radio antennae at Jodrell Bank – the parallels are not exact, but the similarities exist.

At the end of each chapter there are some suggestions for further reading. These are clearly not intended as a comprehensive bibliography, but simply as suggestions of places where the theme of the chapter is developed more fully. At the end of sections or chapters there are also a few short extracts from contemporary sources or later historical works. It is hoped that these will indicate the great variety of narrative material available, usually in English, and will also throw some additional light, direct or oblique, on the subject-matter of the preceding chapter.

xi

Appreciation is expressed to various publishers for permission to quote passages from works still in copyright. The map on page 137 is based on a plate in the *Cambridge Modern History Atlas* with the permission of the Cambridge University Press. Finally, thanks are offered to all those who have helped me with the production of this book.

P.J.H.

I · THE RENAISSANCE PERIOD

Introductory: What was the Renaissance?

BECAUSE the historian, unlike the scientist, uses terms the meaning of which cannot be exactly defined, he must always be sure of two things: first, that he is quite clear in his own mind as to the meaning he is giving to the abstract words he uses; and second, that he makes this meaning clear to others. (He must also, of course, be able to give good reasons for using his terms in the way he does.) 'Liberty', 'feudalism', 'the Reformation', 'Greek democracy' – terms like these are the shorthand of history, but they are imprecise (the degree of imprecision varies) and useless until you, and those to whom you are talking, are clear as to just what you mean when you use them. Then you may still disagree, but at least you will both understand why you are disagreeing.

There has been a long historical debate about the meaning that should be attached to the term 'the Renaissance'. Literally it means a rebirth or revival. Italians of the fourteenth and fifteenth centuries certainly felt that they were living in a time of change, and the more intellectual of them saw as its special characteristic a reawakened interest in, and admiration for, some aspects of Classical civilization. They spoke of a rebirth (*renascita*) of art and letters.

One aspect of this revival was the writing of histories, as distinct from the rather diary-like chronicles of earlier centuries. The writers often divided these histories into three parts; the classical history of Greece and Rome, the period between the sack of Rome in 410 and the fifteenth century, and their own days – 'modern history'. By 1469 they were referring to the second of these divisions as a middle age, sometimes as a '*media tempestas*'. Much later, in the seventeenth century, this division of history into three periods was popularized by a dull German writer, Cellarius (1675). For him the Middle Ages stretched from the death of Constantine in 337 to the capture of Constantinople by the Turks in 1453. This division survived more or less untouched until the nineteenth century.

The idea of a threefold division of history, with the Renaissance lying at the beginning of modern times and marking the recovery of classical civilization and Christian morals, appealed to the eighteenth century age of reason and to the nineteenth century age of common-sense. Most historians took the view that modern times had rediscovered and improved on the virtues of the ancient world, among which they included rationalism, good roads and liberty. By contrast they regarded the Middle Ages as an unfortunate period of darkness, lasting for a thousand years, and characterized by superstition, despotism and deplorable hygiene.

'I have described the triumph of Barbarism and Religion', Gibbon wrote at the end of his *History of the Decline and Fall of the Roman Empire*, published in 1788. In the same century Voltaire had said of Gothic architecture, '. . . what unhappily remains to us of the architecture and sculpture of these times is a fantastic compound of rudeness and filigree.' The following extract from a nineteenth century book neatly summarizes, and does not caricature, the traditional Victorian attitude:

> The Graeco-Roman world had descended into the great hollow which is roughly called the Middle Ages, extending from the fifth to the fifteenth century, a hollow in which many great, beautiful, and heroic things were done and created, but in which knowledge, as we understand it, had no place. The revival of learning and the Renaissance are memorable as the first sturdy breasting by Humanity of the hither slope of the great hollow which lies between us and the Ancient World. The modern man, reformed and regenerated by knowledge, looks across it and recognises on the opposite ridge, in the far-shining cities and stately porticoes, in the art, politics and science of Antiquity, many more ties of kinship and sympathy than in the mighty concave between, wherein dwell his Christian ancestry, in the dim light of scholasticism and theology.[1]

This view of the medieval period, and of the relation of the Renaissance to it, is no longer tenable. The opinion of historians has altered. They do not consider the Middle Ages

[1] J. C. Morison; *The Service of Man*; Kegan Paul, 1887, pp. 177–8.

as uniformly dark, their architecture as quaint and barbarous. The twentieth century regards with a certain nostalgia the medieval emphasis on unity and faith. Historians now recognize that there was intellectual activity, change and development during the period.

At the same time the unique character of 'the Renaissance' has gone. On the one hand, medieval historians have taken over the term and applied it to earlier revivals of learning so that the Renaissance of the fourteenth and fifteenth centuries has become only the last and greatest in the series.[1] On the other hand, the writers of modern history have extended the meaning of the term so that it covers not only the rapid tempo of development in fifteenth century Europe, but also the changes that stemmed from it in the sixteenth and early seventeenth century – the Reformation, the Counter-Reformation, the rise of the nation-state and so on. The Renaissance has become a sort of holdall, stuffed with miscellaneous objects, splitting at the seams and insecurely held together with string.

Are we to regard this Renaissance period as one of rebirth, or as a grand finale – a hopeful sunrise, or a glorious sunset? The answer is that it contains something of both. In the spectrum the colour orange, for instance, lies between red and yellow; it is a colour with its own characteristics, but sharing the qualities of the colours on either side of it. Viewed in one way orange represents 'the decline and fall of red', viewed in another way it shows 'the rise and triumph of yellow' – and both views are correct. It is all a matter of selection. Much the same sort of thing applies to periods of history. The 'colour' of the later seventeenth century is very different from that of the fourteenth, and between the two lies the period of the Renaissance. By isolating different sets of facts it is possible to create a picture of a brilliant sunset or a promising dawn, for both aspects are present. What one can be sure of is that it was a time of rapid change, and it is perhaps most satisfactory to consider the Renaissance as a period in its own right.

Modern scholars have pointed out that in any scheme of periodization the central age of European history from the beginning of the fourteenth century to the end of the

[1] These earlier revivals include the Carolingian in the eighth century and that of the twelfth century based on Paris.

seventeenth, or at any rate to the Peace of Westphalia, should be regarded as a single unit and its culture and institutions studied as a whole.[1]

Within this highly important 'Renaissance period', lies the Renaissance proper, the new developments in art and thought. The term will be used in this restricted sense in Chapter II.

Renaissance Europe

If one takes one's stand at about the midpoint of this 'central age of European history', somewhere towards the close of the fifteenth century, and looks backwards and forwards, what are the salient characteristics that catch the eye? One is a new attitude of mind, that of the humanists, at once antiquarian and original; antiquarian in its devotion to classical models of style and conduct, but original in its critical, detached, impartial interest in the human mind and body, and in the world around it. Humanism found literary expression both in the study of classical and religious texts, and in the original composition of new works in the vernacular; in art men took over and made their own the styles of Greece and Rome, but at the same time they stressed, in sculpture and painting, individual differences and eccentricities of form. Medieval sculptors and miniaturists had observed individual details, but were not able to organize their observations into large compositions as the Renaissance artists could. (See Chapter II.)

Capitalism had begun to develop rapidly. In this context, capitalism may be defined as the use of money, or credit facilities – bills of exchange, etc. – in place of goods or services; as the accumulation of money profits, and as the use of these profits to finance new departures in trade, transport and industry. Examples of all these can be found in the later Middle Ages, but they are not widespread until the fifteenth and sixteenth centuries. Some of the earliest applications of surplus capital were made in the cities that stretched from central Italy to Lombardy and then down the Rhine to the North Sea. At first trade with Asia was firmly in the hands of the Italian ports, notably Venice, and of the Ottoman Turks, but during the fifteenth century first Portugal, and later Spain, broke this monopoly by sailing south round Africa or west across the Atlantic. In the process of explora-

[1] E. F. Jacob; 'Renaissance Origins'; *Times Literary Supplement*, January 6, 1956.

tion new techniques of navigation and shipbuilding were evolved. (See Chapter XIII.)

These new techniques were only one aspect of a wave of practical inventions and scientific speculation. The great age of scientific progress did not begin until the close of the sixteenth century. There were forerunners though, men such as Leonardo da Vinci, Copernicus and Vesalius. The use of gunpowder, and the development of printing, affected the age more directly, the latter by making easy the spread of the new learning, the former by making war so expensive that kings could no longer 'live of their own'. No new sources of power were developed until the close of the seventeenth century., (See Chapter XIV.)

Medieval Europe, though in fact politically fragmentary paid some sort of theoretical lip-service to the over-riding supremacy of Pope and Emperor; it acknowledged legal systems, such as canon law and merchant law, that were common throughout western Europe; the basic types of feudal holding and agricultural practice were modified by geographical differences rather than by state boundaries; the area shared one scholarly language, Latin, and one religion, the Catholic. There was thus a certain common civilization. The forces of change already described led to an emphasis on nationality, on local language and ultimately on local culture and local religions. A whole series of events was set in train. The appeal to the individual conscience was one of the springs of the Reformation. Encouraged by national rulers, the Reformers were successful in northern Europe, and their success helped to bring about the Catholic Counter-Reformation. The struggle between these two movements for the souls of western Europeans led to wars of religion which lasted until the theological subtleties were lost in purely political struggles between absolute monarchs. (See Chapters VI, VII, VIII, IX.)

The process by which the unified culture and restricted sovereignty of medieval Europe gave place to a collection of national, secular autocracies was a long-drawn-out one. It began, on a miniature scale, in fourteenth century Italy; France, Spain and England had acquired most of the characteristics by the early sixteenth century; by the middle of the seventeenth century the process had covered western Europe with the exception of Germany, and the eastern states of Russia and Brandenburg were being drawn into the western orbit. (See Chapters III, IV, V, X, XI, XII.)

Consider the political map of Europe about the year 1470. In the extreme southwest lay Portugal, with the same frontiers as today. Already a nation, she was wealthy and expanding. The fifteenth was her great century, during the next hundred years Spain would overhaul and temporarily (1580–1640) absorb her. The remainder of the peninsula contained four states: Castile, Aragon, Navarre and the Arab kingdom of Granada. In 1469 the marriage of Ferdinand of Aragon to Isabella of Castile led to the union of the two largest areas, and by 1512 Granada and Spanish Navarre had been added, to make up the kingdom of Spain.

North of the Pyrenees the French kings were pursuing a similar policy of consolidation. In 1453 the English had been driven out of all the country except Calais. The lands of the semi-independent vassals were falling under the control of the crown. Here Louis XI (1461–83) played the part that Ferdinand and Isabella were playing in Spain, acquiring Burgundy, Picardy, Anjou, Maine and Provence. His successor Charles VIII added Brittany, so that by 1500 France was much the same shape as she is today, with the exception of a small area of Spanish territory north of the Pyrenees (Roussillon), and with the important difference that her eastern frontier was still some eighty miles to the west of the Rhine.

England had lost her French possessions, and had suffered the civil wars of the Roses. The Yorkist Edward IV (1461–83) began to restore the power of the Crown, a work which was continued by the Tudor Henry VII. To the north, Scotland was still an independent kingdom and had much closer ties with France than with England. Across the North Sea the Scandinavian countries had been united under Danish rule in 1397. They provide an exception to the general process of unification, for Sweden broke away in 1523.

To the south of Scandinavia, in central Europe, lay the Holy Roman Empire. The Emperor was powerful enough to prevent separate independent states emerging, but not powerful enough to unite the area under his own rule. The Empire was a jigsaw puzzle of Dukes, Counts, Margraves, Archbishops, Electors, Free Cities and Imperial Knights.

Not counting the last of these, there were over 300 separate units. The Emperor was chosen by seven Electors, and after 1436 it became customary to elect the Habsburg Archduke of Austria. Although the Empire technically lingered on until 1806, in practice the rulers of Austria had, by the middle of the seventeenth century, created for themselves an independent state on the Middle Danube, while the Elector of Brandenburg was doing the same in north Germany.

The Habsburgs were given an incentive to build up a strong state by the fact that they lay in the path of the Ottoman Turks, who had invaded the Balkans in 1357, captured Constantinople in 1453, and were to reach the gates of Vienna itself in 1529. Throughout our period the Balkans lie outside the main stream of west European history, but the Turkish pressure is a factor which must always be taken into account.

In 1470 the north coast of the Black Sea was still controlled by the Mongol Khans, who penned the Duchy of Moscow into the northern forests. In 1481 the Russians defeated the Mongols and began a process of expansion that was to lead them towards Constantinople and the Baltic in one direction, and across Siberia to the coasts of the Pacific in the other.

Between France and the Empire stretched the richest, most densely populated, most urbanized part of Europe, from Flanders up the Rhine and through Italy as far as Rome. This strip was studded with semi-independent cities and communes. In the fifteenth century the Dukes of Burgundy had united most of this area north of the Alps under their rule, but this embryonic state miscarried on the death of Charles the Bold (1477). The dynastic wars of the next two hundred years largely represent a struggle between France and the Empire for the possession of this strip. In the end the Habsburgs got control of Milan and Flanders, while France obtained the central portion.

Switzerland had begun to break away from the Empire in the thirteenth century and although the Republic was not recognized till 1648, it was by 1470 for all practical purposes a self-governing state, the main export of which was mercenaries, supplied with impartiality to all customers.

The political structure of Italy requires a more detailed description. The seventy or eighty city-states of the late medieval period had by 1470 reduced themselves to five, with a few attendant satellites. All the peninsula south of Rome belonged to the kingdom of Naples. Most of it had been united for four hundred years and its civilization was very different from that of the centre and the north. The Spanish rulers of Aragon and the French dukes of Anjou both had claims to the throne of Naples, claims which were shortly to play an important part in the history of Italy.

North of Naples, and bisecting the peninsula diagonally, lay the Papal States. The strength of this area, and indeed its actual boundaries, varied with the strength of the Papacy. For the next sixty years the Popes were to be much concerned with questions of political power and artistic patronage, and during the second half of that period Rome was the cultural centre of Italy.

Beyond Rome to the north lay Florence. It had grown up as the home of a banking, trading, cloth-making urban middle-class. The city was usually ruled in effect by the house of Medici, bankers and political bosses:

> They were the quintessence of that bourgeois, trading, quick-witted people, adventurous, cautious, unscrupulous, greedy and envious, material and devout, sparing and ostentatious, rakes of a tender conscience, money-grubbers with a passion for art and literature, a coarse-grained folk with an exquisite, unfailing taste, who created ideal beauty through a laborious study of real men in a real world, who thirsted for violent sensations, while they added their accounts and haggled over farthings; . . .[1]

There were two great Medici. The first was Cosimo (1387–1464), who knew how to handle artists – 'One must treat these people of extraordinary genius,' he said, 'as if they were celestial spirits, and not like beasts of burden' – and vineyards too, for in February of each year he would prune his vines himself. He watches us with shrewd bourgeois eyes from *The Journey of the Magi* by Benozzo Gozzoli. In the same painting the other great Medici, his grandson Lorenzo 'Il Magnifico' (1449–92), rides as the youngest of the three kings – a greater patron, but a less successful business man. Under these men Florence became the centre of the cultural Renaissance, the education – as Pericles might have said –of

[1] C. W. Previté-Orton; 'The Medici', *History*, XXXII, No. 116.

Europe. Later Medici became Popes and Grand Dukes, but the family genius was gone – and the family fortunes also.

The north Italian plain was shared and disputed by Milan and Venice. The Duchy of Milan had become a powerful state in the fourteenth century under the Visconti, and Florence and Venice had had to struggle hard to prevent the family conquering all Italy north of the Papal States. In the fifteenth century the Duchy passed into the hands of the Sforzas, a family of *condottieri*. The French dukes of Orleans inherited a claim to the Duchy through the Visconti and this, like the French and Spanish claims to Naples, was soon to lead to war.

Venice was in some ways the most unusual state in Europe. Her government was that of a commercial oligarchy, headed by a Council of Ten, under the nominal leadership of a Doge (duke) elected for life. Based on trade and the control of the sea, her empire had expanded first along the Dalmatian coast, then east towards Syria through the islands of the Mediterranean. At the height of her power she maintained six fleets, 300 ships manned by 36,000 men. She was '. . . a great joint-stock company for the exploitation of the East'.[1]

By now her great days were in fact over. The fear of the Visconti had led her to acquire a large part of the plain of Lombardy; this gave her control of the Brenner Pass and of her food supplies, but it also rendered her vulnerable to attacks by land-based powers already jealous of her seaborne wealth. At the same time her Mediterranean empire put Venice in the forefront of the struggle against the Turks, and in 1479 she was forced for the first time to cede territory to them. This double struggle was eventually to prove too much for her, though the signs of her decline were not obvious to contemporaries, who regarded her with envy and admiration. Commines, writing in the early sixteenth century, called her

. . . the most triumphant city I have ever seen; the city that bestows the greatest honour on ambassadors and on strangers; the city that is most carefully governed; the city wherein the worship of God is most solemnly conducted.

And in the later sixteenth century she was the centre of the dying Renaissance, commissioning paintings from Titian and buildings by Palladio.

[1] *C.M.H.*, I, p. 283.

EUROPE
ABOUT 1490
English Miles
0   100   200   300

SCOTLAND

NORWAY

SWEDEN

Ireland

DENMARK

ENGLAND

NETHERLANDS

Lux-
em-
burg

THE

BO

FRANCE

Franche Comté

SWISS
CONFED.

Tyrol

Aust

Styr

SAVOY

MILAN

VENICE

GENOA

EMPIRE

PORTUGAL

CASTILE

NAVARRE

A

R

A

FLORENCE

PAPAL
STATES

NA

Corsica
To Genoa

O

Sardinia G

GRANADA

N

Sicil

SWEDEN

MUSCOVY

ORDER

TEUTONIC

LITHUANIA

BOHEMIA

POLAND

Austria

ria

HUNGARY

MOLDAVIA

CRIMEA

WALLACHIA

OTTOMAN EMPIRE

NAPLES

Crete
to Venice

Cyprus
to Venice

EXTRACT

The Interpretation of the Renaissance:

The real problem is not what the age should be called, but what were its most characteristic traits and its chronological boundaries. How, in short, can we establish a periodic concept of the Renaissance that will prove a useful tool for the historian, and have practical value for the interpretation of history? . . . Viewing the Renaissance as an age in the history of western Europe, then, I would define it as the age of transition from medieval to modern civilization, a period characterized primarily by the gradual shift from one fairly well co-ordinated and clearly defined type of civilization to another, yet, at the same time, possessing in its own right certain distinct traits and a high degree of cultural vitality. And on the basis of this concept or hypothesis, I would set the arbitrary dates – 1300 to 1600 – as its chronological boundaries. . . .

In the broadest terms, then; the two dominant institutions of the Middle Ages were the feudal system and the universal church. Between them, they determined both the social structure and the ideological content of medieval civilization. And both, in their institutional aspects, were founded upon an agrarian, land-holding economy. . . .

When we turn to the modern age, say by the beginning of the seventeenth century, the general complex of European civilization has changed so radically that it amounts to a change in kind rather than in degree. The economic balance has shifted from agriculture to commerce and industry. Money economy has become almost universal, and capitalism has replaced all but the vestigial remnants of medieval economic organization. On the political side, the national states with centralized government have taken the place of feudal particularism, while at the same time the unity of Christendom has been decisively broken. . . .

Compared with the revolutionary changes in the character of western European civilization between the years 1300 and 1600, the changes in the following three centuries are changes in degree rather than in kind. (W. K. Ferguson, 'The Interpretation of the Renaissance: Suggestions for a Synthesis.' *Journal of the History of Ideas*, XII (1951))

FURTHER READING

O. Halecki, *The Limits and Divisions of European History*, Sheed & Ward, 1950

W. K. Ferguson, *The Renaissance in Historical Thought*, Houghton Mifflin, 1948

K. H. Dannenfeldt, ed., *The Renaissance – Medieval or Modern?*, Harrap, 1959

The New Cambridge Modern History, C.U.P., Vol. I 1957; Chapter I, Introduction

D. Maland: 'The Italian Renaissance – a Problem in Interpretation', *History* June, 1959

II · THE RENAISSANCE, c. 1450–1536

THE Renaissance, in the restricted meaning we have agreed to give to it, refers to the developments in the arts and in thought during the fourteenth, fifteenth and early sixteenth centuries in western Europe. The 'High' Renaissance, when these developments reached their lush maturity, extended from about 1490 to about 1536. To understand it one must consider, very briefly, what had been happening during the preceding century and a half.

The Renaissance in Italy

The complex of changes all – economic, intellectual, artistic – had their origin in urban life, in the towns that stretched in a 'milky way' from Flanders, south up the Rhine valley to the north Italian plain and the manufacturing towns of Tuscany.

The changes came first and fastest in the southern area, between the Alps and Rome. There were several reasons for this. The medieval conflicts of Pope and Emperor had enabled the city-states of north Italy, lying between them, to play off one ruler against the other and so maintain their own political independence. At the same time, their geographical situation at the crossroads of trade, from the north to Byzantium, from Asia to the west, together with the possession of certain valuable natural resources, such as alum (used in the manufacture of cloth), had led to the accumulation of wealth, and the appearance of new economic techniques. Thus Venice had issued government stock as early as 1171, banking had developed at Siena by 1233, and by 1252 Florence was minting a reliable gold coinage. There was a less rigid division between wealth and birth than further north in Europe: dukes became merchants and bankers became dukes. 'In our change-loving Italy where nothing stands firm and no ancient dynasty exists, a servant can easily become a king,' Pius II commented. Political independence combined with wealth and leisure to provide a favourable soil for artistic patronage and cultural experiment.

The classical background of Italy, never completely forgotten, together with a feeling of common identity between the medieval city-states and those of ancient Greece, provided a mental climate favourable to the reception of classical thought. Italy, too, was in intermittent contact with Greek scholars and with the Greek-based culture of the Byzantine Empire: architecture in Venice and painting at Siena, for instance, owed much to these sources before the fourteenth century had opened.

During the fourteenth century all these various factors played their part in fostering the early Italian Renaissance. One can only select a very few names, to indicate the main lines of development. Two men stand on the borders between medieval and Renaissance feeling.

Dante (1265–1321) wrote his *Divine Comedy* in Italian, but his view is not one that would have been possible to a Renaissance man. Similarly, Giotto (1266–1336, Florence) in his paintings began, by the use of perspective and modelling, to 'knock a hole in the wall', but, though modern in technique, his paintings are medieval in feeling.

Petrarch (1304–74), a little later, exhibits in a vestigial form most of the characteristics of the Renaissance humanist. He was born at Arezzo, of Florentine parents, studied law at the universities of Montpellier and Bologna, and, on his father's death in 1326, settled at Avignon. Using Avignon, and later nearby Vaucluse, as a centre, he travelled widely in north and central Italy. He was in love with classical learning, attempting to purify his Latin style, worshipping Cicero, and studying Greek poetry in Latin translation (he could not read Greek). He collected manuscripts, coins, fragments of statuary – any link with what was for him the golden age. He perfected one form of the sonnet, and is said to have helped to produce the first map of Italy. In his interest in the world around him, in his passion for classical culture, in his preoccupation with style, he is the first humanist. With him one may couple Boccaccio (1313–75, Florence), who produced the first great prose work in Italian, the collection of stories called the *Decameron*, who read and wrote widely in Latin, and who was responsible for bringing to Florence in 1360 the first teacher of Greek.

The great innovators in the arts, Brunelleschi, Donatello and Masaccio, all worked in Florence about the turn of the fourteenth century. Brunelleschi (1377–1446) was born in Florence, studied in Rome (where he measured the dome of the Roman Pantheon) and returned to Florence in 1407. He designed the cathedral dome which floats like a bubble over modern Florence. More typical of his use of classical motifs are the Spedale degli Innocenti, the Church of San Lorenzo and the Pazzi Chapel. In these buildings he uses the classical column and arch, reintroduces the Roman 'orders' of column, frieze and cornice, and – a new feature – plays off dark structural features against light-coloured walls. The emphasis is always on proportion, based on the diameter of the column; a preoccupation with 'ideal' proportions is a Renaissance characteristic. Brunelleschi's friend, the sculptor, Donatello (c. 1386–1466), was born in Florence, and accompanied him to Rome. He worked in Florence, Siena, Rome and Padua. His originality is exemplified in his statue of David: it is a nude, accurately-observed young man; it is a technically expert piece of bronze casting; it is designed as a statue in its own right, independent of an architectural setting. In these three ways it was something that had not been attempted for over a thousand years. His equestrian statue at Padua of the *condottiere* Gattamelata was equally revolutionary. The greatness of the painter, Masaccio (1401–*c*.1428) rests almost entirely on six frescoes in the Brancacci chapel of the church of Santa Maria del Carmine in Florence. The figures in these frescoes are sometimes naked, are modelled so that one can feel their weight and are surrounded by air – three innovations. They exercised a great influence on the later painters – they were studied a hundred years later by Michelangelo, whose sketches of the figures still exist.

The great names of the later Renaissance mostly derive, directly or indirectly, from these three. In architecture, Brunelleschi was succeeded by Bramante (1444–1514, Rome), and he by Michelangelo (1475–1564, Florence and Rome). In sculpture Donatello was followed by Verrocchio (1435–88, Florence, Rome and Venice), and he again by Michelangelo. In painting there are two lines of evolution from Masaccio: one, that of classical simplicity, leads through Piero della

Francesca (1416–92, Urbino and Arezzo), to Raphael (1483–1520, Urbino and Rome); the other, more romantic, produces Leonardo da Vinci (1452–1519, Florence and Milan), and ends once again with Michelangelo.

To mention only nine names from the armies of Italian artists is, of course, to over-simplify grossly. The non-expert, though, is liable to get lost in a sea of detail. The other great figures can most of them be fitted into the above scheme of development.

If one looks, in more detail, at the High Renaissance of the later fifteenth century which grew out of the men and trends described above, one becomes aware that the keyword is 'humanism' – one of those shorthand terms which it is easier to use than to define. Renaissance scholars themselves used the word, derived from the Latin *humanitas*, which might be defined as the civilizing influence of culture. This Renaissance humanism is strangely ambivalent in character. On the one hand it is concerned with an interest and skill in academic, abstract, 'ivory tower' knowledge about style and grammar, or mathematical proportion. Browning emphasized this aspect in his *Grammarian's Funeral*:

> So, with the throttling hands of Death at strife,
>   Ground he at grammar;
> Still, thro' the rattle, parts of speech were rife.
>   While he could stammer
> He settled *Hoti's* business – let it be! —
>   Properly based *Oun* –
> Gave us the doctrine of the enclitic *De*,
>   Dead from the waist down.

On the other hand, humanism was also profoundly interested in Man – his nature, his education, his right conduct, his potentialities (often at the expense of its interest in God, and its belief in God's omnipotence). It was fascinated, too, by individual differences in the surrounding physical world: the difference between one face and another, even between one plant and another. This examination of individual detail led also, perhaps inevitably, to an attitude of detachment from the thing observed – what T. S. Eliot has termed a 'dissociation of sensibility'. In these ways humanism weakened the hold that traditional religion had held over men's minds. The humanists were not rational agnostics of the eighteenth century type, however – there was a great vogue for astrology for instance. But Italian humanism was always pulling away from Christianity, and in this it differs strikingly from humanism north of the Alps, which tended to concentrate on relating the New Learning to the Christian religion, and especially perhaps to the writings of St. Paul.

In Italy the humanist sought in the classics for models of literary style and of human conduct, and collected 'brown Greek manuscripts' with the zeal of a philatelist. This led in turn to the founding of great libraries, such as that in the Vatican (1447), and to the rapid progress of textual and grammatical criticism. Old traditions were scrutinized and sometimes destroyed. In 1440, the humanist Lorenzo Valla showed that the Donation of Constantine, on which the Papacy's claims to rule central Italy were based, was a ninth century forgery. Valla also made fun of St. Jerome's Latin style and declared that the Apostles' Creed could not have been written by the Apostles, but this did not prevent Nicholas V making him an apostolic secretary.

The development of printing by movable metal type enabled the humanists to multiply copies and criticism. The earliest presses in Italy were at Subiaco (1465), Rome, Milan and Venice. In the last of these cities Aldo Manuzio (1449–1514) set up the famous Aldine Press in 1490 and by 1515 had printed most of the known Greek and Latin classics. The Italian presses used letters based on the Carolingian handwriting and this alphabet soon spread to northern Europe, driving out the Gothic black letter type, except in Germany. The Italian design is essentially that used in printing today.

To conclude, here is a contemporary description of the academic humanist:

A humanist is one who has a love of things human, one whose regard is centred on the world about him and the best that man has done; one who cares more for art and letters, particularly the art and letters of Greece and Rome, than for the dry light of reason, or the mystic's light into the unknown; one who distrusts allegory; one who adores critical editions with variants and variorum notes; one who has a passion for manuscripts which he would like to discover, beg, borrow, or steal; one who has an eloquent tongue which he frequently exercises, one who has a sharp tongue, which on occasion can let free a flood of good billingsgate or sting an opponent with an epigram.[1]

Parallel with this 'academic' humanism there flourished a 'courtly' humanism in such cities as Naples, Mantua, Urbino, Ferrara and Florence. Platonic Academies – discussion-groups – were set up by the Platonists Ficino and Pico della Mirandola in Florence, and Cosimo de' Medici listened to one of Plato's dialogues as he lay dying. At Mantua Vittorino da Feltre (1378-1446) started a school which embodied many of the ideas of the humanists. It was very different from the monastic schools of earlier centuries: its aim was to form good citizens, rather than men dedicated to life beyond the city. He made three especially startling innovations; science and gymnastics were included in the curriculum as well as the traditional subjects (logic, arithmetic, music,[2] geometry, astronomy and theology), there was a great emphasis on the development of the individual personality, and poor children were educated together with the aristocratic ones. In all this one can trace the influence of Plato's *Republic*, combined with the Renaissance emphasis on the *uomo universale* – the all-rounder. This emphasis on man's potentialities was yet another force weakening the hold of the Church. 'Man can make what he will of himself,' wrote the humanist Alberti, and in the next century Rabelais put over the entrance to his imaginary abbey of Theleme the motto 'Fay ce que voudras' – do what you will. Alberti's attitude led to that of Rabelais and both were a powerful decomposing force on traditional morality.

The artistic achievements of the High Renaissance were inspired by the patronage of Rome, and, to a less extent, Venice and Milan. One can date the capture of Rome by the Renaissance to the Pontificates of Nicholas V (1447-55), and the humanist Aeneas Sylvius Piccolomini – Pius II (1458-64). It was the latter who ordered that the classical monuments in Rome were no longer to be used as quarries for building materials. The passion for classical works of art

---

[1] Quoted by E. K. Rand; *Founders of the Middle Ages*, Harvard U.P., 1928, pp. 102-3.

[2] Music was, of course, affected by the Renaissance. See the work of Dufay (*c.* 1400-74), and Josquin des Prez (d. 1521).

ranked only second to that for manuscripts, and at least two major works were rediscovered; the Apollo Belvedere in about 1479, and the Laocoön on January 14, 1506.

The great Papal patrons of art were Julius II (1502–13), and Leo X (1513–21). After the latter's death the shadow of the Lutheran controversy falls across the city, while in 1527 it was sacked by Charles V's troops. The Sack of Rome marks the end of its great days. Later artistic developments centre round Venice and the painter Titian, but they are not really part of the High Renaissance, which had reached its artistic maturity between about 1490 and 1520. During those years the new learning, and the new technical knowledge of oil painting, perspective and anatomy, had been assimilated to a 'classical' manner, which had not yet passed over into the virtuosity of the Baroque. At the same time the Classical and Christian influences were nicely balanced. The critical, detached, impartial interest in the human body and the world around it led to the development of the portrait and the landscape, so that the Madonna became an Italian woman set against Italian fields, rather than the remote impersonal figure

> . . . standing in God's holy fire
> as in the gold mosaic of a wall,

that she had been in earlier centuries.

Greatest and most typical in their different ways of the High Renaissance are Leonardo da Vinci (1452–1519), Raphael (1483–1520) and Michelangelo (1475–1564). Leonardo stands slightly apart from the other two. He was born in the Republic of Florence and studied in the city under Verrocchio, where he remained until about 1482, when he moved to Milan at the invitation of Lodovico Sforza. He lived there until the Duke was driven out in 1499. The clay model on which he had been working for a great equestrian statue of the Duke's father was shot to pieces by the invading French and Leonardo wrote in his notebooks: 'The Duke has lost his State, his possessions, his liberty, and none of his works was finished.' During the next fourteen years Leonardo moved through Italy, working in Florence, Milan and Rome. In 1516 he went to France at the invitation of the king, and remained there until his death in 1519. Partly because of the unsettled conditions in the area where he worked, partly due to his own nature, experimental, apparently unable to complete one thing at a time, and always seeking for perfection, Leonardo hinted at more than he accomplished, leaving only a handful of paintings, though these are great ones with a unique, mysterious, romantic flavour a little out of key with the typical Renaissance scale. Our understanding of his genius really rests on his notebooks in which, playing Boswell to his own Johnson, he displays in thousands of pages of writing and drawings the universal inquiring mind of the Renaissance at its most acute. Anatomy, physics, geology and geography, engineering, the nature of light and shade, flight, the casting of statues – these are only a few of the fifty headings under which his notes have been analysed. They show a man with an almost unlimited range of interests whose speculations are ahead of his day, and who is at the same time capable of the most exact observation of the contemporary world – the human bones, the insect, the fossil in the rock, the way water flows round an obstacle.

Raphael was born at Urbino in central Italy and studied at Perugia under Perugino. He soon went to Rome, and spent most of his comparatively short life working for Julius II and Leo X. From the historical point of view his most important works are the frescoes he painted in the Stanza della Segnatura in the Vatican (1509–12), since they sum up the balanced Renaissance view of the important forces at work on man. They are a sort of Divine Comedy in paint. On one wall, in the 'School of Athens', are the philosophers of the classical world, many of them with the features of Raphael's contemporaries. On the opposite wall he painted the 'Disputà', in which the philosophers and saints of the Christian world debate the miracle of the Eucharist. On the other two, smaller, walls are 'Justice', the basis of political order, and 'Parnassus', the basis of the artist's imaginative order. It is all there, classical, calm and impersonal, marking the point of balance between the various elements of the Renaissance, '. . . the point at which medieval and modern thought touch one another . . .'[1]

Michelangelo's life spans this point of balance and contact, and stretches on into the next stage of artistic development. He was born at Caprese in Florence and studied under Ghirlandaio. From 1496 to 1534 he oscillated between Rome and

[1] *C.M.H.*, II, p. 14.

Florence, while the last thirty years of his life were spent in
Rome. Michelangelo is the great 'all-rounder' in practice,
as Leonardo is in theory, leaving behind him significant
achievements in poetry, sculpture, painting and architecture.
He is perhaps greatest as a sculptor, his best works including
the colossal marble statue of David in Florence (1504), the
Medici tombs in the same city (1520–34) and the statues
designed for the never completed tomb of Julius II. To the
accurate observation of the human figure that was typical of
the Renaissance he added something else, so that his figures
became giants and titans, full of might and, often, tragedy.
His paintings are criticized for being those of a sculptor rather
than a painter, but in the work which he did for Julius II on
the ceiling of the Sistine Chapel the two arts are satisfactorily
fused. In his later years Michelangelo's art became more
emotional, less serene, a change that suited his volcanic character. It was also a development that was in keeping with
the new styles in art that were appearing – styles that are
known as 'Mannerist' and, later, Baroque. Art now became
'. . . not a self-contained piece of reality, but a passing show
in which the beholder has the good luck to participate just
for a moment . . .'.[1] The difference can be seen by comparing the ceiling of the Sistine Chapel with the fresco of
The Last Judgement, which Michelangelo painted at the east
end of the same chapel between 1536 and 1541; or in architecture by comparing the original plans for the rebuilding of
St. Peter's with Michelangelo's amendments (1547–64). By
the 1530's Renaissance art was developing into something
different.

The Renaissance has its political aspect, characterized by a
growth in the power of nationalism, an increase in the strength
of the ruler, the development of professional diplomacy and
an open admission of the doctrine that the results – in this
case, the safety of the State – justify the means. Nationalism
is absent in Italy, but the other facets are omnipresent.

In the later Middle Ages human society was, in theory, the
society of all Christians, with the Pope at its head, 'to whom
all the kings of Christian people should be subject as to our

[1] H. Wölfflin, *Classic Art: An Introduction to the Italian Renaissance*, Phaidon Press,
1952.

lord Jesus Christ Himself,' as St. Thomas Aquinas wrote in the middle of the thirteenth century. Yet at that time the characteristics of the modern state had already made their appearance in the Kingdom of Sicily under Frederick II (1212–50). These included the creation of a centralized, absolute, bureaucratic rule by divine right; the adoption of Roman law, which cut away feudal privileges; administration by trained, paid officials; a mercenary army; and, the means by which all the former could be maintained, the organization of a regular income based on fixed taxes and accurate accounts.

By the end of the fourteenth century it was difficult to believe in even the theoretical unity of Christendom, when observers were faced with the spectacle of three claimants to the Papacy and three rivals for the title of Emperor! Meanwhile the Italian city-states had been putting into practice the lessons they had learnt from Frederick, so that by the fifteenth century the State, too, had become 'a work of art'. Constitutional theory and practice developed in the political laboratory of north and central Italy for the same reasons that the artistic Renaissance had done so – the existence there of small, independent, rich rulers. Trade led to regular incomes, regular incomes made possible the hiring of mercenary armies, loyal to their paymasters. There were, it is true, drawbacks to the use of mercenaries; fighting for money, their actions tended to be inconclusive, and for a time the professional captains (*condottieri*) were the bane of Italy. In some cases these were able, like Francesco Sforza in Milan, to make themselves heads of states. Political practice combined with the new knowledge of classical history to encourage the discussion of political theory and the study of modern history. The irruption of the French into the peninsula in 1494 led thinkers to debate the possibility of some Italian union able to resist the new giant nation-states which had sprung up to the north and west in France and Spain and now threatened to swallow up the princelets of Italy. Typical of these lines of thought are Guicciardini's *History of Florence* (1509) – perhaps the first really 'modern' history – and the writings of Machiavelli (1469–1527).

It is important not to over-estimate the originality of Machiavelli or his influence on contemporaries. He put into words what many people at the time were thinking or doing, and his main work was not printed until much later (1532):

> He was dead by 1527; his experience was confined to Italy, already a political backwater . . . and it cannot be shown that he influenced anyone – writer or statesman – before 1560. On the other hand, his attitude to politics – universal and narrow at the same time – is particularly typical of the generation after his death . . .[1]

His principal works are *The Prince* (1513) and *The Discourses upon Livy* (1515–17). Machiavelli was born in Florence in 1469, and was an official diplomat from 1498 to 1512. When the Medici were restored he was forced to retire to San Casciano, where he spent most of his time till his death in 1527. It was there that he wrote *The Prince*:

> The evening being come, I return home and go to my study; at the entrance I pull off my peasant-clothes, covered with dust and dirt, and put on my noble court dress, and thus becomingly re-clothed I pass into the ancient courts of the men of old, where, being lovingly received by them, I am fed with that food which is mine alone; where I do not hesitate to speak with them, and to ask the reason for their actions, and they in their benignity answer me; and for four hours I feel no weariness, I forget every trouble, poverty does not dismay, death does not terrify me; I am possessed entirely by these great men.[2]

In *Discourses* Machiavelli drew heavily on classical sources and described his ideal state, a republic defended by a citizen militia; but in *The Prince*, disillusioned, sardonic, he analysed the power-politics of his own day, displaying them without cant or covering, naked and unashamed: 'Medieval tradition dealt with what kings should do in order to be good . . . [Machiavelli] tried to deal with something different, what kings found it most advantageous to do in order to be effective rulers.'[3] His advice had its roots in his own experiences. When he was employed by Florence, the Republic's instructions had been: '. . . we must not allow any consideration to come before that of our survival'. Sent on an embassy

---

[1] *N.C.M.H.*, II, p. 460.
[2] Machiavelli, *The Prince*, ed. W. K. Marriott, Dent, 1908, p. xv.
[3] *N.C.M.H.*, I, p. 5.

to France in 1500 he found that the new nation-state despised the representative of the once powerful merchant-republic, whom they laughed at as *Ser Nihilo*, Mr. Nothing. Two years later he represented Florence at the court of Cesare Borgia, and learnt there that power must rest on strength, on double-dealing or on both. In his dedication to Lorenzo de' Medici he wrote that his object was '. . . . to offer you the opportunity of understanding in the shortest time all that I have learnt in so many years . . .' in order that Lorenzo might be well equipped to liberate Italy from the new barbarians, the foreign invaders, for 'To all of us this barbarous dominion stinks'.

To show how states really become powerful, and to illustrate the demonstration by actual examples – it is these aims that make Machiavelli's *Prince* at once original and typical of the new Renaissance statecraft: '. . . these things, he said, have happened, such is the manner of their happening, and these are the lessons they teach.' [1] These lessons were that the business of a ruler must be to protect and strengthen his state, and that all his actions must be judged by the extent to which they further these objects, and not by the criterion of right or moral conduct. Earlier princes no doubt behaved like this, but they did not say so; what is new is not the principles, but their open acknowledgement.

The Renaissance outside Italy

The problem here is to decide the extent of the debt which the Renaissance in the rest of Europe owed to Italy. There are plenty of signs that, if Italy had not existed, a 'Renaissance' would have occurred just the same. In literature, the poetry of Chaucer (*c.* 1340–1400) shows 'typical' Renaissance characteristics; use of the vernacular, interest in the individual, accurate observation of nature. If we consider realism and observed detail in painting, the miniatures painted for the Duc de Berri (d. 1416) and the outlook of Flemish painters such as Jan van Eyck (d. 1440) are more 'modern' than those of their Italian contemporaries. The technique of oil-painting, too, probably originated in Flanders and spread from there to Italy. If we look for luxury, cruelty and power-politics, the court of the Dukes of Burgundy will stand comparison with that

[1] *N.C.M.H.*, II, p. 460.

of any Italian city-state.   One of the greatest instruments of the
later humanists, the printing-press, originated not in Italy but
north of the Alps in the Rhineland.   One of the pivotal figures
of early humanism, Nicholas of Cusa (1401–64), was a German,
educated near the Zuider Zee.   There are, in short, indications
of a Renaissance in the urban areas of northern Europe, but
they are isolated, there is nowhere the same concentration,
wealth, inspiration as in Italy.

The great contribution of Italy to the northern Renaissance
was humanism, in the widest sense of that term.   To contemporary Europe north of the Alps, the first and greatest
impact of the Italian Renaissance was not artistic but intellectual – the 'New Learning' as they called it.   From this stem
the essential differences between the Italian and the northern
Renaissance.   Throughout, the emphasis in the north is on
philosophy and philology rather than art, and on religious,
rather than secular, models and criticism.

One can see some of the reasons for this.   Philosophy was
the one aspect of the early Renaissance to which the north had
made no real contribution.   At the same time, there was, at
the University of Paris and in Germany, a traditional interest
in philosophical questions.   German culture was based on
Christianity, not on the Roman Empire, in which she had
never been included, so that the classical aspect of the Italian
Renaissance made little appeal to her.

> The literature which the Teutonic mind mainly loved and
> studied and edited was patristic and Christian; but the
> literature which the Latin mind chiefly cultivated was
> classical and pagan. . . . The thought which the Latins
> studied was that of a world into which Christ had not
> entered, though it was one in which Caesar had reigned;
> but the thought which the Teutons cultivated had Christ
> as its source and God as its supreme object.[1]

This natural bias towards an interest in religious matters
had been strengthened by the appearance, in the fifteenth century Rhineland, of the *Devotio moderna*, a new, secular, pietist
movement.   The main organized group, the Brethren of the
Common life, had been recognized by the Papacy in 1431.
They were far from being humanists, but their emphasis on

[1] *C.M.H.*, II, p. 693.

education, and their influence on such men as Nicholas of Cusa and Erasmus, both of whom were educated at their school at Deventer, suggest a link between German Christianity and the later pattern of German humanism.

In the rest of western Europe the effect of the Italian Renaissance was felt late, and usually in such a modified form that national characteristics prevailed over Italian ones, especially as far as the plastic arts were concerned. In Spain the main humanist influences are connected with the name of Cardinal Jiménez (Ximenes) (1437–1517), the able assistant of Ferdinand and Isabella. In 1508 he founded a University at Alcalá, where Greek and Oriental languages were studied, which became an important centre for the Cardinal's twin interests of Catholic reform and Renaissance scholarship. An edition of the Bible in the original languages in which it was written, together with grammars of these languages in Latin and the Vulgate text, was finally published from there in 1520. Perhaps the greatest work of Renaissance co-operative scholarship, it has the fearsome title of the Complutensian Polyglot Bible. The impact of Italian art and architecture was surprisingly late and surprisingly feeble, considering the close contact between Spain and Italy at the time. Even when, in the sixteenth century, the impact was felt, it was soon overlaid by local styles, even as the buildings themselves are overlaid with 'Plateresque' ornamentation.

In France the Sorbonne was printing texts of Italian humanists as early as 1470, but French Renaissance scholarship only became original when Lefèvre d'Étaples (c. 1450–1536) returned in 1493 from Italy. Lefèvre knew Greek, wrote a Latin commentary on St. Paul's Epistles – most of the great northern humanists tackled these sooner or later – and translated the Gospels into French. As a result of his work, Greek was being regularly taught at the University of Paris by 1508. In literature France made significant contributions to the Renaissance. The *Mémoires* of Philippe de Commines (c. 1447–1511) are a first-class history of the events in Burgundy and France between about 1464 and 1494, told in a straightforward style. The greatest French creative writer was Rabelais (1495–1553), whose *Gargantua and Pantagruel* contains somewhere in its enormous length a commentary on almost every aspect of the times.

French painting and architecture were exposed to the radiation of the Renaissance from two opposite directions, Italy and Flanders. In the fifteenth century, for geographical and political reasons, the Flemish influence was the more powerful. There the great innovators had been Jan van Eyck (c. 1380-1441) and Roger van der Weyden (c. 1399-1464), and their innovations were absorbed and displayed by Memling (ob. 1494) in the second half of the century. The style of painters such as these, smooth, tranquil, full of accurate descriptions of individual scenes and faces from everyday life, strongly affected French painting, especially the work of Jean Fouquet (c. 1415- c. 1481) and his followers. The Italian impulse came later, as a by-product of the Italian wars. From the time of Charles VIII's expedition onwards this Italian influence grew in strength until it reached its peak in the reign of Francis I. It has been said that '. . . . the French tried to conquer Italy, while the Italians colonized France . . . The "French Renaissance" was good business for the Italians.' [1]

Leonardo da Vinci spent the last years of his life as a guest of the French court at Amboise. The Château de Chambord, begun in 1519, shows an interesting mixture of Gothic and classical styles; the north wing of Fontainebleau, built between 1528 and 1552, is more purely Renaissance. The court painter, Jean Clouet (?1475-1540), himself a Fleming, produced works in which the northern and Italian influences are both present. There grew up in the first half of the sixteenth century, around the royal palace of Fontainebleau, a strong French school of Renaissance painters and architects.

By 1500 there was in England a group of humanist scholars that could win the respect of Erasmus – men such as Grocyn, Colet and More. John Colet (c. 1466-1519), returned to England in 1496 after having studied in Italy for a couple of years, and lectured at Oxford on St. Paul's Epistles in the 'modern' humanist manner. He founded St. Paul's School in 1510 and took care to equip it with a Latin grammar specially written for it, and a High Master who knew Greek. But if Renaissance scholarship was well established, art and architecture were not. In building there is little to show in the

---

[1] *A History of France*, by L. Romier, translated by A. L. Rowse, Macmillan, 1953, p. 189.

first half of the century apart from isolated works of foreign craftsmen, such as Torrigiano's tomb for Henry VII (1512–18) and the screen at King's. Longleat House (1567 *et seq.*) is one of the first buildings completely influenced by the Renaissance. Painting was represented only by a foreigner, Holbein (1497–1543), who came from Augsburg in 1526 to work at the court of Henry VIII.

It was by way of Augsburg that Germany was most closely connected with the Italian Renaissance. German architecture, like English, never assimilated the pure Renaissance style and remained an uneasy amalgam of Gothic structure and Renaissance detail. One can estimate the gap by comparing the Emperor Maximilian's tomb at Innsbruck with the Medici tombs in Florence. The greatest German artist was Dürer (1471–1528) and his work was greatly affected by Italian examples. Born at Nuremberg, he went to Venice in 1494, and again to Italy for eighteen months in 1505–6. There is plenty of evidence from his notebooks of the influence which these visits had on his art, and by his paintings – and still more by his engravings and woodcuts – he spread that influence through northern Europe.

It was in the spheres of philosophy and humanism that the Netherlands and the Empire were the creative centres of the northern Renaissance. As has already been indicated these were essentially native products, but in southern Germany, at least, they owed something at first to contacts with Italy. These contacts were considerable: students from German universities went to Bologna and Padua, while the Councils of Constance and Basle in the early fifteenth century had forced Italian humanists to travel north. Humanism was early established in the new university at Basle, at Vienna and at Nuremberg, where an observatory was set up.

The outstanding example of this early German humanism is Nicholas of Cusa (1401–64). He was born on the Moselle, educated by the Brethren of the Common Life at Deventer, became a lawyer and then entered the Church. From 1440–7 he was Papal Legate in Germany. He absorbed Italian culture in Italy at Padua and Rome, and went on a mission to Constantinople. The facts conceal the man, with his all-round interests. At the Council of Basle he developed the argument that Councils were superior to the Pope and declared that the Donation of Constantine was a forgery, though he later withdrew the first of these statements. In philosophy, starting from the premise that no two things can be alike, he argued that all human knowledge is therefore only conjecture and that God can be apprehended by intuition, and is in all things. '*Deum esse omnia, ut non possit esse aliud quam est.*' He collected manuscripts and discovered twelve of the plays of Plautus. As a mathematician he thought he had squared the circle, and, for mystical reasons, he suggested that the earth was not at the centre of the universe. He proposed the reform of the calendar a hundred years before it was carried out, and constructed a map of central Europe. Italy has no comparable figure before Leonardo da Vinci.

In the second half of the fifteenth century the most original German humanist was Reuchlin (1455–1522). He had studied Greek at Paris, and travelled in Italy. He made himself an expert in Hebrew scholarship, then undeveloped, and in 1506 produced a Hebrew dictionary and grammar. After 1509 a strong movement developed for the suppression of all Hebrew writings other than the Old Testament, which Reuchlin successfully frustrated, though his attitude was eventually condemned in 1520.

Erasmus

The greatest northern humanist – perhaps the greatest humanist of the entire Renaissance, and certainly the most typical – was Erasmus (*c.* 1466–1536). The illegitimate son of a Dutch priest, he was born near Rotterdam and educated at the school of the Brethren of the Common Life at Deventer. His parents died of plague and his guardians persuaded him to become an Augustinian, a step that he resisted and regretted taking. He hated the life but found opportunities to make himself a good scholar, and so was able to escape from the house, though not the vows, by becoming secretary to the Bishop of Cambrai in about 1493. He went to Paris where he studied in poverty – 'The louse is the scholar's companion,' he wrote – until 1499. He never returned to his monastery, but spent the rest of his life moving about Europe '. . . always close to the pressure points, the great arterial highways, between Oxford, Louvain, Paris, Basle, Venice and Rome.'[1]

[1] *N.C.M.H.*, II, p. 70.

He came to England for six months in 1499 and became a
friend and admirer of the English humanists, More and
Colet. He came back in 1509 and stayed this time until
1514, lecturing on Greek at Cambridge. After 1514 he
lived mainly at Basle, though he continued to make journeys
from there, until his death in 1536. He had now a European
reputation, and corresponded with thinkers and rulers all
over western Europe. In 1516 he at last obtained the much
desired Papal dispensation from monastic discipline. They
could not make him return to the monastery now. During
these years he probably exerted a greater intellectual influence
over a greater area than any other European thinker born
between the days of St. Thomas Aquinas in the thirteenth
century and those of Voltaire in the eighteenth. In thought
he occupies an interesting midway position between the
scholasticism of the former and the agnosticism of the latter.
In some ways detached from his time 'He was neither a courtier
in the age of courts, nor a revolutionary in an age of revolution.' [1]

Two strands coloured all this thinking. One, his attitude
to Christianity, came presumably from the influence of the
Brethren of the Common Life (*Fratres Vitae Communis*, founded
by Geert Groote, *c.* 1380, at Deventer) – an emphasis on simplicity of thought, behaviour and worship and on essentials
rather than on outward ceremonial or hair-splitting argument.
This teaching, which is most clearly accessible in *The Imitation
of Christ* by Thomas à Kempis (1380-1471), is summed up in
these words:

> Of what advantage is it to dispute profoundly about the
> doctrine of the Trinity, if by your lack of humility you are all
> the while displeasing the Trinity? [2]

The other strand was Erasmus's passion for the New Learning, for the study and criticism of Greek and Latin texts – what
he himself always called 'Good Letters' (*bonae literae*). Sometimes the two strands, the religious and the critical, came together, as in his edition of the New Testament. Often they
were tugging in opposite directions, and then, one feels, the
critical took precedence over the religious: 'Religion he loved

---

[1] H. R. Trevor-Roper, *Historical Essays*, Macmillan, 1957, p. 35.
[2] *The Imitation of Christ*; Book I, Chapter 1, verse 3.

for the sake of letters rather than letters for the sake of religion.'[1]

In 1500 Erasmus produced the *Adagia*, a collection of classical proverbs, sayings, epigrams, with his own comments. It became a 'best-seller' – perhaps the first – and he enlarged it greatly in later editions. In his comments the social satirist already appears alongside the scholar, as in the following:

> Priests are said in Scripture to devour the sins of the people, and they find sins so hard to digest that they must have the best wine to wash them down.

Erasmus's *Handbook of a Christian Soldier* (*Enchiridion Militis Christiani*) was published in 1503. This is an entirely serious work, uniting the two strands of humanist worship of letters and religious worship of God in its emphasis on the two weapons of knowledge and prayer – God is mind, and must be worshipped with the mind. The spirit must not be sacrificed to the outward symbol:

> Do you honour the bones of Paul hid in the shrine, and a piece of his carcase shining through glass, and not regard the whole mind of Paul shining through his letters?

In 1509 he returned to the same theme, handled this time satirically, in *The Praise of Folly* (*Encomium Moriae*), a pun on his friend More's name. Writing of the monks at the last Judgement, he says:

> One shows a trough full of fish, another so many bushels of prayers, another boasts of not having touched a penny for sixty years without at least two pairs of gloves on, another that he has lived for fifty-five years like a sponge, always fixed to the same place . . . Christ answers them, 'There is only one law which is truly Mine, and of that I hear nothing.'

In 1513 there appeared an anonymous satire, *Julius Exclusus*, in which the late Pope Julius II found it impossible to get into heaven. One cannot be sure that this was by Erasmus, but contemporaries certainly thought so.

But Erasmus's solvent satire is only one aspect of his work; at the same time he produced editions of the Fathers, of Josephus, of Ptolemy. The most important of these were his corrected texts of St. Jerome, and his Greek text and Latin translation of the New Testament. These appeared in 1516.

[1] *C.M.H.*, II, p. 697.

The New Testament was especially significant, not for its scholarship, since it contained plenty of inaccuracies, but rather as a milestone of progress and a signpost to future events. It came at the psychologically significant moment: the printing press could deal with it; the growing army of educated men could combine their passion for Greek and for Christianity in reading it; the Lutheran revolt, with its appeal to the Scriptures, was to begin the next year. Set against these European movements, the fact that Erasmus, for instance, invented a Greek text for the last six verses of the Book of Revelation, translated from his own Latin MSS., is not important.

Erasmus himself saw the significance of his New Testament in a rather different way. It was his aim to make more accessible what he termed the *philosophia Christi*, the teaching of Christ. He explained this in his preface:

> I wish that all women might read the Gospel, and the Epistles of Paul. I wish that they might be translated into all tongues of all people, so that not only the Scots and the Irish, but also the Turk and the Saracen might read and understand. I wish the countryman might sing them at his plough, the weaver chant them at his loom, the traveller beguile with them the weariness of his journey.

For the first thing, he said, is to know what Christ taught, the next is to follow it (*Primum autem est scire quid docuerit, proximum est praestare*). This, in turn, would lead to religious unity. 'Once accurate lists of the Fathers and above all of the New Testament were available, religious contention was in his opinion bound to come to an end. . . .'[1] In this touching – and misplaced – faith that one has only to show people the right course of action for them to follow it, Erasmus shows his affinity with the Rationalist philosophers of the eighteenth century. And, like theirs, his works provided ammunition for revolution.

Erasmus was attacked for daring to amend the traditional Latin of the Vulgate. This was, he replied, as though a Council should declare that whatever

> . . . shall be corrupted, depraved, added or omitted by any rash and half-educated, or inexperienced, or drunken or vacillating copyists, to that do we give our approval. . . .[2]

[1] *N.C.M.H.*, I, p. 115.
[2] M. M. Phillips, *Erasmus and the Northern Renaissance*, E.U.P., 1950, p. 74.

His New Testament, by touching the Holy of Holies, made it easier for later, more accurate, scholars to produce their amendments.

With the New Testament, Erasmus's creative work was really finished. In 1519 and later years he produced editions of a new work, the *Colloquia*, a collection of imaginary dialogues in which he gave his own commentary on contemporary happenings. The book became a best-seller, like the *Adagia* twenty years before.

The remainder of Erasmus's life was dominated by the Reformation in Germany. In 1517 Luther had attacked the doctrine of Indulgences, and by 1520 when he burnt the Bull in which the Pope had excommunicated him, the argument had reached international and unmanageable proportions. Erasmus had an international reputation as the greatest philosopher, scholar and satirist in western Europe, and it was natural that both sides should seek his support and try to involve him in the quarrel.

Erasmus was affected in three ways. First, his own attitude to Luther changed from one of cautious approval to one of equally cautious disapproval. The change can be traced in his letters.

Luther has said many things excellently well. I could wish, however, that he would be less rude in his manner. He would have stronger support behind him, and might do real good. But, at any rate, unless we stand by him when he is right, no one hereafter will dare to speak the truth. (1518)

Luther's freedom of action is loved by the best in the land; I have no doubt that his prudence will take care lest the affair should turn towards faction or rupture. (1519)

I wish Luther himself would be quiet for a while. He injures learning, and does himself no good, while morals and manners grow worse and worse. (1520)

Luther has been sent into the world by the Genius of discord. Every corner is disturbed by him. All admit that the corruptions of the Church require a drastic medicine. But drugs wrongly given make the sick man worse. (1521)[1]

---

[1] J. A. Froude, *Life and Letters of Erasmus*; Longmans, Green, 1894, p. 215; Phillips, p. 170; Froude, p. 267; Froude, p. 295.

While his attitude of approval for one harried by his own critics, the unlearned monks and friars, had thus given place to distrust for Luther's rough and wild reaction, which was destroying the unity of the Church, both sides continued to press for the powerful support of his name and pen. Erasmus tried to remain detached; he approved of Luther's attacks on the practice of the Church, he disapproved of his manner and of the extension of those attacks from matters of practice to questions of dogma, he feared that truth would be lost as the rival sides grew more enraged. Such a half-and-half attitude naturally infuriated Catholics and Protestants alike:

'I am a heretic to both sides,' he wrote; and again: 'Instead of leading, I have stood naked and unarmed between the javelins of two angry foes'. (1525)

But in fact he had been forced to take sides. As early as 1518 he had shown what his decision would be: 'Erasmus will always be found on the side of the Roman See,' he declared then. Two years later he wrote:

Christ I know: Luther I know not. The Roman Church I know, and death will not part me from it till the Church departs from Christ. . . . I would have the Church purified of evil, lest the good in it suffer by connection with what is indefensible; but in avoiding the Scylla of Luther I would have us also avoid Charybdis. . . . Many great persons have entreated me to support Luther.

I have answered always that I will support him when he is on the Catholic side. They have asked me to draw up a formula of faith. I reply that I know of none save the creed of the Catholic Church, and I advise everyone who consults me to submit to the Pope. (1520)[1]

It is hardly surprising therefore that, when he was at last forced to take part in the controversy, Erasmus wrote against Luther's teaching in his *De Libero Arbitrio* (1524), a book which nevertheless displeased the Papal party by its moderation.

For the third effect of the Lutheran crisis on Erasmus and on humanism had been that the moderate, critical attitude became for the time being no longer tenable and vanished

[1] Froude, pp. 261–3.

from the main stream of European thought. In 1519 Erasmus
had written:

> I am keeping apart, as far as I can, so that I may better
> serve the reflowering of Good Letters.

And it was precisely 'Good Letters' that suffered. Erasmus
was blamed for Luther's revolt. He wrote in 1520 that his
opponents were saying:

> Luther has fallen into his terrible heresies by studying the
> new learning. 'Stand, I warn you, in the old paths, avoid
> novelties, keep to the ancient Vulgate.' This was meant
> for me and my New Testament. I am accused of making
> a new gospel.[1]

After the publication of *De Libero Arbitrio* Erasmus made
renewed efforts to detach himself from the controversy. He
had always been in poor health and now, with old age – he
was sixty, a great age for those days – the illnesses increased.
He continued, though, to correspond voluminously, even with
Pope and Emperor, pleading without success for tolerance, a
breathing space, common-sense. There was a move to make
him a cardinal, or to give him some other dignity; but he
refused all offers.

> A poor, half-dead wretch such as I am cannot be tempted
> into grand idle company merely that I may end my life as a
> rich man. I am pleased by the Pope's letter to me, but the
> ox is not fit for the saddle. (1535)[2]

He died in the following year, at Basle.

Erasmus's importance lies in his immense contemporary influence; in his satirical writings, which certainly played their
part in drawing men's attention to abuses in the Church and
so helped to produce the Reformation – however much he
might protest that this was not his intention; in his letters, with
their eye for the significant detail; in his 'massive erudition',
displayed in his work as an editor of texts – 'He remains aware
of the context, the historical circumstances, and the time and
place of each text that he examines.'[3]

The search for exact dates with which to start and end
historical periods is a snare and a delusion. However, if one

---

[1] Froude, p. 274.   [2] Froude, p. 430.   [3] Phillips, p. 194.

were forced to choose a significant date for the end of the Renaissance, the year 1536 is perhaps the best. It was the year of Erasmus's death, the end of '. . . that golden age which lay between the European discovery of printing and the discovery of its antidote, the *Index Librorum Prohibitorum*'.[1] It was also the year in which the first edition of Calvin's *Institutes* appeared – so different in their attitude to free-will and free thought from that of Erasmus. In 1536, also, Michelangelo began work on his 'Last Judgement', that forerunner of new artistic styles. The work of the Renaissance is done; in art we move on to Mannerist and Baroque constructions, designed to glorify Church and State. The debates are now not over grammar, but over salvation, and they are fought not with books but with cannon-balls. The first religious league of princes has already been established (at Schmalkalden in 1531), and religious and political interests remain inextricably mingled for a hundred years. These religious conflicts are powered by the explosive force of nationalism, expressed in the new nation-states that were emerging in western Europe.

EXTRACTS

1. *Leonardo da Vinci offers his services to Ludovico Sforza, c. 1482:*

Most Illustrious Lord, . . .

1. I have a sort of extremely light and strong bridges, adapted to be most easily carried, and with them you may pursue, and at any time flee from the enemy; and others, secure and indestructible by fire and battle, easy and convenient to lift and place. Also methods of burning and destroying those of the enemy.

2. I know how, when a place is besieged, to take the water out of the trenches, and make endless variety of bridges, and covered ways and ladders, and other machines pertaining to such expeditions.

3. Item. If, by reason, of the height of the banks, or the strength of the place, and its position, it is impossible, when besieging a place, to avail oneself of the plan of bombardment, I have methods for destroying every rock or other fortress, even if it were founded on a rock, etc.

[1] Trevor-Roper, p. 39.

4. Again, I have kinds of mortars; most convenient and easy to carry; and with these I can fling small stones almost resembling a storm; and with the smoke of these cause great terror to the enemy to his great detriment and confusion.

5. Item.   I have means by secret and tortuous mines and ways, made without noise, to reach a designated [spot], even if it were needed to pass under a trench or a river.

6. Item.   I will make covered chariots, safe and unassailable, which, entering among the enemy with their artillery, there is no body of man so great but they would break them.   And behind these, infantry could follow quite unhurt and without any hindrance.

7. Item.   In case of need I will make big guns, mortars, and light ordnance of fine and useful forms, out of the common type.

8. Where the operation of bombardment might fail, I would contrive catapults, mangonels, *trabocchi* [type of catapult], and other machines of marvellous efficiency and not in common use.   And in short, according to the variety of cases, I can contrive various and endless means of offence and defence.

9. And if the fight should be at sea I have many kinds of machines most efficient for offence and defence; and vessels which will resist the attack of the largest guns and powder and fumes.

10. In time of peace I believe I can give perfect satisfaction and to the equal of any other in architecture and the composition of buildings, public and private; and in guiding water from one place to another.

Item.   I can carry out sculpture in marble, bronze, or clay, and also I can do in painting whatever may be done, as well as any other, be he who he may. . . .

And if any of the above-named things seem to any one to be impossible or not feasible, I am most ready to make the experiment in your park, or in whatever place may please your Excellency – to whom I commend myself with the utmost humility, etc.   (*Leonardo da Vinci*, ed. L. Goldscheider; Phaidon Press, 1943, p. 17)

2. *Machiavelli discusses the way in which princes should keep faith, 1513:*

Everyone admits how praiseworthy it is in a prince to keep faith, and to live with integrity and not with craft.   Nevertheless our experience has been that those princes who have done great things have held good faith of little account, and have known how to circumvent the intellect of men by craft, and in the end have overcome those who have relied on their word. You must know there are two ways of contesting, the one by law, the other by force; the first method is proper to men, the second to beasts; but because the first is frequently not sufficient, it is necessary to have recourse to the second. Therefore it is necessary for a prince to understand how to avail himself of the beast and the man . . . A prince, therefore, being compelled knowingly to adopt the beast, ought to choose the fox and the lion; because the lion cannot defend himself against snares and the fox cannot defend himself against wolves. Therefore, it is necessary to be a fox to discover the snares and a lion to terrify the wolves. Those who rely simply on the lion do not understand what they are about. Therefore a wise lord cannot, nor ought he to, keep faith when such observance may be turned against him, and when the reasons that caused him to pledge it exist no longer. If men were entirely good this precept would not hold, but because they are bad, and will not keep faith with you, you too are not bound to observe it with them. Nor will there ever be wanting to a prince legitimate reasons to excuse this non-observance. Of this endless modern examples could be given, showing how many treaties and engagements have been made void and of no effect through the faithlessness of princes; and he who has known best how to employ the fox has succeeded best.

But it is necessary to know well how to disguise this characteristic, and to be a great pretender and dissembler; and men are so simple, and so subject to present necessities, that he who seeks to deceive will always find some one who will allow himself to be deceived. (Machiavelli; *The Prince*, ed. W. K. Marriott; Dent, 1908, Chapter Eighteen, pp. 141–3)

3. *Erasmus defines his attitude to the Reformation, c. 1526:*

The two parties are dragging at the opposite ends of a rope. When it breaks they will both fall on their backs. The reformers turn the images out of the churches, which originally were useful and ornamental. They might have been content to forbid the worship of images and to have removed only the superfluous. They will have no more priests. It would be better to have priests of learning and piety, and to provide that orders are not hastily entered into. There would be fewer of them, but better three good than three hundred bad. They do not like so much ritual. True, but it would be enough to abolish the absurd. Debauched priests who do nothing but mumble masses are generally hated. Do away with these hirelings, and allow but one celebration a day in the churches. Indulgences, with which monks so long fooled the world with the connivance of the theologians, are now exploded. Well, then, let those who have no faith in saints' merits pray to Father, Son and Holy Ghost, imitate Christ in their lives, and leave those alone who do believe in saints. Confession is an ancient custom. Let those who deny that it is a sacrament observe it till the Church decides otherwise. No great harm can come of confession so long as men confess only their own mortal sins. Let men think as they please of purgatory, without quarrelling with others who do not think as they do. Theologians may argue about free will in the Sorbonne. Laymen need not puzzle themselves with conundrums. Whether works justify or faith justifies matters little, since all allow that faith will not save without works. In Baptism let the old rule be kept. Parents may perhaps be left to decide whether it shall be administered in infancy or delayed to maturity. Anabaptists must not be tolerated. The Apostles bade their people obey the magistrates, though the magistrates were heathens. Anabaptists will not obey even Christian princes. Community of goods is a chimera. Charity is a duty, but property must be upheld. As to the Eucharist, let the old opinion stand till a council has provided a new revelation. The Eucharist is only adored so far as Christ is supposed to be present there as God. The human nature is not adored, but the Divine Nature, which is Omnipresent. The thing to be corrected is the abuse of the administration . . . For the rest, let there be moderation in all things, and then we may hope for peace. (J. A. Froude, *Life and Letters of Erasmus*, Longmans, Green, 1894, pp. 344–5)

FURTHER READING

E. Newton, *European Painting and Sculpture*, Penguin, 1941

N. Pevsner, *An Outline of European Architecture*, Penguin, 1950

J. Burckhardt, *The Civilization of the Renaissance in Italy*, Phaidon Press, 1950

K. H. Dannenfeldt, ed., *The Renaissance – Medieval or Modern?*, Harrap, 1959

B. Allsopp, *A History of Renaissance Architecture*, Pitman, 1959

H. Wölfflin, *Classic Art: An Introduction to the Italian Renaissance*, Phaidon Press, 1952

K. Clarke, *Leonardo da Vinci*, C.U.P., 1929

Leonardo da Vinci, *Selections from Notebooks*, ed. I. A. Richter, O.U.P., 1952

N. Machiavelli, *The Prince*, ed. W. K. Marriott, Dent, 1908

J. R. Hale, *Machiavelli and Renaissance Italy*, E.U.P., 1961

J. Huizinga, *The Waning of the Middle Ages*, Arnold, 1924

J. A. Froude, *Life and Letters of Erasmus*, Longmans, Green, 1894

M. M. Phillips, *Erasmus and the Northern Renaissance*, E.U.P., 1950

H. Trevor-Roper, *Historical Essays*, Macmillan, 1958, (*VII Erasmus, VIII Machiavelli*)

III · THE INTERNAL HISTORY OF FRANCE 1461–1559; SPAIN 1474–1516; AND THE EMPIRE 1493–1519

France, 1461–1559

THE history of France during these years falls into three parts: the reign of Louis XI (1461–83), who centralized the government of France in the hands of the Crown and destroyed its rival, the House of Burgundy; the reigns of Charles VIII (1483–98) and Louis XII (1498–1515), when France was mainly concerned with those Italian wars into which she entered so lightheartedly and from which she got so little; and the reigns of Francis I (1515–47) and Henri II (1547–59), when the struggle between Habsburg and Valois, already implicit in the Italian wars, became explicit in the struggle with Charles V. During these last reigns, too, Renaissance culture and Protestant doctrine began to affect profoundly the civilization of France.

The reign of Louis XI spans the gap between medieval and modern France. When Louis came to the throne the country was still essentially a loose collection of feudal liberties, of which the French King's was only sometimes the largest. Twenty years later, when he died, Louis was supreme within his territories, the ruler of a 'modern' nation-state, secure at home and envied abroad, and he left France sufficiently united to survive the misplaced knight-errantry of Charles VIII's Italian expedition.

Before Louis became King three events had occurred in the earlier fifteenth century that strengthened the position of the Crown. By the Pragmatic Sanction of Bourges (1438) the French clergy had declared that general councils were superior in authority to the Pope, that the payments of annates to Rome was to stop and that French chapters were to elect their own nominees as abbots and bishops, subject to royal permission. These declarations gave the Gallican church considerable freedom, and gave French kings a useful counter with which to bargain with the Pope. Secondly, in 1439 the

States-General had authorized the King to raise a standing army and to collect the *taille* [1] necessary to finance it. By thus in fact abdicating their control over taxation they made much easier the task of creating a royal despotism. The third event enabled the King to take advantage of the other two: in 1453 the war with England came to an end at last, leaving to the English only Calais. In 1461 Charles VII was succeeded by his son Louis XI, a man capable of taking full advantage of these events.

Louis XI has been described as Machiavelli's Prince in action. Personally unprepossessing, his face pitted with small-pox, neurotic and possibly epileptic, alternately rash and over-cautious, at the same time cunning, faithless and superstitious – he was nevertheless the first European king to set his country on the road to becoming a modern state, and to initiate those changes that were later adopted (perhaps to some extent imitated) by the Catholic Kings of Spain and the Yorkist and Tudor Kings of England. By the end of his reign his authority was supreme:

> It towered over the great vassals, and even the provincial and popular elements, commanding peace, compelling obedience, concentrating in itself all the interests of the nation, terrible from the suddenness with which it punished, everywhere present, taking counsel from no one, firmly established in itself.[2]

The reign opened inauspiciously. By a series of rash arbitrary moves Louis alarmed the majority of his vassals, who formed in 1465 the League of the Public Good against him. At its head was Charles the Bold, the new Duke of Burgundy. The Dukes of Burgundy had used their own ability, and the strategic position and economic wealth of the area they controlled, to build up a semi-independent state, more powerful than most kingdoms. Most important, their possessions lay athwart the boundaries of France and the Empire, enabling them to play off one ruler against another. Charles continued this policy, until by 1477 he controlled a 'Middle Kingdom' stretching from the Netherlands to the Swiss Alps. It was this over-mighty subject with whom Louis

---

[1] See page 46.

[2] Quoted in A. J. Grant, *The French Monarchy, 1483–1789*, C.U.P., 1925, Vol. I, pp. 3–4.

had to deal. The King gave way, after an indecisive battle at Montlhéry, and at the Peace of Conflans promised the Leaguers what they wanted. Having lost its *raison d'être*, the League melted away, leaving Louis to break his promises and destroy his enemies one by one.[1]

The diplomatic shifts and turns of the succeeding years are too complex to follow in detail. In 1470 Louis' diplomacy resulted in the brief restoration of Henry VI of England, but the project failed and he found himself facing an alliance of Charles the Bold and Edward IV of England. Edward was ultimately bought off at the 'merchant's peace' of Picquigny in 1475, by which the King of England obtained 75,000 crowns, 50,000 crowns a year and the betrothal of the Dauphin to his daughter. (The two Kings met on a bridge and embraced cautiously through a wooden grille halfway across, for assassination was always in the air!)

Quietly, Louis wove his webs – Charles called him 'the universal spider' – to catch Burgundy:

> The harsh administration of Burgundian officials in upper Alsace, the aroused opposition of the Swiss to the growth of Burgundy, the dissatisfaction of René of Lorraine, the hope of Sigismund that he might get his rights and lands back, the cunning of Louis XI, all led to a series of alliances against Charles the Bold.[2]

Charles was defeated by the Swiss in 1474, 1476 and 1477, being killed at Nancy in the last of these battles.

The main danger to Louis was gone; if he had moved cautiously he might have obtained a large share of the Burgundian lands, but he launched an impetuous invasion and drove Charles's daughter Mary into an immediate marriage with the Habsburg Maximilian, son of the Emperor. By the Treaty of Arras (1492) Louis obtained the Duchy of Burgundy, lying within the French frontier, and Picardy – 'the Somme towns'. A French claim to other areas was kept open, but this was all that she got in the end. Guelderland, Utrecht, Liége and Lorraine regained their independence; the rest, consisting of

---

[1] Mazarin adopted similar tactics to destroy the Second Fronde.

[2] J. W. Thompson and E. N. Johnson, *An Introduction to Medieval Europe, 300-1500*, Allen & Unwin, 1938, p. 900.

Flanders, Artois and Franche Comté – the free county of Burgundy outside the French frontiers – passed to the Habsburgs.
Two hundred years later Louis XIV's main efforts were
devoted to obtaining these areas.   Louis XI's failure to acquire
Flanders proved especially disastrous for France.

While Louis XI's chief interest abroad had been this only
partially successful struggle with Burgundy, at home he had
been carrying out major reforms.   Control of the Church
remained securely in his hands.   In 1461 he promised the
Pope that he would abolish the Pragmatic Sanction and in
1472 a Concordat was signed with Sixtus IV, but the King
twisted and turned so dexterously that 'it was impossible to say
whether the Pragmatic was or was not in force',[1] his real aim
being to keep the whole question open.   What was very certain was that he extended the royal control over church jurisdiction, appointments and finance, at the expense of both the
national clergy and the Pope.

Louis seized every opportunity to enlarge the royal domain,
and to put down the independent nobles.   In this he succeeded so well that by his death only Flanders and Brittany
were not controlled by the Crown.   He destroyed Burgundy;
he launched successful expeditions against the southern counts
of Armagnac; in 1481 the last Duke of Anjou died and Louis
obtained Anjou, Maine, Berry and Provence.   In general the
nobles were kept in order by money grants and by fear.   The
secretary to the Duke of Bourbon wrote: 'There was no one
so great in his kingdom that could sleep or rest securely in his
house.'   In England the nobles lost their financial privileges
and kept their political power; in France the reverse happened.

All this needed a strong administration.   The Chancellor
was the official head, and the work was carried out by a King's
Council of salaried, middle-class officials, who owed their
position – and their lives – to the King.   The real burden of
government was supported by Louis alone, so that it was said
that the King's mule carried the King's Council.   He made
no use of the Estates-General; they were only summoned once,
in 1468.   The *Parlement* of Paris, a corporation of lawyers,
claimed the right to register laws, but found it difficult to resist
if the King chose to overrule it.   Lesser *Parlements* existed in

[1] *C.M.H.*, I, 387.

the provinces, and Louis increased their number to eight (Toulouse, Bordeaux, Rouen, Aix, Rennes, Dijon, Grenoble, Perpignan), but local government was really in the hands of crown officials, the *baillis* and *sénéchaux*, exempt from taxation, expecting to make a profit from the local population, men who had bought their offices and were able to keep them in the family. Towns were granted privileges if they behaved themselves, punished fearfully, like Rheims and Bourges, if they showed any independence. The sight of drowned burgesses, floating down the rivers in sacks labelled 'Make way for the King's justice!' discouraged disloyalty.

Louis' security at home and expeditions abroad both required a large and regular income. The approximate details are as follows:

REVENUE

Crown lands	100,000 livres
Aides (duties and excise)	535,000
Gabelle (salt tax)	160,000
Taille (hearth and land tax, from which nobles and clergy were exempt)	1,035,000 in 1461 rising to 3,900,000 in 1483

EXPENDITURE

Pensions	300,000 livres, rising to 500,000
Court expenses	300,000 ,, ,, 400,000
Standing Army	2,700,000 ,, in 1483

Louis financed his government essentially out of the *taille*, which was easy to raise and from which the more powerful classes were exempt. (The burden ultimately became too heavy, and had to be reduced in the next reign.) Although personally miserly, with his old felt hat and greasy robes, Louis thought that money should be made to work for the good of the monarchy and placed his bribes and pensions like investments. Commines remarks: 'He put nothing into his treasury. He took it all and spent it all.' The Lord Chancellor of England was in his pay, and Louis was reputed to have more influence in the Empire than the Emperor Maximilian himself. He developed a diplomatic service, modelled on those of the Italian states. After he had once been let down by

French troops, he concentrated on building up a powerful professional army, which numbered by the end of his reign 16,000, including 6,000 Swiss, the best – and most expensive – troops in Europe.

Louis realized the importance of a prosperous country and initiated, by his policy of interference in economic matters, a primitive form of mercantilism.   In 1462 he developed the fairs at Lyons as rivals to those of Geneva, with the object of tapping the trade which flowed along the great route from Flanders to Italy, and he also established a fair at Rouen to compete with Antwerp.   He encouraged foreign craftsmen to settle in France.   Italians developed silk-manufacture, 'which all idle people ought to be made to work at', at Lyons and (under the royal eye) at Tours.   In 1464 a national system of post-horses was set up to enable the King to obtain and distribute information throughout his kingdom.   In 1470, during the brief restoration of Henry VI, Louis organized an exhibition of French goods in London.   Next year he set up a bureau of mines to encourage prospectors and to grant mining concessions.   In 1479 regulations were issued controlling the cloth trade.   Throughout his reign he tried to attract bullion to the country.   The building of ships and harbours was supervised, notably at Bordeaux and, towards the end of the reign, at Marseilles in the newly acquired district of Provence, where the King had plans to set up a great fleet to get control of the Mediterranean trade.

In the closing year of his reign the neurotic side of Louis' character became dominant.   He shut himself away in his palace at Tours, surrounded by servants who alternately bullied and cringed to him.   The palace grounds were studded with sentries and mantraps.   He suffered from the delusion that he was becoming a leper, and from a genuine paralysis. He had always been superstitious; he would never wear again the clothes he had worn when he heard bad news.   Now as he lay dying, talking, says Commines, a great deal of sense, he was surrounded with ineffective remedies, including the ring of St. Zenobius, a hermit brought all the way from Calabria in southern Italy, and the blood of turtles from the Cape Verde Islands.   These remedies 'though they were not so successful as to recover his life, yet, doubtless, they were very beneficial to his soul' says Commines.

In his shabby old hat and clothes this eaves-dropping,
cheeseparing, cautious monarch, who believed that everyone had his price, but was quick to strike off the head of an
offending nobleman, and even to shut up a treacherous
cardinal in an iron cage, seemed to be an enigmatic compound of craft, cruelty, and vice. . . . His native wit
taught him that a statesman should be a good listener and
greedy for information, that, so far as possible, everybody
of real political importance, both in his own country and in
neighbouring lands, should be known to him personally,
that he should spare no pains to win over an enemy, harbour
no grudges, exercise a long-sighted patience, always be
willing to learn from his own mistakes, and, putting away
pride, to retrace his own steps. . . . In his aversion from
bloodshed, in his distrust of the nobility, in his preferences
for mercenaries . . ., and in his encouragement of trade
and commerce he typifies a new type of statesmanship.[1]

The Valois kings who succeeded Louis XI were, by comparison, all in different ways light-weights. Their energies,
when they had any, were directed to foreign wars. At home
there is less to record in the next four reigns than in that of
Louis XI alone.

The death of Louis found France united, over-taxed, with
a powerful central administration, an efficient army and a
vacillating foreign policy; a country poised, as it were, so
that one might not forecast in what direction she would
develop. In the outcome, the lure of Italian wealth and help-
lessness combined with plausible genealogical claims to draw
her into a series of Italian wars. These adventures in turn
merged in a greater struggle against the enveloping empire of
the Habsburg Charles V. This struggle, too, took place
largely in Italy, and the whole series of wars extended from
1494 to 1559. The foreign policy of the French kings during
these years is described in Chapters IV and V.

The new King, Charles VIII (1483–98), was only thirteen
years old at the time of his father's death and the government
passed into the hands of his sister, Anne de Beaujeu. There
was the usual outbreak of nobles' revolts, including one led by
Charles's brother-in-law, the future Louis XII. These were
suppressed by Anne with a firm hand, and she remained in
control until Charles began to rule in 1491. The important

---

[1] H. A. L. Fisher, *History of Europe*, Arnold, 1936, pp. 459–61.

part she played in tiding over a potentially dangerous minority should not be overlooked.   Her father, who had a low opinion of women, admitted grudgingly that she was 'the least foolish woman' that he knew.

In 1491 Charles married Anne, Duchess of Brittany, thus adding this large and hitherto independent area to the French Crown.   The marriage aroused great opposition abroad and Charles was faced with a dangerous alliance of England, Spain and the Empire.   He bought them off by a series of concessions and left himself, as he thought, with a free hand to invade Italy, which he proceeded to do in 1494.   In 1496 he was back in France, and soon began preparations for a second invasion, but two years later he died, at the age of twenty-eight – a result, it is said, of striking his head against a door lintel at Amboise when on his way to the tennis courts.   Malformed and uneducated – Louis said it was enough if he understood the words '*qui nescit dissimulare, nescit regnare*' – one does not feel that his death was a disaster for France.

Charles left no children and was succeeded by his brother-in-law and distant cousin, Louis XII (1498–1515), who immediately repudiated his own wife Jeanne, in order to marry Charles's widow Anne, thus keeping control of Brittany.[1] Abroad he was involved in Italian wars from 1499 to 1504, and again from 1508 to 1515.   At home his policy was more enlightened.   Few changes were made in the government, Louis even keeping in power those officials who had opposed him in the last reign.   France prospered, enjoying internal peace while the nobles' energies were absorbed in Italy.   The *taille* was reduced by a third; a contemporary, Claude Seyssel, estimated that revenue rose by two-thirds and that a third of the country was cleared for agriculture.   Such figures are not scientific, but they record a strong impression of growing prosperity founded on the maintenance of law and order.   'Merchants now take a journey to Rome, Naples, or London more lightly than formerly to Geneva or Lyons,' he wrote.   The King said that he would rather be laughed at for meanness than blamed for extravagance, and declared in 1513, 'On no account will we lay further burdens on our poor people . . .'

[1] The necessary adjustments were made by Pope Alexander VI, whose son Cesare Borgia received the French title of Duke of Valentinois as part payment for his father's services.

(He had already been hailed by the Estates-General of 1506, as '*Père du peuple*'.)

In both his foreign and home policy Louis was helped by his lifelong friend Georges d'Amboise (1460–1510), who became chief minister and cardinal in 1498. The reduction of taxes, the improved organization of justice, the reform of the monasteries were all carried out by the Cardinal, and his success supports Louis' belief that often the best thing to do was to 'Leave it to Georges'. Machiavelli said of France that it was 'Among the best ordered and governed kingdoms of our time',[1] and some of the credit for this must go to Louis and the Cardinal d'Amboise. Their task was made easier by the natural economic expansion of the period – and by the work of Louis XI. 'The France of Louis XII is the justification of Louis XI.'[2] In 1515 the King's wife died, and he at once married again, his wife being Mary Tudor, sister of Henry VIII. The subsequent round of festivities exhausted Louis and he died within a few weeks of his second marriage. He was succeeded by his son-in-law, Francis I (1515–47).

Young, cultured, handsome – though even contemporaries noticed that monstrous nose, calling him '*le roi grand nez*' – Francis, with Henry VIII and Charles V, makes up the trio of young rulers whose rivalry dominated European politics for thirty years. His foreign policy is a continuation of that of the two previous French kings, though it takes on less the air of an unnecessary luxury and more that of a life and death struggle against the octopus empire of Charles V; a struggle in which France, helped by the German Lutherans and the Muslim Turks, just about manages to hold her own.

At home Francis continued the by now traditional policy of turning the higher nobility into 'a brilliant household of dependants', while the real work of governing was carried on by a small group of professional administrators within the privy council. The central machinery of state continued to function efficiently, while the local government became by the edicts of 1523 and (in the next reign) 1554 an increasingly well-organized bureaucracy. The most important act of creative statesmanship was the centralization of the financial system. Hitherto the greater part of the revenue had been administered

---

[1] Machiavelli, *The Prince*, ed. W. K. Marriott, Dent, 1908, p. 153.
[2] *C.M.H.*, I, p. 416.

by a group of inter-related merchant families who used their position to enrich themselves. In 1523 the head of the most powerful of these, Semblaçay, fell. A new central department was created, the *trésor de l'Epargne*, which administered almost all the revenue. In 1542 the country was divided into eighteen tax districts, and the reorganization was completed in the next reign by the appointment of a single controller-general (1554). Moreover, through the Hôtel de Ville, the King was able to borrow at half the usual rate – 8½ per cent as against 16 per cent. These reforms made the French monarchy the strongest in western Europe. At the end of his reign the Venetian ambassador considered Francis all-powerful. The King, however, was essentially frivolous and unstable, so that his interest in the government was irregular and uncertain, compared with his abiding attachment to hunting, tennis and tournaments.

On the whole economic progress continued, unencouraged but unchecked. The main official action was the establishment of a new port on the north coast in 1517. It was given a grandiloquent Latin name – the Renaissance classical interest was becoming fashionable in France – but the sailors persisted in calling it Le Havre, and Le Havre it has remained. In 1534 a French expedition under Cartier reached the St. Lawrence.

The long-standing tussle with the Pope over the liberties of the French Church was brought to a temporary conclusion by the Concordat of Bologna (1516). The Pope recovered his right to receive the payment of annates, while he recognized the King's right to nominate archbishops, bishops and abbots. The Concordat thus gave the Crown a vested interest in the existing Church and this proved of importance when the Reformation began to affect France.

Francis I was a great patron, and perhaps his most important work, and that which he found most congenial, was to encourage by that patronage the spread of Renaissance culture in France, as described in Chapter II. He appointed Jean Clouet as court painter, and the artist has returned the compliment by immortalizing the King in that portrait (now in the Louvre) from which, rich and self-assured, Francis I regards one sardonically, thin lips made crueller by the narrow moustache that links his beard to the famous nose.

Francis was succeeded by his eldest son, Henri II (1547–59), in character a complete contrast with his father, being 'cold, haughty, melancholy and dull'. The administrative reforms were rounded off; the wars with the Habsburgs continued until the Treaty of Cateau-Cambrésis in 1559. The Treaty ended more than the wars, for Henri was killed in a tournament held to celebrate the return of peace. Throughout his reign he had been under the control of his mistress, Diane de Poitiers, and of the noble families of Montmorency and Guise. The persecution of the Huguenots had become more methodical. In these ways the reign hints at what were to be the dominant themes of French history in the second half of the century – over-powerful nobles and religious wars.

EXTRACT

De Commines describes Louis XI's character, c. 1490

. . . of all the princes that I ever knew, the wisest and most dexterous to extricate himself out of any danger or difficulty in time of adversity, was our master King Louis XI. He was the humblest in his conversation and habit, and the most painful and indefatigable to win over any man to his side that he thought capable of doing him either mischief or service: though he was often refused, he would never give over a man that he wished to gain, but still pressed and continued his insinuations, promising him largely, and presenting him with such sums and honours as he knew would gratify his ambition: . . . He was naturally kind and indulgent to persons of mean estate, and hostile to all great men who had no need of him. Never prince was so conversable, nor so inquisitive as he, for his desire was to know everybody he could; and indeed he knew all persons of any authority or worth in England, Spain, Portugal, and Italy, in the territories of the Dukes of Burgundy and Bretagne, and among his own subjects; and by those qualities he preserved the crown upon his head, which was in much danger by the enemies he had created to himself upon his accession to the throne. But above all, his great bounty and liberality did him the greatest service: and yet, as he behaved himself wisely in time of distress, so when he thought himself a little out of danger, though it were but by a truce, he would disoblige the servants and officers of his court by mean and petty ways, which were little to his advantage; and as for peace, he could hardly endure the thoughts of it.

He spoke slightingly of most people, and rather before their faces, than behind their backs, unless he was afraid of them, and of that sort there were a great many, for he was naturally somewhat timorous. (*The Memoirs of Philip de Commines*, Vol. I, pp. 59–60. Bonn, 1855)

FURTHER READING

A. J. Grant, *The French Monarchy, 1483–1789*, C.U.P., 1925, Vol. I
Cambridge Medieval History, C.U.P., Vol. VIII, 1936, Chapter VIII, Louis XI
The Memoirs of Philip de Commines, 2 vols., Bonn, 1855

Spain, 1474–1516

In the later fifteenth century Spain stood at the parting of the ways: local rulers, local liberties, local privileges might be destroyed or controlled by a unified national state, as was happening to the north in France and England; or local differences might triumph, fragmentation increase, and Spain become, like Italy to the east, only a geographical expression. That she followed the first of these ways rather than the second was due to the work of the 'Catholic Kings' (*los reyes Católicos*), Ferdinand (1479–1516) and Isabella (1474–1504).

Ferdinand of Aragon and Isabella of Castile had married in 1469, but it was not until 1479, the same year in which Ferdinand became King of Aragon, that Isabella was able to make good her power in Castile. From that date they ruled in effect as joint sovereigns. The Iberian Peninsula was then divided between five states. On the west coast was Portugal, already a nation, traditionally hostile to Spain (she had helped to promote the civil war against Isabella), but mainly concerned with the Atlantic and with expansion around Africa to the Indies, which she reached in 1497. In the north, athwart the Pyrenees, lay the small kingdom of Navarre, partly in France, partly in Spain. In the south was the Moorish kingdom of Granada, to which the Arab conquerors of Spain had been confined for two centuries since 1242. The kingdom of Aragon, in north-east Spain, dominated the western Mediterranean. At one time she had had a foothold as far east as southern Greece, and she still ruled Sicily and laid claim to the kingdom of Naples in southern Italy. The central plateau had been unified under the rule of Castile, as the Moors were pushed south. Some idea of the relative importance of these kingdoms can be gained from the following table:

	Area, %	Population, millions
Castile	62	c. 4·5
Portugal	20	c. 1·0 ·
Aragon	15	c. 0·8
Granada	2	c. 1·0
Navarre	1	[uncertain]

The union of Castile and Aragon had occurred almost accidentally, but there was nothing accidental about the way in which Ferdinand and Isabella strengthened their position. Spain remained only a loose confederation of states, held together by the personal union, but there was a consistent policy of centralization of power in the hands of the Crown. In this Isabella led the way, partly because Castile was the larger partner, partly because the local freedoms were more powerful in Aragon – the traditional oath of Aragonese nobles to their king ran as follows:

> We who are as good as you swear to you who are no better than we, to accept you as our king and sovereign lord, provided you observe our statutes and laws; and if not, no.

What follows refers mainly to events in Castile; it is safe to assume, however, that what happened there happened also in Aragon, though often later and in a watered-down form.

The constitutional methods by which the 'Catholic Kings' strengthened their position are typical of the Renaissance 'New Monarchs', echoes of – or echoed by – their French and English contemporaries. To be strong, the monarchy must be financially independent. Isabella increased the financial power of the Crown in Castile by the resumption of crown lands which had been alienated, and by the regular collection of taxes. The chief of these latter were: the *alcabala*, a sales tax, which became a fixed sum in 1494; customs duties; the *subsidio*, a tax on clerical income; and the *Cruzada*. This last, a tax on the sale of indulgences, had been originally authorized in 1482 to finance the war against Granada. It was continued in succeeding years, and everyone was expected to have an up-to-date indulgence, the Crown receiving three-quarters of the net profits. As a result of these actions, the royal revenue rose from 900,000 *reales* in 1474 to 26,000,000 *reales* in 1504.

The collection of this income naturally depended on the efficient administration of the country and, in particular, on the maintenance of law and order. At the beginning of their reign Ferdinand and Isabella found large areas in a condition bordering on anarchy, dominated by independent feudal lords. To deal with this situation the *Santa Hermandad* (Holy Brotherhood) was organized in 1476. Throughout Castile each hundred houses had to supply a mounted archer. In this way a sort of rural police force was established which patrolled the countryside keeping law and order and hunting down law-breakers. The *Hermandad* was greatly feared, punishment being immediate, by mutilation or shooting to death with arrows.[1] It proved such an efficient instrument that by 1498 its work was largely done and it became a more orthodox constabulary.

In its treatment of the nobles the Crown adopted an attitude similar to that of Louis XI: the nobles might have privileges, but not power. They had lost much of their economic strength to the middle classes, and as a result of Isabella's recovery of crown lands. Where necessary, their castles were destroyed by force – forty-six were demolished, for example, in remote Galicia. They were now exempted from taxation, but the business of government was also taken away from them, and they 'were encouraged to appear at court and strive for the purely ornamental honors of palace officialdom. Many came, for those who remained on their estates consigned themselves to obscurity, being without power to improve their fortunes by a revolt as their ancestors had done.'[2] The destruction of the nobles' power was completed by the incorporation of the Grand Masterships of the military orders in the Crown. These orders were composed of the nobility and their dependants and were dangerously strong and wealthy, their members and vassals numbering in 1493 about a million. They had originated as crusading orders against the Muslims,

[1] Compare the Oprichniks, established by Ivan the Terrible.
[2] C. E. Chapman, *A History of Spain*, Macmillan, 1918, p. 211. In 1512 a Palace bodyguard consisting of 200 sons of noblemen was formed.

but had become in effect great independent corporations. They were absorbed by the Crown in 1487 (Calatrava, 200,000 members); in 1493 (Santiago, 700,000); and in 1494 (Alcántara, 100,000).

A machinery of central government by councils was developed. In both Castile and Aragon there existed a *Cortes*, a consultative assembly rather like the early English parliaments. In Aragon especially the medieval *Cortes* had shown signs of developing into something more powerful. These assemblies now declined in importance. The nobles and clergy were exempted from taxation by them, and stopped attending, so that eventually the Castilian *Cortes* had only thirty-six members – 'too large for a council but not large enough for a national assembly'.[1] At the same time the Cortes were summoned less often as the Crown became more secure. Thus the Castilian *Cortes* met only nine times between 1475 and 1503, and not at all during the central period from 1483 to 1497.

The business of government was carried on by the King's Council – the *Consejo Real*. This had been a body of feudal nobles meeting as occasion demanded to advise the king. It now evolved into a department of lawyers sitting permanently to carry out royal policy. These lawyers (*letrados*) became a majority of the Council members in 1480, while in the same year the nobles lost their right to vote, and soon afterwards were excluded altogether. New, lesser councils were created, or developed out of the main body, to handle different departments of royal activity. Some were territorial, such as the councils of Valencia, Catalonia and the Italian territories. Others dealt with new problems which arose as the Crown extended its influence; amongst these were the Council of the Inquisition (1483), the Council of the Military Orders (1489), and rather later the Council of the Indies.

The sphere of local government was also invaded by the power of the Crown. The *Hermandad* patrolled the countryside, while in the towns municipal privileges, embodied in *fueros* (charters) were revoked or not renewed. Those towns that resisted were treated in the same way as rebellious nobles. Local officials were appointed by the central government. The most important link was the *corregidor*. After 1480 the

[1] *N.C.M.H.*, I, p. 332.

corregidores represented the Crown in every town in Castile, acting as 'the omnicompetent servants of an absolute King'. No department of life was exempt from their scrutiny and report:

> We merely kept a Governor for form,
> While this man walked about and took account
> Of all thought, said, and acted, then went home,
> And wrote it fully to our Lord the King
> Who has an itch to know things, He knows why,
> And reads them in His bed-room of a night.[1]

In 1486, by the sentence of Guadeloupe, serfdom had been abolished, and criminal jurisdiction taken out of the hands of the nobles. Spain, like the greater part of western Europe, now adopted the principles of Roman Law, one aspect of which was its emphasis on the power of the ruler – *quod principi placuit legis habet vigorem* (what pleases the prince has the force of law) – an emphasis which was ideally suited to the needs of the royal despots of the fifteenth and sixteenth centuries. The adoption took place in 1505 by the *Leyes de Toro*.

Much depended on the personalities of the rulers. They made good foils for one another. Isabella, determined, proud of herself and of Castile, was never dominated by Ferdinand or by Aragon. On the contrary, she led the way. 'Within thirty years she revolutionized the very rhythm and texture of the nation's life'.[2] She had an honest face, glaucous eyes 'between green and blue', and the peasant's tenacity and bluntness of speech. 'What,' she said when she was presented with the first Spanish Grammar, 'what's its use?' Ferdinand, handsome, an excellent horseman, and quite illiterate, was nevertheless the most astute diplomatist of his day. His methods won the approval of Machiavelli, who called him 'the foremost king in Christendom'. Under their combined sign of the yoke and the arrows (Y for Yugo and Ysabel, F for Flecha and Fernando) they drove and disciplined Spain.[3]

The Catholic Kings were assisted by Isabella's confessor, Cardinal Jiménez (Ximenes), who was in a position of power and trust from 1492 till his death in 1517. He was largely

---

[1] 'How It Strikes A Contemporary', Robert Browning, 1855.
[2] W. C. Atkinson, *Spain*, Methuen, 1934, p. 81.
[3] The yoke and arrows have been adopted as a symbol in Franco's Spain.

responsible for the peaceful accession of their successor Charles V. He was created Archbishop of Toledo in 1495 and Cardinal Inquisitor-General in 1507. He reformed the morals and behaviour of the Church, especially of the orders of nuns and friars, while the freedoms of the Church in lay matters were reduced in the same way as those of the nobles. At the same time, the Church was gradually withdrawn from the normal system of taxation, contributing the *subsidio* and a proportion of the *Cruzada* instead. Jiménez was also strongly influenced by Renaissance humanism, and was responsible for the creation of a new University at Alcalá, where the Complutensian Bible was produced.

While the Catholic kings were occupied in reforming the government by concentrating all power in the Crown, they were simultaneously engaged in strengthening the country by expansion abroad, and by the imposition of an outward unity on the different races and religions that existed within Spain.

The second task was the more complex. During the Middle Ages there had arrived in the peninsula two alien elements – the Arabs as conquerors, and the Jews as traders. The later reconquest by the native Spanish had produced no fewer than seven national-religious groupings. The Arabs were divided into Muslims, living in the still independent kingdom of Granada; *Mudejares*, Muslims living in Catholic Spain; and *Moriscos*, Muslims who had become converted to Christianity. There were practising Jews, and Jews who had become Christians, *Marranos*. There were the Catholic Spanish, of course, and also those Christians who had lived for a long time under Muslim rule and acquired a hybrid culture, known as *Mozarabes*. Faced with these divisions, it is not surprising that Ferdinand and Isabella adopted the policy of imposing religious unity by force, though in fact that policy proved in the long run politically ineffective and economically disastrous. War with the Moorish kingdom of Granada broke out in 1480 and after hard fighting the capital was taken and the war ended in 1492. The Muslims were promised religious toleration, but, when an attempt at forced conversion had led to a rising, those who still refused to accept Christianity were expelled from Castile (1502), though not from Aragon.

Within three months of the fall of Granada Ferdinand and

Isabella had ordered the conversion or expulsion of the Jews from Castile and Aragon. It is said that 20,000 lost their lives, 165,000 emigrated and 50,000 accepted baptism and became *Marranos*. The fact that this name meant 'pigs' suggests how little they were assimilated.

To enforce their religious policy the Catholic kings in 1478 asked the Pope to establish an Inquisition in Castile.[1] It was set up first at Seville in 1480 and in the following year the first *auto de fé* took place there, at which six people were burnt. Tribunals were soon set up in other towns, under the control of an Inquisitor-General, Torquemada (1483–94). There were reputedly a considerable number of burnings between 1480 and 1504. The religious problem was not solved, as later events showed, but the Inquisition became a most efficient instrument for imposing unity and royal control on the whole country.

In the expansion of their influence and territories the Catholic kings proved more successful than in their handling of the domestic religious problem. They began to compete successfully with the Portuguese, who were ruled, Erasmus said, by a 'Grocer-King'. In 1492, that seminal year in Spanish history, Columbus made his first voyage, under the patronage of Castile, and reached the West Indies. In 1493 the Spanish Pope, Alexander VI, gave Spain authority over all lands more than one hundred leagues west of the Cape Verde Islands, but by the Treaty of Tordesillas the next year the boundary was finally drawn three hundred and seventy leagues to the west. In 1494 the Canary Islands were conquered, and between 1508 and 1510 Oran and other points on the North African Mediterranean coast were captured from the Muslims. In 1503 the *Casa de Contratación* was set up at Seville to control all American trade.

In Europe Ferdinand played a dominant part in the Italian wars from 1494 to 1516. In 1493 the French king, Charles VIII, who was already planning to invade Italy, reached an agreement with him by which Ferdinand promised not to interfere in the affairs of the kingdom of Naples – the area in Italy to which both France and Aragon laid claim. In return Charles ceded to Aragon the districts of Cerdagne and

---

[1] The Inquisition had originally been set up in 1233, and there had been a court in Spain, but it had died out.

Roussillon, Catalan-speaking but lying to the north of the Pyrenees. The French did not recover these areas for over a hundred and fifty years, but within twelve months Ferdinand had broken his word and was helping to form an alliance against Charles, the League of Venice. From then onwards, with the exception of the years 1508–10, the one clear thread in the tangled skein of events in Italy was the opposition of France and Spain.

From the Spanish point of view the most important period was from 1502 to 1504. During these years a Spanish army under 'the great captain' (*il Gran Capitano*) Gonzalo de Córdoba drove the French from Naples, winning a decisive victory at Cerignola in 1503. The secret of Gonzalo's success lay partly in his own genius, partly in the fact that the French were far from their base, but mainly in the successful reorganization of the Spanish army. In 1496 a standing army had been set up, in which a twelfth of all men between twenty and forty were liable for service. Gonzalo modelled his pikemen on those of the Swiss, his light infantry on the Italian arquebusiers, and made of both a powerful force, which gave the first indication that the Spanish soldier would soon replace the Swiss as the best in Europe. As a result of the Spanish victories France renounced her claim to Naples by the Treaty of Blois (1505) and southern Italy remained in the hands of Spain for two centuries, until 1713.

On the death of Isabella in 1504 Ferdinand married Germaine de Foix, the niece of Louis XII of France. In 1512 the death of her brother left Ferdinand with a claim to the throne of Navarre. Ferdinand overran Spanish Navarre at once and the area was officially annexed in 1515. Thus when he died in the following year Ferdinand left behind a peninsula united except for Portugal. Spain controlled the western Mediterranean and held south Italy, points along the north African coast, and huge, though as yet uncertain, areas of the New World. The rivalry of France and Spain, which was to continue with hardly a pause until the Treaty of the Pyrenees in 1659, had begun and Spain had won the first round. France had been duped and held at bay with the minimum of expense. Ferdinand was justly annoyed when he heard that Louis XII had accused him of having twice deceived the French king. 'He lies,' said Ferdinand, 'I have deceived him ten times!'

In material and intellectual progress, the reign of the Catholic kings was less remarkable. The artistic Renaissance made surprisingly little impact on Spain. The influence of Erasmian humanism was more widespread, but was destined to fade away. The importance of economic matters was not really recognized. And so, though Spain led the way with great success in the realms of national unification, administration and government, and though the sixteenth century was in many ways her golden age, she was never as completely dominant as one might expect, and her rivals overhauled and passed her one by one. The reasons for this lie partly in the details of later political history – the peculiar difficulties of Charles V, the disastrous revolt of the Netherlands – but economic weakness played a large part and this had its origin in the reigns of Ferdinand and Isabella. The expulsion of the Jews had shaken the commercial structure of the country, the expulsion of the Muslims led to the decline of irrigation and hence of agriculture in Andalusia. In the fourteenth century the sheep-breeders had been allowed to form a great corporation, the *Mesta*. This corporation was now encouraged by Ferdinand and Isabella, and its privileges codified in 1511. The aim was good, to encourage the production of native wool and cloth, but the privileges proved most disastrous. In April the sheep-flocks moved from their winter pasture in Estremadura and La Mancha north to Leon and the Asturias. In September they moved south again. A great strip of country, the royal sheepwalk, was set aside for the practice of this horizontal transhumance, in which other forms of agriculture were rendered impossible. The damage done by the passage of these huge flocks (in 1477, 2,694,042 sheep) was enormous; and the *Mesta* found it profitable to export raw wool to Italy, so that in fact a cloth industry did not develop in Spain. A rigid class-structure made for stability but not for economic progress. An emphasis on *limpiezza* (purity of blood) and noble birth encouraged an unproductive lesser nobility – the *hidalgo* [1] and the *caballero* – too poor to produce a surplus themselves, too proud to work for others.

Isabella and Ferdinand had five children: Isabella and Mary married into the Portuguese royal family, Catherine into the English house of Tudor, John and Joanna into that of

---

[1] Who numbered perhaps 540,000 (10%) in Castile alone.

the German Habsburgs.   On Isabella's death Joanna and her
Habsburg husband Philip became rulers of Castile, but Philip
died within two years and Joanna was declared mad.   Ferdinand resumed the rule of Castile, as Regent for Joanna's son,
the future Charles V, who succeeded Ferdinand on the latter's
death in 1516.

Extract

A Florentine looks at Spain, 1513:

The natives do not devote themselves to trade, which they
look upon as degrading; the pride of the hidalgo goes to his
head, and he would rather turn to arms with little chance of
gain, or serve a grandee in wretchedness and poverty, or, before the times of the present king, even assault wayfarers,
than engage in trade or any other business.   Recently, however, some attention is beginning to be given in a few places
to trade, and already in parts of Spain cloth and silks are
manufactured; . . .

But the whole nation is opposed to industry.   Accordingly
the artisans only work when they are driven to do so by necessity, and then they take their ease until they have spent their
earnings; this is the reason why manual labour is so dear. . . .

Aside from a few grandees of the kingdom who display
great luxury, it must be remembered that the rest of the
people live at home in the utmost straits; and if they have a
little to spend they put it all on their backs or in purchasing
a mule, thus making a great show before the world when they
have scarce anything at home, where their surroundings are
mean in the extreme and where they exercise an economy
truly astonishing. (Guicciardini, *Opere inedite*, Vol. VI,
quoted by J. H. Robinson, *Readings in European History*, Vol. II,
Ginn, 1906, pp. 25–6)

Further Reading

C. E. Chapman, *A History of Spain*, Macmillan, 1918
J. B. Trend, *The Civilization of Spain*, O.U.P., 1944
A. Turberville, *The Spanish Inquisition*, O.U.P., 1932
R. T. Davies, *The Golden Century of Spain*, Macmillan, 1937; Chapter I

The Empire, 1493-1519

The political history of western Europe at this time is largely that of the attempt to create stable nation-states. France and Spain succeeded in this task while, for different reasons, Italy and the Empire failed. It is not difficult to discover some at least of the causes for the failure of the latter. For one thing, it was the wrong size. The new states had to be large enough to be powerful, but small enough to be easily united. The Empire sprawled. Then too there was no natural centre round which national feeling could easily coalesce. The Emperor had great theoretical prestige, but he was in fact only a territorial prince, his lands lying largely in one corner of the Empire, his power regarded with jealousy by his peers. Even in the Middle Ages the Empire had ceased to correspond to any political reality, its theoretical pretensions increasing as its real power declined. The last Emperor to make some attempt to reconcile theory and practice, Sigismund, had died in 1438.

The Empire had grown into a jigsaw puzzle of bits and pieces; there were said to be 365 of them, and there were certainly over 200 relatively important ones. At its head was the Emperor. He was elected, and in theory need not be a German prince: Henry VIII, for instance, contested the election of 1519. In fact, from 1438 until the Empire vanished in 1806, the title was always held by the Austrian Habsburgs, who gradually carved a smaller empire for themselves out of the chaos of the larger one. At a time when a national ruler needed an organized administration, an army and a regular system of taxation, the Emperor – as Emperor – possessed none of these things. What power the Habsburgs possessed was theirs as rulers of Austria and its associated territories. That power was sufficient to prevent the Empire breaking up into local units (Austria, Bavaria, Saxony and so on), but insufficient to establish a united country at the expense of those areas. The history of the Empire in the sixteenth and early seventeenth centuries is largely the history of the process by which the larger units within it used religious pretexts to increase their own particular power at the expense of that of the Emperor. As for the latter, it is more realistic to regard him simply as the ruler of Austria – a ruler for whom the possession of the Empire was more often a source of weakness than of strength.

Next in theoretical importance to the Emperor were the seven Electors, who had been given by the Golden Bull of 1356 the right of electing the Emperor. Of these, three were the Archbishops of Cologne, Mainz and Trier, spiritual princes of the Rhineland. Of the four lay Electors one, the King of Bohemia, was a foreigner; the Count Palatine ruled the middle Rhineland; the Duke of Saxony ruled the area to the northwest of modern Czechoslovakia; the Margrave of Brandenburg that to the north of Saxony. These seven made up the College of Electors.

About 120 spiritual princes and 170 lay ones had the right to be represented in the Imperial Diet. Their territories varied greatly in importance, from sizeable states like the territories of the Bishop of Liége, or the Landgrave of Hesse, to the merest inconsiderable scraps of land.

This patchwork was studded with Free and Imperial Cities, the latter built on royal demesne. Their numbers fluctuated but, with the growth of commerce, tended to increase. In the second half of the fifteenth century they began to form Leagues to protect their trade and increase their power; these often included the local nobility, such as the Swabian League on the upper Rhine, formed in 1488, which at one time possessed an army of over 12,000 men. In 1489 the Imperial Cities obtained the right to be represented at the Diet.

Lastly, probably most numerous, and certainly most destructive of law and order, were the Imperial Knights. In some ways similar to Scottish lairds, these held directly of the Emperor and often 'ruled' little more than the castle from which they exercised their trade of highway robbery.

This tangle of feudal liberties and nascent states was in theory united by the Emperor and the Imperial Diet. The latter consisted of three Estates: the seven Electors; the lay and spiritual princes, about 290 in number; the Imperial Cities (85). There was no agreement on the Diet's power and procedure. When it had reached a decision there followed 'negotiations between Diet and Emperor, and the result reached was like a treaty between independent Powers'.[1]

[1] A. J. Grant, *The French Monarchy, 1483–1789*, C.U.P., 1925, Vol. I, p. 7.

Maximilian had married Mary of Burgundy, the daughter of Charles the Bold, in 1477 when Louis XI's ill-judged aggression had driven her to seek protection from France. By this marriage he added to the traditional Austrian Habsburg lands on the Danube (Austria, Carinthia, Styria, the Tyrol) the Burgundian Rhineland possessions of Franche Comté, Luxemburg and the Netherlands. Besides its obvious advantage to Austria, this marriage had two important long-term results. It gave Austria territory in the west and prevented her becoming a purely southeastern power, interested only in the Danube and the Turks. It also ensured that France and Austria would normally be enemies, since France would try to recover these Burgundian territories. This enmity remained a fairly constant factor until the middle of the eighteenth century.

In 1486 Maximilian was elected King of the Romans – a title the significance of which was rather like that of 'Prince of Wales', and in effect ruled the Empire for his father, Frederick III. On the latter's death in 1493 Maximilian became Emperor,[1] and in the same year Charles VIII of France ceded Flanders to him. In 1496 Maximilian arranged the marriage of his son Philip to Joanna, the daughter of Ferdinand and Isabella of Spain. The child of this marriage, Charles V, thus united in his own person the Austrian and Burgundian territories and those of Spain (Aragon, Castile, Navarre, the Balearic Islands, Sardinia, Sicily and the Indies). His empire in Europe was greater than any since the days of Charlemagne and was the most successful result of Maximilian's tortuous and often far-fetched diplomacy. The Habsburg emblem A.E.I.O.U., was said to stand for *Austriae est imperare orbi universo*, Austria will rule the world, and a Latin verse ran *Alii bella gerant; tu, felix Austria, nube; Namque Mars aliis, dat tibi regna Venus* (others wage war; you, lucky Austria, marry; and while Mars helps the others, Venus provides your power).

As a dynastic ruler, waging war by marriage, Maximilian was successful. As an Emperor his complex, interfering, haphazard foreign policy achieved nothing.[2] Its only importance in Imperial history was that the need for money for his Italian

---

[1] The last Emperor to be crowned in Rome.
[2] It is not described here, but can in part be disentangled from Chapter IV.

escapades led Maximilian to compromise in his struggle with the princes in Germany.

Before Maximilian's accession there had already appeared in the Empire a reform party led by the elector Berthold, Archbishop of Mainz. The essence of Berthold's various plans was the creation of a federal Germany, ruled by a Council of Regency in which the power of the Emperor would be outweighed by that of the princes, of whom the Archbishop was naturally one. Had Berthold achieved his aim the Empire would have become in effect an oligarchy. The attitude of the greater princes to the problem of reform was similar to that of the nobles in fifteenth century England. They, too, wanted central institutions of government, provided these were under their own control.

In 1495 Maximilian joined the League of Venice against the French in Italy and a Diet was called at Worms to pay for the Imperial army. There Maximilian and the reform party under Berthold manoeuvred for twenty-six weeks until eventually a compromise was agreed upon. Maximilian refused to accept the plan for a Council of Regency (*Reichsregiment*) which would have provided the Empire with a central administrative authority, since he would only have been allowed to nominate three of its twenty members. Control would thus have passed to the princes, and the Emperor would have become merely an executive officer. He accepted instead a plan for the calling of an annual Diet which he promised to consult. In return he obtained a grant of the proceeds of the Common Penny for four years. (The Common Penny was a graduated property tax, and its expenditure was to be controlled by the Diet.) Both sides agreed to the development of the powers of the Imperial Court of Justice (*Reichskammergericht*) so that it might deal with disputes between the princes and make easier the adoption of Roman Law throughout the Empire. A Perpetual Peace was declared inside the Empire, forbidding private wars and the use of private armies, a reform aimed particularly at the lawless Imperial Knights.

The collection of the Common Penny proved impossible: in Switzerland there was a revolt of such widespread proportions that Maximilian was forced to recognize the Swiss cantons' *de facto* independence by the Treaty of Basle (1499). The other reforms faded away. It had been fatal to entrust them to the Diet, a body which had already proved its uselessness.

Nevertheless, shortage of money and renewed fighting in Italy (where Louis XII had invaded Milan) forced Maximilian to meet the Diet at Augsburg in 1500. The Estates agreed to provide an Imperial army of 34,000, while Maximilian had to accept Berthold's Council of Regency. The Empire was to be divided into six 'circles', excluding Habsburg territory, responsible for carrying out the decisions of the Council. The plan worked briefly and then, in 1502, Berthold and Maximilian quarrelled. Two years later the Archbishop died, and the Emperor was able to divide and destroy the purpose of the other Electors, by providing his own 'reforms'. In general they fared no better than Berthold's had done. In 1507 the Empire was divided for administrative purposes into ten 'circles'. These survived and were of some limited value, but otherwise the old anarchy returned.

The truth of the matter was that Maximilian wanted money, the princes wanted power, but no one now wanted a strong central government. In other countries the local liberties were extinguished by the King – Ferdinand, or Louis or Henry – but 'Germany was not a unity; the Empire was not a government'.[1] The character of Maximilian played its part in this failure. Affable, easy-going, he was popular wherever he went, but he wasted time and money in disastrously mismanaged wars. As with the medieval emperors, wars in Italy gave scope for disunion in Germany. Maximilian fluttered in too many directions and flew in none – he even considered, apparently seriously, the possibility of becoming Pope (and of making himself King of Sweden). Stubbs has described his attractively inefficient personality:

> The most delightfully unprincipled hero of the age of transition, always in every feast and every fray, always wanting money and selling himself for promises, and never getting the money and never keeping his engagements; a good deal of the rake and a good deal of the knight-errant.[2]

As a purely dynastic prince of the house of Habsburg, however, Maximilian was not unsuccessful. True, at his death the French had got control of Milan; but within his Austrian

---

[1] Grant, p. 18.

[2] Stubbs, *Lectures on European History*, Longmans, Green, 1904, p. 337.

territories he carried out reforms, possibly adopted from Burgundy, and centralized the administration at Innsbruck. He left to his grandson Charles strength there and in the Netherlands.

EXTRACT

A Venetian Ambassador describes the princes and knights of the Empire, 1507:

The princes are in the habit of remaining in their own territories far from the court, where they support by their income, so far as they can, the nobles of the region. These princes are almost continually at strife with one another or with some of the free towns. If they are poor, they generally permit their retainers to attack and rob on the highways. They are naturally proud and insolent, and feel resentment toward any one who is able to rival them in any respect . . .

Moreover the chief temporal princes are in the habit of leaving their principality to the eldest son and then providing for the rest of their children with other territories, or ecclesiastical benefices; so that if a duke has ten sons, all demand to be dukes like their father. The result is that there are an infinite number of counts, dukes and margraves in Germany . . .

The knights are accustomed to live in some castle far from a town, or at the court of some prince, or among the mountains in solitary regions. They live and dress wretchedly, hate the burghers, and are poor, but so proud that nothing in the world would induce them to engage in commerce. They are devoted to fighting; and when that is wanting they have nothing to do but to hunt or set to plundering on the highways. (Quirini; quoted by J. H. Robinson, *Readings in European History*, Ginn, Vol. II, p. 31)

FURTHER READING

New Cambridge Modern History, C.U.P., Vol. I, 1957, Chapter VII: The Empire under Maximilian I

IV · THE ITALIAN WARS, 1494–1559

The Expedition of Charles VIII, 1494–5

THE European wars fought between 1453, when England's struggle with France came to an end, and the Treaty of Cateau-Cambrésis in 1559, took place largely in, and for possession of, that debatable land starred with independent urban communities, which stretched across Europe from the Netherlands to Sicily. The greater part of the fighting was concentrated in an even smaller area between Naples and the Alpine foothills. It is arguable that this checked the growth of a national state in Italy as effectively as the political structure of the Empire prevented the rise of a united Germany.

North Italy offered obvious attractions to the invader. The area was superficially rich, and full of portable loot. It was politically weak and divided, unable to defend itself and prone to look for foreign aid in its domestic quarrels, while the surrounding powers, France, Spain and the Empire, all laid claim to parts of the peninsula.

None of this was obvious to contemporaries. The seventy or eighty states of the fourteenth century had reduced themselves to five giants [1] and a number of satellites by the middle of the fifteenth century. On the whole these states were uneasily peaceful. North and central Italy was prosperous, and it was civilized; the artistic innovations of earlier days had given place to the assured control of the High Renaissance. Guicciardini, looking back on the period, wrote that for a thousand years

> *Italy* had at no Time enjoy'd a State of such compleat Prosperity and Repose, as in the Year 1490, and some time before and after.

After describing the political scene, he continued:

> Such then was the State of Affairs; these were the Foundations for the Tranquillity of *Italy*; so connected, and counter-

---

[1] Milan, Venice, Florence, the Papal States, and the kingdom of Naples. See Chapter I.

poised, that there was not only no Appearance of a present Change, but the most discerning Person could not devise, by what Counsels, Accidents, or Powers, such a Peace could be disturbed.[1]

Nevertheless the situation was not so stable as it appeared. The hindsight of the historian can see more than 'the most discerning Person'. In Milan the usurping house of Sforza ruled, and the Duke, Ludovico, had himself usurped his nephew's throne. The French house of Orleans had a claim to the Duchy, derived from the expelled Visconti, while at the same time the area was technically within the Empire. There was plenty of room for discord there. To the east, Venice was feared and envied by her neighbours, who would be glad of a chance to check her expansion and share her wealth. In the south, the kingdom of Naples had passed to an illegitimate branch of the house of Aragon, but Ferdinand of Spain still ruled Sicily and looked with envy across the Straits of Messina to the north. There too the French had a claim, which passed to the Crown on the death of the Duke of Anjou in 1481.

Central Italy, dominated by the Papal States and the republic of Florence, had begun to show symptoms of instability. In Rome the Spaniard, Rodrigo Borgia, had become Pope as Alexander VI, and was already suspected of intending to carve out of the Papal States a temporal kingdom for his family. In Florence the Medici had controlled the republic, in fact if not in theory, for most of the fifteenth century, but there were signs that this control was now weakening. Their enemies, especially in Pisa (which Florence had annexed in 1406) looked to France for help. The Prior of San Marco, Savonarola, by his attacks on the luxury of the city and by his prophecies of impending doom, spread social discord, and weakened morale. In 1492 the ruling Medici, Lorenzo the Magnificent, died and was succeeded by the relatively incompetent Piero. In these ways there was created a Florence ripe for revolution.

All that was wanted was some action to liberate the tensions concealed within an apparently peaceful Italy. It was provided by Charles VIII of France. Small in mind and body, he had determined, against the advice of his counsellors, to

[1] F. Guicciardini, *History of Italy*, trans. A. Goddard; London, 1755, Vol. I.

assert the French claim to Naples. The Duke of Milan had invited him to invade the Peninsula. He felt that it was a Crusade, that he might recapture Constantinople from the Turks. He called himself King of Jerusalem and put on his banners *Voluntas Dei; missus a Deo*. His marriage to Anne of Brittany had raised up a powerful coalition against him. Charles bought it off in a reckless series of treaties. By the Treaty of Étaples (1492) Henry VII received 50,000 francs a year; by the Treaty of Barcelona (1493) Ferdinand got the provinces of Roussillon and Cerdagne to the north of the Pyrenees; by the Treaty of Senlis the Emperor Maximilian obtained Artois and Franche Comté.

Having thus secured his rear, Charles, with the main French army, crossed the Alps on the second of September, 1494, while a quarter of his force went by sea to Genoa. The army met no serious opposition and moved south by way of Turin and Pavia to Florence, which Charles occupied on November 17. Piero de' Medici had fled. On the last day of the year Charles entered Rome. Having made terms with Alexander VI, he moved on south and reached Naples on February 22. Europe had watched his march with amazement. He had come 600 miles in six months. Men said that the French did not need weapons, only chalk to mark up their billets. But this very success helped to destroy the invaders. All who felt themselves in danger united, in the League of Venice,[1] against Charles. The French army, short of supplies, weakened by disease, its lines of communication extended to breaking-point, retreated almost as quickly as it had advanced. There was an indecisive battle at Fornovo in north Italy and then Charles withdrew to France. Within the next year the garrisons he had left behind in Naples had been driven out by the Spanish under Gonzalo de Córdoba.

This brief prologue ushered in a period of thirty years of fighting. The pattern changed in detail but remained basically the same. An Italian state would open the door to the invader, who would be successful, and then the Italians would unite and with the help of the other great powers drive the invader out again. In the long run it was Italy and

---

[1] The main members were the Pope, Alexander VI; the Emperor, Maximilian; Ferdinand of Aragon; Venice and Milan.

Italian unity that suffered, and the Spanish Habsburgs who gained.[1]

An immediate result of Charles VIII's expedition had been the expulsion of the Medici from Florence and the establishment there of a new constitution, modelled to some extent on that of Venice. This was drawn up with the help of Savonarola. Born in 1452, he had become Prior of the Dominican convent of San Marco in 1491. In his sermons he attacked the Medici for destroying the liberty of Florence, Pope Alexander for his temporal wickedness, and the Florentines themselves for their luxurious sins, prophesying doom for all three. He told his own priory that God had revealed to him that twenty-five of its twenty-eight members would be damned. His sermons, perhaps surprisingly, were very popular. Now, however, his descent into the political arena, his support of the French, and the puritan rule which he imposed on Florence, destroyed his influence. In 1497 he was excommunicated by Alexander VI, and in the following year the Florentine mob rose against him. He was tried by Papal commissioners in Florence for heresy – he had declared 'a Pope who errs does not represent the Church' – and was burnt in 1498 in the same square where the year before the people had, on his instructions, burnt their 'vanities' – cards, false hair, paintings and books – and sung 'Go mad, go mad for Jesus'.[2]

The Expeditions of Louis XII, 1499–1504 and 1508–16

In 1499 a second invasion of Italy took place under the new French king, Louis XII. He had inherited the Orleanist claims to Milan as well as the Angevin claims to Naples. His army of 17,000 defeated the unpopular Duke of Milan, Ludovico Sforza. Ludovico was exiled and France divided the Duchy of Milan with Venice. Then Louis marched south to Naples where he agreed, by the Treaty of Granada (1500), to divide that kingdom with Ferdinand of Aragon. The boundary between the northern French and southern Spanish shares was, perhaps deliberately, vague and there was also disagreement over the movement of flocks from their summer pastures in the French Abruzzi and southern Appenines to

---

[1] One incidental consequence was the spread of Italian culture to France.
[2] *Che per zelo e per amore*
De Gesù, diventar pazzo.

their winter grazing in Spanish Capitanata and Apulia. As a result war broke out in 1502, and by 1504 the Spanish had driven the French out of Naples. The success of the Spanish was partly due to their new army which had been modelled on the best Italian and Swiss lines, partly to the genius of their general Gonzalo de Córdoba, and partly to the proximity of their base in Sicily. The acquisition of Naples by the Spanish was one of the few permanent consequences of the Italian fighting, for it remained in their hands until 1713.

While the French had been acquiring Milan and the Spanish Naples, Cesare Borgia, the son of Pope Alexander VI, had been making use of his father's French alliance and the temporary acquisition of 300 French 'lances' which it brought him, to restore Papal control over the cities of the Romagna, the northern part of the Papal states. In this he was eminently successful, using a mixture of force and cunning that has been anatomized by Machiavelli in *The Prince*. It is possible that he hoped to establish there a state for himself, but his father died in 1503 before the work was completed, and the Papacy passed almost immediately into the hands of his enemy, Giulio della Rovere, who took the name of Julius II. Cesare was imprisoned, subsequently went to Spain and died in an obscure skirmish in Navarre in 1507. Julius meanwhile completed the work of restoring the Pope's power throughout the Papal States – a task which he seems to have enjoyed.

It was Julius II's desire to complete the reconquest of the Romagna by recovering Rimini and Faenza from Venice. This was indeed the main cause of the next Italian war. In 1508 he encouraged for this purpose the formation of the League of Cambrai, composed of all those who feared Venice, or hoped to benefit from her partition.[1] Since 1495 she had held part of Spanish Naples; she had quarrelled with the Pope on ecclesiastical matters and with Maximilian over the control of Padua and Verona; now the French intended to add eastern Milan to their territory in the west. Worst of all, Venice was rich, powerful and arrogant.

The Venetians retreated from their mainland possessions and withdrew to the lagoons. Louis and Maximilian divided the conquered mainland between them, but almost at once

---

[1] The main members were the Pope, Julius II; the Emperor, Maximilian; Ferdinand of Aragon; Louis XII of France, and Henry VIII of England.

the familiar Italian pattern repeated itself, and an alliance was created to drive out the foreigner. The mainland cities, oppressed by Maximilian, wished they had not opened their gates to him quite so quickly and yearned for the return of Venice's humane rule. Julius II, having gained his territory and being, as the Venetian ambassador, Domenico Trevisiano observed, 'determined to be the lord and master of the world's game', joined Venice and Spain, in a Holy League,[1] the prime object of which was to drive the French out of Italy.

At first all went well for the League; the French were decisively defeated by Swiss mercenaries at Novara and forced to evacuate Milan, which was restored to the Sforza family, and the French party was overthrown in Florence, to which the Medici returned in 1512. Meanwhile Pope Julius II had died in 1513 before the battle of Novara, and been succeeded by Leo X, himself a Medici. Louis XII died in 1515 and was succeeded by Francis I. Four years later, in 1519, the Emperor Maximilian died. The old actors were replaced by a new cast but the play went on.

Immediately on his accession Francis I led his armies into Italy and defeated the Swiss in a two-day battle at Marignano (1515). The French recovered Milan which they held until 1522. The battle marked the end of the period during which the Swiss had been the best soldiers in Europe, a period that had lasted since 1470. They now signed a perpetual peace with France (1516) by which their boundaries with Milan were adjusted, and a little later they became in effect a neutral nation. For the moment the success of Francis seemed complete, but for that very reason it was not lasting.

The Decisive Struggle in Italy, 1521–9

In 1519 the Habsburg Charles V was elected Emperor, thus winning the first victory in a struggle with Francis that was to continue for almost thirty years.[2] Fighting broke out between the rivals in 1521 when the French invaded Spanish Navarre. The Holy League was more or less reconstituted in its original form – the new Pope, Adrian VI, had been Charles's right-hand man in Spain – and the French were driven from Milan. In the following year the Duke of Bour-

---

[1] To which the Emperor Maximilian and Henry VIII adhered later.
[2] See Chapter V.

bon quarrelled with Francis, joined Charles, and was put in charge of the Italian armies. Francis I invaded Italy again (1524) and reoccupied Milan, but in the following year he suffered the most decisive defeat of the wars at Pavia. Francis was besieging this Lombard city when he found himself in danger of being trapped between the forces inside the walls and a relieving army under Bourbon. He rashly attacked the latter and was routed. (At one point he silenced his own artillery by getting between them and the enemy.) Francis himself was taken prisoner and sent to Madrid.[1] There, after some delay, he signed a treaty in 1526 by which he gave up all France's claims in Italy and to the entire Burgundian inheritance, including the Duchy of Burgundy within France and French Flanders in the north. His two sons were handed to Charles as hostages and he was allowed to return to France.

The battle of Pavia (won on Charles's birthday, February 24) had been too complete a victory for one who was already apparently the most powerful ruler in Europe. As soon as Francis had left Spain he claimed that he had signed the Treaty of Madrid under pressure and that his oath was not valid. Other states, alarmed at Charles's power, supported the King of France, and he was able to create the League of Cognac against the Emperor.[2] For three years there was hard but unco-ordinated fighting in Italy, in the course of which the Imperial army took Rome. Bourbon was killed in the assault and his troops, unpaid and uncontrolled, sacked the city (1527). In the following year the Genoese leader, Andrea Doria, led Genoa to the side of Charles V. This was an important event. The Emperor obtained not only a fleet, but also a port vital for communications between Spain and Milan, and control over the coastal route into French Provence. By 1529 both sides had fought themselves to a standstill, while Charles also needed peace in order to deal with the problems of German Protestantism and of the Turkish pressure up the Danube.

The resulting Peace of Cambrai (1529) in effect settled the outstanding problems in Italy, though it took another thirty years' antagonism (until the Treaty of Cateau-Cambrésis in

---

[1] From whence he wrote: '. . . *de toutes choses ne m'est demeuré que l'honneur et la vie qui est sauve*'.

[2] Supported by Francesco Sforza; Pope Clement VII; Florence and Venice.

1559) for Habsburg and Valois to recognize this. The terms were to a large extent a repetition of those signed at Madrid in 1526. Francis again renounced all claims in Italy, Artois and the Netherlands, but this time he was not required to give up French Burgundy or French Flanders. In return Charles released Francis's two sons, who were still in Madrid, in exchange for two million gold crowns. The money was brought to the frontier in barrels and exchanged on the spot for the princes – neither side trusted the other very far. There were the usual proposals for a marriage alliance and for a Crusade against the Turks. The marriage – of Charles's sister Eleonora to Francis – actually took place. Charles now went to Italy and in 1530 was crowned Emperor by Pope Clement VII at Bologna (once again it was his birthday), having received the iron crown of Lombardy two days before.

The Aftermath; 1536–8; 1542–4; 1552–9

The Treaty of Cambrai was relatively long-lived and when fighting did break out again, the wars had changed their character. The French had lost control of Italy and the Habsburgs were now firmly established there. During the remainder of Francis's reign there were only two brief periods of warfare and although the French made efforts in the traditional directions of Naples and Milan, they were more successful in the Alpine duchy of Savoy, while the area of conflict tended to leave Italy altogether and move to France's northeast frontier.

The death of Francesco Sforza in 1535 led to a revival of the old French claims to Milan. A brief war followed (1536–8) in the course of which the French occupied Savoy while Charles invaded Provence from his new base in Genoa. The French adopted a 'scorched earth' policy and Charles was forced to retreat again. The Truce of Nice repeated the terms of Cambrai but left Francis in control of Savoy.

In 1541 Charles suffered a disastrous defeat at the hands of the Turks in Algiers and, partly for this reason, Francis was encouraged to open hostilities once more (1542–4). Neither side gained any advantage from the fighting, which, as far as Italy was concerned, was confined to Savoy. Francis had made an alliance with the Ottoman Turks in 1536, and in 1543 a Turkish fleet wintered at Toulon. This scandalized Europe – French citizens were evacuated to provide billets for the infidel – but it failed to enable the French to take Nice. In 1544 the Treaty of Crépy once more repeated essentially the terms of the Peace of Cambrai, the French, in addition, giving up Savoy.

In 1547 Francis I died and was succeeded by his son Henri II, who had been the younger of the two hostages in Madrid. That same year Charles won a decisive victory in Germany over the Protestant rebels there. His success had been partly due to the help of Maurice of Saxony, but Maurice was a Protestant and a politician. He was not satisfied with his reward, and he was alarmed at the indications that Charles intended to enforce religious unity in Germany. He turned to Henri and, by the Treaty of Chambord (1552), the King of France promised to help the Protestants in return for the strategically invaluable bishoprics of Metz, Toul and Verdun.

The new war lasted from 1552 to 1559. Apart from unsuccessful attempts by the French to help Florence and to invade Naples, and a brief Imperial brush with the Pope, this was not really an 'Italian war'. The centre of the fighting had moved north of the Alps to Lorraine and the Netherlands, where it was to remain for the next hundred and fifty years. In 1555 Charles began the long process of abdication, and the war became one between Henri II and Charles's son, Philip II. In 1557 there were financial crises in both France and Spain and in the following year the long struggle was finally brought to an end, at least as far as Italy was concerned, by the Treaty of Cateau-Cambrésis. The Spanish kept all their acquisitions in Italy, while France surrendered Savoy, but kept five valuable sally-ports there, the cities of Turin, Pinerolo, Chieri, Chivasso and Villanova, together with Saluzzo.[1]

What were the final consequences of these long, confusing and often tedious wars in Italy? The peninsula became almost a part of the Spanish empire. The Spanish held Naples and Milan and also had control of the client-states of Genoa (1528) and Florence (1537).[2] The outlines of the territorial success of the Spanish Habsburgs had been sketched at least

---

[1] For the other terms of the Treaty, see Chapter V.

[2] An enlarged version of which was renamed the Grand Duchy of Tuscany in 1569.

as early as 1529 and their Italian empire lasted until the extinction of their house in 1700.

France had exhausted herself to no purpose territorially, but it can be argued that the Habsburgs would have been overpoweringly strong if she had not fought them. She failed to obtain any of the areas to which she had laid claim, but the control of the Italian cities in Savoy was turned to advantage by Richelieu in the next century. The earlier wars had encouraged, accidentally, the spread of Italian artistic fashions to France.

Italy suffered most. She had provided the battleground, and experienced the horrors such as those which attended the Sack of Rome by the Imperial troops in 1527. The wars may have checked at a critical moment her development into a single nation-state. Instead she became virtually a Spanish colony. At least she obtained peace; in the second half of the century religious wars were fought in France and the Netherlands, but 'For central Europe there was paralysis, and soon for Italy, the Italy of golden cities, decadence'.[1]

EXTRACTS

1. *Savonarola preaches a sermon:*

O Italy! O Rome! I give you over to the hands of a people who will wipe you out from among the nations! I see them descending like lions. Pestilence comes marching hand in hand with war. The deaths will be so many that the buriers shall go through the streets crying out: Who hath dead, who hath dead? and one will bring his father and another his son. O Rome! I cry again to you to repent! Repent, Venice! Milan, repent! . . . The prophets a hundred years ago proclaimed to you the flagellation of the church. For five years I have been announcing it: and now again I cry to you. The Lord is full of wrath. . . . The saints of Italy, the angels, are leagued with the barbarians. Those who called them in have put the saddles to the horses. Italy is in confusion, saith the Lord; this time she shall be yours. And the Lord cometh above his saints, above the blessed ones who march in battle-array, who are drawn up in squadrons. Whither are they bound? St. Peter is for Rome, crying: To Rome, to Rome!

[1] *N.C.M.H.*, II, p. 358.

and St. Paul and St. Gregory march, crying: To Rome!
And behind them go the sword, the pestilence, the famine.
(Adapted from J. A. Symonds, *The Age of the Despots*; Smith &
Elder, 1906)

2. *Erasmus satirizes the condition of Europe, 1522:*

Alastor: But what says *Fame* upon the whole matter?
Charon: She speaks of Three Great Potentates, that are
mortally bent upon the ruin of one another, insomuch that
they have possessed every part of Christendom with this fury

of *Rage* and *Ambition*. These Three are sufficient to engage
all the lesser Princes and States in their quarrel; and so *wilful*
that they'll rather perish than yield. The *Dane*, the *Pole*,
the *Scot*, nay, and the *Turk Himself*, are dipt in the broil and
the design. The contagion is got into *Spain*, *Britany*, *Italy* and
France: nay, besides these feuds of hostility and arms, there's
a worse matter yet behind: that is to say, there is a malignity
that takes its rise from a diversity of *opinions*, which has debauched men's minds and manners to so unnatural a degree,
and insociable that it has left neither *faith* nor friendship in
the world. . . . For these controversies of the *tongue* and of
the *pen* will come at last to be tried by the *sword's point*. . . .

Alastor: You may observe up and down in the courts of
Princes certain Animals; some of them tricked up with
feathers, others in *white*, *russet*, *ash-coloured frocks*, *gowns*, *habits*;
or call 'em what you will. These are the instruments, you
must know, that are still irritating *Kings* to the thirst of *War*
and *Blood* under the splendid notion of *Empire* and *Glory*: and
with the same art and industry they inflame the spirits of the
Nobility likewise and of the *Common People*. Their sermons are
only *harangues* in honour of the outrages of *Fire* and *Sword* under
the character of a *just*, a *religious*, or a *holy war*. And which is
yet more wonderful, they make it to be *God's Cause* on *both
sides*. *God fights for us*, is the cry of the *French* pulpits; *and
what have they to fear that have the Lord of Hosts for their Protector?
Acquit yourselves like men*, say the *English*, and the *Spaniard*,
and the victory is certain; for this is God's cause, not Caesar's. As
for those that fall in the battle, their souls mount as directly
to Heaven, as if they had wings to carry 'em thither, arms and
all. (From the *Colloquies*; Hell Broke Loose; in Roger
L'Estrange's translation, 1699)

FURTHER READING

A. J. Grant, *The French Monarchy, 1483–1789*, C.U.P., 1925, Vol. I
New Cambridge Modern History, C.U.P., Vol. I, 1957, Chapter XII: The
    Invasions of Italy. Vol. II, 1958, Chapter XI: The Habsburg-
    Valois Struggle
Machiavelli, *The Prince*, ed. W. K. Marriott, Dent, 1908

V · CHARLES V, 1516–58

CHARLES V, the son of Joanna of Spain and the Archduke Philip of Austria, was born at Ghent on February 24, 1500. As a consequence of the death of his father in 1506 and the insanity of his mother he became sole ruler of Spain when his grandfather, Ferdinand of Aragon, died in 1516. Three years later, when his other grandfather, Maximilian, also died he succeeded to the Burgundian inheritance and the lands of the Austrian Habsburgs. Later in the same year, helped by the judicious expenditure of 850,000 florins, he was elected Emperor – 'the dearest merchandise that was ever bought,' wrote Pace, who had been sent to Germany to see how the land lay by Henry VIII. At the age of nineteen Charles ruled a larger empire than any European since the days of Charlemagne.

The very nature of Charles's empire made it impossible for him to control it. His possessions sprawled in disconnected patches across the map of Europe. There was no means of getting from the Austrian lands to Spain, from Spain to Burgundy, except by sea or by long overland marches across the Alps and through other peoples' territory, and whichever way he went his flank was exposed to possible attacks from the French. The magnitude of Charles's inheritance was the measure of its weakness. The problems it implied were greater than the strength it contained. As an Austrian ruler Charles's main preoccupation should be to develop Maximilian's institutions there. In Spain he would have to establish his rule, as a foreigner, over the proudest and most independent race in Europe. As Emperor, as ruler of the Burgundian lands, as King of Spain, he inherited three separate quarrels with France and he would be committed to a war for possession of the scattered territories in Italy and the Netherlands involved in those quarrels. Within the Empire his interests and his beliefs alike ran contrary to the two main currents of the time, local nationalism and Protestantism. Within two years the Turks would take Belgrade and begin to exert their pressure on central Europe.

Faced with such a collection of problems, it is not surprising that Charles failed to solve them. Throughout his reign he hurried anxiously from one group of his possessions to another. After 1529 he was never in one country for more than three and a half years at a time. It was like trying to compress a huge mattress – where he was there might be control, but everywhere else troubles rose around him.

Spain

When Charles went to Spain in 1517, more than eighteen months after the death of Ferdinand, he was 'Charles of Ghent', unable to speak the language and accompanied by foreign advisers. His younger brother, Ferdinand, knew Spanish and had been brought up by his Spanish grandfather, after whom he had been named, but he was packed off to Flanders (and eventually became ruler of the Austrian lands). The aged Cardinal Jiménez, who had been governing Spain since the death of the King, was dismissed. Charles was surrounded by Burgundians, or by Spanish who had lived in the Netherlands. To the native Spanish he appeared remote and extravagant.

To this general impression Charles soon added by his acts particular grievances. He was under the control of his Burgundian adviser, Chièvres; the Archbishopric of Toledo, the most important in Spain, was given to the latter's young absentee nephew. When the Castilian Cortes met they found a Burgundian, the Chancellor Le Sauvage, presiding. They refused to continue proceedings until he left. (Nevertheless they voted Charles a *servicio* (subsidy) of 600,000 ducats.) The Cortes of Aragon and of Catalonia were also suspicious, and Charles left Spain, in order to be crowned King of the Romans, without meeting the Cortes of Valencia. He confirmed the privileges of the guilds (*Germanía*) there, then withdrew the confirmation, confirmed them again, and then once more withdrew his confirmation. When he left Spain he had promised to appoint a Spanish regent, but he left behind instead a Fleming, his old tutor Adrian of Utrecht, later Pope.

This series of *gaffes*, each relatively unimportant in itself, together produced an explosive situation. Within a few months of Charles's departure Spain was torn by two revolts, that of the *Comuneros* in Castile, and the *Germanía* in Valencia.

The Castilian outbreak was one of towns and nobles. The rebels freed Charles's mother, Joanna, but she refused her support and appeared madder than her followers had suspected. The rebels now called for the return of Charles – 'If the King comes back he can govern the whole world from these kingdoms, as his forefathers did before him.' A royal army, led by Spaniards, defeated the rebels at Villalar (1521), and the opposition collapsed. Nobles and towns could not work together, one district distrusted the next, the fatal separatism of Spain showed itself. Meanwhile, in Valencia a rising of the *Germanía* (guilds), in protest against Charles's failure to confirm their privileges, soon took on the character of a social war, townspeople against nobles: 'The ideas of the nobility and of the heathen belong to the past. The whole Kingdom shall live in peace and justice, as one brotherhood under one King and one law.' Though potentially less dangerous than the Castilian revolt, it took longer to suppress, but by the time Charles, now Emperor, returned to Spain in 1522, the country was once more at peace. The disturbances had been to some extent a last protest against the centralizing policy of Ferdinand and Isabella, and it is a tribute to their work that order was so easily re-established. The chief gainer was the Crown, which now found itself unchallenged.

Charles showed that he had learned by his mistakes. His task was made easier by the fact that his Burgundian advisers, Chièvres and Le Sauvage, were dead (as, providentially, was the young Burgundian Archbishop of Toledo), and his new Chancellor, Gattinara, was a southerner from Piedmont. Charles now spent seven years in Spain, longer than he was ever to spend at one time in any other country. He did not again insult Spanish national sensibilities; indeed, by the end of his life Spain had absorbed him, and he had become more Spanish than the Spanish themselves. Of the next twenty-one years (1522–43) Charles spent altogether thirteen and a half in Spain.[1] It was a good centre from which to conduct the struggle against Francis in Italy and the Turks in North Africa. In 1543 he appointed his son Philip as Regent, and he did not return to Spain again until his retirement to Estremadura in 1556.

[1] 1522–9; 1533–5; 1536–9 (with the exception of three months in the summer of 1538); and 1541–3.

Spain remained peaceful, but the process began by which she became fossilized. The political power of the nobles continued to decline, since they refused to be taxed; the Cortes met fairly regularly, Charles listened to their petitions and obtained from them the grant of a *servicio* which trebled in amount and came to form one of the most important sources of his income. The powers of the Inquisition grew as it became not only a religious court but also increasingly a *de facto* instrument of royal power. The Council grew smaller (unlike the Tudor Council, for instance) and less specialized. Half a dozen lawyers began to exercise the functions simultaneously of executive, judiciary and high court of appeal. The dead hand of bureaucracy started to throttle Spanish development. These tendencies were exaggerated when Philip, who had a passion for personal administration, became Regent.

Spain was in many ways a source of strength to Charles. It formed the base from which to carry on the wars against the Frenchman and the Turk. It provided the money for those wars – not so much money as the Netherlands, and certainly not so much as was needed, but nevertheless a sizeable amount. The exploits of the *Conquistadores* in Mexico and Peru led to an influx of gold and silver which, though it was not an unmixed blessing to Spain, provided Charles with an income that may have averaged 300,000 ducats a year. Spain also supplied men. The Spanish soldier replaced the Swiss as the best in Europe. The early reforms of Gonzalo de Córdoba were continued and the organization of the army in *tercios* (regiments of pikemen and arquebusiers) became standard practice for a hundred years (1534–1631). Spain, too, produced most of Charles's generals, for 'The double lure of knight-errantry and plunder made the Spanish imperialists in Europe as it made them *conquistadores* in America'.[1]

The Empire

In January 1519 the Emperor Maximilian died. There followed six months of bribery and wire-pulling among the Electors before Charles was finally elected. Francis I bid hard for his own election, and in May Henry VIII toyed with the idea of becoming a candidate, but in fact a foreigner had

[1] *N.C.M.H.*, II, p. 314.

little chance.   A German Prince such as Frederick of Saxony
might have been considered, but he refused to stand.   Nevertheless, the Electors took Charles's money before voting for
him, the most greedy and unfaithful being the Elector of
Mainz.   Charles spent about 850,000 florins, of which 543,000
was provided by the Augsburg banker Jacob Fugger.[1]

Charles left Spain in 1520 and, after a brief visit to England,
where he met Henry VIII at Canterbury, was crowned King
of the Romans at Aix in the autumn of that year.   In 1521 he
presided at Worms over the first of the great Diets held during
his reign.   Three problems faced him: constitutional, the
perennial problem of the government of the Empire; religious,
the new problem of Lutheranism; personal, the problem of
the administration of the Habsburg lands attached to Austria.

The struggle between Maximilian and the reform party
under Berthold of Mainz had produced no decisive reforms
and, with the certainty of an absentee Emperor, it now became
important to create some central administrative machinery.
After a prolonged period of bargaining between the Emperor
and the Princes it was agreed that the Council of Regency
(*Reichsregiment*) should be revived, that the Habsburg lands
should be included in its sphere of influence, and that it should
rule in Charles's absence but have only advisory powers when
he was in Germany.   The Imperial Chamber was restored as
in 1507, only now its members were to be paid by the Empire
not the Emperor.   These reforms came to nothing.   In 1522
a Diet at Nuremberg imposed a 4 per cent duty on imports
and exports, customs houses were to be put up along the
Imperial frontier, and the money raised was to be used to
finance the central government.   The idea of a customs union
is particularly significant when one remembers that German
unity in the nineteenth century was made much easier by the
creation of just such a union, the *Zollverein*.   But in 1522 the
Princes went on to attack the privileges of the Imperial Cities
and of the capitalists in general.   The opposition of the
latter, especially of the Fuggers of Augsburg, led to the collapse
of the whole scheme.   (Jacob Fugger reminded Charles of the
debt the latter owed him: 'It is well known that Your Imperial

---

[1] *N.C.M.H.*, II, p. 338; the banking house of the Welsers also supplied 143,000
florins; the Elector of Mainz received 100,000 florins, the Swabian League,
171,360; Cologne, 52,810; Saxony, 70,000; the Palatinate, 184,000.

Majesty could never have won the Roman Crown without my help.') Any strengthening of the administration really depended for even a limited success on the continuous presence in Germany of a strong Emperor: Charles was only in the Empire for seven months and then in the summer of 1521 he left and did not return until 1530. An absence of nine years was asking too much. The *Reichsregiment* proved itself incapable of dealing with the social and religious crises through which the Empire was passing during the years 1521–32, – perhaps the most critical decade in German history –, and was thoroughly discredited by its failure to deal with the Knights' War of 1523, though it dragged on a tenuous existence till about 1530.

The second problem which faced Charles in 1521 was that of Lutheranism. Luther had nailed his ninety-five theses to the church door at Wittenberg in 1517, had been excommunicated in 1520, and had appealed to the 'German nation' in the autumn of that year.[1] He had not yet become involved in the political rivalry of the Princes and his reputation was at its height. At Worms a compromise was widely hoped for, indeed expected, and might have proved a politically wise expedient. On April 16 Luther reached the city, escorted by Imperial robber-knights under Franz von Sickingen – a significant fact. Already the political advantages of Lutheranism, as a weapon against the Emperor, were becoming recognized. On the 17th and 18th he was confronted with his writings, which he refused to repudiate, and on the following day Charles declared his own position:

> What my forefathers established at Constance and other Councils it is my privilege to uphold. . . . I have therefore resolved to stake upon this cause all my dominions, my friends, my body and blood, my life and soul.

For a few days there was some attempt to reach a compromise, but the Emperor's support for the traditions of the Church, and Luther's dependence on a conscience 'captive to the word of God' had no common ground. The reference to the Council of Constance swung many middle-of-the-way Princes to Charles's side. When Luther rode out from Worms under the ban of the Empire he was kidnapped by the forces

[1] For Luther, and the religious aspect of his protest, see Chapter VI.

of the Elector of Saxony and the process of taking sides had begun. The rejection of Luther by Charles had made a religious war almost inevitable, though its outbreak was postponed for another twenty-five years. It has been argued that the Emperor ought to have put himself at the head of Lutheranism as a national movement, but this is to demand of Charles a different character. His brother Ferdinand might just possibly have done so.

The third problem that Charles had to consider was dynastic, the administration of the Austrian Habsburg lands. These were now formally ceded to Ferdinand (1522). He administered them admirably for over forty years, and also held the eastern gate of Europe against the Turk. Some writers have considered it unfortunate that he was not elected Emperor instead of Charles, but the added prestige would have been more than counter-balanced by the problems involved, and his attention would have been inevitably distracted from the two tasks he carried out so successfully.

While Luther was at Worms France had declared war on Charles and in the following months he left the Empire and returned to Spain by way of Bruges and London. The wars in Italy absorbed his attention for the greater part of the next decade. The critical events which took place in Germany during the Emperor's absence are described in Chapter VI.

When Charles returned to Germany by way of the Brenner Pass in the spring of 1530, his prestige was great. South of the Alps he had been everywhere successful; by the Peace of Cambrai he had established his power in Italy at the expense of France, and at Bologna the Pope had crowned him Emperor. In the Empire, though, things had been going badly. True the Turks had failed, the year before, to capture Vienna after a seventeen days' siege, but it was probable that they would come again – as they did, in 1532. Meanwhile Lutheranism had been gaining princely converts, and in 1526 a Diet held at Speier had been forced to announce a compromise; deciding unanimously that, until a General Council of the Church should meet, each Prince should so conduct himself 'as he hopes and trusts to answer to God and his Imperial Majesty'. In 1529 a second Diet at Speier had withdrawn this concession and the Electors of Saxony and Brandenburg, together with Philip of Hesse, three other princes and fourteen cities, had 'protested' that in matters of conscience each man has the right to stand alone and present his true account before God.

On his arrival Charles immediately summoned a Diet at Augsburg with the object of reuniting the German Catholics and these 'protestants'. Some have seen in this aim the dominating theme of the years after 1530:

> From 1530 onwards, the restoration of religious unity in Germany becomes the paramount object of Imperial policy, and everything is gradually subordinated to it. . . . The thread which links up the diverse and multifarious political manoeuvres, and which decides the ultimate grouping of parties, is Charles's determination to attempt the reunion of Christendom by means of a General Council.[1]

Melanchthon, an Erasmian Lutheran if this is not a contradiction in terms, drew up a statement of Lutheran doctrine, embodying the maximum concessions that the Protestants were prepared to make – the Confession of Augsburg. The Catholic theologians refused to accept this statement and called on Charles 'to take fire and sword in hand and root out these noxious and venomous weeds'. The Protestants were given six months to return to the Catholic Church, and the Imperial Chamber was reorganized to enforce that return. At the same time Charles wrote to the Pope, Clement VII, demanding the calling of a General Council.

Charles remained in either the Empire or the Low Countries until the autumn of 1532, during which time this apparently simple situation became more complex. In January 1531 Ferdinand was crowned King of the Romans and thus recognized as Charles's successor – but next month the Protestant princes and cities came together in the League of Schmalkalden, a town of Saxony. 'From this point the Protestants were a political power, and from this point too the validity of the gospel became a question of power.'[2] By the end of 1531 the military organization of this League was complete. The command was to be shared by Philip of Hesse and the Elector of Saxony. The Imperial attempt to discipline the members of the League was delayed for fifteen years, partly due to the external dangers from 'the Frenchman and the Turk'. Early

---

[1] W. L. McElwee, *The Reign of Charles the Fifth*, Macmillan, 1936, pp. 112, 115.
[2] *N.C.M.H.*, II, p. 162.

in 1532 Charles summoned a Diet at Nuremberg to establish a religious truce and to obtain an Imperial army to meet the coming Turkish advance into Hungary. He achieved these aims, but all action against the Protestants was to be suspended until a General Council of the Church should meet. The Turks were turned back (in fact before the Imperial army arrived, by the heroic defence of Güns) and in October Charles left for Italy. Once more he was absent for almost ten years, returning in January 1541.

During this decade Charles was involved in his successful expedition against Tunis and in war with France from 1536 to 1538. The Turkish pressure ebbed and flowed in the Balkans, while in the west the King of France and the Turks were allied against Charles from 1535 to 1543. Meanwhile within the Empire religious rivalry smouldered on, intermittently threatening to blaze into civil war. One such occasion was in 1534 when Philip of Hesse seized Württemberg from the Habsburgs and restored the exiled Duke, who joined the Protestant camp. Peace was patched up at Kadan, but Ferdinand had his hands full in the east and the League of Schmalkalden spread across the map, having taken the decisive step in 1535 of opening membership to all states that would accept the Confession of Augsburg. 'As always with Ferdinand, infidels were more important than heretics, and he was prepared to make almost any sacrifice to avoid civil war.' [1] In 1539 the new Duke of Saxony became a Lutheran and at about the same time the Elector of Brandenburg carried through a series of religious changes in his lands similar to those of Henry VIII in England. The Emperor had lost the support of the two largest states hitherto on his side.

So when Charles returned to Germany in 1541 he found that the situation had deteriorated. A Diet was called at Ratisbon at which a committee of theologians from both camps tried for the last time to reach a compromise that would satisfy everyone. Understandably they failed. They agreed among themselves, and Charles was prepared to accept their elaborate formularies, but the extremists – Catholic and Protestant alike – rejected the compromise, and Charles lacked the power with which to enforce it. Once more the absence of effective Imperial government had proved disastrous to unity.

[1] McElwee, p. 209.

Spain was loyal and peaceful, Italy securely held, the later wars with France were fought from bases in Flanders and Lorraine. For all these reasons, Charles remained in the Empire or the Low Countries for the last thirteen years of his reign (1543–56). Flanders was threatened from two sides, by the French from the south and by the Protestant prince William of Cleves, who had built up a powerful state for himself, to the east. At about this time, events began to move in Charles's favour. The most consistent Protestant leader and enemy of the Emperor, Philip of Hesse, played into his hands. Married for almost twenty years to a woman he did not love, he obtained from Luther permission, based on rather dubious Old Testament parallels, to commit bigamy, an arrangement that was to be kept secret. Naturally everyone heard about it. Protestant morale was dangerously weakened; also, bigamy was a capital offence and Philip was forced – in return for an imperial pardon – to desert for the time being his Protestant allies and in particular the Duke of Cleves. In the ensuing war against the Duke, Charles achieved perhaps the most clear-cut and lasting success of his reign. In a brief and brilliant campaign (1543) William was defeated. He was attached to the Catholic party and Guelderland was added permanently to the Low Countries.

In 1544 the Treaty of Crépy marked the final defeat of Francis. After the Frenchman, the Turk; in 1545 Charles's agents signed a truce with Suleiman the Magnificent, which in 1547 became a seven years' treaty. Finally, the German Council of the Church for which Charles had been pressing for so long, opened at Trent in December 1545. For the first time, Charles was really free to move against the Protestants, and when they failed to attend the Diet of Ratisbon (1546) John Frederick of Saxony and Philip of Hesse were outlawed, and war became inevitable.

The Schmalkaldic War (1546–7) was waged against Saxony, Hesse, Duke Ulrich of Württemberg, and the cities of Ulm, Strasburg, Constance and Augsburg. While John Frederick and Philip argued, Charles concentrated Papal, Spanish, Italian and Netherlands troops at Ingolstadt, but both sides found it difficult to keep their forces in the field and feared to take decisive action. Then, suddenly, on a misty spring morning in 1547 Charles's troops unexpectedly crossed the river Elbe and destroyed the Saxon army at Mühlberg. The victory was complete. Charles's prayer before the battle – '*Exsurge Domine, et judica causam Tuam*' – had been answered, for a third of the army of the League had perished and the Elector was his prisoner. And yet, as after Pavia, there is a sense of anti-climax. Nothing decisive happened.

The emptiness of Charles's victory at Mühlberg was partly the fault of the Emperor himself. 'He could work to restore the old order on a more efficient basis; but he could not contemplate setting up a new order.' [1] In 1548, at Augsburg, he tried to enforce a religious compromise, the Interim – seventeen years too late. It conceded to the Protestants the right of clerical marriage and Communion in both kinds; too little to please them, too much for the Catholics to accept. At the same time, Charles attempted to overhaul the machinery of government. The *Reichskammergericht* (Imperial Chamber of Justice) was reformed, rigid rules of procedure were drawn up and controversial ecclesiastical cases were to be dealt with in Charles's own courts. The Emperor, remembering how the Swabian League had helped him in his youth, attempted to introduce reforms to the Imperial constitution '. . . by the creation of a powerful League of a federal kind among a number of German states and cities with the territories of the House of Habsburg serving as a flywheel', [2] and the imperial towns of Ulm and Augsburg as a nucleus. The Princes would have none of it. The only positive concession that Charles obtained at Augsburg was the removal, in effect, of the former Burgundian lands together with Guelderland and Utrecht from the control of the Empire.

Charles's plans to remodel the Empire had been wrecked on the political ambitions of the Princes. Mühlberg, like Pavia, had been too decisive a victory. The Italian triumph had called forth the League of Cognac, the German one led to the creation in 1550 of a league of German Princes against the possibility of an over-mighty Emperor. The moving spirit was Maurice of Saxony. His support for Charles had been bought by the grant of the Electorate, and having been paid he returned to the Protestant camp. In 1552 Maurice and the League signed the Treaty of Chambord with Henri II of France. While Henri occupied Metz, Toul and Verdun

[1] McElwee, p. 196.   [2] *E.H.R.*, Jan. 1955, p. 149.

with an army of 35,000 men, Maurice advanced into southern
Germany, and Charles with a few followers fled before him
through storms of rain over the Brenner Pass to Villach in
Carinthia.   It was like one of those reversals of fortune to be
found in Greek tragedies.   But then the pendulum swung
back again, for Maurice's lines of communications were
extended and his allies were plundering and burning.   Charles
recrossed the Alps and, by the Treaty of Passau, allowed the
Protestants toleration until a German Diet should settle the
religious question, and released their leaders, Philip of Hesse
and John Frederick of Saxony.   Within six months of his
flight the Emperor was back in front of Metz, besieging the
city with a huge army.

It was Charles's last positive action in the Empire.   The
siege of Metz failed, but Maurice died in the summer of 1553.
Charles retired to Brussels, from which city he carried on the
war against the French and prepared for his own abdication,
while the real power in Germany was exercised by his brother
Ferdinand.   The Peace of Augsburg, which was declared in
September 1555, a month before Charles abdicated his
sovereignty over the Low Countries, was thus the result of
negotiations between Ferdinand and the Princes.

The religious settlement was not the last act in the reign
of Charles V.   It was the first in the reign of Ferdinand I.[1]

It was the consequence, however, of Charles's rule, and marks
a temporary resolution of the religious and political problems
with which he had been faced.

The Peace of Augsburg contained three important decisions:
each Prince was to resolve whether the religion of his state
should be Catholic, or that of the Augsburg Confession
(Lutheran); no other religious choice was allowed,

all such as do not belong to the two above-named religions
shall not be included in the present peace but shall be totally
excluded from it;

and

where an Archbishop, Bishop, or other priest of our old
religion shall abandon the same, his archbishopric, etc., and
other benefices shall be abandoned by him.   The chapters

[1] K. Brandi, *The Emperor Charles V*, Cape, 1939, p. 629.

and such as are entitled to it by common law shall elect a person espousing the old religion who may enter on the possession of all the rights and incomes of the place.

This last, known as the 'ecclesiastical reservation', was to apply to all Church lands after 1552, the date of the Treaty of Passau.

The Peace marked the triumph of the Princes at the expense of the Emperor, of separatism at the expense of religious unity. *Cuius regio, eius religio*, was the later pithy summary. It marked the recognition of Lutheranism as a politically respectable faith; but it did not establish toleration. The Peace was successful, as such things go, lasting for two generations until 1618, though it contained within itself the seeds of later conflict in the exclusion of all other religions (notably Calvinism) from the settlement, and in the ecclesiastical reservation. It was a peace of exhaustion, in which no one quite got what they wanted. It marked the end of the German phase of the Reformation and of the expansion of Lutheranism. It was the end also of the Empire, which became from now only a polite fiction, behind which grew up the reality of the Austrian Habsburg Monarchy.

It has been said of the Reformation in general that it 'began with ideas and ended in force' and that in Germany 'There was no more disappointing epoch . . . it had hoped to re-form the Church and renew the Empire; instead it split the one and destroyed the other'. These words might be applied without modification, respectively to Charles's aims and to his achievements within the Empire.

The Frenchman

The most important events in the Habsburg–Valois struggle have already been considered, either in Chapter IV or in the earlier pages of this chapter. Here it is only necessary, there-fore, to indicate the structure of that struggle and to mention more particularly those isolated events not already described. The wars fall into three clearly defined blocks of events: first there is the fighting in Italy, from 1521 to 1529, punctuated by Charles's victory at Pavia in 1525 and terminated by the Treaty of Cambrai in 1529, by which France lost control of Flanders, Milan and Naples. During these years only a little of the fighting occurred outside Italy, some skirmishing in

Navarre in 1521 and 1523 and English raids into northern France in 1522 and 1523.

The second block of events contains the wars of 1536 to 1538 and 1542 to 1544. The character of the struggle began to change. The French obtained largely accidental help from the disturbed state of Germany and, more deliberately, a new – and to sixteenth century eyes – notorious ally in the Turks (1536). In the first of these two wars the fighting was still mainly confined to Italy, but in the second there was a significant shift to the north of the Alps. In this second war Francis launched armies against Artois, Brabant, Luxemburg, Piedmont and Roussillon. Luxemburg was twice overrun, in 1542 and 1543, while in the latter year Charles destroyed the forces of Francis's ally, William of Cleves. In 1544 a joint invasion of France by Charles and Henry VIII was undertaken. The English forces spent too long capturing Boulogne, but Charles from his base at Metz reached Soissons, within sixty miles of Paris. As a result, the terms of the Treaty of Crépy (1544) were favourable to the Emperor.

The third block consists of the wars from 1552 to 1559. The fighting was centred to the north of the Alps, in Lorraine and Flanders. The French were on the whole more successful than in either of the preceding periods. The protagonists were different, Francis I giving place to Henri II, Charles V to Ferdinand; but the peace which closed the war was the end-product of the earlier fighting and must be regarded as the natural terminus of Charles's struggle with France.

In 1552 Maurice of Saxony and the Schmalkaldic League made the Treaty of Chambord with Henri II. By this Henri was to provide the League with 240,000 crowns for the first three months and after that 70,000 crowns a month. In return he was to have possession of Cambrai, and the three Lorraine bishoprics of Metz, Toul and Verdun – towns which were 'not of German speech'. These Lorraine bishoprics had a double strategic value, for they gave France control of a route into Germany by way of the Moselle, and at the same time they threatened the Imperial line of communications between the Netherlands and Franche Comté.

Fighting began in the spring. While the French advanced towards the Rhine, Maurice and the Protestant Princes marched south against Charles. By the time Charles had

made his peace at Passau with the Princes, the Duke of Guise
had entered and fortified Metz, a city that was now to remain
in French hands till 1870. Charles knew its importance.

'From this city,' he wrote, 'they will have a clear road to
the Rhine and so will be able to cut off my communications
from south Germany to the Netherlands, besides which they
can threaten Thionville and the whole province of Luxem-
bourg. From Metz, too, they can tamper with the communications between the Netherlands and Franche Comté.
Their fortifications cannot yet be finished so that we might
have good hope of taking the town.' [1]

From November to January Charles besieged Metz, but he
failed to take it – the siege had started too late in the year
and, as Charles said, the fortunes of war favoured 'a young
King rather than an old Emperor'.

The war continued, punctuated by a truce in 1556
(Vaucelles), until 1559. There was desultory fighting in
Italy, and more decisive battles in the north, where the Imperial forces won a great victory at St. Quentin in 1557, and
the French under the Duke of Guise captured Calais from the
English (1558). More important were the great bankruptcies
of France and Spain in 1557, since they really brought to an
end this long series of wars.

By the Peace of Cateau-Cambrésis (1559) France gave up
her claims in Italy and returned Savoy to its Duke, but kept
a handful of valuable towns on the Italian side of the Alps.
She was to hold Calais for eight years; and she kept Metz,
Toul and Verdun. Philip II of Spain was to marry Elizabeth
of France, daughter of Henri II, and the Duke of Savoy was
to marry the French king's sister, Margaret. Philip and
Henri were to work together to put down heresy in their
dominions. French opinion at the time declared that she
'lost as many provinces as she regained cities', but in fact
Calais and the Lorraine bishoprics proved of great value.
Spain was left in control of Italy, while Flanders now became a part of the Habsburg Netherlands. The clause about
heresy (anticipated in 1544 at Crépy) indicated the beginning
of the political campaign of the Counter-Reformation. For
almost thirty years there was peace between France and Spain

[1] Brandi, p. 618.

and the terms of the treaty largely endured until the Peace of
Westphalia in 1648. The Peace closes one epoch, that of
Habsburg–Valois rivalry in Italy and religious–political war-
fare in the Empire, and ushers in another, that of the Counter-
Reformation and the dominance of Spain.

The Turk

The expansion of the Ottoman Empire is dealt with more
completely in Chapter XIV, here it is only necessary to consider it as an added complication for Charles V. 'Protestantism,' the historical cliché runs, 'was saved by the Frenchman
and the Turk.'

The Turkish menace took three forms: naval, the struggle
to control the western Mediterranean; political, the alliance
with Francis I; and territorial, the expansion up the Danube
valley towards Vienna. Of these three, the Danubian
advance was the most dangerous and the most permanent.
It was Ferdinand rather than Charles who had to deal with
this threat which in some ways promoted rather than weakened German unity, Protestant and Catholic tending to sink
their differences when the danger became imminent. In
1526 the Turks had destroyed Hungary at the battle of Mohacz
and in the same year Ferdinand became king of that third of
the country which remained free. In 1529 and again in
1532 Suleiman launched campaigns against Vienna. They
failed, but the Turkish pressure remained a constant threat,
with the frontier only eighty miles from the city.

The naval and political aspects were to some extent inter-
locked. In 1529 the corsair Khair ad-Din Barbarossa had
seized Algiers. Four years later, as grand admiral of the
Turkish fleet, he captured Tunis. From these places he was
in a position to threaten both Italy and the western Mediterranean. In 1535 Charles achieved one of the few clear-cut
victories of his reign when he recaptured Tunis. It was now
the West's turn to menace the communications between
Barbarossa and Constantinople. The western Mediterranean
became the scene of a series of duels between the Genoese
imperial admiral, Doria, and Barbarossa. It was at this
point that the French entered the story. Francis had been
flirting with the idea of a Turkish alliance ever since his
disastrous defeat at Pavia in 1525. A treaty was finally signed

in 1536 and Christian Europe held up its hands in pious, but hypocritical horror. In 1541 Charles failed disastrously to take Algiers. Two years later Barbarossa burnt Reggio, in the toe of Italy, and in conjunction with the French captured Nice. This was the most positive achievement of the alliance. Barbarossa wintered at Toulon, but next year France was forced to sign the Peace of Crépy. Barbarossa died in 1546 and in the following year Suleiman made a truce with Ferdinand. In sum, Charles had been hampered by having to deal with yet one more problem, but had emerged as dominant in the western Mediterranean while the Austrian Habsburg state had held the Turks, weakened by their extended lines of communication, on the Danube.

The Low Countries

Charles was born at Ghent, and named after the great Duke of Burgundy, Charles the Bold. He spent twenty-eight years of his life in the Low Countries, during twelve of which he was their ruler. Only in Spain was he present as ruler for a longer period. He was very conscious of himself as the heir to the Burgundian lands; in 1526 when Francis was his prisoner, Charles's demand was for 'Burgundy, no more, no less'. In the 'twenties too he spoke of his wish to be buried in the Grande Chartreuse at Dijon, the capital of French Burgundy, when it should be recaptured; and much later, in 1548, when writing to his son Philip he referred to the Low Countries as *nuestra patria*. It is not altogether a coincidence that his rule there was the brightest spot in a troubled reign.

When Charles became Duke of Burgundy in 1515, Flanders and Artois were still acknowledged to be French fiefs, and the other nine states were fiefs of the Empire. When Charles abdicated in 1555 Flanders and Artois were no longer French while the other states had been virtually withdrawn from the Empire in 1548, and in the north and east Charles had added six new states; Friesland (1524), Overyssel and Utrecht (1528), Drenthe and Groningen (1536), and Guelderland (1543). The effect had been to create a block of territory independent of both France and the Empire, one which has survived to the present day as the countries of Holland and Belgium. It was perhaps the most permanent of Charles's achievements, and one of prime importance to the English, menaced by the French absorption of Flanders – much of English foreign policy can be read as a determination to keep the Low Countries weak and independent.

Of course, Charles's interest in the Netherlands was not only sentimental, but also strategic and financial. They controlled parts of the Rhine route, and protected that flank of the Empire which was geographically the most open. One has only to plot Charles's journeys to see how often an expedition to the Empire began or ended at Brussels. Financially the area was one of the richest, most highly commercialized parts of Europe, with Antwerp as its centre. Towards the end of his reign especially, Charles came to rely to an increasing extent on his income from these parts and in 1552 they contributed over six million florins.[1]

Such an area needed wise government, and Charles was well served by his Regents; his aunt Margaret (1509–30), and his sister Mary (1530–55). A policy of religious and political centralization was pursued. Later in the century this policy was to be one of the causes of the revolt of the Netherlands, but during Charles's reign the Regents acted with cautious prudence. There was only one outburst when, in 1539, Ghent rebelled against increased taxation. The city was in some ways a special case; for one thing, its constitution was unusually democratic, for another it was suffering an economic crisis, having lost to Antwerp its position as one of the economic hubs of the area. When news of the revolt reached Charles in Spain he moved north across France (it was one of the rare occasions when he and Francis were on good terms), punished the rebels, took away the city's charter – and its great bell Roland – and only consented to issue a new one after the town's representatives, barefoot, in their shirts and with halters round their necks, had begged for pardon. There was no further trouble from the municipalities.

Charles V

In the autumn of 1555 Charles began the long process of abdicating his various sovereignties. The Empire was to be ruled by his brother Ferdinand (though it was not until April 1558 that the latter became Emperor); his son Philip received the remainder – Spain and the Indies, Naples and Milan,

[1] R. Tyler, *The Emperor Charles the Fifth*, Allen & Unwin, 1956, p. 164.

Franche Comté and the Netherlands. In February 1557
Charles retired to the villa which he had had built near the
monastery of San Jeronimo de Yuste, in Estremadura, with a
little court of fifty people. 'The interior of the villa was rich
with costly hangings, tapestries from the Netherlands, embroidered scenes and paintings in oils, statues and curious
jewels, clocks and scientific instruments, beautiful and luxurious
furniture. Charles had no intention of leading the life of an
ascetic and a monk.' [1] The dignity of his life there was only
marred by his habit of eating too much – notably pickled
anchovies.

Historical convention requires that one should summarize
the problems and achievements of Charles. Yet their only
common denominator is the person of the Emperor himself,
he is the only cord which binds together this bale of sixteenth
century merchandise. He triumphed in Italy, though perhaps more by luck than judgement, and the peninsula remained within the Spanish sphere of influence for a hundred
and fifty years. He failed to provide political or religious
unity for the Empire, and the consequences of his failure were
not worked out till 1648. He achieved local successes of
great practical value at Tunis and in the Netherlands. Spain
became the political centre of Europe; and Charles to some
extent grew to be a Spaniard, while the Spanish court in its
turn acquired the habit of Burgundian luxury.

The three great complications that hampered Charles
were those of communications, heresy and debt. The first
two have already been considered, less obvious but for that
very reason more insidious were his financial difficulties.
Charles was at war almost continuously in some part or other
of his scattered territories, at a time when war was becoming
vastly more expensive while the revenues of the new national
monarchies were only just starting to expand. It is not
possible to unravel in a small space the tangled skein of the
Emperor's finances, but certain points should be noted. The
main sources of income were Spain, the Netherlands and the
German bankers. In Spain Charles V's income was perhaps
three times that enjoyed by Ferdinand and Isabella. It was
made up from clerical taxes and the *Cruzada*; from the *alcabala*,
which was now a fixed quota paid by each town and village;

[1] Brandi, p. 639.

from the leases of revenues of the estates of the military orders; from the grant by the *Cortes* of a *servicio*; and from the imports of gold and silver from Mexico and Peru, of which the government's share (fixed in 1504 at one-fifth) appears to have averaged about 300,000 ducats per annum for the period from 1503 to 1560.[1]   From the Netherlands Charles drew an ever-increasing surplus to meet his deficits in other areas.   'Normal receipts averaged about one million gold florins from 1515 to 1541; by 1545 they had risen above five million . . . to reach 6·7 million in 1556, the year Charles left for Yuste. Navagero, the Venetian ambassador, estimated that in twenty years the Emperor took twenty million gold florins abroad. . . .'[2] And in 1559 another Venetian, Soriano, wrote of the Netherlands:

> These are the treasures of the king of Spain, these his mines, these his Indies which have sustained all the emperor's enterprises.[3]

Yet Charles's debts mounted as the great European price-rise cut into his receipts (prices in Spain doubled during the first half of the century), and he was forced to borrow from the great German bankers, especially the Fuggers of Augsburg. Jacob Fugger had helped to finance the Imperial election in 1519; over thirty years later another member of the family, Anton, lent Charles 400,000 ducats in the critical days of 1552. They received their reward in the shape of commercial privileges in lands from Hungary to Spain, but the rates at which Charles might borrow rose disastrously all the same, and seem to have reached the fantastic figure of over 40 per cent in the fifties.[4]   Bankruptcy followed hard on the heels of the Emperor's abdication.

To list the achievements and the difficulties of Charles V is to describe the political history of the first half of the sixteenth century and to recognize the problems that, to a greater or lesser degree, faced all its rulers.   The Emperor's life had not equipped him to comprehend these problems.

Charles V was himself neither a diplomatist nor a commander.   By birth and education he was a knight and a

---

[1] Tyler, pp. 249–50.   The Castilian revenue, according to the Venetian ambassadors, rose from about 1,000,000 ducats in 1525 to about 2,750,000 in 1551.
[2] Tyler, p. 164.   [3] *N.C.M.H.*, II, p. 333.   [4] Tyler, p. 244.

nobleman, taking delight in arms and very brave, but he had not the experience of a youth spent in armies, nor the education which might have made him into a military leader. . . .

His diplomacy was equally limited. He was a good judge of men, but his reserved character, the inheritance of all his family, had been trained too soon on the open stage of a Court, to enable him to move among men with any natural ease. His private notes and reflections, like his letters, are deliberate, earnest and questioning. His strength was in his regal virtues of sureness of purpose and a high sense of honour; with these his growing self-confidence now went hand in hand, not always for his good. Delicate, unhealthy, slow in his movements and on the whole ugly in his person, Charles nevertheless expressed in his outward manners something of these inner forces: undeniably there was about him something impressive, something of the leader.[1]

He was well served by his ministers, Chièvres (1458–1521), Gattinara (1521–30) and Granvelle (1530–50), and as the years went by he himself acquired a fund of political experience and *expertise*. After 1530, though he might call Granvelle 'his soul', he became increasingly his own adviser:

More than ever Charles, and Charles only, represented the empire. He governed it like the head of one of the great sixteenth-century merchant houses where the junior members of the family served as heads of the foreign branches of the firm. There were great advantages in having members of the Habsburg family as governors-general, regents or even kings in his dominions. They were locally more acceptable than even the greatest nobles of non-royal blood and much less likely to be involved in local feuds; their employment as his personal representatives accorded with Charles's own views of the central role of the dynasty in his whole position. The Netherlands, the Empire and Spain after 1529 were always, at least nominally, entrusted to a Habsburg or his consort.[2]

Charles regarded his responsibilities with a high seriousness, and worked immensely hard at his job of ruling – what Louis XIV was to call *mon métier du roi*. Notice the tired eyes in Titian's portrait, painted when the Emperor was forty-eight.

[1] Brandi, pp. 393–4.   [2] *N.C.M.H.*, II, p. 309.

Tens of thousands of letters bearing the imperial signature have survived, and of these a not inconsiderable part are written in Charles's hand.[1]

He could not command success but at least he deserved it, and it was not his fault if, as Montesquieu was to say of that same Louis XIV, *'il avait l'âme plus grande que l'esprit'*. For Charles was 'not quite a great man, nor quite a good man, but . . . an honourable Christian gentleman, striving, in spite of physical defects, moral temptations and political impossibilities, to do his duty. . . .'[2]

Extracts

1. *Clauses relating to the Augsburg Confession, Sept. 25, 1555:*

. . . we (Ferdinand), and the electors, princes, and estates of the Holy Empire will not make war upon any estate of the empire on account of the Augsburg Confession and the doctrine, religion and faith of the same, nor injure nor do violence to those estates that hold it, nor force them, against their conscience, knowledge, and will, to abandon the religion, faith, church usages, ordinances, and ceremonies of the Augsburg Confession, where these have been established, or may hereafter be established, in their principalities, lands, and dominions. . . .

On the other hand, the estates that have accepted the Augsburg Confession shall suffer his Imperial Majesty, us, and the electors, princes, and other estates of the Holy Empire, adhering to the old religion, to abide in like manner by their religion, faith, church usages, ordinances, and ceremonies. . . .

But since in many free and imperial cities both religions – namely our old religion and that of the Augsburg Confession – have hitherto come into existence and practice, the same shall remain hereafter and be held in the same cities; and citizens . . . shall peacefully and quietly dwell with one another. . . .
(Quoted by J. H. Robinson, *Readings in European History*, Ginn, Vol. II, pp. 114–6)

2. *Charles's speech of abdication at Brussels, Oct. 25, 1555:*

I have carried out what God has permitted – for the outcome of our efforts depends upon the will of God. We human

---

[1] Brandi, p. 16.
[2] E. Armstrong, *The Emperor Charles V*, Macmillan, 1902, Vol. 2, p. 383.

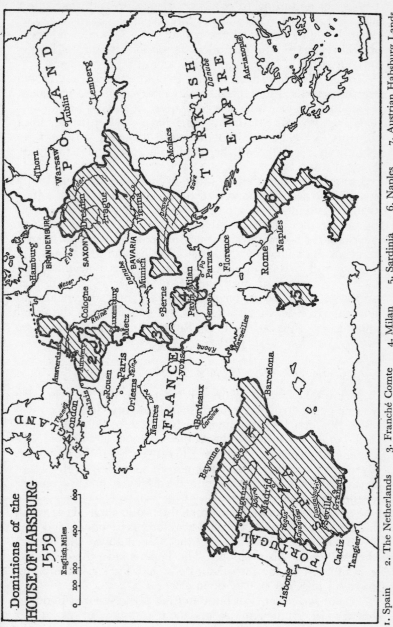

Dominions of the
HOUSE OF HABSBURG
1559

English Miles
0   100 200   400   600

1. Spain   2. The Netherlands   3. Franché Comte   4. Milan   5. Sardinia   6. Naples   7. Austrian Habsburg Lands

beings act according to our powers, our strength, our spirit, and God awards victory or permits defeat. I have ever done what I could, and God has aided me. I – and you, too – should return to Him boundless thanks for His aid, for having succoured me in my greatest trials and in all my dangers.

Today I feel so exhausted that I could not help you, as you see yourselves. In my present state of dejection and weakness, I should have to render a serious account to God and man if I did not lay aside authority, as I have resolved to do, since my son, King Philip, is of an age sufficiently advanced to govern you; and he will be, I hope, a good prince to all my beloved subjects.

I am determined then to retire to Spain and to yield to my son Philip the possession of all my Belgian provinces. I particularly commend my son to you, and I ask of you, in remembrance of me, that you extend to him the love which you have always borne towards me; moreover I ask you to preserve among yourselves the same affection and harmony . . .

Above all, beware of infection from the sects of neighbouring lands. Extirpate at once the germs of heresy, should they appear in your midst, for fear lest they may spread abroad and utterly ruin your state, and lest you fall into the direst calamities. (Quoted by J. H. Robinson, *Readings in European History*, Ginn, Vol. II, p. 167)

3. *Charles gives advice to Philip*, (*1548*):

Seeing that human affairs are beset with doubt, I can give you no general rules save to trust in Almighty God. You will show this best by defending the faith. After all our trouble and labour in bringing back the German heretics, I have come to the conclusion that a general council is the only way. Even the German Estates have agreed to submit to it. Have a care, therefore, that the council continues, in all reverence to the Holy See. . . .

You yourself know how unreliable Pope Paul III is in all his treaties, how sadly he lacks zeal for Christendom, and how ill he has acted in this affair of the council above all. Nevertheless, honour his position. The Pope is old; therefore take careful heed to the instructions which I have given my ambassador in Rome in case of an election. . . .

France has never kept faith and has always sought to do me hurt. The young King seems about to follow in his father's footsteps. But act cautiously and try to keep the peace for the weal of Christendom and your own subjects. The French will always be casting about for excuses to resume their royal claims on Naples, Flanders, Artois, Tournai and Milan. Never yield to them, not so much as an inch; they will take an ell. From the beginning of time these French Kings have been greedy for their neighbours' land. Defend Milan with good artillery, Naples with a good fleet, and remember that the French are discouraged if they do not immediately succeed in anything they undertake. . . . To preserve peace I have allowed my demands for our ancient hereditary land (*nuestria patria*), for the duchy of Bourgogne, to drop. But do not altogether renounce your rights.

You cannot be everywhere, you must find good viceroys and such as will not overstep their instructions. . . . The best way is to hold your kingdom together by making use of your own children. For this you will have to have more children and must contract a new marriage. (Charles V's Political Testament, January 18, 1548. K. Brandi, *The Emperor Charles V*, Cape, 1939, pp. 583–5)

FURTHER READING

W. L. McElwee, *The Reign of Charles V, 1516–1558*, Macmillan, 1936

R. Tyler, *The Emperor Charles the Fifth*, Allen & Unwin, 1956

K. Brandi, *The Emperor Charles V*, trans. C. V. Wedgwood, Cape, 1939

New Cambridge Modern History, C.U.P., Vol. II, 1958, Chapter X; The Empire of Charles V in Europe

VI · THE REFORMATION, 1517–64

Catholic Europe on the Eve of the Reformation

THE organization of the Catholic Church which had grown up during the first five centuries of the Christian era had remained the official, universal, religious establishment for a thousand years after the fall of the equally universal Roman Empire. There had, of course, been change: the practice of the Church had developed in both dogma and ritual a complexity unknown in the earlier centuries; religious orders of monks, and later friars, had become increasingly numerous; religious disputes between eastern and western Europe had led eventually to schism in 1054 and to the establishment in the east of the Orthodox Church. Yet in spite of these changes the Catholic Church was essentially the same as at any time in the preceding millennium. Now, in the short space of fifty years, it was to lose, apparently for ever, its control over great areas of western and northern Europe, through the sequence of events known collectively as the Reformation.

At first sight the cause of this surprising reversal of fortune appears obvious; the Church in 1500 was worldly and corrupt, so that earnest Christians reacted by rediscovering older, simpler, purer methods of worship. Unfortunately, this explanation is open to several objections. For one thing, this was not the first time that the Church had become corrupt. In the tenth century

> the papacy became first the plaything of rival factions within the papal *Curia* itself, and finally the tool of a local Roman family. . . . What thus happened to the papacy is in fact what was happening to archbishoprics, bishoprics, parishes, and monasteries all over western Europe.[1]

The state of affairs then was a good deal more startling than that in Renaissance days, and similar, though less extreme, conditions can be found in other periods. In the past the

---

[1] J. W. Thompson, and E. N. Johnson, *An Introduction to Medieval Europe*, Allen & Unwin, 1938, p. 289.

Church had always put its house in order in the end, often as a result of lay pressure. Some of the monastic orders had originated as a protest against laxity and luxury, as an attempt to get back to the austerity of the original Rule. In the Renaissance period there was a growing demand within the Church for a reform of morals such as had occurred in earlier centuries and this demand in the end produced the Counter-Reformation, but not before the Church had been overtaken by the rapid development of the Reformation. Thus the cause of the success of the Reformation does not lie entirely in the corruption of the Church. Neither does it appear to lie in the initial complaints of the Reformers. Under the pressure of opposition they later developed dogmas that could not be accepted without radically altering the teaching of the Church, but initially their reaction was against corruption of morals rather than matters of faith. In the past the Church had been able to deal with criticisms of this type by assimilating the critics; St. Francis for example had been absorbed in this way in the thirteenth century. (Criticism of dogma, on the other hand, such as that of John Hus (1369–1415) of Bohemia, or philosophical schemes at variance with Christianity, such as that of the Albigensians (c. 1200), had always been ruthlessly suppressed). Philosophies which were not basically anti-Christian were also assimilated successfully. In the thirteenth century the 'new' Aristotelian philosophy had been synthesized with the teaching of the Church by St. Thomas Aquinas.

The success of the Reformers does not lie, then, in the corruption of the Church, but in its failure to deal with their protests either by assimilation or by suppression. The six-teenth century church was unable to control a situation which the thirteenth century church had mastered. That she was unable to do so was partly the result of secular peculiarities of the period. The success of the Reformers was due to the fact that they were born at the right time.

Among the non-religious elements which made easier the success of the Reformation one may single out the Renaissance critical approach to authority; the invention of printing; the financial needs of the Papacy; and the development of nation-states. The effects of these can be seen in what follows.

Let us turn now to the state of Catholic Europe on the eve of the Reformation. The most obvious, widespread and long

standing scandal had been the secularization of clerical behaviour and morals. Complaints on these grounds had
appeared steadily from the fourteenth century onwards, where
they can be found in English in the writings of Chaucer
(d. 1400) and Langland (d. *c.* 1400). Most of the complaints
fall under one of two headings; sins of the flesh, and ignorance. Priests had mistresses and illegitimate children, ate
and drank too much, were proud and lazy. They preached
poverty and the virtue of charity, while they lived idle and
luxurious lives themselves. More serious, essentially, was the
complaint that priests were too often ignorant men, no better
than the peasants among whom they lived, mumbling the
services inaccurately in only half-understood Latin. The
picture naturally varied in detail from place to place, but
these, in summary, were the ordinary people's criticisms. In
general, it appears that it was among the monks and friars that
conditions were worst; both Chaucer and Langland are full
of admiration for the parish priest, doing his duty, and as
poor as his flock.

The Papacy and the Roman administration had their own
particular abuses in addition to those already described –
abuses which spread downwards to lesser office-holders.
One might perhaps call them 'sins of bureaucracy'. The
chief of these were simony, pluralism and nepotism. Simony
(called after the sin of Simon Magus, described in Acts 8) was
the technical term for the sale of church offices. In 1500
Alexander VI, for instance, created twelve Cardinals in return
for 120,000 ducats. Pluralism was the practice of holding
several offices at once. Cardinal Wolsey was simultaneously
Archbishop of York, Bishop of Lincoln, Bishop of Tournai,
and in 1521 became abbot of St. Albans, the richest monastery
in England. Pluralists had much the same interest in their
pluralities as shareholders have in the companies in which
they invest. Nepotism was the name applied to the custom
of giving church preferment to relatives – often, though not
necessarily, illegitimate sons. The future Pope Julius II was
created a Cardinal by his uncle, Pope Sixtus IV, who also
made him archbishop of Avignon, and bishop of Bologna,
Coutances, Lausanne, Mende, Ostia, Velletri and Viviers, and
abbot of Nonantola and Grottaferrata.

This was the situation which confronted the critical eyes of the

Renaissance humanist, agnostic in Italy, more devout to the north of the Alps. Neither type of humanist saw anything of which they might approve, and the new art of printing enabled them to broadcast their reactions, whether these were critical, as in the work of Lefèvre d'Étaples on the Epistles of St. Paul and Erasmus's New Testament; or satirical like Erasmus's *Praise of Folly* and Ulrich von Hutten's *Letters of Obscure Men*; or simply books of pure devotion, the writings of lay mystics, such as the Brethren of the Common Life. All reached a new audience, notably among the urban middle classes.[1]

At the same time, the Papacy was caught in the net of more insidious difficulties which arose from the fact that the Pope was not only a spiritual leader, but also a temporal monarch ruling a large slice of central Italy. The temporal possessions of the Papacy had always tended to involve it in secular trouble, but these acquired a new dimension with the ending of the Great Schism in 1417. The treasury was then empty, the income only a quarter of that of former days:

. . . the decay of the whole tax-collecting system meant that a steep moral price had to be paid in order to maintain even this modest income. The chancery taxes, imposed on anyone who had to seek an official document from the Papal court, were much increased. Dispensations and compositions of various kinds were charged at a high rate; the indulgence became financially important. . . . The sale of offices, an institution more respectable in the Middle Ages than now, but even then rather shocking in a clerical context, had begun seriously in the Papal court during the Schism. . . . The salaries of the venal offices were on the average about eleven per cent of the purchase price; percentage charges were made when an office was sold by one holder to another. The capital invested grew by 1520 to between two and a half and three million ducats, and the annual interest absorbed a huge sum. Thus there grew up a kind of privileged stock exchange, to which entry was reserved for the officials of the Roman curia – a fact that had disastrous results for the many attempts made by the Popes to reform the curia.[2]

[1] Later, printing also helped to spread the Reformed teaching. In 1523 German presses issued ten times as many books as in 1513; 80 per cent of these books were devoted to the new movement.

[2] *History Today*, November 1957: P. Partner, 'Papal Finance and the Papal State,' pp. 773–4.

The Papal income was augmented by the profits of jurisdiction in accordance with the normal practice of rulers – for *justitia magnum emolumentum est* (justice is a great source of income) – so whenever possible cases were referred to Rome; and by the clerical taxes of annates (a charge on the revenue of a benefice whenever it changed hands), and tenths (a tithe of all church revenues) levied originally for a crusade but now collected whenever money was needed. To these regular clerical taxes must be added the revenues obtained from laymen; the sale of dispensations for breaches of the canon law, of pardon for offences, and of indulgences.

It was in these extensions of her judicial and financial activities that the Church came in conflict with the new force of nationalism. The claim to control temporal princes, the claim to administer all clerical patronage, the claim of clerical immunity from lay jurisdiction, the claim that clerical property was exempt from lay taxation, the indirect taxation of the laity – even in the high Middle Ages these had provoked opposition from local rulers. Now, with the growth of the new national monarchies intent on centralizing their control, bringing all their subjects under their jurisdiction, and increasing their revenue by all possible means, the Papal and clerical claims seemed intolerable. At the same time the Pope, since he was himself a temporal ruler, felt the need to augment his own income and strengthen his own position in Italy, at the very time when such actions must arouse the greatest irritation.

There was no machinery by which the Church might automatically reform itself. Great crises in the past had sometimes been dealt with by the device of calling a General Council.[1] Unfortunately for the prospects of internal reform the first half of the fifteenth century had witnessed the Conciliar Movement, an attempt to put the Pope under the control of such Councils. This had naturally alarmed the Papacy, which was disposed to regard the demand for a General Council with great suspicion, and in 1460 to appeal from the authority of a Pope to a Council was declared heresy in the Bull *Execrabilis*. Some historians see in the collapse of the Conciliar Movement a disastrous failure on the part of the Church to adapt itself to changed conditions.

---

[1] There had been eighteen General Councils, from that of Nicaea in 325 to that of Basle in 1443.

The calling of a General Council depended on the election of a reforming Pope – and too many people had a vested interest in the existing system for this to be easy.   The Church had what engineers call a 'built-in' system against reform. The Popes during the critical years between 1471 and 1534 were the natural products of this system.   Sixtus IV (1471–84) was a 'passionate imperious unscrupulous Franciscan' – and at the same time an eager nepotist.   His successor, Innocent VIII (1484–92), colourless, affable, tender towards his daughter, made little impact on contemporaries, and was buried *lasso singultu, modicis lacrimis et ejulato nullo*.   Alexander VI (1492–1503) was an efficient worldly administrator without apparent control over the weaknesses of the flesh. He and Julius II (1503–13) concentrated their energies on making effective the temporal power in central Italy and obtaining from that area an adequate revenue.   In this task they may have been mistaken, but they were at least successful:

> The effect of this seems to have been that, from the pontificate of Julius II, Papal revenues rose steeply, and for the first time regained the level they had in their heyday in the fourteenth century – but with the difference that, instead of being drawn from the clerical estate all over Europe, they were provided mainly by the inhabitants of the Papal State. . . . From the financial point of view the Reformation is therefore a paradox; the final outburst against Papal money-grabbing came at the moment when the Popes were less guilty under this charge. . . .[1]

The two Popes whose Pontificates spanned the years during which the Reformation established itself were men quite unfitted to weather the storm that broke about their heads. Leo X (1513–21), a Medici, charming and ineffective, was mainly concerned to encourage Renaissance culture and learning, a task which he performed admirably; Clement VII (1523–34), another Medici, was '. . . a cold soul, lacking all strong feeling, never unfolding itself', faint-hearted, vacillating, undecided.   His successor, Paul III (1534–49), exhibits the Papal paradox at its clearest.   On the one hand, he was a product of the movement for reform within the Church, the Counter-Reformation.   On the other hand, his practical politics were controlled by his desire to further the fortunes of

[1] Partner, p. 774.

the family to which he belonged, the Farnese. When these two motives came into conflict, as they constantly did, family feeling invariably triumphed, and his shifting policy exasperated Charles V as it destroyed the last possibility of a German religious settlement.

These were the men on whose shoulders rested the burden of solving the unique and complex problem of reform; perhaps no one could have succeeded but it is hardly surprising that they failed.

The Reformation in Germany, 1517–55

Germany presented in several ways an ideal field for religious revolt. Politically, she had inherited anti-Papal sympathies from the medieval struggles of Pope and Emperor. It was natural that the Princes, the rulers of the fragments into which Germany was broken, should see in religious war a political weapon, a means of extending their territory at the expense of their neighbour and their powers at the expense of those of the Emperor. In western Germany economic changes had led to urban self-consciousness in the towns and peasant uprisings in the country, which might alike seek religious justification. The 'German nation' as a whole looked askance at the flow of wealth and perquisites to Italy.

From the religious point of view, there already existed strong currents in favour of reform. The *devotio moderna*, of which the Brethren of the Common Life were only the most potent example, spread in a broad band of mysticism and lay reform throughout the Rhineland from Switzerland to the North Sea. Farther east in Bohemia the Hussites had kept a form of 'protestantism' alive for a century in the face of persecution. German Renaissance scholarship was Christian and critical, and the works of Erasmus, and of lesser satirists such as Ulrich von Hutten and Sebastian Brandt (*The Ship of Fools*), were widely read.

All that was required was a man to set the match to this potentially explosive situation.

Martin Luther (1483–1546) was born at Eisleben in Saxony, the son of a miner sufficiently well-to-do to rent three smelting furnaces. From 1501 to 1505 he studied law at Erfurt University, where he acquired a lasting distaste for Aristotle.

Then, suddenly, he gave up his secular career and became an Augustinian friar. This, the first of the three great emotional crises of his life, seems to have been produced by the fear of damnation, perhaps triggered off by his experience of a violent thunderstorm in July of that year. Luther described his state of mind at that time as '. . . walled around by the terror and agony of sudden death (*terrore et agone mortis subitae circumvallatus*). . . .'

Luther remained attached to the Augustinian house at Erfurt until 1512. During these years he tried by the continuous practice of confession and penance to quiet his feelings of guilt and come to terms with what he regarded as a jealous God. 'If ever a monk got to heaven by monkery,' he said later, 'I resolved that it would be I.' During these years he experienced continuous thunderstorms of the spirit, in which the keywords are temptation (*Anfechtung*) and terror, 'For I am dust and ashes and full of sin and I am speaking to the living, eternal, true God.' In 1510 he was sent, with two colleagues, to represent the Erfurt Augustinians in a lawsuit at Rome. He went with great enthusiasm and returned depressed and disappointed by the worldly atmosphere of the Holy City. The following year he was transferred to the new small university of Wittenberg. Although he became Professor of Theology and sub-prior there, his private miseries continued to plunge him into '. . . the very abyss of despair so that I wished I had never been created. Love God? I hated Him!' He told his difficulties to the vicar of the order, Staupitz. The latter prescribed a cure in the shape of hard intellectual work, lecturing on the Bible and reading for his doctor's degree.

The cure worked, though not in quite the way intended. As Luther lectured on the Psalms, on Romans and on Galatians, he developed privately most of the theology he was later to express publicly. The evidence is there in the notes for his lectures, often written in the margin of his Bible. The key to this theology, so far as Luther's personal problem was concerned, is in these two comments on Romans: 'Nobody knows whether he loves God purely unless he would be willing not to be saved but rather to be damned if it so please God', and 'If you have a true faith that Christ is your Saviour, then at once you have a gracious God'. This, the mechanics of

'Justification by Faith' solved Luther's personal problem, the dilemma of how corrupt man can ever satisfy a perfect God.

Luther had reached this position by 1516. In the following year he attacked the misuse of Indulgences, which was connected with just this problem of salvation. The practice of issuing Indulgences had become increasingly common since 1300, when Boniface VIII issued a great jubilee Indulgence. The theory behind the issue of Indulgences was, briefly, that by the payment of money a layman might purchase the removal of Church punishments and of the pains of purgatory – though not, of course, the guilt of sin, or sufferings in hell. The Church was able to do this by drawing on the 'treasury of merits', composed of the inexhaustible merits of Christ which were sufficient in themselves to wipe out all sin, and to which were added the merits of the saints. It was essential to feel true sorrow (contrition), the payment being a part of the penance.

During the fourteenth and fifteenth centuries the practice of selling Indulgences had been abused in two ways. First by the buyers, who forgot, or did not understand, the theological argument and thought that they were buying salvation, and then by the sellers, whose sales talk tended to encourage such thoughts. The growing importance of money led Popes to encourage, and secular rulers to resent, these activities.

In 1517 a Dominican, Tetzel, was selling Indulgences in the neighbourhood of Wittenberg; part of the profits was to go to the Pope, to pay for the rebuilding of St. Peter's. Tetzel's speeches were crude:

> Listen to the voices of your dear dead relatives and friends, beseeching you and saying, 'Pity us, pity us, We are in dire torment from which you can redeem us for a pittance.'
> Remember that you are able to release them . . .[1]

The effect of these words on a man who believed he had found the true way of salvation may be imagined. Luther drew up ninety-five theses against Indulgences and nailed them to the church door at Wittenberg – a normal academic proceeding. The theses asserted that the Church could only remit what the Church had imposed, and therefore could remove neither guilt nor divine punishment for sin, on the

[1] R. H. Bainton, *Here I Stand*, Hodder & Stoughton, 1951, p. 78.

other hand the Christian who had truly repented would be pardoned by God without an Indulgence.

Within a few months Luther found himself unexpectedly famous. The invention of printing sent his theses speeding throughout Germany and releasing a great flood of religious energy. He became the object during 1518 and 1519 of attempts to obtain his submission by promises, arguments, threats. A counter-attack was mounted by Prierias, one of the Dominicans, the traditional enemies of the Augustinians, who regarded themselves as the watchdogs of orthodoxy (*Domini canes*, the hounds of God). In 1518 Luther met the Papal legate, Cardinal Cajetan, at Augsburg. The Cardinal tried to intimidate Luther by stressing Papal authority, and as a result Luther was compelled to admit that he felt even the Pope might be fallible. His thought had made another leap forward. In the spring of 1519 the support of Luther's protector, the Elector of Saxony, was needed in the Imperial election and Cajetan's assistant, Miltitz, tried to flatter Luther into surrender; but neither threats nor blandishments had any effect.

The critical debate took place in 1519 at Leipzig, between Luther and John Eck, a professor from Ingolstadt. It lasted for eighteen days and in the course of this intellectual contest Luther found himself defending in public what he had so far only thought in private, and being made to press his ideas to their logical conclusion. In a sense Eck won the debate, since he forced Luther to declare himself a heretic, and to admit that he believed the individual's interpretation of the Bible was more important than that of Pope or Council. 'We are all Hussites,' Luther said, 'without knowing it.' Eck wrote triumphantly to Rome, and in due course Luther was excommunicated in the Bull *Exsurge*. Published in the summer, it reached Luther in October, and sixty days later, when the period of grace had expired, he burnt it, together with the canon law, exclaiming, 'Since they have burnt my books, I burn theirs.'

Meanwhile, the most important and most constructive part of Luther's public work had taken place between the end of the Leipzig debate and the arrival of the Papal Bull. It consisted of the three pamphlets Luther wrote at this time. They are as near as he ever came to issuing a connected statement of his views and policy. In August he composed *An Appeal to the Christian Nobility of the German Nation*. It is an appeal to Charles V and the rulers of Germany to resist the Papal tyranny which claims that the spiritual power is superior to the temporal; that only the Pope may interpret the Scriptures; that only the Pope may call a general council. It had the greatest effect on popular secular opinion, being written in German and invoking national feeling: 'It is time the glorious Teutonic people should cease to be the puppet of the Roman pontiff.' [1] In October Luther issued *A Prelude concerning the Babylonish Captivity of the Church*, written in Latin and addressed to the clergy. In this he reduced the seven Catholic sacraments to three: baptism, the Eucharist, and penance. Within the Eucharist, he denounced the withdrawal of the cup from the laity, and defined in what sense Christ was present in the bread and wine: 'Fire and iron are two substances; yet they are so mingled in red-hot iron that any part is at once iron and fire.' [2] With this pamphlet Luther lost the support of those, such as Erasmus, who hoped for reform from within the Catholic Church. Also in October Luther wrote *Of the Liberty of a Christian Man*, a positive statement of the code of behaviour involved in the doctrine of Justification by Faith. In it he wrote to the Pope 'beware of those who would make you not just a man but half a god'; he also defined the relation between faith and works – 'Good works do not make a good man, but a good man does good works.' [3]

In the spring of 1521 Charles V came to Germany to be crowned. At the Diet which he held at Worms one of the problems to be considered was what to do with the now excommunicated Luther. On April 16, under a safe-conduct from Charles, Luther rode into the city.

A man of middle height, with a strong face, a sturdy build of body, with eyes that scintillated and were never still. He was clad in the robe of the Augustinian Order, but with a belt of hide, with a large tonsure, newly shaven, and a coronal of short thick hair,

---

[1] H. Bettenson, *Documents of the Christian Church*, O.U.P., 1943, p. 276.

[2] Bettenson, p. 277. Henry VIII received from the Pope the title *Fidei Defensor* for a reply to the *Babylonish Captivity*.

[3] R. H. Bainton, p. 164.

wrote a Spanish observer.[1] On Wednesday the 17th, at
about 4 p.m., he was shown his books and asked if he would
retract his opinions; he asked for time to get ready an answer,
and was given twenty-four hours. On the following day he
replied, concluding,

> I will answer without frills. Unless I am proved wrong
> by Scripture or reasoning – I do not accept the decisions
> of Councils or Popes, for they err and contradict each
> other – my conscience is captive to the word of God; and,
> because it is neither safe nor honest to go against one's con-
> science, I neither will nor can revoke anything. *Gott hilf mir*.
> Amen.

Next day the Emperor rejected Luther's doctrine, and in
May Luther was placed under the ban of the Empire. Meanwhile, however, he had left Worms and disappeared. The
rumour ran that he had been murdered, but in fact he had
been spirited away at the command of that enigma, the Elector
of Saxony, and hidden in the castle of the Wartburg. Luther
lived there for nine months, left off his monk's habit, let his
hair grow, and hid his identity under the name of Junker
Georg. He spent his time translating the New Testament
into German, a work that was printed in 1522.

During the slow development of the crisis from 1517 to
1521, Luther's struggle had become a *cause célèbre*. As his fame
grew it fired the explosive situation existing in Germany, and
when it became clear that the Emperor was not going to put
himself at the head of a national German revolt, local elements
began to declare for Luther, and local reformers to develop
each their own simplified brand of Christianity.

The Imperial Knights, those amateur highwaymen, were
the first to try to kidnap Lutheranism for their own ends.
One, Ulrich von Hutten, had written in 1519:

> Three things maintain the dignity of Rome – the authority
> of the Pope, the relics of the saints, the sale of indulgences.
> Three things are feared at Rome – a General Council, a
> reform of the Church, the opening of the eyes of the Ger-
> mans. Three things are excommunicated at Rome –
> indigence, the primitive Church, the preaching of truth.

[1] Quoted in T. M. Lindsay's *The History of the Reformation*, Clark, Vol. I, 1907,
pp. 279–80.

Another, Franz von Sickingen, had escorted Luther to Worms. These two now planned to secularize the Church lands and give them to the deserving knights. In earlier days von Sickingen had attacked Worms (1513) and Mainz (1518), now in 1522 he organized a League of the Knights of the Upper Rhine and led it against Trier. The *Reichsregiment* seemed powerless, and the Princes, alarmed at the turn events were taking, raised a force commanded by the Elector Philip of Hesse which defeated and killed von Sickingen. The Knights' War is important as demonstrating so early the mixture of religious and political motives, and the power of the Princes – two factors that were to dominate the German Reformation.

In the summer of 1524 a more disturbing outburst occurred. Peasant risings broke out in west and south Germany. These in themselves were nothing new; they had been frequent in the second half of the fifteenth century, brought on by excessive taxation and the adoption of Roman law which obliterated the nice distinctions of feudalism and degraded all not entirely free to the status of serf. Their emblem was the peasant's clog, the *Bundschuh*. What was new was the religious element in the risings; to the peasants Luther, with his doctrine of heavenly freedom and his attacks on earthly custom, appeared as the apostle of social revolution – *Lord Christ has freed us all* (*Dan Christus hat uns alle befriet*) they declared. The town priest of Zwickau, Thomas Münzer, with whom Luther had already quarrelled (Münzer called him 'Father Sit on the Fence'), put himself at the head of the Saxon peasants at Mühlhausen. In 1524 he was preaching as follows:

> Behold, at the bottom of all the usury, the thieving, the robbery, are our great lords and masters, who take all creatures for their own, the fishes in the water, the birds in the air, the plants on the earth; all must be theirs. Thereupon they let God's command go abroad among the poor people and say: 'God hath spoken, thou shalt not steal'; but it serves them nothing. And while that from all men, the poor ploughman, the journeyman, and all that lives, they pluck their skin from off them, and their flesh from off their bones; should these transgress against the Most-Holy, they must hang. Thereto 'Amen' saith Doctor Lugner (liar). The masters are themselves the cause that the poor man is their foe. They will not do away with the

cause of the rebellion; how can the matter turn out well in the long run? As I say this, so I must be rebellious, come what may.[1]

Luther and the Princes were alike horrified, and once more it was the latter who restored order in their own interests. Luther supported them, writing

. . . let everyone who can, smite, slay, and stab, secretly or openly, remembering that nothing can be more poisonous, hurtful, or devilish than a rebel. . . . Their ears must be opened with musket balls, so that their heads fly into the air.[2]

Meanwhile, Münzer was exhorting the peasants:

If you be only three wholly committed unto God, you need not fear one hundred thousand. On! On! On! Spare not! Pity not the godless when they cry. Remember the command of God to Moses to destroy utterly and show no mercy. The whole countryside is in commotion. Strike! Clang! Clang! On! On![3]

The main rebellion came to an end with the defeat of Münzer at Frankenhausen in 1525 and in the reprisals which followed it is estimated that over 100,000 peasants were executed.

The decade 1521–30 was a critical one. By 1525 Lutheranism was firmly established, but it now depended for its existence on the backing of the Princes against both the Emperor above and the peasants and urban middle-class below. It was especially powerful in Swabia and on the north coast, being supported by the Duke of Pomerania, Christian IV of Denmark, John Elector of Saxony, Philip of Hesse and Albert of Brandenburg. The Empire was splitting in two, and the line of division echoed an earlier one.

. . . the frontiers of the Latin Church ultimately coincided to a remarkable extent with those of the old Roman Empire. Where the legions of the Caesars had planted their standards and founded their colonies . . . there in the sixteenth century the Roman Church retained its hold. The limits of

---

[1] Münzer at Mülhausen; quoted by R. Pascal, *The Social Basis of the German Reformation*, Watts, 1933.
[2] Bainton, p. 280.   [3] Bainton, p. 278.

the Roman Empire are in the main the boundaries between Teutonic and Latin Christianity.[1]

Between 1525 and 1530 religious compromise failed, fragmentation increased, the Reformers acquired a creed and a name and the struggle became to some extent political rather than religious.

In 1526 the Princes, meeting at Speier, declared unanimously:

> We, the Electors, Princes, Estates of the Empire . . . while waiting for a Council, (have agreed that) everyone (is) so to live, govern and conduct himself as he hopes and trusts to answer to God and his Imperial Majesty.[2]

This indirect encouragement to political and religious disagreement foreshadowed the compromise finally reached a generation later at Augsburg. At the second Diet of Speier (1529) the Princes decided, but not unanimously, that the previous concession should be withdrawn. There should be no further innovations; toleration for Catholics in Lutheran states, but not for Lutherans in Catholic ones. (The minority faiths of Zwingli and the Anabaptists were, of course, to be tolerated nowhere.) The Lutherans objected that a unanimous decision could not be repealed by a simple majority, and recorded their formal protest:

> In matters concerning God's honour and the salvation of our souls, each man has the right to stand alone and present his true account before God. On the last day no man will be able to take shelter behind the power of another. . . .[3]

In 1530 Charles V called a Diet at Augsburg and attempted to heal the growing split between 'the old religion' and 'the Protestants'. The latter submitted a *Confession* designed to minimize their differences with the Catholics and to exaggerate those between themselves and the Zwinglians. Thus it did

---

[1] *C.M.H.*, II, p. 168.   [2] *N.C.M.H.*, II, p. 340.

[3] K. Brandi, *The Emperor Charles V*, Cape, 1939, p. 300. The original 'Protestants' were the Elector John of Saxony, Margrave George of Brandenburg, Dukes Ernest and Francis of Brunswick-Luneburg, Landgrave Philip of Hesse and Prince Wolfgang of Anhalt; and fourteen cities, Strasburg, Ulm, Nuremberg, Constance, Lindau, Memmingen, Kempten, Nordlingen, Heilbronn, Reutlingen, Isny, St. Gallen, Weissenburg and Windesheim.

not deny the seven Sacraments (as Luther had earlier done) and described the Lord's Supper ambiguously:

> They (the Lutherans) teach that the body and blood of Christ are truly present and are distributed to those who partake in the Lord's Supper; and they reject those that teach otherwise.[1]

The Lutheran theologians were prepared to make further concessions, but the Protestant Princes were not, and ultimately withdrew from the city. A canon of Mainz wrote at the time:

> . . . each single Elector and Prince of the Empire wants to be Emperor and King in his own principality. . . . God give that all may end well. It is urgent.

The Diet then condemned Lutheranism, and the Princes' secularization of Church property.

Luther, being under the ban of the Empire, was unable to come to Augsburg. The Protestant leader there and the man responsible for drawing up the Confession which became the firm and permanent foundation of the Lutheran Church, was Melanchthon. Philip Melanchthon (1497–1560), a humanist prodigy, Professor of Greek at the age of twenty-one, had come to Wittenberg in 1518. Three years later, in his *Loci Communes*, he had provided a much-needed summary of the Lutheran doctrines, and in 1529 he had accompanied Luther to Marburg for the debate with Zwingli. This 'little shrimp of a man', as Luther called him, provided the intellectual, humanist element in the Lutheran movement.

During the winter of 1530–1 the Protestants formed the League of Schmalkalden, a defensive political alliance of most of the Princes and cities that had 'protested'. The Lutheran cause now had teeth as well as a creed. With the creation of the League the Reformation entered its third phase, in which the question was not so much if the new religion would survive, but rather what part of Germany 'the old religion' might retain. This phase, covering the years from 1531 to 1555 is, inevitably, one of political manoeuvre – and, ultimately, war – rather than one of religious development. It is therefore intimately connected with the Emperor Charles V, and with his other problems. In the hackneyed phrase –

[1] Bettenson, pp. 295–6.

'Protestantism was saved by the Frenchman and the Turk'. The main events have already been considered in Chapter V, and it is therefore only necessary to give here the briefest outline.

During the thirties Charles V was out of Germany, the Schmalkaldic League grew in strength and on several occasions the Empire came within an ace of civil war. In 1541 Charles returned and a conference was held at Ratisbon – a final attempt to come to terms. It failed, and in 1546 the long-expected war broke out, in which Charles won an overwhelming victory at Mühlberg. As a result he tried in 1548 to enforce his own religious compromise, the Interim. This satisfied nobody and in 1552 the Protestants, under their new leader Maurice of Saxony, obtained French help in exchange for Metz, Toul and Verdun. The ensuing war lasted till 1559, but in 1555 the Germans settled their internal differences by the Peace of Augsburg. It was a compromise peace; each Prince might choose between Lutheranism and Catholicism, no other religions would be tolerated, and all ecclesiastical territories held by the Catholics in 1552 were reserved for them in perpetuity. The two sides had stopped fighting only because they were tired, and the compromise held the seeds of future war. Nevertheless it endured for sixty years.

While Germany was agreeing to differ, Lutheranism had unobtrusively become the official religion of Scandinavia, being adopted, for rather mixed motives, by the kingdom of Sweden in 1536, of Denmark in 1537. Lutheranism also profoundly coloured the English Reformation, but in France, Switzerland and Holland its influence was soon replaced by that of Calvinism.

What of the man who had fired the explosive charge? The historically significant part of Luther's work had been completed by 1526. Had he died in that year, it seems improbable that the later history of the German Reformation would have been greatly different. In 1525 he had married a former nun, Catherine von Bora – a demonstration which proved more successful than one might perhaps have expected. In 1529, together with Melanchthon, he played a decisive part in the Marburg conference with Zwingli. In 1540 Philip of Hesse, one of the earliest and most influential of the Protestant leaders, perhaps with an eye on events in England where Henry VIII was king, asked Luther if he might divorce his wife. Luther, basing his decision on Old Testament examples, answered that Philip might commit bigamy. The ensuing scandal adversely affected the prestige of Lutheranism.

In 1546 Luther died at Eisleben, where he had been born. As he had remained under the Imperial ban all his life, he had been unable to take a direct part in the religious discussions with the Imperial authorities, but he had kept a watchful eye on their proceedings. During these years he had also finished his translation of the Bible into German, composed a Lutheran liturgy and written a number of great hymns, including *Ein feste Burg* ('A safe stronghold our God is still') which has been called the *Marseillaise* of the German Reformation. Luther's position was that of the great figurehead, the father-image of the Reformers, a man to consult and talk with.

It is difficult to assess Luther's character and influence. Centuries later Heine wrote: 'The refinement of Erasmus, the mildness of Melanchthon, could never have brought us so far as the brutality of Brother Martin.' Certainly his explosive, emotional, egocentric toughness, springing from the heart rather than the intellect, was a superb equipment for the work of destruction which was Luther's primary achievement, but these very qualities did not fit him for the role of a constructive or original thinker. His was an essentially medieval mind, concerned with a typically medieval question, 'What shall I do to be saved?' which he answered in an essentially conservative way. For the mechanical process of reasoning he had a supreme contempt, calling it 'the devil's whore'.

The centre of his religious thought is the relationship of the individual to God, and this emphasis on religion as something personal and inward – 'Not the performance of a rite, but the experience of a presence' [1] – is the most original part of his doctrine. From it stemmed his two main points of emphasis; the priesthood of all believers – 'the one outstanding difference between the followers of the reformed and the medieval religion', [2] and Justification (a technical term, the acquittal of the guilty) by Faith, 'Such faith,' he wrote, 'which throws itself upon God, whether in life or death, alone

[1] Bainton, p. 139.   [2] Lindsay, I, p. 444.

makes a Christian man.' He based his teaching on the Scriptures, but this raised the problem of how they were to be interpreted, and he himself gave greater weight to those parts that were in accord, such as St. Paul's Epistles, and neglected those, like St. James's Epistle, of which he disapproved.

Luther was not able to create institutions and his impact on the temporal sphere was limited. His repudiation of the Canon Law may have aided the growth of capitalism, but this is debatable and the consequence was certainly fortuitous. His influence on the development of the modern state was equally accidental, but potent, strengthening the power of the national monarch. As early as 1522 (before the Peasants' War) Luther had declared that rebellion could not be justified, basing his argument on Romans xiii; 'the powers that be are ordained of God'.[1] In his struggle with Rome, his appeal was often to specifically national feelings: 'What,' he said, 'have we Germans to do with St. Peter?' These two strands of thought led naturally to the glorification of the national ruler – always provided that he supported the right religion. Perhaps there is a touch of envy in Luther's gibe at Henry VIII, 'Squire Harry thinks he is God', but there is also some truth, for now 'the godly prince is *summus episcopus*,' the head of the Church. An early twentieth century historian wrote: 'The supreme achievement of the Reformation is the modern State.' Today we may feel that this is not necessarily a compliment; it remains true that Luther and Machiavelli (or the tendencies of thought symbolized by those names) were the co-architects of seventeenth century absolutism.[2]

The Reformation in Switzerland; Zwingli, 1484–1531

In Switzerland there developed a Reformed church that was at first independent of events in Germany. Its creator, Ulrich Zwingli, was a humanist who had studied at Berne, Vienna and Basle, had learnt Greek, and had fallen under

---

[1] He modified this view later. One can trace the evolution of Luther's political thought in these two quotations: 'No prince shall war against his over-lord, that is, his King and Emperor . . . (1523); When Emperor and ruler wage war against God and right, then shall no man pay obedience to them' (1531).

[2] A Lutheran anthem began: *Vivat, Vivat, Vivat, Vivat, Vivat, Johannes Friderich, Elector et Dux Saxonum, Defensor Veri Dogmatis, Pacisque Custos Pervigil, Vivat per omne seculum* (Bainton, p. 381).

the spell of Erasmus. In 1506 he became a priest, and during the next ten years went with the Swiss mercenaries to the Italian wars as their chaplain. In 1518 he was appointed to Zurich, where he immediately began to attack the local sale of indulgences. Steadily, unobtrusively, but fundamentally, he widened the scope of his attacks until they included the Pope's authority, transubstantiation, the doctrine of purgatory, celibacy, fasting and the invocation of saints. In 1522 his followers began to eat meat in Lent; and in the same year Zwingli married. By 1525 the Zwinglian reformation was complete and the 'Reformed service' had begun to spread from the canton of Zurich to Berne, Basle and northwards to the towns of south Germany.

The political structure of Switzerland was unique in Europe. It comprised a confederation of thirteen cantons and a number of 'protected' areas, the whole being theoretically part of the Empire, but in practice independent. There were many local differences between the cantons. The whole area had become in the late fifteenth century a valuable mine of mercenaries. The fact that Zwingli's doctrines were allowed to spread unchecked was partly due to these special circumstances, partly to the calm, unexplosive way in which he had proceeded.

Opposition came first from within the confederation. The five Catholic cantons of Lucerne, Uri, Schwyz, Unterwalden and Zug united against the areas that had adopted the Reformed service, and war almost broke out in 1529 over the question of the spread of this service to the protected areas. A treaty was agreed to at Kappel, but it only postponed the crisis. The religious clauses were ambiguously worded and in 1531 war came. Zwingli himself was killed in the only battle; by the second treaty of Kappel (1531), which followed within a few weeks, each canton was to choose which religion it would allow. The result was to divide the confederation into two parties, and to check the spread of Zwingli's teachings in south Germany, while the leadership of the Protestant cantons passed from Zurich to Berne and Geneva.

Zwingli's reforms, like those of Luther, were based on his reading of St. Paul and St. Augustine, but there the resemblance ends. He himself stressed his independence of Luther: 'I began to preach the Gospel of Christ in the year 1516, before anyone in my locality had so much as heard the name of

Luther.' The two men were totally different in temperament. Luther was in many ways a medieval Schoolman, Zwingli a classical humanist. Where Luther rested his church on the protection of the Princes, Zwingli of necessity based his on the democratic middle-class town, in which the church was the congregation, united by faith, and in direct communion with God. Zwingli's humanist training led him to emphasize the words of the Bible – while Luther would allow whatever was not specifically forbidden by the Scriptures, Zwingli, would accept only what they specifically authorized; 'I will try everything by the touchstone of the Gospel,' he wrote. This led to a 'Puritan' emphasis in his teaching, which was absent from Luther's; images, pictures, choirs and church music, for instance, must all go.[1] The mind, not the flesh, was the key to salvation.

The contrast between Luther and Zwingli is seen most clearly in their respective attitude to the Eucharist. In 1529, when his teaching was spreading to south Germany, a discussion between Zwingli and Luther was held at Marburg in an attempt to hammer out a common programme. In spite of the profound differences that existed, agreement was reached on fourteen points, but on the fifteenth, the significance of the Eucharist, there was no common ground. Where Luther saw the mysteries of consubstantiation, Zwingli understood only a commemorative feast, bare symbols (*nuda signa*). Luther quoted the Latin Vulgate, chalking on the table between them, *Hoc est Corpus meum*, This is my Body. Zwingli replied with the Aramaic – *This my Body*. The absent verb, he said, was not 'is', but 'signifies'. Neither would budge. Luther refused Zwingli's proffered hand, and when the conference broke up it had achieved nothing.

In 1519 Zwingli had written his first hymn. It included the words:

> Thy cup am I,
> To make or break.

He and his church were broken at Kappel, and it was left to a later reformer, Calvin, 'to gather up the fragments of Zwingli's German party, and to establish an ultra-Protestant opposition to the Lutheran Church.' [2]

---

[1] Zwingli himself was a good musician, and could play six instruments.
[2] *C.M.H.*, II, p. 216.

The Reformation in Switzerland; Calvin, 1509–64

John Calvin, who thus built on the ruins of Zwingli's church, as a Reformer of the second generation; he was also a foreigner, a Frenchman. These two facts, at first sight incidental, deeply affected his thought and career.

France occupies a halfway position in the history of the Reformation, neither militantly Catholic like Spain, nor astutely Protestant like northern Europe. The Pragmatic Sanction of Bourges (1438) had left the French Church largely independent of both royal and Papal control. In 1516 Francis I concluded the Concordat of Bologna with Leo X by which the King was given virtual control over French clerical appointments. From that moment it was in the Crown's own interests to support the Catholic Church in France.

At first the movement for reform stemmed from the French humanists, such as Lefèvre d'Étaples, and was characterized by an emphasis on the Scriptures, on the straightforward nature of salvation and on the criticisms of Erasmus. Such a programme was almost respectable, and it inspired a local reform within the Church, carried out by the Bishop of Meaux (1517–25). Meanwhile, however, Luther's books were entering France along the trade routes from the great international fairs at Frankfurt and Lyons. As a result, attempts by the government to suppress anti-Catholic teaching commenced in 1523; but Francis's constant preoccupation with Italy, and his unstable character, made royal persecution ineffectively intermittent. In 1534 posters appeared one night in many of the chief towns of France – '*The truth about the horrible, great, unbearable abuses in the Papal Mass introduced in direct contradiction of the Last Supper of Our Lord, the only mediator and saviour Jesus-Christ.*' One was found on the door of the King's bedroom at Amboise. Not surprisingly there was a renewed burst of persecution.

It was against this background that Calvin grew up. He was the son of a Picard lawyer, and was educated at Paris, where he studied theology, and at Orleans and Bourges, where he read law. On the death of his father he went back to Paris and his first love, theology. His education had been strongly humanist and he had learnt both Greek and Hebrew.

Then, probably in 1533, he experienced what he termed 'a sudden conversion' in which God subdued the humanist to the theologian.   Later in the year he composed a Protestant lecture for a friend and in November, as a result, he had to disappear.   The wave of persecution following the affair of the posters forced Calvin to leave France, and in 1535 he went to Basle.   From there he moved to Italy, back to France during a brief amnesty and then on to Geneva, which he reached in 1536 – accidentally, since he was heading for Strasburg but had to make a long detour to avoid the Imperial troops.   Intending to spend one night in the city, he spent twenty-six out of the remaining twenty-eight years of his life there.

Geneva was a city-state outside the confederation of Switzerland, under the titular control of the Duke of Savoy.   The direct ruler had been the Bishop of Geneva, but essentially political causes had led the city councils to overthrow, with the help of the Bernese, the authority of both Duke and Bishop.   The city was now divided between those who wanted freedom but no change in religion, and those, many of them former Zwinglians, who wanted a *godly thorough reformation*.   Another Frenchman, Farel, 'the red-bearded Elijah', had already established Reformed doctrines there in 1535.   Farel persuaded Calvin to stay and help him, and the latter immediately tried to tidy up this confused situation. His demands for greater disciplinary powers were resented, and in 1538 Farel and Calvin were both expelled from the city.   Calvin went to Strasburg, where he came under the influence of the Lutheran Bucer, married and lived there from 1538 to 1541 as the minister of French Huguenot refugees. Then, out of the blue, the citizens of Geneva asked him to come back.   'Better death a thousand times,' Calvin exclaimed, but he went back all the same, and what has been called a 'marriage of convenience' between the Frenchman and the city lasted for twenty-four years.   During this time Calvin carried out a unique political, religious – and therefore social – experiment.   Whatever he might preach as the ideal practice, Geneva became in fact a theocracy, dominated by Calvin, 'the Pope and Emperor of Protestantism'.   Yet his power rested solely on his personality, for he was only once a magistrate and was not even a full citizen of Geneva until 1559.

In 1541 a committee, led by Calvin, drew up a constitution, the *Ecclesiastical Ordinances of Geneva*. This blueprint of the machinery of Church and State provided that all citizens [1] must be orthodox followers of the Calvinist faith. As such they were the Church, independent and responsible for church matters and church discipline, their officers divided into pastors (preachers), doctors (teachers), elders (responsible for moral discipline) and deacons (responsible for the poor). Church discipline was applied to everyday conduct – dress, food, entertainment, private vices and opinions were all investigated as well as the more obvious public acts, like drunkenness or non-attendance at church. The body ultimately responsible for the maintenance of this discipline was the Consistory, made up of six pastors or doctors and twelve co-opted laymen. It was able to impose spiritual punishments, such as public confession and excommunication, and could also hand over those found guilty to the secular arm, the city councils.

It was in this machinery of government that Calvin's originality is most apparent. His theology, like that of so many of the Reformers, rests on an interpretation of the Bible coloured by his reading of St. Augustine. In 1536 Calvin had published his *Institutes of the Christian Religion* (*Institutio Religionis Christianae*). It was a lawyer's brief in defence of his faith, and a plan for a Reformed Church to embody that faith. Although Calvin wrote much else (the standard edition of his works runs to forty-nine volumes), he remains essentially a one-book man, never needing to replace this original statement, made when he was only twenty-seven – though he expanded it from six to eighty chapters in the course of his life. His theology is completely expressed in the original edition of the *Institutes*, with the clear and ruthless logic of the engineer or lawyer. It has the precision and inevitability of a piece of machinery – and, his opponents sometimes claim, the same inhumanity. Basing his reasoning on the Scriptures, he gave greater emphasis to the Old Testament than earlier Reformers had done, replacing the authority of the Catholic Church by that of the whole Bible. The interpretation of this depended on the Holy Ghost – and the Elect would have no difficulty in recognizing the voice of

[1] The population of Geneva was about 13,000, but only about 1,500 could vote.

God. But who were the Elect? Calvin felt that his own strong will had been mastered and broken by the Will of God, and he saw in the operation of that Will the mainspring of the universe.

> Hence we declare, that by His providence, not only heaven and earth and inanimate creatures, but also the counsels and wills of men are governed so as to move precisely to that end destined by Him. . . . For the will of God is the highest rule of justice; so that what He wills must be considered just, for this very reason because He wills it. When it is inquired, therefore, why the Lord did so, the answer must be: Because He would. [1]

These two passages express the basis of Calvin's theology. On it he built, using as materials the word of the Bible and the fact that God must have every good quality in infinite quantity.

From the height of absolute goodness, the difference between the best and the worst of men becomes infinitely small, since all men are corrupted by the Fall. Therefore salvation can come only from God, the all-powerful, while man can do nothing towards it. From this logical train of argument there followed the two doctrines peculiar to Calvinism; Election, and Predestination. God is all-merciful, but He is also all-just. His mercy would save all, His justice condemn all. To demonstrate both qualities He has Elected some to eternal salvation, regardless of their merits on earth, while others have been condemned to the eternal damnation which all men deserve. It is impossible to know who the Elect are, but a high external standard of behaviour combined with an equally high spiritual life are perhaps hopeful signs. This, in crude outline, was Calvin's doctrine of Predestination – powered by God's will and working like a great machine – 'Interdependence absolute, foreseen, ordained, decreed,' as M'Andrew, the Calvinist engineer, said of his ship's engines, in Rudyard Kipling's *M'Andrew's Hymn*.

The idea of Predestination was no new one; it was in the writings of St. Augustine, and hence in the theology of the medieval Schoolmen and, of course, of the other Reformers. What was new was the especial emphasis that Calvin gave to it, pushing the doctrine to its logical limits, and extracting the

[1] *Institutes*, Bk. I.

extreme conclusions that could be drawn from it. Calvin stressed that the workings of God's will could not be understood by man, they could only be accepted. He himself called the doctrine of Predestination a 'labyrinth', and God's eternal decision 'this hair-raising decree' (*decretum quidem horribile*). One might have expected that such an iron-fisted doctrine could lead only to passive despair or careless immorality of the sort described in Browning's *Johannes Agricola in Meditation*:

> I have God's warrant, could I blend
> All hideous sins, as in a cup,
> To drink the mingled venoms up,
> Secure my nature will convert
> The draught to blossoming gladness fast. . . .

In fact, just the reverse happened. The Reformers now had a certainty with which to fight the certainty of Rome, and everywhere Calvinists became the shock-troops of Protestantism.

Calvin's view of the relations between Church and State was similar to that held by the Papacy in the Middle Ages. The temporal and spiritual powers were like two swords, one entrusted to the Church and one to the State. Neither trustee must normally interfere with the wielder of the other, but the State must be prepared to use its power to protect the Church and to enforce its decisions. In Geneva the Councils of the city were in theory supreme in political matters, but in fact, such was Calvin's influence, the pastors controlled the city-state in both its spiritual and temporal affairs. In the second half of the century, under the stimulus of persecution, Calvinism became 'the creed of rebels', but there was no place in Calvin's own teaching for active resistance to the ruler:

> 'The most wicked kings,' he wrote, 'are placed on their thrones by the same law which has established the authority of all kings.'

In Calvin's thought there could be no hint of religious toleration. In this he was, of course, at one with the Catholic Church and all the major Reformed churches. People must worship God in the best – indeed the only possible – way, and if they refused they must be compelled to do so by legal pains and penalties. Thus when Servetus, a sort of Spanish Unitarian, was so imprudent as to come to Geneva in 1553 he was tried for blasphemy and burnt – though Calvin asked that he be only beheaded. This action must be seen in the historical context of its time. The Roman Inquisition burnt Giordano Bruno for pantheism in 1600, and James I burnt two Unitarians in England in 1612.

Calvin's emphasis on education was something a little new in the Reformation. It helped to transform Geneva, and the city became one to which men came from all over western Europe and from which they went out again to disseminate Calvinism. The obscure little Savoyard town grew into a cosmopolitan European city, peaceful, pious and learned, 'the Protestant Rome'; in the eyes of Catholics 'the mine whence came the ore of heresy', as the Venetian Suriano wrote.

The preachers who left this sixteenth century Moscow affected decisively not only the religious but also the political history of western Europe in the second half of the century. In the Empire they won over states from the Lutherans, in spite of the fact that Calvinists were not included in the Peace of Augsburg, complicated the religious pattern, and helped to produce the situation that led to the Thirty Years' War. In France they formed an important minority and their conflict with the Crown led to civil war, which continued sporadically from 1562 to 1598. In Scotland John Knox successfully established Calvinism in the south in 1561 and the Catholic Mary, Queen of Scots, was forced to flee to England a few years later. In England itself they were a thorn in the side of Elizabeth – and something much more dangerous to the early Stuarts. In the Netherlands they kept the revolt against Spain alive from 1572 to 1609, and ultimately set up an independent Calvinist confederation in the North.

The Anabaptists

Through the breach that Luther had made in the walls of Rome there poured, besides the Lutherans and Zwinglians, besides the Calvinists, a mixed band of lesser men – 'the sects'. This is not surprising. In replacing the authoritarian discipline of Rome by the judgement of the individual conscience the Reformers ran the risk that there would be as many religions as there were individuals. Among these groups the name that occurs most often is that of the Anabaptists, and when it does so it is always coupled with the extremes of hostility and persecution. However much the other Reformers and the Catholics might differ among themselves, on one thing they were all agreed – that the only good Anabaptist was a dead one.

At first sight this hostility seems inexplicable. Instead of infant baptism, the Anabaptists believed that children should be consecrated to God, and baptized when they grew up – an innocent enough Protestant variation, one would have thought. The real reasons for the hatred that the Anabaptists inspired are complex. For one thing, the name 'Anabaptist' was used to describe any extreme religious practice of which the speaker disapproved. It became a political 'swear-word', in the same way that the words 'capitalist' and 'communist' have done in the twentieth century. It thus came to include a vast range of individual, eccentric beliefs, which had little or nothing to do with the question of adult baptism. What most of those who were termed Anabaptists did have in common, however, was a fanatical faith in their own vision and a determination to sacrifice everything to that vision. They therefore threatened the established social order, which in turn sought their extermination.

The majority of these religious extremists seem to have derived their beliefs partly from medieval mysticism, partly from a Christian communism for which they could find justification in Christ's teaching, and partly from that desire to believe in an imminent end to the world and its miseries that has so often powered religious enthusiasm. But '. . . attempts to realise the millennium, if successful, would be fatal to most forms of government. . . . The revolutionist becomes a believer in the brotherhood of man, in the perfectibility of the race, and in the practicability of the millennium. The narrower his experience of men and affairs, the wider his flights of fancy.' [1] Under the pressure of the intense persecution which these threats led the forces of law and order to practise, the doctrine of passive resistance to which most Anabaptists were committed broke down, and their 'quiet spiritual dramdrinking' turned into a literal attempt to realize the Apocalyptic vision upon earth. This, in turn, provided the excuse for more violent persecution by the authorities.

It will be obvious that much of this coloured the events in the

[1] *C.M.H.*, II, p. 222.

Peasants' War of 1524, but there were many other outbursts both before and after that date. The most dramatic, though not the most typical, of these occurred at Münster in 1534, where there had already been revolts of the townspeople in 1525, 1527 and 1529. Early in the year the Anabaptists obtained a majority on the city Council and under the leadership of two Netherlanders, Jan Matthys and Jan of Leyden, began to introduce a new social order. The city was besieged, and the inhabitants lived under martial law. All goods belonged to the community; at first there was 'simply an abundant Christian charity enforced by public opinion, and latterly a requisitioning of everything that could be used to support the whole population of a besieged city'.[1] When Jan Matthys was killed in the fighting, Jan of Leyden took command. He introduced polygamy – there were far more women than men in the town. Under the strain of events his own unstable character rapidly disintegrated. Eventually the Anabaptists surrendered on promise of a safe-conduct – and the leaders were then tortured to death, while all those who had played a prominent part in the resistance were executed.

Most of the Anabaptists, though, were not such dramatic figures as Jan of Leyden, but weavers and handworkers, poor men preaching at crossroads, groups of artisans praying in back rooms. A Swiss observer wrote:

> They avoided costly clothing, despised costly food and drink, clothed themselves with coarse cloth, covered their heads with broad felt hats; their walk and conduct was altogether humble. . . .[2]

Their persecution was everywhere the same, however:

> 'Some,' wrote their leaders, 'they have executed by hanging, some they have tortured with inhuman tyranny, and afterwards choked with cords at the stake. Some they have roasted and burned alive. . . . No human being was able to take away out of their hearts what they had experienced. . . . The fire of God burned within them.'[3]

Mysterious and persecuted, the Anabaptists occur again and again in the sixteenth and seventeenth centuries, at once a

[1] Lindsay, II (1908), p. 462.
[2] R. H. Bainton, *The Reformation of the Sixteenth Century*, Hodder & Stoughton, 1953, pp. 100–101.
[3] Bainton, p. 102.

symbol and a product of the social crisis that accompanied the change from medieval to modern Europe.

The Consequences of the Reformation

The forces of the Reformation destroyed the spiritual unity of western Europe in the same way that the forces of nationalism had intensified regional differences. The two sets of changes were of course connected, acting and reacting upon one another. By 1600 the new religious pattern was fairly stable; there were few significant changes in the seventeenth century. Eastern Europe had been unaffected and remained nominally Orthodox in the north, Muslim in the south. For the rest, southern Europe – Spain, and Portugal, Italy, south Germany and the Austrian Habsburg lands – had remained Catholic. Northern Europe – Scandinavia, north Germany, Scotland and England – had become Protestant; Lutheran, Calvinist or Anglican. France and the Netherlands were emerging from civil wars that resulted in a kind of toleration in the former, while the latter split into a Calvinist north and a Catholic south.

The religious pattern was everywhere linked, to a greater or lesser extent, with the nation state. This was least true in the south, but even there the actions of Philip II of Spain were inspired by a compound of religious and national motives, and the Spanish Inquisition was in effect a department of state. In the north the link was closer: in Germany the religious settlement was tied to the Prince – *cuius regio, eius religio*; in France it took the form of a royal decree, the Edict of Nantes: the Church of England was a state church, a political compromise.

In one way, therefore, the Reformation had strengthened the power of the State. At the same time, however, many states contained large religious minorities, and the position of these minorities led them to demand religious toleration – though this was no part of their programme when they were themselves in power – and to declare that armed resistance to a religious tyrant, or the assassination of a heretic ruler were justifiable actions. In this way they unintentionally fought a battle for toleration and democracy. 'Political liberty was the child of the Reformation, though not of the Reformers.'[1]

The effect of the Reformation on political history is clear,

[1] See also Chapter XIV.

though contradictory. There is no such agreed view as to its effect on economic life, and in particular on the development of capitalism. A generation ago many historians thought they had found a close causal connection between Protestantism and capitalism. Capitalism, it was argued, flourished in countries where Protestantism, and particularly Calvinism, triumphed. A rather over-simplified summary of the general argument would be that the Catholic Church had prohibited usury, and that when the Protestants overthrew the canon law they created a mental climate in which it was easier for capitalists to develop to the full the new financial techniques.

Other historians were not so sure. They pointed out that capitalism had begun to develop in the Middle Ages in spite of the Church, and that Jesuit thinkers, later, were able to reconcile the two ethics. As so often in history, it seems probable that the true picture is more complicated; perhaps it is something like this: capitalism antedated Protestantism but both developments were expressions of the same forces, interacting on one another. Protestantism developed often in urban areas, where the new financial techniques were already being practised. There it helped to free the capitalist from the control of the priest, and to break down old class barriers.

An accidental by-product of the Reformation was its effect on the development of national literatures. Translations into the vernacular moulded the literary style of those that read them. Luther's Bible and hymns, and the English Authorized Version of 1611 exercised a powerful influence on later writers in Germany and England. The other arts, with the doubtful exception of music, probably suffered rather than benefited from the spread of the new creeds.

The Reformation hastened the process of reform within the Catholic Church. It also, by the sources on which it drew, such as St. Augustine, and the problems with which it was primarily concerned – Justification, Predestination, the Eucharist, decided to some extent the pattern which that reform would take, the problems with which the Counter-Reformation would particularly concern itself.

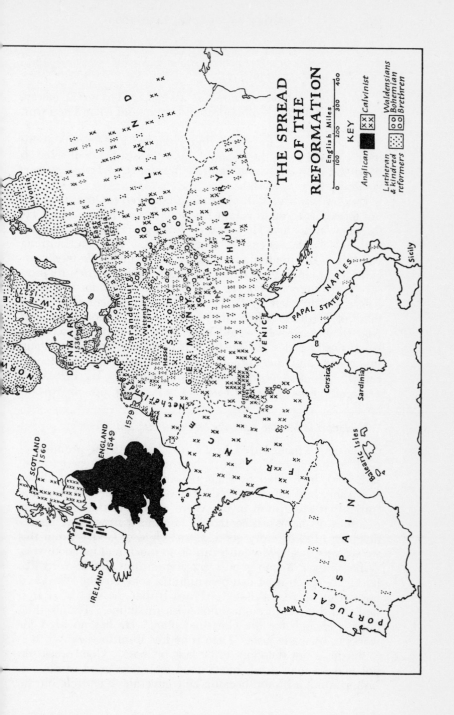

THE SPREAD
OF THE
REFORMATION

English Miles
0   100   200   300   400

KEY

■ Anglican   ✕✕ Calvinist
                    ✕✕

⋯ Lutheran   ⊙⊙ Waldensians
  & kindred   ⊙⊙ Bohemian
  reformers   Brethren

EXTRACTS

1. *St. Augustine (396–430):*

On Faith: I have no hope at all but in Thy great mercy. Grant what Thou commandest and command what Thou wilt. (*Confessions*, X. 40.)

On Grace: . . . for them that were weak He reserved his own gift whereby they should most irresistibly will what is good and most irresistibly refuse to forsake it. (*De correptione et gratia*, 34–8.)

On Predestination: Will any man presume to say that God did not foreknow those to whom He would grant belief? and if He foreknew this, then He certainly foreknew His own kindness, with which He vouchsafes to deliver us. This, and nothing but this, is the predestination of saints; namely, the foreknowledge and planning of God's kindnesses, by which they are most surely delivered, whoever are delivered. As for the rest, where are they left by God's righteous judgement save in the mass of perdition where they of Tyre and Sidon were left? And they, moreover, would have believed, had they seen the wondrous miracles of Christ. But it was not granted to them to believe, and therefore the means of believing was denied them. (*De dono perseverantiae*, 35, quoted in H. Bettenson, *Documents of the Christian Church*, O.U.P., 1943, pp. 76, 79–80)

2. *Luther defines the difference between Faith and Works:*

The soul which with a firm faith cleaves to the promises of God is united with them, absorbed by them, penetrated, saturated, inebriated by their power. If the touch of Christ is healing, how much more does that most tender touch in the spirit, that absorption in the Word convey to the soul all the qualities of the Word so that it becomes trustworthy, peaceable, free, full of every good, a true child of God. From this we see very easily why faith can do so much and no good work is like unto it, for no good work comes from God's Word like faith. No good work can be within the soul, but the Word and faith reign there. What the Word is that the soul is, as iron becomes fire-red through union with the flame. Plainly then faith is enough for the Christian man. He has no need for works to be made just. Then is he free from the law.

But he is not therefore to be lazy or loose. Good works do not make a man good, but a good man does good works. A bishop is not a bishop because he consecrates a church, but he consecrates a church because he is a bishop. Unless a man is already a believer and a Christian, his works have no value at all. They are foolish, idle, damnable sins, because when good works are brought forward as ground for justification, they are no longer good. Understand that we do not reject good works, but praise them highly. (*Of the Liberty of a Christian Man* quoted in R. H. Bainton, *Here I Stand: A life of Martin Luther*, Hodder & Stoughton, 1951, pp. 111–12)

3. *Calvin defines Predestination:*

No one who wishes to be thought religious dares outright to deny predestination, by which God chooses some for the hope of life, and condemns others to eternal death. But men entangle it with captious quibbles; and especially those who make foreknowledge the ground of it. We indeed attribute to God both predestination and foreknowledge; but we call it absurd to subordinate one to the other. When we attribute foreknowledge to God we mean that all things have ever been, and eternally remain, before His eyes; so that to His knowledge nothing is future or past, but all things are present; and present not in the sense that they are reproduced in imagination (as we are aware of past events which are retained in our memory), but present in the sense that He really sees and observes them placed, as it were, before His eyes. And this foreknowledge extends over the whole universe and over every creature. By predestination we mean the eternal decree of God, by which He has decided in His own mind what He wishes to happen in the case of each individual. For all men are not created on an equal footing, but for some eternal life is preordained, and for others eternal damnation. . . . (*Institutio, Book III, cap. xxi* quoted in H. Bettenson, *Documents of the Christian Church*, O.U.P., 1943, pp. 299–300)

4. *The Significance of the Last Supper:*

(*a*) And He took bread, and gave thanks, and brake it, and gave unto them, saying, This is my body which is given for you: this do in remembrance of me. (*St. Luke XXII, v. 19: Authorized Version, 1611*)

(*b*) What is the Sacrament of the Altar?

Answer: It is the very Body and Blood of our Lord Jesus Christ, under the Bread and Wine, for us Christians to eat and to drink, under the institution of Christ Himself. (*Luther's Short Catechism*, 1529.)

(c) *The Minister.*   You do not understand then that the body is enclosed in the bread, or the blood in the cup?

The Child.   No.   On the contrary, in order that the reality of the sacrament be achieved our hearts must be raised to heaven, where Jesus Christ dwells in the glory of the Father, whence we await Him for our redemption; we are not to seek Him in these corruptible elements. (*The Geneva Catechism,* 1541)

(d) I profess likewise that true God is offered in the Mass, a proper and propitiatory sacrifice for the living and the dead, and that in the most Holy Eucharist there are truly, really and substantially the body and blood, together with the soul and divinity of Our Lord Jesus Christ, and that a conversion is made of the whole substance of bread into His body and of the whole substance of wine into His blood, which conversion the Catholic Church calls transubstantiation. (*Profession of Faith, 1564; based on the statement of the Council of Trent in 1551*)

(b) and (d) from H. Bettenson, *Documents of the Christian Church,* O.U.P., 1943, pp. 291, and 372–3. (c) from L. Bernard and T. R. Hodges, *Readings in European History,* The Macmillan Company, N.Y., 1958, p. 236)

FURTHER READING

R. H. Bainton, *The Reformation of the Sixteenth Century,* Hodder & Stoughton, 1953

T. M. Lindsay, *The History of the Reformation,* 2 vols., Clark, 1907–8

R. H. Bainton, *Here I Stand: A Life of Martin Luther,* Hodder & Stoughton, 1951

J. Mackinnon, *Calvin and the Reformation,* Longmans, Green, 1936

H. Bettenson, *Documents of the Christian Church,* O.U.P., 1943

B. Hall, *John Calvin,* Historical Association Pamphlet, G.33, 1956

R. Pascal, *The Social Basis of the German Reformation,* Watts, 1933

L. W. Spitz, ed., *The Reformation: Material or Spiritual?,* Harrap, 1962

VII · THE COUNTER-REFORMATION, 1534–98

Spain and Italy

THE condition of the Catholic Church in the fifteenth century, described at the beginning of Chapter VI, produced not only the Reformation, but also a number of movements for reform from within. The outcome of these is usually known as the Counter-Reformation.

Attempts at reform had begun in Spain and to a lesser extent in Italy before the Protestant Reformation had started, yet they did not achieve their aim until the second half of the sixteenth century, by which time they were acting under a new stimulus – the success of that Reformation. Starting from the same terminus, corruption in the Church, the slow-moving demand for reform from within had been overtaken and passed by the more speedy Protestant movement outside. The relative slowness with which the Catholics put their own house in order was mainly due to three causes: the notorious difficulty any bureaucracy of vested interests finds in reforming itself; the fact that the call for reform came from isolated groups, unable to act officially until the Papal throne was occupied by one who thought as they did; and the absence of any sense of urgency, until the Protestant Reformation was well established.

The work of the Counter-Reformation falls chronologically into three distinct phases. First there were the early attempts at a reform of morals, attempts that had their origin in the fifteenth century, their inspiration in Erasmian humanism, and their conclusion with the accession of Pope Paul III in 1534. Between 1534 and 1563 lies the heart of the Catholic revival – the Counter-Reformation in the narrower sense of the term. During these years the movement gathered speed, captured the Papacy, took the vital decision not to compromise with the Protestants on matters of dogma, created new weapons and sharpened up old ones. Finally, between 1563 and the end of the century, the forces of the Counter-Reformation moved over to the attack and attempted to win back those parts of Europe that the Catholic Church had lost. The struggle became one in which religious and political motives were inextricably mingled. The main temporal power involved was that of Philip II of Spain, whose wars with France, England and the Netherlands combined religious enthusiasm and political expediency; but Spain often found itself at loggerheads with the Papacy. The death of Philip in 1598 may be taken as marking the close of the Counter-Reformation.

The first attempt to reform from within the sad state into which the Church had fallen took place in Spain. There, between 1492 and 1517, Cardinal Jiménez was largely successful in first restoring the morals of the clergy and then overcoming their ignorance and lack of polish by a planned system of education.[1] The comparative ease with which he was able to do this can be explained, in part at least, by the peculiar history of the country. In Spain the new force of Nationalism was not opposed to the Church. On the contrary the centuries-long struggle with the Moors had made Spanish patriotism synonymous with support for Catholicism. Ferdinand and Isabella were *los reyes Católicos*, the Catholic kings. Jiménez' work was also made easier by the influence of Erasmian humanism, very fashionable in Spain at this time, and by the existence of the Spanish Inquisition, re-established there in 1480, a terrible and effective weapon.

In Italy, lacking a central government, where humanists were often agnostics, and where the secularization of the Papacy was accepted as part of the established political scene, attempts to reform the Church naturally followed a different pattern. They were essentially, at first, private and un-official. Many of them were initiated by members of the society known as the *Oratory of Divine Love*. This consisted of a group of about fifty humanist reformers, who began to meet in Rome about 1517. It included those who were later active in the Counter-Reformation and, as with the Protestants, their thought was strongly influenced by the writings of St. Augustine. In 1527 the sack of Rome scattered the members, though some of the leaders later reassembled in Venice.

During these years there also took place in Italy the creation or reform of a number of religious orders, of which the most significant were the Theatines and the Capuchins. The Theatines were a small order of secular clergy, living in the

[1] See also Chapter III.

world but bound by monastic vows, who were to go among the unreformed clergy and act as leaven by example and instruction. They were started by Cardinals Cajetan and Caraffa in 1524 and took their name from the latter's see of Chieti (Theate). Confined at first to Venice and Naples, their blameless lives made the word *Chietino* synonymous with 'puritan'. The Capuchins, reformed Franciscans, began as a spontaneous movement in Umbria and were officially recognized in 1528. Their influence was much more widespread than that of the Theatines and their order was next in importance to that of the Jesuits in its contribution to the Counter-Reformation.

At this time the movement for reform from within became complicated by the impact of the Protestant movement for reform from without. Shaken by this impact, Catholic reformers began to divide into two groups. On the one hand were those that one might perhaps call liberal churchmen, who desired to reach some sort of compromise with the more moderate Protestants and to find a common ground for definition of dogma which would take into account the new ideas of the humanists. On the other hand were those who agreed with the first group on the necessity for moral reform, but were opposed to any compromise with Protestant or humanist on matters of dogma, and saw the only possibility for success in a programme of increased centralization and vigorous counter-attack. In the end it was this second group which got control, for '. . . the whole temper of the age was against reconciliation by the ignoring of differences. . . . It was not the spirit of Erasmus that triumphed, but the spirit of Calvin and Ignatius Loyola. Men desired certainty in religion, and believed that it was obtainable.' [1]

Representative of the two groups were the Cardinals Contarini and Caraffa, both members of the Oratory of Divine Love. The liberal Contarini was the descendant of an ancient Venetian family, had studied at Padua and become a diplomat. He felt able to reconcile Aristotelian Scholasticism, Erasmian humanism, and at least some of Luther's earlier pronouncements. He represented the Catholics at the Diet of Regensburg in 1541 and helped to prepare there the compromise which came twenty years too late and was rejected by the extremists on

[1] Grant, *The French Monarchy, 1483–1789,* C.U.P. 1925, Vol. I, p. 262.

both sides. He died in the following year. His friend and rival, Cardinal Caraffa, was an aristocratic Neapolitan and an accomplished humanist scholar. In 1524 he had helped to start the Theatines in the wild Abruzzi. Later he was Papal Nuncio in Spain and came back full of admiration for the work of the Inquisition. In 1542 he persuaded Paul III to establish the Roman Inquisition and was one of its Inquisitors-General. In 1555, a fierce-tempered, very old man, he became Paul IV (1555–9). The militant Counter-Reformation had triumphed.

For the crux of the problem of reform was the attitude of the Papacy, and the Papal throne was perhaps the last place where the necessity for reform would be recognized. The transformation was slow and spasmodic. Thus, although it is not until the Pontificate of Paul IV that the Papacy became finally committed, Paul III (1534–49) for all his worldly ambitions has a good claim to be regarded as the first Pope of the Counter-Reformation, since it was during his Pontificate that all the essential steps were taken. In 1536 he ordered a Commission of Cardinals (it included both Contarini and Caraffa) to inquire into abuses. On receiving its report in the following year he set in motion the machinery for calling a General Council of the Church, which finally met in 1545. Later he licensed the Jesuits. The Counter-Reformation received its form and its weapons from him.

Paul III's immediate successors, Julius III (1550–5) and Marcellus II (1555), were lesser men, but with Paul IV the threads are picked up again. When he at last banished his nephews from Rome in 1559 the Counter-Reformation came of age. Later Popes, Pius IV (1559–65), Pius V (1565–72), Gregory XIII (1572–85) and Sixtus V (1585–90) moved over to the political counter-attack against the Reformers. That they were able to do this was largely due to the work of the Jesuits, the Inquisition, and the Council of Trent.

The Jesuits

Don Iñigo Lopez de Loyola (1491–1556), the son of a Basque nobleman, became St. Ignatius Loyola, the founder of the Jesuits. He grew up fond of games, tales of chivalry, women, fighting – a normal young Spanish aristocrat. Then in 1521, when he was defending Pamplona against the invading French, he was struck by a cannon-ball which shattered one leg and damaged the other. The break failed to set properly, so he had it broken and re-set.

'And now,' he wrote later, 'the bones beginning to knit together, one just below the knee was found to be over-lapping another, thus shortening the leg; and there it remained, protruding. . . . The flesh and the protruding bone having been cut away, remedies were applied so that the leg might not remain shorter than the other. . . .' [1]

The operation was unsuccessful. The man of war was unable to fight, the gallant was no longer a handsome athlete, the extrovert was forced to brood. This was the crisis in his life. Within three months he had a vision in which he believed that the Virgin and Child had appeared to him. He left at once for Montserrat, the holy hill in Aragon, and lived like a hermit at Manresa, close by. There he confessed continuously, practised austerities and tried to drag salvation from God – 'I will follow like a puppy-dog if I can only find the way to salva-tion' – before at last he stopped struggling and threw himself on God's mercy. Later he wrote:

All the helps God gave him during his whole life . . . were less than the graces he received that day sitting by the river. Moreover this enlightenment remained with him so that he seemed to himself afterwards a different man, possessed of a new intellect. [2]

A psychological crisis, an attempt to work for salvation, ulti-mately passive acceptance – the parallel with Luther's spiritual history is striking, and may be explained on either theological or psychological grounds. Now the history of the two men parts company; Luther had to construct, partially and empiric-ally, a satisfactory creed, Loyola was able to accept what was already available. 'I saw, felt within me, and penetrated with my mind all the mysteries of the Christian faith.'

There followed almost twenty years of preparation and struggle before the new Order that Loyola had already dimly conceived was established. There were several false starts. First he went on a pilgrimage to Jerusalem, intending to begin a

[1] From the autobiography dictated 1553–5; quoted in M. Purcell, *The First Jesuit*, Gill, 1956, p. 43.
[2] Purcell, p. 93.

mission, but the Franciscans quickly sent him back to Italy. He decided he must educate himself, learn Latin and study theology, and this he did for eleven years, first in Spain at Barcelona, Alcalá and Salamanca, and then at Paris (1528–35). (He was there at the same time as Calvin.)

While Loyola was in Paris he gathered six companions: another Basque, Xavier; three Castilians, including Lainez, later the second General of the Order; a Savoyard and a Portuguese. In 1534 they vowed together to go to Palestine if possible, failing that to do whatever the Pope might order. They got to Venice, but the way to Palestine was blocked by war and so they went instead to Rome, where they were befriended by Contarini. There Loyola met opposition from the Vatican bureaucrats, but at last, in 1540, Paul III licensed the Society of Jesus. Its aims were described in the draft constitution that Loyola had drawn up:

> That the members will consecrate their lives to the continual service of Christ and of the Pope, will fight under the banner of the Cross, and will serve the Lord and the Roman Pontiff as God's Vicar upon earth, in such wise that they shall be bound to execute immediately and without hesitation or excuse all that the reigning Pontiff or his successors may enjoin upon them for the profit of souls or for the propagation of the faith, and shall do so in all provinces whithersoever he may send them among Turks or any other infidels, to the farthest Ind, as well as in the region of heretics, schismatics, or unbelievers of any kind.[1]

The faith is to be spread by preaching, spiritual exercises, charity, 'and especially by the training of boys and the uneducated in Christianity'. In 1541 Loyola was elected as the first General. Membership was at first limited to sixty, but the limitation was removed in 1544. The detailed constitution of the Society was developed gradually and did not reach its final form until 1558. The Jesuits were essentially an order of priests – clerks regular like the Theatines – but there were important differences which aroused the opposition of many Catholics. They did not wear a special habit; fasting and extreme mortifications were avoided; they were excused from the communal recitation of the church offices and the regular singing of high masses, activities which took up a great part of

---

[1] T. M. Lindsay, *The History of the Reformation*, Clark, Vol. II, 1908, p. 547.

the time and energy of most orders.   They were to spend their time instead as soldiers of Christ and of the Holy See, vowed to poverty, chastity and obedience to the elected General of the Order, and working as preachers, teachers and missionaries.

The training of a Jesuit was long, arduous and detailed. The period of probation for Novices lasted two years instead of one as in the other orders, and the time was not all spent in theoretical training, but partly in the practical experience of hospital work, pilgrimage and begging. This was followed by another innovation, a period, which might last ten or twelve years, as a Scholastic. The years were devoted to education in theology, philosophy and the humanities, together with practice in the teaching of others. At the end those considered suitable became full members of the Society. Of these a few, the spiritual and intellectual élite, took a fourth vow of direct personal obedience to the Pope. The 'Professed of the Four Vows' numbered in 1556 only forty-three out of a total of about 1,500 people attached to the Society.

Loyola left behind him two monuments; a body of men, the Jesuits; and a book, the *Spiritual Exercises*. The latter is at least as important and remarkable as the former – one of the half dozen most significant books of the sixteenth century. Loyola began to compose the *Exercises* at Manresa in 1522, but they did not reach their final form until 1548. At Manresa he had read, and been deeply impressed by, Thomas à Kempis's *Imitation of Christ*, that classic of Christian mysticism. To become a mystic one must lose one's attachment to the things of the world, and the *Exercises* are designed to help one to achieve this, 'to master the soul by manipulating the body'.[1] They are not a book to be read, but a series of mental exercises to be carried out, preferably under the supervision of a superior. Their full title reads: *Spiritual Exercises for overcoming oneself and for regulating one's life without being swayed by any inordinate attachment*. They were designed to last for four 'weeks' (though each 'week' might continue for an indefinite length of time) during which attention was concentrated on sin and conscience; the life of Christ; the Passion and the Resurrection. The correct posture for meditation, both mental and physical, an exact order of procedure, the appreciation of intangible mysteries by considering their material aspects – these are the special

[1] Lindsay, II, p. 542.

characteristics of the *Exercises*. They are a sort of spiritual circuit-training, a religious assault course and the first European manual of applied psychology.

To systematize the techniques of mysticism was an unconventional idea, the end to which they were put was equally so. For the ordinary mystic withdrawal from the world is the conclusion of the process, but for the Jesuit this experience must become the source of inspiration for an active life. Having completed the *Exercises* he must come down from the heights he has so arduously reached and work in the world, his spirit tamed so that he is 'as a corpse' under the control of his superiors, his mind toughened so that if the Church defines 'anything to be black which to our eyes appears to be white, we ought in like manner to pronounce it to be black'.

Loyola himself had been elected the first General of the Order in 1541 and held that office until his death in 1556. He has been called 'a mixture of St. Paul, Don Quixote and Lenin'. One might add that he also manages to combine the characteristics of Luther and Calvin. The emotional nature of his conversion, and the later signs of that emotional temperament – the nervous indigestion from which he suffered, the ease with which he blushed and wept – are Luther's; the iron logic, the emphasis on education, the creation of a powerful machine, are the methods of Calvin. His emphasis on authority is typical of the sixteenth century spirit of autocracy: 'We must put aside all judgement of our own and keep the mind ever ready and prompt to obey the Church in all things.'

The Jesuits encountered much opposition from the other Orders, which resented their relative freedom from religious routine, from Paul IV who regarded them as an unnecessary imitation of his own Theatines; and from the old-fashioned university of Paris. Nevertheless they rapidly became the most powerful weapon of the Counter-Reformation and of the reformed Papacy, and dominated the later sessions of the Council of Trent. Their influence was not confined to Italy. Already at the time of Loyola's death they were scattered over Spain, Portugal, France, Germany, the Low Countries, India, Japan, Brazil and the Congo.

At first the Jesuits were famous as teachers and missionaries. Their colleges, providing a sort of advanced secondary education for lay scholars as well as members, were soon as good as the best in Europe, employing the latest techniques of humanist scholarship and Renaissance learning. Outside Italy the earliest and most important were those at Cologne (1545), Vienna (1551) and Ingolstadt (1556). Jesuit missionaries moved out from these centres and the Catholics began to win back ground from the Protestants, first in the Rhineland, then on the Danube and in Poland. Jesuit agents were active in the religious struggles in the Netherlands and in France, and in Elizabethan England.

The Order had been founded to combat paganism as well as Protestantism, and Jesuits went as missionaries to the new lands being opened up by the Portuguese and Spanish. Francis Xavier left Europe in 1541 and travelled through Asia for ten years, from Goa to Malaya and on to Japan, dying when he was just preparing to enter China in 1552; by 1580 there were eighty-five Jesuit missionaries in Japan.

In the seventeenth century the Jesuit influence continued to grow, but their prestige began to decline. They were too powerful, too successful, their skill in argument became casuistry, their general 'the black Pope'. They were the confessors of kings, who perhaps appreciated their doctrine of Probabilism, by which the sinner must be given the benefit of every possible doubt. (Loyola's instructions to two Jesuits going to Ireland included the advice, '. . . when conversing with persons of note see – in order to win them for the greater glory of God – of what temperament they are and adapt yourselves to them'.[1])

Macaulay has described the vast paradox of the later Jesuits:

> There was no region of the globe, no walk of speculative or of active life, in which Jesuits were not to be found. They guided the counsels of Kings. They deciphered Latin inscriptions. They observed the motions of Jupiter's satellites. They published whole libraries, controversy, casuistry, history, treatises on optics, Alcaic odes, editions of the fathers, madrigals, catechisms, and lampoons. The liberal education of youth passed almost entirely into their hands, and was conducted by them with conspicuous ability. They appear to have discovered the precise point to which intellectual culture can be carried without risk of intellectual

[1] *Letters*, Vol. I, quoted in Purcell, p. 290.

emancipation. . . . They were to be found in the garb of Mandarins, superintending the observatory at Pekin. They were to be found, spade in hand, teaching the rudiments of agriculture to the savages of Paraguay. . . . Whether the Jesuit should live under the arctic circle or under the equator, whether he should pass his life in arranging gems and collating manuscripts at the Vatican or in persuading naked barbarians in the southern hemisphere not to eat each other, were matters which he left with profound submission to the decision of others. If he was wanted at Lima, he was on the Atlantic in the next fleet. If he was wanted at Bagdad, he was toiling through the desert with the next caravan.

But with the admirable energy, disinterestedness, and self-sacrifice which were characteristic of the Society, great vices were mingled. It was alleged, and not without foundation, that the ardent public spirit which made the Jesuit regardless of his ease, of his liberty, and of his life, made him also regardless of truth and of mercy; that no means which could promote the interest of his religion seemed to him unlawful, and that by the interest of his religion he too often meant the interest of his Society. . . .

So strangely were good and evil intermixed in the character of these celebrated brethren; and the intermixture was the secret of their gigantic power. That power could never have belonged to mere hypocrites. It could never have belonged to rigid moralists. It was to be attained only by men sincerely enthusiastic in the pursuit of a great end, and at the same time unscrupulous as to the choice of means.[1]

The Inquisition

The Inquisition had been revived in Spain in 1480. Cardinal Caraffa had seen it at work there, and in 1542 he persuaded Paul III to set up the Roman Inquisition. The Holy Office, as it was called, consisted of six (later twelve) cardinals, with powers 'in all the states of the Christian Commonwealth' over all people, whatever their rank. These powers included the right to imprison before trial, to interrogate in private, to use torture and to withhold from the accused the nature of the charge against him. If guilt was proved, the Inquisitors might impose canonical punishments, or confiscation of goods, or

---

[1] Macaulay, *History of England*, Dent, 1953, Vol. I, pp. 542–4.

they might hand the accused over to the secular authorities, who would inflict the death penalty.

The Roman Inquisition acted in a similar way to the Spanish one, but it was in practice a less extreme body. This was partly due to the fact that the Protestant danger in Italy was less acute than the danger from the infidel in Spain, where the identification of religion and nationalism led to the deterioration of the Spanish Inquisition into a sort of secret police, often at loggerheads with Rome. There was for instance the case of Carranza, Archbishop of Toledo, who made certain errors in his commentary on the catechism, was denounced to the Spanish Inquisition and became a victim of that body for seventeen years, despite protests from the Jesuits, the Pope and the Council of Trent.

In Italy, on the other hand, the Roman Inquisition did a useful job, from the Catholic point of view, in suppressing the small Protestant groups which had appeared at places in the north such as Parma and Lucca. Its main function was to act as a centralized machine, supervising the measures taken to check the spread of dangerous thought. As such, its most notorious acts were its burning in 1600 of the philosopher, Giordano Bruno, and the later trial of Galileo. While indefensible in twentieth century eyes, neither of these *causes célèbres* was remarkable when set against the general background of intolerance in sixteenth and seventeenth century Europe.

The Inquisition was concerned with the enforcement of the censorship of books, that answer of established authority to the invention of the printing press. In 1559 Paul IV issued the first *Index Librorum Prohibitorum*, replaced in 1564, after the Council of Trent, by the Tridentine Index. In these lists Erasmus and Luther, Calvin and Rabelais, rub shoulders. The consequence was to ensure that modern thought developed to some extent in isolation from the influence of the Catholic Church. Today at the front of Catholic books, there are still the licences of the censorship; *Nil obstat* (Nothing stands in the way), and *Imprimatur* (Let it be printed).

The Council of Trent, 1545–63

The demand for a General Council of the Church had been increasing for a generation: Protestants; the Emperor Charles

V; those who desired to restore the unity of Christendom by agreement and those who wished for reform of morals in order that the Church might fight back the better – all pressed for a General Council. After the Commission of Cardinals appointed by Paul III had issued their report on abuses within the Church, the *Consilium de emendenda ecclesia*, the Pope began to consider the calling of such a Council. But the geographical problem of its site – which implied the political problem of who was to control it – together with the interminable wars between the Emperor and the King of France, delayed proceedings.

Trent was the place eventually chosen, a bishopric on the River Adige in the Dolomites, politically in the Empire, but geographically part of Italy. In 1544 the Peace of Crépy temporarily ended the wars and made it possible for the Council to meet. It sat, on and off, for eighteen years and its chronology is complicated. The sessions fall into three groups: sessions i to x, held between December 1545 and June 1547, while Paul III was Pope; sessions xi to xvi, held between May 1551 and April 1552, during the Pontificate of Julius III; and sessions xvii to xxv, held between January 1562 and December 1563, under Pius IV. The Bull summoning the Council outlines three aims; to end the religious schism, to reform the Church, and to call the re-united, reformed Church to a crusade against the infidel; but only the second of these was achieved.

At the opening sessions, matters of procedure were settled. It was decided, after prolonged bickering, that only bishops and the heads of religious orders might vote, and that voting was to be by individuals and not by 'nations'. This gave an immediate numerical majority to the Italians, who were in general poorer, less intellectual and more Papal than the representatives from beyond the Alps. These decisions having been made, there followed a long debate as to whether reform or dogma should be dealt with first. Eventually it was decided to discuss both at the same time, but in fact questions of dogma were, on the whole, settled before questions of reform.

During the first period of the Council's life it was agreed that the basis of authority should be the Bible as expounded by the Church, together with the Church's traditions, and that these two sources should be regarded as of equal authority, (a

decision which would obviously be unacceptable to the Reformers.) The official text of the Bible was to be that of the
Vulgate, though each country might decide for itself whether
or not it would also permit the use of translations. The longest
and most technical debates in this first period concerned the
doctrine of Justification by Faith, which was eventually defined
in such a way as to exclude the Lutheran interpretation. In
1547 the Pope, alarmed at the growing influence of the
Emperor, used an outbreak of spotted fever in Trent as an
excuse to transfer the Council to Bologna. Charles ordered
the Spanish bishops to stay where they were, and in this way
the first chapter in the Council's life came to an end.

In 1551 the Council reopened at Trent. Protestant delegates attended, but their claim that a General Council was
superior to the Pope was rejected, and their presence was disregarded. The Catholics reasserted and defined the seven
Sacraments. The definition of the Eucharist included a firm
statement of the doctrine of transubstantiation – that Christ is
'truly, really and in substance' (*vere, realiter ac substantialiter*)
contained in the bread and wine. In 1552 renewed fighting
between Charles V and France led to the suspension of the
Council once more.

The last group of sessions was attended by Catholics only.
The traditional doctrines concerning indulgences, the position
of the priesthood, celibacy, the invocation of saints, and purgatory, were all reaffirmed. At the same time most of the
administrative abuses, such as nepotism, simony and pluralism, were denounced. Bishops might only hold one diocese,
were to reside in it and were to be held responsible for the
state of the Church there. These sessions were dominated
by the Jesuits, notably Lainez, and they were mainly responsible for the emphasis laid in the closing session on the power of
the Pope. The profession of faith drawn up by the Council
included the clause '. . . I promise and swear true obedience
to the Bishop of Rome . . .', while the Council's concluding
act was to declare its will '. . . that confirmation of all that
has been decreed should be requested of the most blessed
Roman pontiff . . .'.

Whatever differences of opinion there may be on the other
consequences of the Council's work, there can be no doubt that
it confirmed the Pope's theoretical position and greatly

strengthened his actual power. The decisions of the Council represent to varying degrees the different forces of sixteenth century Catholicism: the reformed Spanish Church; the revived interest in the philosophy of St. Thomas Aquinas; mysticism; humanism; the influence of the Papal Court; the interest of the temporal rulers; and the new power of the Jesuits. Through those decisions the Church acquired a clearly-defined, compact body of doctrine and a hierarchy that would soon be reformed and educated – the whole inspired by a spirit of dogmatic certainty.

The Effects of the Counter-Reformation

With the close of the Council of Trent the formative period came to an end and the forces of the Counter-Reformation moved over to the attack. The tide of Protestantism was checked and in some places swept back. The Catholic south of Europe was held, and parts of the Empire, notably south Germany and the Austrian Habsburg lands, together with Poland, were cleared of Protestants or regained from them. In Germany the dominating figure was a Jesuit, Peter Canisius. In the fifties his journeys through the Empire averaged fifteen hundred miles a year, and his *Summary of Christian Doctrine* was the best known book produced by the Counter-Reformation. The Catholic successes were only partial, however. In France thirty years of civil war ended in a form of religious toleration, while in the Netherlands a national revolt led to the division of the country into two states, a Calvinist north and a Catholic south. In England and Scotland the movement met with no success at all.

The Counter-Reformation stimulated the arts, the help of which was enlisted, especially by the Jesuits, in what can be regarded as one of the great advertising campaigns of history. Palestrina, the Master of the Pope's choir, composed the *Mass for Pope Marcellus* (*Missa Papae Marcelli*) in 1562–3. In painting and architecture the Mannerist tendencies already visible in the late work of Michelangelo were developing into a new ornate emotional style, the Baroque. The Catholic Church did not create the Baroque style, but it found in it a powerful ally. It was in architecture that the influence of religion on art was greatest; Baroque architecture started when Vignola's Jesuit church in Rome was begun in 1568. Soon statues floated upwards, their robes caught in a heavenly whirlwind, the faces of saints shone from paintings in dramatic contrasts of light and shade, the exterior of churches became patterned and ornate, the interior stirred the senses and led the eye towards the altar.[1]

Philip II of Spain (1556–98)

The partial success of both the Reformation and the Counter-Reformation had made almost inevitable a series of wars in which the religious struggle would be complicated by a parallel political struggle. 'Neither would tolerate the other, and Europe was doomed to be the battlefield of the contending principles. The sword alone could be the arbiter.' [2] In that struggle the King of Spain was destined to play an important, if sometimes ambiguous, role.

The events of Philip II's reign, like those of his father Charles V, fill a large canvas, sprawling from the islands of Greece to those of western Scotland, and covering forty years in time. As with his father's reign, there is the same need to recognize the connection between events so widely separated.

Philip's wars against France and in the Netherlands are described in detail in Chapter VIII. Here it is more convenient to give a general outline of the history of Spain under his rule as the supreme example of a Catholic country deeply involved in the wars produced by this head-on collision of Reformation and Counter-Reformation. Not that Philip was an entirely satisfactory supporter of the Papacy – he was too much inclined to behave as if the Spanish had invented Catholicism.

> To Philip, no doubt, all his policy was consciously directed to the glory of God and the good of his Church; but these things were identical in his mind with the exaltation of the power of Spain. . . . Whenever political interest and religious zeal clashed, religion almost invariably gave way.[3]

Yet, in general, religious orthodoxy and political expediency went hand in hand, particularly in the second half of his reign when Spain fought against the Calvinist Dutch, against the Anglican Elizabeth, against the French Huguenots.

---

[1] See Chapter XIV.   [2] *C.M.H.*, II, p. 689.
[3] R. T. Davies, *The Golden Century of Spain*, Macmillan, 1937, p. 131.

There was, though, constant friction with the Papacy, for the royal control of the Church was almost as absolute as that of Henry VIII had been.   The Pope objected to the Spanish claim to examine Papal bulls and briefs before they were admitted to the country.   In 1581 there was a quarrel over the royal right to appoint bishops which led to the expulsion of the Papal Nuncio.   Pius V summed up the situation when he said bitterly: 'In Spain you all want to be Popes and bring the king into everything.'

From his father Philip had inherited an impressive, though scattered, Empire;   the Netherlands, Luxemburg, Franche Comté, Milan, Naples, Sicily, Spain and the Spanish colonial territories.   To these he added in 1580 Portugal and her overseas empire.   Philip inherited also the dying stages of the Habsburg–Valois wars and, consequent on these, a rapidly approaching bankruptcy that brought the fighting to an end in the Treaty of Cateau-Cambrésis (1559).

The King had directed the closing stages of the war from the Netherlands.   Now he returned to Spain, where he was to remain throughout his long, busy reign.   In appearance he was a northerner, with fair hair and blue eyes, and there is something Germanic also in his inflexibility, and his passion for bureaucratic methods and administrative routine;   but the emotional side of his nature, introverted, much concerned with death and religion, seems more typically Spanish.   His days were divided between the psychological consolations of religion and the reassuring contemplation of exact detail, and this division was repeated in his behaviour, unmoved by public disasters and victories, yet in private deeply attached to his wife, Elizabeth of France, and capable of writing human and charming letters to his children.

If there is a curious dichotomy in Philip's character, there is one too in the history of Spain at this time.   On the one hand it is *il siglo d'Oro*, 'the Golden Age of Spain', during which Europe was dominated by the movements of Spanish troops, impressed by the wealth of the Spanish empire, and influenced by Spanish habits in everything from methods of fighting to manners of dressing.   (With the significant exception of shipbuilding: the Spanish began to imitate British galleons after 1588.)   On the other hand, this 'Golden Age' was followed immediately by a sensational decline in the seventeenth century, and historians are agreed in finding the underlying causes of this in the Golden Age itself, where they had been spreading, like dry rot, beneath the gilded surface. When considering the events of Philip's reign, therefore, one must try to strike a balance between the superficial strength and the underlying weakness.

Born in 1527, Philip had been brought up to administer; in 1543 he had become a member of the Council of Castile and Duke of Milan, in 1549 the Netherlands had sworn an oath of allegiance to him and in 1556 he succeeded his father on the throne of Spain. His first wife, Maria of Portugal, died in 1545 leaving behind an only child, Don Carlos, who grew up a hydrocephalic idiot. His second wife, Mary I of England, died childless in 1558. The Treaty of Cateau-Cambrésis included in its terms the marriage of Elizabeth of France to Philip. She died in 1568, leaving two daughters, Isabella and Catharine. Philip's fourth wife, Anne of Austria, his niece and a daughter of the Emperor Maximilian II, died in 1580 leaving a son, Philip, who later became Philip III. It was always the Habsburg policy to rule through relatives, and to extend their power by family alliances, but none of these connections brought Philip any lasting gain.

When Philip II returned to Spain in 1559 he found that the Crown's power had weakened a little. He was quick to restore centralized control. The death of Paul IV in 1559 made it possible to end for the time being the domestic religious bickering which had been going on between the Spanish administration and the Papacy. The activities of the Spanish Inquisition, combining as they did bureaucratic procedure, national solidarity and religious enthusiasm, were calculated to appeal to Philip, and his return to Spain was celebrated with a great *auto de fé* at Valladolid. And in 1565 he wrote to the Governor of the Netherlands:

As to the Inquisition, my will is that it be enforced by the Inquisitors as of old, and as is required by all law, human and divine. This lies very near my heart, and I require you to carry out my orders. Let all prisoners be put to death, and suffer them no longer to escape through the neglect, weakness, and bad faith of the judges. If any are too timid to execute the edicts, I will replace them by men who have more heart and zeal.[1]

Philip considered the *Moriscos* to be a source of national and spiritual weakness. In 1566 an edict of 1526, no longer observed, was re-enacted. National songs and dances and the use of Arabic were forbidden, women were to appear in public with their faces unveiled, Christian midwives were to attend *Morisco* births, and the public baths were to be pulled down. In ways such as these Philip hoped to destroy their distinctive civilization. The measures provoked a revolt, as perhaps they were intended to do, and a bloody civil war broke out which lasted from 1568 until 1570, when the *Morisco* resistance was finally destroyed by Don John of Austria, the illegitimate son of Charles V. The remaining Castilian *Moriscos* were deported to the centre and north of Spain, and the agricultural prosperity of Andalusia, potentially the most fruitful area in Spain, declined. The policy was not even a success in its attempt to destroy the Moorish influence in Spain, for between 1609 and 1614 perhaps half a million *Moriscos* had to be expelled in a renewed effort to 'purify' the Spanish blood. Yet later in the ˚century they began to return again from North Africa.

Technically part of Philip's foreign policy, but closely connected with the events already described, were the wars against the Moors of North Africa and the Ottoman Turks of the Eastern Mediterranean. The maritime possessions of Aragon involved a struggle for control of the sea-routes. Between 1560 and 1564 a series of abortive raids was launched against the Barbary corsairs and their bases in North Africa. These were followed in 1565 by a more successful operation, the relief of Malta, which was being besieged by the Turks. Five years later the Turks attacked the Venetian island of Cyprus, and took it in 1571. (The Christian commander was skinned alive, his skin stuffed with straw and sent to Constantinople as a trophy.)

This disaster persuaded the Christian powers to forget, briefly, their own rivalry. A combined Venetian and Spanish fleet, consisting of about 270 galleys, 50,000 sailors and 30,000 soldiers was assembled at Messina under the command of Don

---

[1] Acton, *Lectures on Modern History*, Macmillan, 1906, p. 144.

John. It destroyed the Turkish fleet in the battle of Lepanto (1571) off the Gulf of Corinth. The victory gave a valuable psychological stimulus to the morale of the European Mediterranean countries and is historically significant as the last battle in which galleys, dominant for nearly two thousand years, played a major role, but it was not followed up. As a result the Turks continued to control the Eastern Mediterranean, and Cyprus remained in their hands until 1878.

In another area the struggle against the Moors had an important, though accidental, consequence for Spain. In 1578 the young King of Portugal, Sebastian, was killed when the expeditionary force which he was leading was defeated in Morocco. His great-uncle, the Cardinal Henry, died two years later, and the Portuguese were left with no immediate heir to the throne. There were several possible successors, but Philip's geographical position enabled him to enforce his own claim, derived from his mother Isabella of Portugal. The Portuguese were never friendly to the Spanish, and the Duke of Alva had to occupy Lisbon by force, after which Philip was crowned there in 1581. (The chief pretender, Don Antonio, fled abroad and received support at different periods from both England and France.)

Spain and Portugal remained united for sixty years. The union greatly strengthened the power of Spain. The whole peninsula was under one man. The Portuguese Empire included Brazil in the west, control of the coast of Africa, and the Spice Islands in the east. At least as important as these territorial acquisitions was the fact that Spain became an Atlantic sea-power, controlling the Azores, the Portuguese harbours and an experienced fleet. It is one of the ironies of history that this new naval power also made possible the disaster of the Armada.

The three rulers who in their very different ways dominated European politics in the second half of the sixteenth century were Philip, Elizabeth I and the Queen Mother of France, Catherine de' Medici. They all began to exercise real power at about the same time, Philip in 1559, Elizabeth in 1558 and Catherine in 1560, and they all moved with a certain caution. There the resemblance ends. Spain was a world power. England had been weakened by two disastrous reigns, the country was divided on religious matters, the ruler a woman; in France the king was a minor, the real ruler was again a woman, the country was tottering on the verge of a religious civil war. 'So long as France was kept divided both England and Spain were secure; and, if in addition English religious dissensions were fomented by the Spanish encouragement of Catholic revolt, there would be no power in Europe to counteract Philip's plans.' [1]

The Netherlands had replaced Italy as the key area in Europe, while the chief danger that Philip was anxious to reduce was 'the auld alliance' between France and Scotland, since Mary, Queen of Scots, was the widow of the late King of France, and her mother a member of the powerful Guise family. This was the pattern in 1559, but fifty years later France, England and the Netherlands had all triumphed at the expense of Spain.

For the first ten years the situation remained outwardly little altered. The Guise connection between France and Scotland forced Philip to sustain Elizabeth – it was largely through his efforts that the bull of excommunication against her was delayed until 1570. Then between 1568 and 1578 the pattern changed. In Scotland Mary lost her throne in 1568 and became Elizabeth's prisoner; and as early as 1569 Philip was writing to Alva:

> We think here that the best course will be to encourage with money and secret favour the Catholics of the north, and to help those in Ireland to take up arms against the heretics and deliver the crown to the Queen of Scotland, to whom it belongs.[2]

In the Netherlands local opposition grew into national revolt when the Sea Beggars seized Brill in 1572. In England events moved more slowly, but the uneasy alliance with Spain turned gradually into a cold war as the fundamental contradictions between the two countries revealed themselves.

Religion, politics, economics – all played their part in the destruction of the Anglo-Spanish *entente*. As early as 1562 John Hawkins had traded in slaves between West Africa and the Spanish West Indies – the first in a series of English merchant-

[1] *C.M.H.*, III, p. 487.
[2] M. A. S. Hume, *Philip II of Spain*, Macmillan, 1897, p. 141.

trespassers there.   Later Spanish officials attacked and largely destroyed one of Hawkins's trading expeditions at San Juan d' Ulloa (1568).   In the same year, when they were forced to put in to English ports, Elizabeth 'borrowed' £85,000 from Spanish ships, which were carrying the money as a loan from Genoese bankers to pay the army in the Netherlands.   In 1570 the bull excommunicating Elizabeth was at last published. Next year the Ridolfi plot to replace Elizabeth as Queen of England by Mary, Queen of Scots, was discovered.   Ridolfi, a Florentine banker, had been in touch with Philip, Alva and the Spanish ambassador in London.   By events such as these one can measure the destruction of the friendly relations that had once existed between Spain and England, and trace the birth of the period of unofficial guerrilla warfare.   The common link between the two countries, the Netherlands, had now become a 'sentimental obstruction', while their common fear of France and Scotland had vanished now that Mary was in English hands, and in 1578 Philip reached an understanding with the Guise family, still incomparably the most powerful factor in French politics.

From 1578 to 1588 Philip's foreign policy was at its most positive and most successful.   Portugal was acquired, and the defeat in 1582 of the Pretender's fleet in the Azores was as great a naval victory as Lepanto.   In France the understanding with the Guises was replaced by a formal alliance in 1585 which left the King of France a mere figurehead.   In the Netherlands the war was going well; by 1579 the south had been reconquered and the seven northern states were left fighting alone.   Their leader, William the Silent, was assassinated in 1584, while the Spanish troops continued to win victories under the command of the most successful and brilliant of Philip's generals, Alexander Farnese, Duke of Parma.

During these years England and Spain slid rapidly into open war.   In 1579 Drake took the treasures of Peru and Mexico, while in the next year an 'Italian' expedition left Lisbon in an unsuccessful attempt to invade Ireland by way of Dingle Bay. In 1583 the exposure of Throckmorton's plot against Elizabeth led to the expulsion of the Spanish ambassador from London, and normal diplomatic relationships were not resumed until peace was signed in 1604.   'The enterprise of England,' the plan to invade the island, first mentioned in 1583, began to

take shape.   Meanwhile an English expeditionary force under
Leicester was giving some rather inefficient help to the Dutch
rebels in the Netherlands.

Drake raided Cadiz and Lisbon in 1587 and delayed the
proposed invasion for a year, but at last in the following spring
an Armada of about 130 ships, carrying 30,000 men, set sail.
Its instructions were to transport Farnese's army from Nieuport
and Dunkirk to England.   The English use of fireships at
Cadiz, the fact that Parma was blockaded by the Dutch fleet,
the English naval strategy in the ensuing battle near Gravelines,
the weather – these were the main factors in the story of its
destruction, a detailed account of which belongs rather to
English than to European history.   Of the Spanish fleet about
half eventually limped back around Scotland and Ireland to
Spain.

For Philip, the nineties did not justify the promise of the
eighties.   In France the assassinations of the Duke of Guise and
the King of France left the French people with the invidious
choice of a Spanish princess, Philip's daughter Isabella, or the
Huguenot, Henri of Navarre.   Henri's military ability, and
his conversion to Catholicism, decided the issue.   Philip's
dreams of partitioning France, or of adding it to the Habsburg
family business (there had been a suggestion that Isabella
should, after succeeding to the throne of France, marry the
Emperor's son) faded away, and peace was eventually signed at
Vervins in 1598, four months before his death.

In the Netherlands, too, Spanish victories gave place to
defeats.   Parma died in 1592, by which time the Dutch had
discovered in Maurice of Nassau and Oldenbarneveldt a
soldier and a statesman capable between them of uniting the
northern provinces and driving back the Spanish armies.   By
1594 the area that was to become the United Provinces was
virtually clear of Spanish troops, though a truce was not signed
until 1609.

The struggle with England, too, continued into the next
century (1604).   Both sides really underestimated the problems
of sea-borne expeditions.   An English force sent to Portugal in
1589 lost 11,000 men; more successful was the sack of Cadiz
in 1596.   Philip planned a series of 'Armadas' to Ireland, only
to be prevented by poverty or the weather.   Elizabeth
launched five expeditions to help Henri of Navarre.   Both

countries made big gestures, spent money they could ill-afford and achieved nothing.

In foreign policy it is arguable that Spain failed through attempting too much; at home it is indisputable that the wheels of government turned too slowly because Philip tried to do everything himself. The words of his father, Charles V, had been: 'Trust nobody but yourself', and Philip was temperamentally inclined to follow this advice.

The government of Spain, like that of the rest of western Europe, continued to be carried on by Councils (of which there were eventually twelve), while the influence of the *Cortes* steadily declined.[1] Some of the Councils were territorial, dealing with the affairs of Castile, Aragon, Portugal, Italy, the Indies and Flanders, while the remainder were departmental, concerned with finance, justice, the Inquisition and the military orders. The keystone was the Council of State, a consultative body with the King as President, composed of the men he chose to summon. Its members were in fact mainly Spaniards, the only important exception being the Burgundian, Cardinal Granvelle (1517-86). Philip picked advisers of varying opinions between whom he held a sort of balance of power. 'The whole system,' it has been said, 'seems like a fantastic prototype of the party government of nineteenth-century England. And it had some of its advantages. Thus, for example, it achieved Philip's purpose of getting every proposal well canvassed.' [2] But the Council had no executive powers. Philip alone could take action. His secretaries were only secretaries and not, as in England, chief ministers in disguise. Every decision from the most trivial to the most important went through the King's hands, usually several times. The information or advice was sent to the King on paper with very large margins. There he could make his own comments, even going so far as to correct the spelling. The annotated document would next be sent to the appropriate council for discussion and would then return to the King, together with more sheets containing the council's advice. Philip would re-read the entire file – and if necessary the whole

---

[1] In 1544 the Castilian *Cortes* had begged, on the grounds of expense, that they might not be summoned more than once in three years.

[2] Davies, pp. 123-4.

process could be gone through again. Philip – like his rival Elizabeth – saw advantages in a policy of procrastination. 'Time and I,' he would say, 'are a match for any other two.' But the papers piled up more quickly than they could be dealt with, the wheels of government slowed down, and the administration suffered a progressive hardening of the arteries.

The disasters in North Africa were due to delays in Spain; Malta was only relieved in the nick of time; 'If death came from Spain,' said a Spanish viceroy in Italy, 'we should live for a very long time.'

By 1600 the population of Spain had perhaps topped 8,000,000. This represented an increase of about 1,000,000 during the century, most of which had probably taken place in the first fifty years. Quite large numbers emigrated to the New World, and there may have been as many as 150,000 there by 1574.

Meanwhile the economic weaknesses already noticed in the time of Charles V became more apparent. The finances of the Crown were by the end of Philip II's reign in a deplorable state, due to the fact that Spain's strength had to be used to support the whole of his empire. Italy brought in nothing; Aragon stood stiffly on its privileges; the Netherlands, the main source of revenue in earlier times, had now become the main cause of expenditure, the war there costing even in its early stages an average of 2,000,000 ducats a year. Castile was taxed up to the hilt, and the exemption of the nobles and clergy meant that this taxation fell with ruinous severity on the agricultural and industrial classes.

The only source of income that was increasing was the import of treasure, now mainly silver, from America, a quarter of which was the Crown's share. The following figures give a picture of rapid and continuous development:

Period	Total Value
1556–60	£4,599,400
1576–80	9,919,300
1596–1600	19,795,000[1]

Yet the bullion did not seem to make the country any richer. It was most peculiar.[2] The value of the treasure was in fact

---

[1] Davies, pp. 299–300.

[2] Though one Spaniard at least had discovered the right answer as early as 1558. See Chapter XIII.

offset by a corresponding rise in prices, which nearly doubled in the second half of the century:

	Index Number
1551–60	68·21
1571–80	100
1591–1600	118·77[1]

At the same time Spain's foreign entanglements ensured that money soaked away from Spain to foreign bankers and traders – even to the Dutch themselves, who continued to trade by sea with the Spanish-controlled part of the Netherlands.

The returns from agriculture continued to fall. After about 1520 Spain, instead of having a surplus of wheat, began to have to import it from abroad. The expulsion of the *Moriscos* from Granada had weakened the most prosperous Spanish province. The herds of the great sheep-owning corporation, the Mesta, were declining in numbers:

1516	2,775,250
1526	3,433,168
1562	1,673,551

The pressure of rising taxation had stifled the embryonic industries which had begun to develop in Castile during Spain's brief period of prosperity between 1520 and 1550. More and more Spaniards were too well-born, or too devout, to work. At the end of the century all the male population of Guipuzcoa were *hidalgos*, while it has been estimated that in 1570 one quarter of the adult male population of the country was clerical. Spain was rapidly becoming a land of noble beggars, of rocks and of saints (*tierra de cantos y santos*).

The economic condition of Spain, coupled with expensive foreign wars, involved Philip in a policy of rising taxation punctuated by bankruptcy. The *alcabala* was supplemented by an excise on necessities such as food and drink, known as the *millónes* since its yield was reckoned in millions of ducats. The existing taxes were already pledged to pay the interest on money borrowed by the government in the form of annuities paid out of the State's income (*juros*), a type of national debt which had increased five-fold during the reign of Charles V. The Venetian ambassador reported that taxation in Castile had risen from 2,750,000 ducats in 1551 to 5,250,000 in 1573.

[1] Davies, p. 266.

The continuing expense of the wars – the Armada alone cost 10,000,000 ducats – had to be met by borrowing from foreign bankers, and this in turn led to bankruptcy. Three times during his reign Philip was forced to suspend the payment of interest on the national debt and each time one can detect repercussions in foreign affairs. The First Decree, in 1557, brought the long wars with France to an abrupt end. The Second Decree, in 1575, helped to ruin Antwerp, and led to the sack of that city in the 'Spanish Fury', a sack which played its part in uniting the whole Netherlands for a short time against Spain. The Third Decree, in 1596, paved the way for the Peace of Vervins with France two years later. When Philip died in that year his son was faced with a debt of 100,000,000 ducats.

Within the Spanish peninsula the forces of separatism continued to threaten the power of the Crown, notably – as usual – in Aragon. In 1563 the *Cortes* there had refused to make a grant of 1,350,000 ducats until Philip promised an inquiry into the activities of the Inquisition, which was disliked as a Castilian institution. In 1585 a former secretary of Philip's, Antonio Perez, was imprisoned for selling State secrets. Five years later he fled to Aragon and pleaded the judicial liberties of that country. Eventually he was arrested by the Inquisition there, whereupon the people of Saragossa burnt down its headquarters. Perez escaped to France and England where he kept himself alive by manufacturing and selling State secrets. The case demonstrates the surprising impotence of the royal power in Aragon.

Most of the hidden causes of Spain's weakness have now been described. They may be summarized as follows: separatism, the continued tendency of such areas as Portugal and Aragon to break away; a clericalism to which everyone paid lip-service, in which 'everyone believed, no one enquired'; a financial system, crippling in its intensity and in the type of taxes imposed, such as the *alcabala* and the local tolls; a bureaucracy, corrupt in the provinces, honest but slow-moving at the centre where limited and mediocre men took refuge in administrative detail submitted to the leaden-footed deliberation of a half-German bureaucrat; above all to the disparity between the means and the end, between the relative under-development of Spain and the immense tasks that she attempted.

But the financial and political strains to which Spain was subject are more clear to the hindsight of the historian than they could be to contemporaries. To the Spanish, Philip was Philip the Prudent, the King who had united the peninsula, thrown back the infidel, supported the true – the Spanish – religion against heretics in France, the Netherlands and England; whose ships came yearly into Seville laden with treasure from the four quarters of the world.[1]

Learning and the arts flourished, while the more slow-moving forces of economic decay were sapping the foundations on which they rested. Twenty-one new universities were opened in the sixteenth century, those already established at Salamanca and Alcalá were internationally famous, while even the English were prepared to study the work produced by the school of nautical science controlled by the *Casa de Contratación* in Seville. There treatises were produced on eclipses, the exact calculation of latitude, the magnetic variation of the compass and similar topics. Spanish scholars assisted at the Gregorian correction of the calendar. Although the country had the first index of prohibited books in Europe and the Inquisition may have stifled the spirit of inquiry, it had also the only *Index Expurgatorius* – a list of books that might be published, provided that offending passages were taken out. Spain was thus in an odd way more liberal than other Catholic countries, where one phrase could damn a book, and in the seventeenth century Hobbes, Bruno, Galileo and Copernicus could all, surprisingly, be read there.

The religious climate in Spain naturally encouraged the emotional aspect of the Counter-Reformation, and there was a sudden flowering of mysticism. The greatest names are those of St. Teresa of Avila (1515–82), a woman of considerable humour and common-sense, and her disciple, the poet St. John of the Cross (1542–91).

Philip himself was a considerable patron of the arts, especially painting and architecture. He collected the works of the Flemish masters, such as Bosch and Breugel (but he is said to have disapproved of the flame-like figures that El Greco was painting at Toledo from 1577 onwards). The King's collection was housed in the Prado, one of the new buildings commissioned by him.

[1] Though an Elizabethan, it is true, called Spain 'a colossus stuffed with clouts'.

In architecture the dominant figure was Juan de Herrera (1530–97). He was mainly responsible for the construction of the Escorial (1563–84), the great palace in the Guadarrama mountains thirty miles northwest of Madrid. The Escorial is often described as 'grim' or 'austere', but in fact it represents the arrival in Spain of Renaissance classical architecture – and when one compares it with contemporary Portuguese extravagance one is very thankful for the restraint displayed. The Escorial is what modern architects would call 'a unit of habitation'; it contains a little of everything, laid out in a rather rigid pattern which perhaps owes something to Philip's card-index mind. It measures 675 by 525 feet and includes a palace, a church larger than many cathedrals, a college, a monastery and a crypt where the Habsburgs lie neatly filed in marble coffins. Philip's own tiny suite of rooms adjoined the church, so that from his bedroom he could look down onto the high altar. As the years went by he spent more and more time there, where he boasted that he could rule the world with a stroke of his pen. Here are two twentieth century accounts, in contrasting mood:

King Philip sat working in the Escorial – the gigantic palace that he had built for himself, all of stone, far away, high up, amid the desolation of the rocky Guadarrama. He worked incessantly, as no monarch had ever worked before, controlling from his desk a vast empire – Spain and Portugal, half Italy, the Netherlands, the Western Indies. He had grown old and white-haired in his labours, but he worked on. Diseases had attacked him; he was tortured by the gout; his skin was cankered, he was the prey of a mysterious and terrible paralysis; but his hand moved over the paper from morning till night. He never emerged now. He had withdrawn into this inner room of his palace – a small room, hung with dark green tapestries – and there he reigned, secret, silent, indefatigable, dying. He had one distraction, and only one; sometimes he tottered through a low door into his oratory beyond, and kneeling, looked out, through an inner window, as it were from a box of an opera, into the enormous spaces of a church. It was the centre of his great building, half palace and half monastery, and there, operatic too in their vestments and their strange singings, the priests performed at the altar close below him, intent upon their holy work. . . .[1]

[1] L. Strachey, *Elizabeth and Essex*, Chatto & Windus, 1928, pp. 135–6.

It is an inspiring situation, for Philip was an aesthete and had inherited the taste of the Burgundian line: the enormous palace-monastery high up on a half-moon spur of the hills, hard sunlight upon stone by day, the shadows becoming more intensely blue – blue of the sea he could not subdue – with evening, the light pale gold in the chapel of the monks of St. Laurence, and the dark figure, almost always in black, taking his place quietly along with them in his stall for vespers, some intermission from the affairs of this world, his mind now fixed upon the next, where his heart already was. . . .[1]

EXTRACTS

1. *Loyola's teaching:*

Spiritual Exercises, Part II. Rules for Thinking with the Church: Number 13. That we may be altogether of the same mind and in conformity with the Church herself, if she shall have defined anything to be black which to our eyes appears to be white, we ought in like manner to pronounce it to be black. For we must undoubtingly believe, that the Spirit of our Lord Jesus Christ, and the Spirit of the Orthodox Church His Spouse, by which Spirit we are governed and directed to Salvation, is the same. . . .

Constitution VI. 1 :

And let each one persuade himself that they that live under obedience ought to allow themselves to be borne and ruled by divine providence working through their Superiors exactly as if they were a corpse which suffers itself to be borne and handled in any way whatsoever; or just as an old man's stick which serves him who holds it in his hand wherever and for whatever purpose he wish to use it. . . .

(Both from H. Bettenson, *Documents of the Christian Church,* O.U.P., 1943, pp. 363 and 364)

Third Exercise on Death:

Application of the *smell* and the *touch*. Imagine yourself respiring the odour your body exhales when the soul is departed; the infection it would give out, if it were taken from the coffin a few months after your death. Imagine you touch this damp earth, where they have laid you; this shroud in which they have wrapped you, and which is now in rags; this bare skull, once the seat of thought; these dismembered limbs,

[1] A. L. Rowse, *The Expansion of Elizabethan England,* Macmillan, 1955, pp. 245–6.

which once obeyed the orders of your will; – in fine, this mass
of corruption, which the sepulchre has enclosed a few months,
and the sight of which is horrible.   In presence of this terrible
scene, ask yourself what are health, fortune, friendship of the
world, pleasures of the senses, life itself: 'Vanity of vanities,
all is vanity' (Eccles. i, v. 2).

End by a colloquy with our Saviour dying: 'Into Thy hands
I commend my spirit, O Lord.' (L. Bernard and T. B.
Hodges, *Readings in European History*, The Macmillan Company,
N.Y., 1958, p. 256)

2. *The Authority of the Pope and of tradition reasserted (1564):*

I recognize the Holy Catholic and Apostolic Roman Church
as the mother and mistress of all churches; and I vow and
swear true obedience to the Roman Pontiff, the successor of
blessed Peter, the chief of the Apostles and the representative
of Jesus Christ.

I accept and profess, without doubting, the traditions,
definitions and declarations of the sacred Canons and Oecu-
menical Councils and especially those of the Holy Council of
Trent; and at the same time I condemn, reject and anathe-
matize all things contrary hereto, and all heresies condemned,
rejected and anathematized by the Church. This true
Catholic Faith (without which no one can be in a state of
salvation), which at this time I of my own will profess and
truly hold, I. *N*, vow and swear, God helping me, most constantly to keep and confess entire and undefiled to my life's
last breath, and that I will endeavour, as far as in me shall lie,
that it be held, taught and preached by my subordinates or
by those who shall be placed under my care: so help me God
and these Holy Gospels of God.   (The Tridentine Profession
of Faith, to be recited publicly by all clergy; from the Bull of
Pius IV.   Quoted by H. Bettenson, *Documents of the Christian
Church*, O.U.P., 1943, pp. 373–4)

3. *Philip II writes from Lisbon to his daughter:*

Lisbon, January 15, 1582.

It is good news for me to learn that you are so well.   It seems
to me that your little sister is getting her eye teeth pretty early.
Perhaps they are in place of the two which I am on the point of
losing. . . .

We are having terrible weather here; torrents of rain fall,
sometimes with fearful claps of thunder and flashes of lightning.

I have never seen such weather at this season.   It would be a good thing for you, my elder daughter, if you are still afraid of thunder. . . .

The other day some one gave me what I have enclosed in this box and said it was a sweet lime.   I think, just the same, that it is only a lemon, but nevertheless wanted to send it to you.   If it is really a sweet lime, I have never seen one so big. I do not know if it will still be good when it gets to you.   If it is, taste it and let me know what it proved to be, for I cannot believe that a lime ever was so big, and consequently shall be pleased to be enlightened by you.   The little lemon which is in the box with it is only to fill up space.   (Quoted in J. H. Robinson, *Readings in European History*, Ginn, Vol. II, pp. 170–1)

4. *The Venetian Ambassador announces Philip II's death:*

His majesty expired at the Escorial this morning at daybreak, after having received all the sacraments of the Church with every sign of devoutness, piety and religion. . . . He was a Prince who fought with gold rather than with steel, by his brain rather than by his arms.   He has acquired more by sitting still, by negotiation, by diplomacy, than his father did by armies and by war. . . . Profoundly religious, he loved peace and quiet.   He displayed great calmness and professed himself unmoved in good and bad fortune alike. . . . On great occasions . . . he never counted the cost;   he was no close reckoner, but lavished gold without a thought;   but in small matters, in the government of his household, in his presents and rewards, he was more parsimonious than became his station. . . . He held his desires in absolute control and showed an immutable and unalterable temper. . . . No one ever saw him in a rage, being always patient, phlegmatic, temperate, melancholy.   In short, he left a glorious memory of his royal name, which may serve as an example, not only unto his posterity and his successors, but unto strangers as well. (Quoted in R. T. Davies, *The Golden Century of Spain*, Macmillan, 1937, pp. 224–5)

FURTHER READING

J. Brodrick, *The Origin of the Jesuits*, Longmans, Green, 1947

The New Cambridge Modern History, C.U.P., Vol. II, 1958, Chapter IX, The New Orders

T. M. Lindsay, *The History of the Reformation*, Clark, Vol. II, 1908, Book VI, The Counter-Reformation

R. T. Davies, *The Golden Century of Spain*, Macmillan, 1937

B. J. Kidd, *The Counter-Reformation*, S.P.C.K., 1933

VIII · WARS OF RELIGION, 1562–1609

Introduction

THE reign of Charles V spans the period between two types of wars fought, at any rate superficially, for different kinds of reasons. The early conflicts with Francis I have a personal, dynastic flavour, each man fighting to add to the possessions of his 'house'. In this way they look back to struggles such as the Hundred Years' War between England and France – and some of the incidents, as when Charles challenged Francis to a duel, or Francis appeared unexpectedly on Charles's ship at Aigues-Mortes, might have come straight out of Froissart.

The last war in which the Emperor was engaged, however, bore a different character. The War of the League of Schmalkalden, which broke out in 1547, could not have occurred in the form it did if the German Reformation had not taken place. Its causes were partly religious, it was in some ways a civil war between rival ideologies. At the same time, like all wars, it had its political and economic aspects, and these are inextricably confused with the religious battle-cries. One can never be sure to what extent the protagonists were inspired by selfish motives. The Lutheran Maurice is surely also a self-seeking man on the make, the Most Christian King of France supports the Protestants in Germany while he is persecuting their co-religionists at home, and the war is ultimately brought to an end not by the triumph of a faith, but by religious compromise and economic disaster.

The two dominant themes of the first half of the sixteenth century are ended – the German Reformation in 1555 and the struggle between Habsburg and Valois in 1559; but since they are ended by compromises, they reappear in the changed conditions of the seventeenth century. Meanwhile the second half of the sixteenth century is dominated by the Counter-Reformation. The issues are made sharper, the struggle more bitter, by the enthusiasm of on the one hand the Jesuits, and on the other the Calvinists – the 'shock-troops' of rival ideologies.

172

In the south of Europe, in Spain and Italy, there is no conflict, Catholicism is almost unchallenged. In the north of Europe, in Scandinavia and Scotland, Protestantism is easily triumphant. In the great middle belt the struggle is fought out. In Germany it is postponed for fifty years, and then plays its part in the early stages of the Thirty Years' War (Chapter IX). In England there is the threat of civil war or foreign invasion hanging over the greater part of Elizabeth's reign. In France and in the Spanish Netherlands the explosive mixture of political ambition and religious zeal leads to conflict – the wars of religion in France (1562–98) and the revolt of the Netherlands (1572–1609). It is only when these civil wars are over that France and Spain can give their full attention to their old occupation of fighting one another.

Beneath the general similarity there are profound differences between the two struggles. In France the war is for the most part a civil war, religious motives are more important at its commencement than at its close when Spanish intervention gives it something of an international character, and it is finally ended by a religious compromise; in the Netherlands, on the other hand, the war is from the start powered by local resentment of an alien government, religious divisions only become clear as the fighting progresses, and it is eventually brought to an end by the political division of the area into two parts.

The Wars of Religion in France, 1562–98

On the death of Henri II in 1559 the throne passed to his eldest son Francis II, the husband of Mary, Queen of Scots. Within a year he was dead of an abscess in the ear – '. . . that deaf ear that never could hear the truth of God,' John Knox commented sourly – and Mary had been packed off back to Scotland. The new King, Francis's brother Charles IX (1560–74), was only nine and the regency was soon in the hands of the Queen-Mother, the Italian Catherine de' Medici (1519–89). Royal power was to remain with her for over a quarter of a century.

France in 1560 was at peace with the Habsburgs, but she was exhausted by the struggle and bankrupt. During the reign of Catherine's husband powerful nobles, such as the families of Guise and Montmorency, had already shown a tendency to meddle in the affairs of government, and a regency provided the classic field for such activities. The Huguenots though persecuted were nevertheless increasing in numbers and in strength. It was Catherine's destiny to struggle with this complex of problems, unhelped by her weak and degenerate 'Italian' sons, while France moved through that series of civil disturbances of which an English historian has written: 'French historians distinguish eight "wars", but some simplification seems desirable'!

Catherine de' Medici failed to solve the problems that confronted her and many writers have blamed this failure on the defects of her character. A contemporary declared that '. . . she had too much wit for a woman, and too little honesty for a Queen',[1] while many modern historians have seen a stupid Italian matriarch, intent only on securing the fortunes of her children. Yet her lack of success is not greater than that of Charles V in Germany, faced by a rather similar situation, and Catherine suffered from the double disability of being a woman and a middle-class foreigner, 'born of a simple house, altogether beneath the dignity of the King of France' said a contemporary ambassador. Henri of Navarre's comment seems in the circumstances an appropriate one:

> I ask you, what could one poor woman do, left by the death of her husband with five little children on her hands, and two families in France who were planning to seize the crown – ours and the Guises? Was she not forced to play strange parts, to deceive first one and then the other, in order to guard (as she has done) her sons, who have successively reigned by the wise conduct of that shrewd woman? I am surprised she never did worse.

Catherine is said to have introduced the custom of riding sidesaddle into France – is it altogether fanciful to see in this a symbol of her oblique approach to problems, and of her common-sense love of a compromise between extremes – which so often took the form of 'getting folk together and making them shake hands'? [2]

The great nobles against whom Catherine had to defend her children fell into three main groups. Undoubtedly the most

---

[1] Dallington, 1598.
[2] J. E. Neale, *The Age of Catherine de Medici*, Cape, 1943, p. 41.

dangerous were the Catholic Guises from Lorraine, richer than the crown and represented in 1559 by the military Francis, Duke of Guise, fresh from the capture of Calais, and by the politician Charles, Cardinal of Lorraine. Half-foreign, the family owed its influence to the patronage of Frances I and the support of Henri II's mistress, Diane de Poitiers.

The second group, that of the Bourbons, was linked by marriage to the royal family and was next in the line of succession. Its leaders were the weak Anthony, King of Navarre, and his ambitious younger brother Louis, Prince of Condé, who had been 'converted' to Calvinism in 1558. The strength of the Bourbons lay in the south, and in the Huguenots. The third great family, that of Montmorency, was divided in religion but united in their opposition to the Guises; their leader was the Constable Anne, a Catholic whose reputation had been under a cloud since his defeat by the Spanish at St. Quentin, their most active member was Anne's nephew, the Huguenot Gaspard de Coligny. The natural feudal antagonisms between these three groups of nobles found expression in religious disagreement.

The link between Calvin at Geneva and the French Protestants was close both emotionally and geographically. Persecuted Huguenots found refuge in Switzerland, while Calvinist ministers moved in the reverse direction as missionaries. The Concordat of Bologna (1516) between Leo X and Francis I had given the King control over Church appointments. There was thus no incentive to become a French Henry VIII, and therefore French Protestantism, since it was not acting in the interests of the King, was almost compelled to turn to rebellion.

In 1555 the Calvinist churches in France acquired a regular organization, and in 1559 the first National Synod was held secretly in Paris. Calvin claimed 300,000 supporters and although this seems to have been an exaggeration, the Calvinists probably numbered eventually about 10 per cent of the population. They were most numerous in that part of France which lies west of the Rhone and south of the Loire. Their organization followed the normal Calvinist pyramidal structure of the local congregation with its disciplinary committee, the Consistory; the regional 'Colloquy'; and the National Synod – a structure ideally suited for the organization of revolutionary activities. As in other countries, the Calvinist strength lay in the urban artisan, the professional class and the rural lesser nobility, those bankrupt 'hedge squires' who are the surprising supporters of Calvinism alike in France, the Netherlands and Scotland.   There were only too many of them in France where the absence of a firm law of entail and the ban on entry into trade left men with undiminished rank but with dwindling lands and income.   These local nobles, penniless, discontented and accustomed to bear arms, became the leaders of provincial resistance.

In 1560 the country seemed to be slipping into civil war and economic disaster.   The Crown's debt was four times its annual income, and during that year the Bourbon family tried to stage a palace revolution, the Conspiracy of Amboise, with the object of supplanting the Guises at court.   Catherine's first attempt to deal with the situation was to summon the States-General, which had not met for eighty years.   The Third Estate put forward a plan to solve the economic crisis, and perhaps the religious one too, by nationalizing the Church lands.   This, they estimated, would produce a surplus of 72,000,000 livres – an attractive scheme, when the Crown's income was only about 12,000,000 livres.   The clergy hastily offered 16,000,000 livres.   Their offer was accepted, and the States-General dissolved.

Catherine's second move was to arrange a conference between Huguenots and Catholics, the Colloquy of Poissy (1561). The Queen-Mother and her Chancellor, L'Hôpital, took the view that, at least until the Council of Trent had reached some conclusion, toleration was better than oppression.   'Kindness,' the Chancellor said, 'will do more than persecution.' The Calvinists' chief spokesman was Beza, sent from Geneva, the Catholics being led by the Cardinal of Lorraine.   The conference lasted about a month and while it was going on the new General of the Jesuits, Lainez, was hurriedly sent from Rome to strengthen the party of no compromise.   A formula was drawn up by five moderates from each side, and rejected by the extremists.   Catherine was repeating the experiences of Charles V in 1548.

Early in 1562, Catherine made her third effort.   A special Council was persuaded to pass the Edict of St. Germain.   The Huguenots were ordered to surrender all the ecclesiastical buildings they had occupied, and were not to meet within the walls of any city. On the other hand, their existence was officially recognized for the first time, and they were given the right to worship freely in the suburbs of towns and in the countryside. The Edict was an attempt to put into practice L'Hôpital's maxim 'a man may be a citizen without being a Christian'.

The Edict was a statesmanlike compromise which satisfied no one and alarmed the extreme Catholics. Within six weeks the Duke of Guise, finding Huguenots worshipping in a prohibited place, had massacred them and unleashed the forces of civil war: 'To arrest this surrender of Counter-Reformation policy and the ruin which it portended to the Church in France, Guise fell upon a congregation of Protestants, and mingled their blood with their sacrifices' was how Lord Acton described this Massacre at Vassy.

The first period of the wars lasted from 1562 to 1570.[1] The details are of little significance. The Huguenots looked for support to Elizabeth I, whose forces occupied Le Havre (1562–3). The Duke of Guise was assassinated, and Coligny was suspected of having known of the plot – a suspicion which was to have important consequences in 1572. Montmorency was killed in battle, Condé was taken prisoner and shot. With the death of the original leaders the time seemed ripe for a second attempt at toleration. A new party was beginning to appear, the *Politiques*, or political Catholics, contrasted with the religious Catholics, the *Religieux*. Their enemies declared that the Politiques

> . . . were those who preferred the repose of their kingdom or their own homes to the salvation of their souls; who would rather that the kingdom remained at peace without God than at war for him.[2]

The Peace of St. Germain (1570), which marked a pause in the fighting, was a *Politique* peace. The Huguenots received four towns (La Rochelle, Cognac, Montauban and La Charité) for two years, and the right to hold public office, and to worship openly in two towns in each province, though not in Paris. These terms marked an advance for them over those which

---

[1] The dates of the eight wars are: 1562–3; 1567–8; 1568–70; 1572–3; 1574–6; 1577; 1580; 1585–9.
[2] Marshal Tavannes.

they had obtained eight years earlier, and further alarmed the Catholics. Pope Gregory XIV called the Peace '. . . the most deadly blow that the faith has received since the beginning of the religious troubles'.

St. Germain indicated a temporary change in Catherine's political policy. The war had strengthened the power of the Guise family and of Spain. The Queen-Mother was by temperament a *Politique*, and knew that peace was needed to strengthen her own position. In pursuance of this policy, she planned a double marriage. Her daughter, Marguerite, was to marry the Bourbon Huguenot Henri of Navarre, her second son was to marry the Protestant Queen Elizabeth. This latter match fell through – it was an uncertain business wooing Elizabeth – but Catherine obtained instead, an English alliance against Spain the Treaty of Blois. Meanwhile, the outbreak of fighting in the Netherlands (1572) offered an opportunity for the French to make good their claim to Flanders.

The new policy implied a suspension of internal disagreement – in the 1560's a *Politique* had observed; 'With the men whom we have lost in these wars we could have driven the Spaniards out of the Low Countries' – and a war against Spain in alliance with the heretics of England and the Netherlands. This would have been a daring, and yet in a way a traditional, plan. Catherine, however, withdrew her support almost before it was under way. The reason was as follows. Coligny had come to court in 1571, and Charles IX had fallen completely under his influence, and had allowed him to organize a Huguenot expedition against the Spanish. The troops met disaster at Mons, while the Queen-Mother was appalled at the prospect of her son coming under an alien influence. She had not plotted against the Guises in order that he might fall into the hands of the Huguenots instead. Coligny must be removed.

Catherine moved swiftly. In August 1572, all the nobility were in Paris for the wedding of Marguerite and Henri. 'There can be very little doubt that she authorised the Guise family to carry out their blood feud and assassinate Coligny.'[1] Unfortunately for Catherine, Coligny, shot from a window by an arquebusier, was only wounded and the King supported the demand for a full enquiry. It seemed to the Queen-Mother that the only way to maintain her influence was to

[1] Neale, p. 77.

conceal the lesser crime by a greater.   Charles was persuaded
of the existence of a Huguenot plot against him.   On the morning of August 24 a general slaughter of Huguenots in Paris
took place, arranged by the Duke of Guise with royal approval.
The news spread to the provinces, where many towns followed
suit.   Coligny died and so did about 4,000 Huguenots in
Paris, and perhaps as many more in the rest of France.

The news of the Massacre of St. Bartholomew was received
with approval by Catholics.   Charles IX explained to the
Parlement of Paris that it had been the only means of crushing
'. . . a conspiracy for the extermination of the royal family'.
Catherine wrote to her relative the Duke of Tuscany: 'I am
sure you will be exceedingly pleased to hear of the successful
execution of the Admiral and his followers . . .'; Philip II
sent word to Catherine '. . . that to hear of it was for me the
best and most cheerful news which at present could come to
me'; while the Pope had a special *Te Deum* sung in St. Peter's.
Meanwhile, Protestant states reacted with horror; Queen
Elizabeth, with her instinct for the dramatic, ordered the
English court to wear mourning when she received the French
ambassador.

But the international repercussions of the Massacre were
brief – Elizabeth was soon standing godmother to Charles IX's
daughter, and the old Franco-Spanish rivalry quickly reasserted itself.   The real importance of the Massacre lay in its
effect inside France.   There it lay like a sword between the
two main parties for the best part of a generation.   The
Huguenots were sure it was the result of a long-premeditated
plot.   It is true that there had been talk of a general action
against Huguenots for the past ten years, as an abstract possibility, talk in which Catherine had joined, but

> Most scholars today are agreed that in a desperate situa-
> tion she seized on a desperate plan – a plan which had been
> talked of by many people beforehand, and must have been
> there, ready to assert itself in her mind.[1]

There could be no immediate peace in France, while the
methods of Italian despots were elevated into principles of
statecraft.   The Massacre, it has been truly said, was not only
a crime but a blunder.

[1] Neale, p. 81.

The immediate result was a fresh series of civil wars, occurring intermittently from 1572 to 1580. Charles IX died in 1574, haunted – the Huguenot legend ran – by the memories of St. Bartholomew, and was succeeded by Catherine's third son, Henri III (1574–89), the effeminate lover of lapdogs and male favourites, his life divided between religious penances and secular debauchery. During this period the *Politiques* found themselves fighting increasingly often on the same side as the Huguenots, whose acknowledged leader was now Henri of Navarre. He was also the next heir but one to the throne and as a heretic quite unacceptable to the Guises and the extreme Catholics. And so, in order to prevent his accession, they created the 'League' in 1576:

> Beginning with a statement that it was formed for the protection of Henry III and his successors, its articles established an *imperium in imperio*, claiming an allegiance more peremptory than that due to the King, and even threatening the lives and goods of recalcitrant members.[1]

Two years later a Huguenot statement of political theory, the *Vindiciae contra Tyrannos*, set out to justify the act of rebellion against a religious tyrant. The kingdom was falling apart. In 1577 a temporary agreement was reached in the Treaty of Bergerac, the terms of which anticipated the final settlement of 1598. The Huguenots were to be allowed freedom of worship in one town in each district, and mixed judicial tribunals (*chambres mi-parties*) were set up in the south, where the Huguenots were most numerous. They were also given control of eight 'towns of refuge'.

The Treaty of Bergerac provided a measure of peace for seven years, though frequent 'incidents' occurred during that time. One reason for the comparative calm was that the heir to the throne, Catherine's fourth son Alençon, who had adopted *Politique* principles, was for much of the time in the Netherlands or in England, struggling against the Spanish and for the hand of Elizabeth. But with his death from fever in 1584 Henri of Navarre became the heir to the throne.

The League took immediate steps to meet this threat. A close understanding was reached with Philip of Spain by which the two parties agreed to combine for the extirpation of heresy

[1] *C.M.H.*, III, p. 31.

and to recognize the Cardinal of Bourbon (Henri of Navarre's uncle) as the King's successor, while Philip was to provide the League with a subsidy of 50,000 crowns a month. The French King, Henri III, allied himself with the League, and withdrew toleration from the Huguenots.

As a result, full-scale fighting broke out again in the summer of 1585 – the 'War of the Three Henries'. The League was most powerful in the north and east, where it held a string of towns stretching across France; Châlons-sur-Marne, Verdun, Dijon, Lyons, Bourges, Orleans and Angers. A new factor was the appearance of Paris as an almost independent element in the already complicated situation. There the Catholics divided the city into sections, the leaders of which formed a 'Council of Sixteen', pledged to support the League. The dominating, autonomous attitude of the capital anticipates its political behaviour in the Fronde of the seventeenth century, and the French Revolution of the eighteenth.

Once more, civil war strengthened the power of the Guise family and of Philip, while Henri III became only a figurehead. The situation was made clear to him in May 1588, when he forbade the Duke of Guise to enter Paris. Barricades rose throughout the city and the royal forces stood impotently by while the Duke rode unarmed through the streets, a self-evident 'King of Paris'. Henri III fled to Blois, where he called a meeting of the States-General. The speakers proved all ardent Leaguers, and the King began to revolve in his mind an alternative plan to restore the royal power. The Duke of Guise and his brother the Cardinal were summoned to Blois and there assassinated. Henri wrote to his mother, Catherine, that *he* was now 'King of Paris'. The shrewd old woman replied: 'God grant it may be so, my son, but what about the other towns?' The League seized 'the other towns' and in April 1589, the King was forced by events to sign an agreement with Henri of Navarre, recognizing him as the heir to the throne. In August Henri III was assassinated by a Jacobin friar. Catherine had died earlier in the year.

The struggle now became increasingly one of faction (the League) and the foreigner (Philip II) against the natural heir to the throne, but it took Henri of Navarre nine more years to become Henri IV (1593), to sign a peace treaty at Vervins with the Spanish (1598), and to settle for a century the religious question on a basis of toleration by the Edict of Nantes (1598). These events, the conclusion to a generation of civil war, are also an integral part of Henri's reign and will be found in Chapter X.

Here it is only necessary to consider briefly the effect of the wars on France. Perhaps the most important consequences had been vastly to increase the extent of royal indebtedness, illustrated by the following figures:

	Royal debt, in millions of livres
1560	43·5
1576	101
1598	350

A more unexpected consequence was the subsequent revival of the royal authority. The country was tired of fighting and afraid of the growing danger from her old enemy Spain. In consequence, the way was clear to lay the foundations of power of an absolute monarchy. The twelve years remaining to Henri IV after 1598 were too brief to make these foundations secure – Richelieu encountered the opposition of the nobles and the Huguenots, Mazarin that of the nobles and the city of Paris – but the first steps were taken.

EXTRACT

Marguerite de Valois describes the morning of the Massacre of St. Bartholomew :

Seeing that it was daylight, and thinking that the danger of which my sister had spoken was now past, and overcome with sleep, I told my nurse to shut the door, so that I could sleep quietly. An hour later, when I was fast asleep, there came a man beating on the door with his hands and feet, crying 'Navarre! Navarre!' My nurse, thinking it was my husband the King, ran quickly to the door and opened it. It was a gentleman named M. de Leran, with a sword-wound on his elbow and another from a halberd on his arm; and he was still being pursued by four archers, who all came after him into my room. To save his life, he threw himself on my bed. . . . At last, thank God, M. de Nancay, the captain of the Guard, came up . . . he abused the archers for their indiscretion, and got rid of them, and granted me the life of the poor man who was holding on to me. So I put him to bed, and nursed his wounds in my room, till he was completely recovered. I changed my nightgown, too, because the man had covered it with his blood: and M. de Nancay told me what had happened, and assured me that my husband was in the King's room, and would come to no harm. So I threw on a dressing gown, and he took me to my sister's room, where I arrived more dead than alive; for just as I reached the lobby, all the doors of which were open, a gentleman named Bourse, trying to escape from some archers who were pursuing him, was run through by a halberd-stroke three paces from me; I fell the opposite way, half fainting, into the arms of M. de Nancay, and thought that the blow had pierced us both. Whilst I was there, M. de Moissans, my husband's first gentleman, and Armagnac, his first footman, came to look for me, to beg me to save their lives. I went and threw myself on my knees before the King and my mother the Queen, to ask this favour, which at last they granted. (Marguerite de Valois, *Memoires et Lettres*; ed. Guescard; Paris, 1842; quoted in J. M. Thompson, *Lectures in Foreign History*, Blackwell, 1925, p. 109)

FURTHER READING

A. J. Grant, *The French Monarchy, 1483–1789*, C.U.P., 1925, Vol.
A. J. Grant, *The Huguenots*, Thornton Butterworth, 1934
J. E. Neale, *The Age of Catherine de Medici*, Cape, 1943

The Revolt of the Netherlands, 1572–1609

Although many of the elements present in the French wars of religion are also to be found in the revolt of the Netherlands, they are combined in a different way, and a different pattern naturally results. The causes arise from national feeling rather than from religious discord, the fortunes of war are dependent to a large extent on the brute facts of geography, and the ultimate solution is not one of toleration, but of grudging division.

The seventeen states of the Netherlands owed their unity in the first place to the Dukes of Burgundy, notably Philip the Good (1421–67), who added to the nucleus of Artois and Flanders the states of Namur, Brabant, Limburg, North Holland and Luxemburg. The brilliant Burgundian court and civilization provided a superficial glitter which concealed a world of local differences. On the death of Philip's son, Charles the Bold (1477), the French King Louis XI had hoped to seize at least Flanders and Artois, but he was frustrated by the marriage of Charles's daughter Mary to the Habsburg Emperor Maximilian (see Chapter III).

Maximilian's grandson and successor, the Emperor Charles V, had been born in Ghent, spoke Flemish, and regarded himself as a Burgundian. In his attitude to the Netherlands family feeling was nicely combined with political and economic considerations, for the area was politically invaluable and economically profitable. Except for the revolt of Ghent in 1540 the area presented few problems for the Emperor, compared with those which he faced in the rest of his dominions and he was able to enlarge its boundaries to the east. Yet when Charles resigned the government to his son Philip in 1555 there were already signs that there would be trouble in the future.

The grounds of unrest were financial, political and religious. The wealth of the Netherlands had made them for some time the financiers of wars elsewhere, and the revolt of Ghent had provided evidence that the limits of taxation by consent were being reached. The Lutheran and Anabaptist doctrines had been spreading through the states since about 1530, and Charles had reacted by issuing a series of *placaten* (edicts) against heresy, culminating in the 'edict of blood' in 1550 and the introduction of the Inquisition in the same year – actions that struck at the heretic and alarmed the nationalist, intent on preserving his 'liberties'. In 1548, at the Diet of Augsburg, Charles had obtained the removal in effect of the Netherlands from the control of the Empire. Now these lands passed with Spain to his son Philip. Thus an area where local feeling was so strong that one province would hardly co-operate with its neighbour, was detached from its natural context, to become the milch-cow of a foreign ruler. This political rearrangement lent a new meaning to the tensions that already existed between the Habsburg rulers and the states of the Low Countries – the *'pays de par deça'*.

This north European area which a Spanish king had inherited was remarkable for the extent of its wealth and the maturity of its economic development. That development was partly encouraged by, and had partly helped to produce, the liberties of the local city communes in the later Middle Ages. By the time of Charles the Bold, the Netherlands included the mining areas of Namur and Liége, the textile towns of Ghent and Ypres, and the ports of Amsterdam and Antwerp; and each of these was only the planet round which lesser satellite towns revolved. There were naturally great local variations in wealth: in 1570 the Duke of Alva discovered that the total annual value of manufactured articles was about forty-five million florins, and that out of this total Brabant contributed about eleven million florins, and Flanders about ten and a half. In trade, however, the balance of wealth was tipping north-wards, from Bruges to Antwerp, and later to Amsterdam. By 1550 80 per cent of the total exports of the area passed through Antwerp, and only one half per cent through Bruges.

Areas of wealth might shift, but the general economic power of the Netherlands had been evident for three centuries. 'These lands are rooted above all in commerce. . . . We must not lose sight of this,' wrote Charles V. Through it the Burgundian dukes of the fifteenth century had been enabled to build up their 'modern' state, civilized, ostentatious, cruel.[1] But the cities, accustomed to fight off or play off against one another France and the Empire, retained great local freedom. The most obvious expression of this lay in the great cloth-halls and belfries which dominated each town. In the hall the merchants met to administer the town, in the belfry hung the bells to call out the citizens to a meeting – or a riot. Both the dukes and the merchant princes are immortalized in the works of the artists who flourished under their patronage in the fifteenth century; Jan van Eyck (c. 1380–1441) and Memling (c. 1434–94) at Bruges; and Roger van der Weyden (c. 1399–1464) at Brussels.

The Netherlands had a tradition of religious inquiry. The lower Rhine, from Cologne to the North Sea, had long been a centre of German Catholic mysticism. In the Middle Ages there had been such men as Meister Eckart of Cologne (d. 1327) and Jan of Ruysbroeck (d. 1381). The most influential development had been the foundation of a secular *fraterhuis* by Geert Groote at Deventer in about the year 1380. From this centre the Brethren of the Common Life had influenced such

[1] For the fifteenth century Burgundian state, see J. Huizinga, *The Waning of the Middle Ages*, Arnold, 1924.

men as Thomas à Kempis, Nicholas of Cusa and Erasmus. This living tradition of secular religious inquiry made the Netherlands more susceptible to the new teachings of the sixteenth century.

One last characteristic of the area remains to be mentioned. This was the existence of a fairly clear-cut linguistic division between the states of the south and east (Artois, Hainault, Namur, Luxemburg and the southern parts of Flanders and Brabant), speaking the French dialect of Walloon, and those to the north and west speaking Flemish or Dutch.

The Netherlands, then, was a rich, densely populated region, possessing a more distinct character – or rather collection of characters – than any other area of comparable size north of the Alps. This area now passed to Philip of Spain, a ruler who knew no Flemish and little French and who left the country in 1559 as soon as peace had been made with France, and never came back. As Regent there remained his half-sister, Margaret of Parma, the illegitimate daughter of Charles V by a Flemish woman.

Even before Philip's departure there had been plenty of expressions of local discontent to act as danger signals, and now distaste for Charles's religious policy combined with dislike for Philip to stimulate a determination not to be bled white in order to finance a foreign king's economy. When Philip on the eve of his departure asked the States-General for a grant of 1,300,000 florins, and the imposition of taxes of 1 per cent on land and 2 per cent on movable property, he met with a blank refusal. He was forced to compromise, and to accept a subsidy spread over nine years, to be collected by the States' own commissioners. In return, he had to promise to withdraw the 3,000 Spanish troops still stationed in the Netherlands. A contemporary describes him turning to William of Orange whose wrist he shook, exclaiming '*No los estados, ma vos, vos, vos*' – 'It is not the States-General, but you, who are responsible.'

Philip's absence did not improve matters, for he left behind a councillor and a scheme. The councillor was Cardinal Granvelle, the son of Charles V's great minister, unpopular both as a foreigner and as the real power behind Margaret of Parma. The scheme was concerned with the ecclesiastical organization of the country. The existing bishoprics did not correspond to territorial divisions, and were subject to archbishops in France (Rheims) and the Empire (Cologne). It was proposed to create three archbishoprics and a number of new bishoprics, to recognize the linguistic division of the country, and in general to see that religious and political divisions corresponded more closely. It was a sensible, statesmanlike measure, yet it raised a storm of opposition. It was regarded as the first step towards fastening the rule of the Inquisition securely on to the country, and moreover the bishops would be appointed by Philip and the lay nobles would lose a valuable source of income. It thus, unintentionally, aroused religious, financial and national apprehensions. It was not the measure which stirred up opposition but fear of foreign dictatorship.

For five years the situation deteriorated. The nobles felt that they were being edged out of control. There was constant friction in which financial demands, national feeling, constitutional privileges and religious persecution were inextricably mingled. At first Philip was forced to temporize. In 1561 the Spanish troops left at last; in 1564 Granvelle too was withdrawn. But Philip had no intention of giving way permanently. To complaints about the influence of foreign councillors he replied, 'I, too, am a foreigner; will they refuse to obey me as their Sovereign!' It is the sort of politically insensitive remark that one associates with the Stuart kings.

In 1565 Philip decided that the time had come to enforce the *placaten* and the decisions of the Council of Trent. 'I would rather lose all my states, and even a hundred lives, if I had them, than rule over heretics,' he wrote from Segovia. Against this may be set the reaction of William of Orange:

I cannot approve of princes trying to rule the conscience of their subjects and desiring to rob them of their faith.

to which he added, writing to Margaret a few weeks later:

If His Majesty and your Highness insist on carrying out these edicts, which I see may lead to the utter ruin of the country, I ask leave to resign my offices and avoid the stain of failure on me and mine.

Meanwhile the lesser nobles, whose incomes were suffering from the price-rise (and who were the backbone of so many revolts in the sixteenth century) formed a Confederation and

drew up a petition to Philip, known as the *Compromis*, demanding a more tolerant religious policy.   Many of the signatories
were Calvinists, none were of great importance, the most influential name being that of William's younger brother, Louis
of Nassau, who constituted himself the leader of the movement.
The significance of the *Compromis* lay not in itself, but in the fact
that it provided a point at which the various complaints might
fuse into open opposition.   In 1566, the document was presented to Margaret at Brussels.   It was then that one of her
advisers unintentionally christened the new movement:

> *Quoi, Madame, peur de ces gueux?* . . . By God, if you take
> my advice, their petition should be endorsed by a sound
> thrashing, and they would go down the steps of the court
> more quickly than they came up.[1]

He had given the movement a name – 'the Beggars', and a
rallying cry, *Vivent les Gueux!*

Margaret agreed to suspend the religious programme, pending a deputation to Philip.   The news of the Beggars' success
encouraged more widespread opposition.   Refugees came
back from Calvinist Geneva and from the Rhineland.   Amongst
the well-to-do, miniature beggars' bowls were fashionable as
ear-rings or cap-badges.   There was an outburst of icono-
clasm.

> The movement started on the linguistic frontier, in the
> area where the new cloth manufacture had created an in-
> dustrial proletariat, particularly amenable to the propaga-
> tion of a new creed, and whose religious ecstasy was nearly
> allied to social unrest.[2]

The centre of the disturbances was Antwerp, where in August
the cathedral was sacked.   Margaret wrote despairingly to
Philip: 'Everything is in such disorder that in the greater
part of the country there is neither law, faith, nor King.'   She
depended on William to maintain some sort of order, and in
fact the movement had alarmed the politically privileged, who
now helped to put it down.

William of Orange had been born in 1533, the eldest son of
the Lutheran Count of Nassau; his home lay to the east of

---

[1] *C.M.H.*, III, p. 203.
[2] P. Geyl, *The Revolt of the Netherlands*, Williams & Norgate, 1932, p. 92.

the middle Rhine. He had been brought up as a Catholic at Brussels from 1544 to 1553, living at the very heart of the Catholic court. The Emperor Charles had leant upon his shoulder during the abdication ceremony. In 1551 he had married Anne of Egmont, the daughter of one of the great Netherlands nobles. So far his career had been a conventional one, and he seemed destined to become assistant manager of a branch of the Habsburg family business.

Between 1559 and 1567 all this was changed. In the former year William was in France as a hostage during the negotiations for the peace of Cateau-Cambrésis. Riding in the woods at Chantilly the cold French King Henri II spoke of the plans, now that peace was assured, for an international campaign to eradicate heresy. William listened, and said nothing (thus earning his nickname of the 'Silent' – which would be better translated 'the Cautious'), but the mutual dislike of William and Philip was hardening into mistrust.

In 1561 William, whose first wife had died in 1558, married again. His second wife was Anne, daughter of Maurice of Saxony, the old Lutheran enemy of Charles V. It was not a tactful move. A little later Granvelle wrote to Philip:

> The Prince is a dangerous man, subtle, politic, professing to stand by the people, to champion their interests, even against your edicts, but seeking only the favour of the mob, giving himself out sometimes as a Catholic, sometimes as a Calvinist or Lutheran. He is a man to undertake any enterprise in secret which his own vast ambition and inordinate suspicion may suggest. Better not leave such a man in Flanders.[1]

This was how William was presented to Philip, two thousand miles away. Meanwhile, in the Netherlands, he was helping Margaret to restore order in Antwerp.

William's position became increasingly unsafe, and in April 1567, he left for his home at Nassau. Four months later Spanish troops from Italy marched into Antwerp. Their leader, the Duke of Alva, had left Spain in April and brought his army of 10,000 men over the Mont Cenis pass and north through Burgundy, Lorraine and Luxemburg to restore order.

[1] F. Harrison, *William the Silent*, Macmillan, 1897, p. 34.

For a few months Margaret remained Regent, but all real power was in the hands of the Captain-General. 'I have tamed men of iron in my day,' he is reported to have said. 'I shall know how to deal with these men of butter.'

Alva set up an emergency tribunal, with an overriding authority, yet without any legal status, soon known as the 'Council of Blood'. The Duke was president and, together with two Spanish lawyers, alone had the right of voting, while seven Netherlanders might sit but not vote. Two of the greater nobles who had been associated with William of Orange in the protests against Spain's policy, Egmont and Hoorn, were arrested and a period of repression followed. Later, Alva claimed to have had 18,600 persons put to death in the Netherlands. The policy was, in the short view, successful. It put down opposition, forced Margaret to resign, and provoked unsuccessful invasions by Louis of Nassau from Friesland and by William of Orange from across the Meuse, thus providing the Spanish with an excuse to execute Egmont and Hoorn. By 1569 (the year when Breugel painted his *Massacre of the Innocents*) it appeared that the Spanish had triumphed.

In fact the situation had worsened. William had been declared a traitor early in 1568. He had replied with his *Justification*, an outline of events leading to the crisis, in order that Philip

> . . . may learn rightly to understand the actions of his good and faithful servants and subjects, at this present wrongly slandered, persecuted and oppressed.

Although formally addressed to Philip the fifty-page pamphlet was really intended for the rest of Europe and was circulated in German, Latin, Dutch, English, Spanish and French. When the University of Louvain protested that Alva was infringing their liberties by seizing William's son who was studying there, his Spanish lawyer replied (in bad Latin) *Non curamus privilegios vestros*, (We take no account of your liberties). This seemed to the Netherlanders to sum up neatly the Spanish attitude, which events had yearly made more clear. An Englishman wrote home

> Now the very Papists do perceive that the Duke of Alva doth go about to make them all slaves

and Louis of Nassau's proclamation in 1568 had declared

> We have come . . . to drive out the intruding, foreign and
> shameful tyranny of these cruel ravishers and persecutors of
> Christian blood, to bring back your old privileges. . . .

The emphasis is everywhere the same; on 'liberties', 'slavery',
'privileges', rather than on directly religious matters. Although these latter provided much of the fuel of discontent, it is
a mistake to see the revolt as primarily religious, rather than –
in the first instance – as the reaction to a foreign despotism.

In 1569 Alva proposed new taxes, partly at least in order to
cover the costs of his army. There was to be a tax of 1 per
cent on all property, of 5 per cent on all sales of landed property,
and of 10 per cent on every sale of moveables. This last, the
Spanish *alcabala*, provoked the most intense opposition. It
would have stifled the life of a country which depended upon
commerce. In the end both it and the 5 per cent tax were
postponed for two years in return for a fixed sum, but Alva
insisted on their introduction in 1571. Opposition was widespread, and trade began to come to a standstill. Then an
event occurred that altered the pattern of resistance. In
April 1572 the 'Beggars of the Sea' seized Brill. The revolt of
the Netherlands had begun.

In 1568 the 'Land Beggars', the forces of the lesser nobles, had
been defeated. But William, as a sovereign prince, had the
right to arm ships, and letters of marque were issued by him in
1569 to eighteen privateers. The number had increased to
eighty-four by the following spring. These 'Beggars of the
Sea' at first used English ports in which to victual and refit, but
in 1572 this practice was forbidden by the English:

> No manner of victual from henceforth shall pass to be
> carried to the sea for the victualling or relief of the fleet
> now serving the Prince of Orange.

The Beggars therefore put in to Brill in the Meuse estuary and,
finding the Spanish garrison absent, took over the town. Six
days later Flushing, a much more important place, joined them.
At once Louis of Nassau crossed the frontier from the south,
taking Mons and Valenciennes, while William moved from
Germany through Guelderland to Brabant. Spanish rule

seemed to be crumbling, but William was defeated and Louis had to surrender Mons, while France withdrew her support. This French reversal of policy, after St. Bartholomew, was called by William a 'hammer-blow' (*coup de massue*). He wrote to his brother John, however,

> I am bent on going to Holland and Zeeland, being resolved to maintain the affair there as long as possible and to find there my grave.

Alva marched north, burning and terrorizing, but his army was held at Alkmaar, which was saved from surrender when the dykes were cut. The action is symbolic; it was by water that the northern Netherlands obtained its independence.

In 1573 Alva was recalled to Spain. His inflexible policy had led to revolt; behind him he left a reputation for cruelty, and the Dutch name for a mooring-post, *dukdalf* – a suitably satirical comment on his failure! Alva was succeeded as Governor by the Castilian Requesens who entered into negotiations with William, but was unable to accept the latter's terms: religious toleration; the restoration of the old constitutional liberties; the removal of the Spanish army and of foreigners from all official posts. In 1574 the siege of Leyden was raised by a fleet of 200 flat-bottomed barges, which sailed across the flooded fields. As a reward for its heroic resistance the town was given a university, which became one of the main centres of science in the next century. Soon William held most of Holland and Zeeland. Meanwhile in the south Louis of Nassau had been killed in a disastrous battle at Mook Heide on the Maas.

The death of Requesens from typhus in 1576 left the Spanish army unpaid and ill-led. Mutineers sacked Antwerp:

> Within three days Antwerp, which was one of the richest towns in Europe, had now no money nor treasure to be found therein, but only in the hands of the murderers and strumpets: for every Don Diego must walk jetting up and down the streets with his harlot by him in her chain and bracelets of gold. And the notable *Bourse* which was wont to be a safe assembly for merchants, had now none other merchandise therein, but as many dicing tables as might be placed round about it.[1]

[1] Gascoigne, *The Spoyle of Antwerpe*, quoted by C. V. Wedgwood, *William the Silent*, Cape, 1944, p. 166.

The Spanish Fury, as it was called, had the effect of hastening the union of 'the Entire Fatherland' against the foreigner.   The established authorities felt themselves threatened, and sixteen of the seventeen provinces (the exception was Luxemburg, which never played a significant part in the revolt) signed the Pacification of Ghent (1576).   By this they agreed to unite to expel the Spanish; to recognize William as general in Holland and Zeeland; and to suspend the edicts against Protestants, pending a final settlement.   The Pacification was impressive on paper, less so in actual fact.   It was not a union so much as 'a treaty of peace between the provinces of the States-General on the one side and Holland and Zeeland on the other',[1] and some of the twenty-five clauses indicate a new source of dis-union, for they implied the exclusive rule of Calvinism in the two northern states.   Four years of guerrilla fighting had exaggerated the differences which already existed between the north and the south.

In 1577 the new Governor, Don John of Austria, arrived. He had as it were been kicked upstairs by Philip, who found him insufferable after his victory at Lepanto.   Don John's policy in the Netherlands was not unintelligent.   He signed the Perpetual Edict, by which he accepted many of the terms of the Pacification of Ghent, agreeing to withdraw the Spanish army and to respect traditional liberties, and declaring his intention to uphold the Catholic faith.   William resisted these siren songs and Don John was naturally irritated – an English observer said William's behaviour 'fretted him to the guts'. He wrote to Spain:

> The Prince of Orange has bewitched the minds of all men . . . that which the Prince loathes most in the world is your Majesty; if he could, he would drink your Majesty's blood.

Then Don John made the mistake of snatching at Namur and thus alienated many of his supporters.   But before the situation could resolve itself he was dead of fever.   He was succeeded by Alexander Farnese, Duke of Parma (1578–92), the most able and successful of Philip's representatives in the Netherlands.

Meanwhile the States-General, encouraged by William, had been looking around for some foreign sponsor.   Their choice

[1] Geyl, p. 150.

fell on the Archduke Matthias, brother of the Emperor.   As an Austrian Habsburg this was a diplomatic choice, but in spite of William's support Matthias remained a colourless figurehead.

The Pacification of Ghent had broken down.   The Walloon-speaking southern provinces had accepted Don John's compromise, and now formed the Union of Arras (1579).   William remained convinced that, whatever the Spanish might promise, they intended in the end to destroy the liberties of the Netherlands, and he was able to persuade the seven northern provinces to continue the struggle.   They banded together in the Union of Utrecht (1579).   Six of the seven provinces were now controlled by their Calvinist minorities, and the revolt began to be a struggle between a Catholic-controlled south and a Calvinist-dominated north.

Next year William was outlawed by Philip:

> We empower all and every to seize the person and goods of this William of Nassau, as enemy of the human race; and hereby, on the word of a king and as minister of God, we promise to any one who has the heart to free us of this pest, and who will deliver him dead or alive, or take his life, the sum of 25,000 crowns in gold or in estates for himself and his heirs; we will pardon him any crime if he has been guilty, and give him a patent of nobility, if he be not noble. . . .

William retorted with a hundred-page *Apology*, printed in Dutch, Latin and French.   The *Apology*'s argument was based on the new Calvinist political doctrine that the people had a moral obligation to get rid of an undutiful ruler, which had been outlined in the *Vindiciae contra Tyrannos* (1578).   The *Apology* therefore opened with an attack on Philip, designed to show that he had broken this unwritten agreement, and continued:

> The mischief has all arisen from the cruelty and arrogance of the Spaniard, who thinks he can make slaves of us, as if we were Indians or Italians; of us who have never been a conquered people, but have accepted a ruler under definite conditions.   This is the cancer that we have sought to cauterise.

The natural sequel to the *Apology* was an Act of Abjuration (1581) by those states that had signed the Union of Utrecht, which stated the new doctrine even more clearly:

A prince is constituted by God to be the ruler of a people, to defend them from oppression and violence, as the shepherd his sheep; and whereas God did not create the people slaves to their prince, to obey his commands, whether right or wrong, but rather the prince for the sake of the subjects, to love and support them as a father his children, or a shepherd his flock . . . and when he does not behave thus but . . . oppresses them, seeking opportunities to infringe their ancient customs, exacting from them slavish compliance, then he is no longer a prince but a tyrant, and they may not only disallow his authority, but legally proceed to the choice of another prince for their defence.[1]

This the Estates proceeded to do. Matthias was packed off to Germany, William was confirmed in his titles of Count of Holland and Zeeland and the supreme rule was offered to Francis, Duke of Anjou, brother of the King of France.

The years from 1582–88 were the most disastrous period for the Netherlands. Anjou proved impossibly slippery (Henri of Navarre had once said of him – 'He's deceiving me if he doesn't deceive everybody who puts any trust in him') and in 1583 tried to seize power by a series of *coups d'état*. This 'French Fury' failed. Two thousand French were cut down in Antwerp alone, and Anjou retired to France, where he fortunately died in the following year. About the same time William was assassinated in Delft by a cabinet-maker's apprentice, Balthasar Gerard – there had been five attempts on his life since 1580. He died almost at once, crying '*Mon Dieu, ayez pitie de mon âme: mon Dieu, ayez pitie de ce pauvre peuple.*'

William was fifty-one when he was killed. A print by Cornelis Anthoniszoon, shows 'the noble Prince William' at the age of twelve, a smooth-faced, foppish little prince on horseback. Ten years later Antonio Moro painted him: auburn curly hair, bright brown eyes, long nose, strong chin, mouth a little full and solemn – the total effect is of a handsome, solemn, undistinguished man. A third picture attributed to Adriaen Key, shows William at the age of forty-eight. One can hardly believe it has any connection with the other two. The face is that of a very old man, heavy pouched eyes, wrinkled lids and forehead, lantern jaws covered with grey stubble,

[1] Wedgwood, p. 224.

sparse hair – (William described himself as '*Calvus et Calvinista*', bald and a Calvinist). The portrait illustrates the effect of almost twenty years of life as a guerrilla leader.

That is the significance of William. He was not a very good general, his life seemed at the time unsuccessful; but he was a great worker, immensely patient and tolerant, a statesman and diplomat who could keep the flame of resistance alive, working towards a limited objective – freedom from political and religious oppression, his aim as he said in the early days being '. . . to restore the entire fatherland in its old liberty and prosperity out of the clutches of the Spanish vultures and wolves.' He was one of the new *Politique* rulers, like Henri of Navarre and Elizabeth of England.

'If,' a contemporary Catholic writer commented, 'you look at his inconsistency on religious questions, as shown in his speeches and despatches, you will see that he put the State as something above the Christian religion. . . .' [1]

He stands, as Miss Wedgwood has stressed, between two eras:

He belonged in spirit to an earlier, a more generous and more cultured age than this of narrowness and authority, and thin, sectarian hatred. But he belonged also to a later age; his deep and genuine interest in the people he ruled, his faith in their development, his toleration, his convinced belief in government by consent – all these reach out from the mediaeval world towards a wider time. [2]

The decline in the fortunes of the Netherlands continued for another four years after William's death. Parma was everywhere successful and by the close of 1585 he held all the main towns to the south of the rivers Waal, Maas and Rhine, except Ostend and Sluys. In despair the States-General offered their sovereignty to Henri III of France, who refused the offer, and then to Elizabeth of England. By the Treaty of Greenwich Elizabeth accepted a partial interest in their fate, Leicester being sent over with 4,000 foot, in return for the towns of Flushing and Brill as pledges. The British help was of little value. Treacherous captains gave up Deventer and Zutphen (1587) to the Spanish, Leicester quarrelled simultaneously with his Dutch masters and his English mistress and meanwhile

[1] Harrison, p. 38.   [2] Wedgwood, p. 253.

Parma moved north of the rivers and began to conquer the area to the east of the Zuider Zee – the back door to Holland. After two years Leicester was summoned back to England.

The final stage in the revolt lasted from 1588 to 1609. In the former year the tide began to turn. Parma was recalled to the southern Netherlands to play his part in the invasion of England – a plan which ended in the defeat of the Spanish Armada. By that year, too, the control of the seven northern provinces had passed into the hands of the two men who were to exercise it for the next thirty years. These were Oldenbarneveldt (b. 1547), the Advocate of Holland, and William's eighteen-year old son, Maurice (b. 1567). Although of differing age, temperament and religious views, the two men worked well together at this time. Oldenbarneveldt disposed of the wealth and civil influence in Holland, which supplied 50 per cent of the war effort, while Maurice, elected as Stadtholder and Captain-General, proved himself a military genius. They were helped in their task by Maurice's cousin, Louis William, Stadtholder of Friesland. At about the same period Henri of Navarre became the legitimate King of France and the civil war there slowly turned into a national war against Spain.

All these factors combined to transform the balance of power in the Netherlands. The consequences were dramatic. In a series of campaigns between 1590 and 1594 Maurice practically cleared the Spanish from the area to the north of the Rivers Rhine, Waal and Maas, winning victories at Breda (1590); Zutphen, Deventer and Nymwegen (1591); Guelderland and Overyssel (1592); Gertruidenberg (1593); and Groningen (1594). Twice Parma was distracted from his proper work by Philip's demands that he intervene in France, where he spent nine months campaigning between 1590 and his death in 1592.

In his years as Captain-General Maurice transformed the art of war, adopting and adapting the new ideas on mobility, and on the proper relation between musketeers, cavalry and pikemen. Instead of using his men in clumsy uneconomic columns, he arranged them in shallower, linear formations, about five ranks deep. The musketeers were organized in separate groups, detached from the pikemen. The army was divided into units of about 500 men, a much more flexible arrangement than the Spanish unit of 3,000. New methods of fighting were accompanied by regular pay, training and drill. Maurice was quick to develop also new techniques of fortification, of the use of artillery and scientific devices such as the telescope. His example influenced the methods of the great commanders of the next century: Gustavus Adolphus, Cromwell and Turenne.

In spite of Parma's death and Maurice's successes, the war continued for another fifteen years (1594–1609) without affecting the final issue or the lines of division that had been reached in 1594. The fact was that in that year Spain and Holland already each held as much as they could hope to gain. Later events, although they seemed important to contemporary eyes, did not effect the historical pattern. In 1596 the United Provinces entered into a Triple League with England and France against Spain, being treated for the first time as diplomatic equals. In the following year Maurice won a brilliant victory over the Spanish at Turnhout, with the help of English troops. In 1598 Philip virtually handed over the Netherlands to his daughter Isabella and her husband, the Archduke Albert, one of the Austrian Habsburgs. In 1600 Maurice won a further important victory at Nieuport. Four years later he encountered an opponent worthy of his strength, when the command of the Spanish forces passed to Spinola Marquis de los Balbases, of the ancient family of Genoese bankers, with a flair for fighting. Spinola took Ostend, but the war was dying on its feet, and in 1609 the Spanish at last consented to sign a Twelve Years' Truce with their rebellious northern provinces.

Although technically only a truce, the Spanish had in fact recognized that they could not recapture the north, but legal recognition of its independence had to wait until 1648. The terms were favourable to the United Provinces; they were allowed to trade with the Spanish Indies, and the River Scheldt was to remain closed, thus sealing off their southern rival, Antwerp. The final lines of division had been decided by geographical rather than religious or national considerations. The Spanish had always been well-established in the Walloon-speaking provinces of the south. From there they had, under Parma, reconquered the Flemish-speaking provinces to the north as far as the great tangled estuary of the Maas, Waal and Rhine. Beyond, the states to the west and south of the Zuider

Zee (Holland, Utrecht and Zeeland) could protect themselves by river, flood-water and sea. Those states to the east of the Zuider Zee (Guelderland, Overyssel, Friesland, Drenthe and Groningen) could be reached more easily by the northern armies than by the Spanish, and the latter had been driven from their precarious foothold there by Maurice.

. . . Calvinism was no less strong in Flanders and Brabant than it was in the Northern provinces. If it was established as the ruling religion in Holland and Zeeland first . . . this was due to the fact that the Sea Beggars, the shock-troops of Calvinism, recruited from all over the Netherlands, selected those provinces as the stronghold where they had the best chance of resisting. . . . Their choice was determined . . . by the geographical situation of Holland and Zeeland, further away from Spanish military power, possessing in the rivers, lakes and marshes splendid natural advantages for defence, and offering above all the inestimable advantage of open communication with the sea. . . .

. . . The final distribution of the two religions, Catholicism prevailing to the exclusion of everything else south of the rivers, Protestantism in a dominant position north of them, resulted from the course of the war. . . . Parma succeeded in re-establishing Spanish power in Flanders and Brabant not because they were more inclined to Catholicism than the northern provinces, but because they were more exposed to his attack.

It was the rivers which brought about a strategic stalemate; it was this stalemate, in the end confirmed by the Truce, which enabled the secular power on either side to strengthen the position, here of Catholicism, there of Protestantism. . . .[1]

The new state was in several ways an oddity in seventeenth century Europe. For one thing it was a republic, and moreover a republic, as it were, of town councils. The nearest parallels were Switzerland and Venice. Each of the states that composed the United Provinces was theoretically sovereign. Within these states the real power was in the hands of the towns. At the Hague there was a Council of State of twelve members, but it never exercised much authority. More powerful was the central States-General, which also met at the

[1] P. Geyl, *The Netherlands Divided, 1609–1648*, Williams & Norgate, 1936, pp. 15–17.

Hague, and to which each state sent delegates.   This weak
confederation was able to behave as a unit for two largely
accidental reasons.   One was the over-riding importance of
Holland, where Oldenbarneveldt was supreme.   If Holland
and Zeeland could agree on a course of action, the remaining
states had little alternative but to support them.   The other
factor making for unity was the special position of the House of
Orange.   William had made the state, Maurice had saved it.
Maurice was Stadtholder in six of the seven states.   As long as
all the states were prepared to place the chief power in the
hands of the same man, he would be in effect the head of the
United Provinces.

William had striven for toleration, but the new republic
was a Calvinist one.   By a process of historical osmosis the two
religions had to some extent sorted themselves out, Calvinists
moving north from the southern states (where they were persecuted), and Catholics moving south from the northern
ones (where they were barely tolerated).   Nevertheless in the
United Provinces probably not more than a third of the population were Calvinists.

The new state was very prosperous.   The Dutch boasted:

It is known to all the world that whereas it is generally
the nature of war to ruin land and people, these countries on
the contrary have been naturally improved thereby.[1]

During the war they had set up the Dutch East India Company
(1602), and at its close Amsterdam, flourishing at the expense
of Antwerp, was equipped with a Bank and a Bourse (1609).
This commercial prosperity was concentrated in the states of
Holland and Zeeland – for instance, they supplied twelve of
the seventeen directors of the East India Company.

National feeling; religious enthusiasm; the courage and
statesmanship of William and the military ability of Maurice;
the physical geography of the area; Philip's attitude to the
revolt, which was a curious combination of interference and
off-handedness – all these varying influences had played their
part in bringing into existence a new type of state.

[1] Geyl, *Revolt*, p. 233.

THE NETHERLANDS
in the 16th. Century

English Miles

0   20   40   60   80   100

GRONINGEN

FRIESLAND

DRENTHE

OVERYSSEL

Alkmaar

Haarlem
Amsterdam
Naarden

Leyden
Delft
UTRECHT
Utrecht
Zutphen
GELDERLAND

Rotterdam
Brill

Mook

ZEELAND
Geertruidenberg

UPPER
GELDERLAND

Middelburg
Flushing

Turnhout

R. Rhine

Bruges
Ghent
Antwerp

B R A N T

Mechlin

F L A N D E R S
Schelde

Brussels

LIÈGE

OF

LIMBURG

Lille

Gembloura

Liège

ARTOIS
Orchies
Mons
Namur

B

Donai
HAINAULT
NAMUR
BISHOPRIC

Arras

CAMBRAI
(Bp.)

to Liège

R.

LUXEMBURG

F R A N C E

R. Meuse

R. Moselle

▨ States which made up the United Provinces (Holland)

〰〰〰 Present French Frontier

EXTRACTS

1. *The Northern Provinces form the Union of Utrecht, January 29, 1579:*

In as much as it has been experienced, that since the Pacification of Ghent, by which almost all the Provinces of these
Netherlands have bound themselves to stand by one another
with life and goods, and to drive the Spaniards and other
foreign nations, together with their following, out of these
lands, the same Spaniards, with Don John of Austria and other
of their chiefs and captains, have endeavoured all means, and
still daily essay to reduce the aforesaid Provinces, in whole and
in part, under their subjection, tyrannical rule and slavery; and
not by arms so much as by machinations to divide the same
Provinces one from another, and dismember them; and to
bring to nothing and subvert the union brought about by the
aforesaid pacification. . . .

Therefore [the Northern Provinces] . . . have esteemed it
advisable to bind and unite themselves one with another more
nearly and particularly, not in order to sever themselves from
the general Union brought about at the Pacification of Ghent,
but rather even more to strengthen the same, . . . the following
articles have been settled . . .

I. And firstly, that the aforesaid Provinces shall unite, bind
and confederate one with the other, . . . and stand for ever
by the others, in all ways and manners as if they were one
Province alone. . . .

XIII. And in point of Religion, those of Holland and Zeeland
shall deport themselves as best they think, and the other
Provinces of this Union shall regulate themselves according to
the contents of the religious-peace by the Archduke Matthias,
Governor and Captain-General of all these lands, . . . already
drawn up, . . . in order that each individual shall remain free
in his religion, and that no one shall suffer any tribulation on
account of his religion, in accordance with the Pacification of
Ghent. (E. Reich; *Select Documents illustrating Mediaeval and
Modern History,* King, 1905, pp. 605–6, 610)

2. *Antwerp hears of the assassination of William, July 1584:*

On the evening of the twelfth of this month we received the
news, the truth of which was subsequently confirmed, that on
the tenth the Prince of Orange was murdered at Delft by a
Burgundian called . . . Gerard. The latter had been de-

spatched the day before as ambassador to the States and to William of Orange from France, to announce the death of the Duke of Alençon. And about a quarter of an hour later the Prince was no longer living. While I am writing this the news has come that the aforesaid Gerard has been tortured at Delft and has confessed that he was induced to kill the Prince of Orange by a Jesuit in Italy, in the name of the King of Spain. The Jesuit had promised him 30,000 pounds for it, and if he lost his life, his friends were to have the money. . . . (Fugger News-Letter from Antwerp, 16 July, 1584. Quoted by W. F. Reddaway, *Select Documents of European History*, Vol. II, Methuen, 1930, p. 110)

FURTHER READING

P. Geyl, *The Revolt of the Netherlands (1555–1609)*, Williams & Norgate, 1932
F. Harrison, *William the Silent*, Macmillan, 1897
C. V. Wedgwood, *William the Silent*, Cape, 1944
G. N. Clark, *The Birth of the Dutch Republic:* Raleigh Lecture on History; British Academy, 1946

IX · THE THIRTY YEARS' WAR, 1618–48

Introduction

THE first half of the seventeenth century witnessed the revival, in an acute form, of the two conflicts which had bedevilled the first half of the sixteenth century: the religious–political struggle between the German Princes and the Emperor, and the dynastic rivalry between France and the Habsburgs for dominance in western Europe. The first round in these clashes had been brought to an end, respectively, by the Peace of Augsburg in 1555 and the Treaty of Cateau-Cambrésis in 1559. Both these settlements were in the nature of a compromise rather than a solution. For half a century the antagonisms lay dormant, partly because some at least of the contestants had been satisfied temporarily, partly because Spain and France had domestic problems to deal with – the revolt of the Spanish Netherlands (1572–1609) and the French wars of religion (1562–98). Philip II's intervention in the closing stage of those wars was a prelude to the second round of the fight – a round from which France was to emerge triumphant.

In the seventeenth century domestic affairs inside the Empire, and international ones outside, were linked in the Thirty Years' War. Indeed the clue to that sprawling, tangled affair lies in realizing that it was not one but half a dozen irrelevant contests fought across the prostrate body of the Empire. Besides the conflict of Habsburg and Valois, there was the constitutional struggle for political power between the Emperor and the Princes; the religious conflict between the forces of the Counter-Reformation and the Calvinists; and a rivalry, part-political, part-economic, for control of the Baltic and the north German coastline. The appearance for the first time in the European contest of this area was a consequence of the political vacuum left by the decline of the Hanseatic League of north German cities. (Their last register was drawn up in 1604, though the League maintained a ghostly existence till 1669.) It had controlled the Baltic, and now that it could no longer do so, Denmark, Sweden and the Habsburgs all had their eyes on the valuable Sound dues and on the naval supplies which were passing through to the United Provinces.

Religious friction seemed most likely to provide a cause, or an excuse, for war. The Peace of Augsburg had contained three sources of possible conflict. The principle of *cuius regio, eius religio* had been confined to the creeds of Catholicism and Lutheranism, thus excluding the Calvinists. Nevertheless, Calvinism had become the official religion in a number of German states and demanded recognition. Secondly, by the principle of 'ecclesiastical reservation' states that became Protestant after 1552 might not secularize Church lands, and if an ecclesiastic became a Protestant he must give up his lands and his position – but these limitations were regularly disregarded. Finally, by a curious chance, the terms of the Peace had never been officially confirmed by the Emperor.

The success of the Counter-Reformation in winning back parts of the Empire had led to a revival of Catholic morale, and a series of crises occurred. In 1606 after a clash between Protestants and Catholics at Donauwörth the Emperor Rudolf II put the town under the ban of the Empire, and the Catholic Maximilian of Bavaria forced it to yield in 1607. It lost its position as an Imperial city, was given to Bavaria and provided with a majority of Catholics on the town council. Protestants were everywhere indignant.

In 1608 the Calvinists formed an Evangelical Union of Protestant states, nominally open to all, but in fact confined almost entirely to Calvinists, since the Lutherans were on the whole satisfied with their own position. The main state in the Union was the Palatinate. The Electors Palatine had changed the religion of their subjects three times between 1559 and 1583, but had finally settled for Calvinism. The Elector Frederick was only fourteen and the prime mover in the Union was his chief minister, Christian of Anhalt, a bustling, efficient, red-haired little man. In 1609 Maximilian of Bavaria retorted with a Catholic League and next year obtained the support of Spain, which promised the League subsidies for three years. At first both these religious groups were instruments of their founders' ambitions rather than societies of zealots, but they provided centres round which religious antagonisms might cohere.

A second and more dangerous crisis occurred in 1610 on the death of the Duke of Cleves-Jülich. This owed its danger and its significance to the fact that it became more than a domestic issue and involved the hopes and fears of powers outside the Empire. Their interest in what should have been a purely German problem was an omen of things to come. The lands concerned lay across the Rhine, stretching from the frontiers of the United Provinces to the area east and west of Cologne. Controlling the lower Rhine, they had an obvious economic importance. They were also strategically significant, for in the hands of a Protestant ruler they would cut off the Spanish Netherlands from the land-route up the Rhine to the Tyrol and Spanish Milan, while in the hands of a Catholic power they would turn the flank of the United Provinces. The succession was disputed and uncertain. The two main claimants were Protestants, and the Emperor therefore hastened to occupy the Duchies, pending a settlement. From 1610 to 1614 the fate of the area seemed likely to provoke a European War. Henri IV of France was preparing to intervene when he was assassinated; Maurice of Nassau and Spinola, the Spanish general in the Netherlands, came within an ace of fighting, but a compromise solution was then reached by the Treaty of Xanten. The Duchies were divided between the two claimants; William of Neuberg (who had become a Catholic) received Jülich and Berg, while his opponent the Elector of Brandenburg (who had become a Calvinist) obtained Cleves, Mark and Ravensberg.

Meanwhile the political condition of the Empire was a standing encouragement to disunity. Its haphazard composition and ineffective constitution remained much as it had been at the opening of the sixteenth century.[1] The fact that one can thus describe it in the terms of a hundred years earlier is itself a criticism and a demonstration of a fatal failure to evolve – it would be impossible, for instance, to describe the government of James I's England in terms of that of Henry VII's (though contemporary Englishmen sometimes attempted to do so). The fragmentation of territories had continued – Anhalt, an area only a little larger than Essex, was divided into four principalities. In 1608 the *Reichsregiment*, one of the few central institutions, was paralysed when, a Protestant

[1] See Chapter III.

having been elected as president, the Catholics refused any longer to recognize its jurisdiction. The Protestants would not recognize the Catholic reform of the calendar; it was idle to talk about union between states which might be living in different months because of a difference in faith.

The Emperor Rudolf II (1576–1612) had given up trying to rule. He had ceased attending Diets in 1598 and became such a recluse that he had to show himself periodically at the windows of his palace in Prague to scotch the rumours that he was dead. His private zoo contained, symbolically, a living dodo from Mauritius. He

> . . . passed the darkening later years of his reign among the astrolabes and celestial diagrams of his laboratories, filling the stables with horses he never rode, the imperial apartments with concubines he seldom saw and never touched; closeting himself for hours with his astrologers and astronomers, while edicts and dispatches accumulated the dust of weeks, unsigned upon his desk.[1]

He was succeeded by his brother Matthias (1612–19), weak, irritating and childless, primarily concerned to end his days in peace.

The Emperor Matthias did not get his wish however, for the third and final crisis exploded into war ten months before his death. This time the dispute was over Bohemia. The crown of the Kingdom of Bohemia was elective, not hereditary, and – though outside the Empire – it carried with it the right to be one of the seven Electors of the Emperor. The Bohemians had, since the fourteenth century, regularly chosen a Habsburg, and the taxes from Bohemia covered half the cost of the Imperial administration: for political and economic reasons, it was not a territory of which a Habsburg would wish to lose control.

Nevertheless, the Bohemians had remained strongly independent in their political institutions, their religious views, and – as Czechs – their national feeling: 'Like a caterpillar in a cabbage, a serpent in the breast, a rat in the granary, a goat in the garden, so in Bohemia the German steals, cheats and deceives,' [2] they said. In religion they had a tradition of

---

[1] C. V. Wedgwood, *The Thirty Years' War*, Cape, 1938, p. 71.
[2] D. Ogg, *Europe in the Seventeenth Century*, Black, 8th edn., 1960, p. 113.

Protestantism that went back beyond the time of Luther to
John Hus, burnt for heresy in 1415. By 1600 Calvinists,
Lutherans and the followers of Hus were all well established
in the kingdom, and in 1609 a threat of religious revolt forced
the Emperor Rudolf to issue the *Letter of Majesty*, guaranteeing
religious freedom to the Bohemian Protestants. Nevertheless,
two years later the Bohemians deposed Rudolf and elected
Matthias in his place. He proved a disappointment to them,
yet his cousin Ferdinand was elected as his successor in 1617,
having promised to observe the *Letter of Majesty*.

The Bohemians could hardly have made a worse choice.
Ferdinand had been educated by the Jesuits at their College at
Ingolstadt and was known as a highly religious man – or as some
put it, 'a silly, Jesuited soul' – who had already wiped out
Protestantism in Styria, saying 'Better a desert than a country
full of heretics!' He at once began to pursue a similar policy in
Bohemia, and throughout the royal territories the Protestants
lost their rights.

In 1618 the Calvinist Count Thurn and his followers entered
the palace in Prague and threw Ferdinand's two Regents and
their secretary out of the window. The three men fell about
fifty feet, but were not killed. Catholics said that the Virgin
Mary, on whom they had called, had saved them, while
Protestants declared that their fall had been broken by a pile of
manure heaped against the castle wall! Whatever the truth of
the matter, the 'defenestration' of Prague proved to be the
final cause of a series of wars which were to last for thirty
years.

One can subdivide the Thirty Years' War into a German
period (1618–29); a Swedish period (1630–35); and a French
period (1635–48). Each was ended by a Peace: the Peace of
Lübeck in 1629; the Peace of Prague in 1635; and, finally, the
Peace of Westphalia in 1648.

The German Period, 1618–29

The Bohemian rebels set up a provisional government, and
in 1619 declared Ferdinand deposed. Nine days later he was
elected Emperor, the news of his deposition by the Bohemians
reaching Frankfurt as his new title was being announced.

Having overthrown Ferdinand, the Bohemians looked for a
new King. They invited Frederick, Elector Palatine, leader

of the Evangelical Union and son-in-law of James I of England, to accept the Crown. In spite of his apparently powerful position and connections Frederick proved to be a man of straw, quite unsuited to lead a revolutionary cause; the prime movers in the Union were the ambitious Christian of Anhalt and the Margrave of Ansbach, who exclaimed: 'We have in our hands the means to overturn the world.' He spoke more truly than he knew.

Frederick had the support of Mansfeld, a mercenary leader whose services the rebels had bought. (The illegitimate son of a former Imperial Governor of Luxemburg, he hoped to carve out a principality for himself but was destined to die in 1625, fleeing south through Bosnia with a handful of followers.) Frederick also had an alliance with the unreliable, half-Tartar half-Calvinist prince of Transylvania, Bethlen Gabor. Against these doubtful forces Tilly, the general of the Catholic League, moved 25,000 men in the summer of 1620, while Spinola occupied the Lower Palatinate with a further 25,000. In November 1620 Mansfeld and the Bohemians were defeated by Tilly in the Battle of the White Hill, just outside Prague. Frederick fled in the nick of time and began a life of exile which was to last until his death in 1632.

Bohemia was absorbed into the Habsburg dominions. Its coinage was disastrously debased and great areas of forfeited land confiscated; new men such as Wallenstein and an early Metternich, made their fortunes out of these obscure financial transactions. Protestantism was forbidden, 160,000 inhabitants went into exile, and in 1627 the country received a new constitution, establishing German law and hereditary Habsburg rule, which remained in force till 1848. Bohemia did not reappear as part of an independent state till the creation of Czechoslovakia in 1918.

The war ought to have finished in 1620, for its main aim – the expulsion of Frederick from Bohemia – had been attained, but it proved easier to raise armies than to disband them. Mansfeld retreated to the United Provinces, where the Twelve Years' Truce with Spain had just expired. Maximilian of Bavaria had been promised the Upper Palatinate in exchange for his military help, and parts of that had still to be conquered. Meanwhile he held in pawn the Habsburg territory of Upper Austria. Spinola's troops had not yet reduced all the Lower Palatinate. The Elector Frederick was in north Germany, trying to create an alliance of Protestant states there. Many of the German Princes were alarmed at Ferdinand's illegal action in putting Frederick under the ban of the Empire without consulting them. This confusion of interests produced a confusion of campaigns. The years from 1621 to 1629 are the most complex in detail of the whole war. Fortunately, the details are not important.

In the spring of 1621, the Protestant Union broke up. A number of lesser Princes, who felt themselves threatened by recent events, went to the help of the Palatinate, but Tilly with the army of the Catholic League had cleared the area by 1623. The Emperor Ferdinand then honoured his pledge to Maximilian, giving him Frederick's Electorate for life together with the Upper Palatinate. The apparent triumph of the Austrian and Spanish Habsburgs, the deposition of Frederick and the Emperor's growing tendency to act without regard for the constitution of the Empire alarmed the Princes. However the Lutherans on the whole continued neutral, notably the Elector John George of Saxony, whom some have seen as a wise *Politique* and others as a slow, self-seeking Saxon. He had added Lusatia, originally part of Bohemia, to Saxony, so he was hardly in a position to resist and his refusal to play a leading part halved the Protestant strength. The Protestant rulers of north Germany (the Lower Saxon Circle) consequently looked for support to those foreign powers that might be expected to oppose the Habsburgs, especially to France and Denmark.

The struggle moved into a new, more ominous phase. The protagonists were now Richelieu, Christian IV of Denmark, and Wallenstein. A fresh set of alliances was created, of which Richelieu was the prime architect. France, England, the United Provinces, Christian IV and the Lower Saxon Circle were linked together, while in southern Europe Richelieu's diplomacy resulted in the temporary blocking of the Valtelline, the Habsburg link with Italy.

Four armies were now involved. Christian IV, a hard fighter, a hard drinker, the cheerful father of innumerable illegitimate children – 'One could hardly believe he had been born in so cold a climate,' said Cardinal Bentivoglio – hoped to extend his territory to Verden and Halberstadt and get control of the Elbe and Oder. He faced the veteran Tilly and in 1626 was routed at the battle of Lutter in north Germany. Meanwhile the other Protestant army under Mansfeld had been easily defeated by a new Imperial force under the command of Wallenstein.

Wallenstein is an ambiguous figure, at the same time a *condottiere* of the fifteenth century and an economic *entrepreneur* of the eighteenth. He was born in Bohemia in 1583, educated at Lutheran schools, travelled in Italy, became a Catholic about 1602, and in 1604 was serving in a minor capacity with the Imperial forces in Hungary. In 1609 he laid the foundations of his fortune when he married Lucretia von Wishkow, a widow and one of the wealthiest noblewomen in Moravia. The years between 1609 and 1620 are obscure, but it is clear that he used his wife's fortune (she had died in 1614) to build up a web of commercial interests. In 1617 he was able to bring help to the Emperor's forces besieged by the Venetians in Gradisca. 'Herr von Wallenstein,' he wrote, with superb confidence, 'will wait upon Archduke Ferdinand in the camp with 180 cuirassiers and 80 musketeers maintained at his own cost.'[1] He was able to save Gradisca and, as so often with his actions, the expenditure proved a wise investment, for by 1620 he was in command of 2,000 men and had acquired the reputation that 'whatever he has in mind to perform is bound to be accomplished'.

In 1622 Wallenstein was in charge of the organization in conquered Prague, using the contacts he had made in the obscure years to provide 'powder from Poland, cuirasses from Leipzig, matchlints from Nuremberg and pikes from Liége'. He had profited greatly from the destruction of Bohemian independence. The details are uncertain, but he appears to have made a profit of 450,000 gulden out of the depreciation of the coinage, to have laid out this profit in loans to the Emperor and to have received the lands of the dispossessed rebels in exchange. Ferdinand now created him Count of Friedland (for 150,000 gulden, less 85,000 already lent on the estate). In the following year Wallenstein married again and added in one year forty-nine estates to his lands in Friedland,

---

[1] F. Watson, *Wallenstein, Soldier under Saturn*, Chatto & Windus, 1938, p. 70. All the detailed information about Wallenstein in this section is taken from Mr. Watson's book.

filling in the gaps between his existing holdings. The new Count took as his motto the proud prophetic words *Invita Invidia*, Welcome Envy.

This was the man who was now created by Ferdinand 'Independent General over this our Expedition despatched into the Holy Roman Empire'. The army Wallenstein led numbered about 35,000 foot and 17,000 horse, supplied from his own lands. His agent, Gerhard von Taxis, collected supplies at Reichenberg in north Friedland, where the volume of trade quadrupled, and sent them north. Wallenstein wrote regularly letters giving minute instructions as to the improvement of agriculture, the supply of manure and so forth – a spate of regulations which reminds one of the activities of such men as the Great Elector:

> Have a keen eye in all ends and places of our duchy, that the beer is not overcharged, also that bread and other victuals and all things else that man cannot forgo in his undertakings are brought and kept to a cheap rate.

The defeat of Mansfeld showed that Wallenstein was more than just a business man playing at soldiers, as his enemies had said. The Emperor now had his own successful army, independent of Maximilian and the League. Wallenstein planned to move north into the Lands of the Lower Saxon Circle and to make the Habsburg power supreme on the Baltic. In 1627 he wrote: 'There are twenty-eight ports in Pomerania. We must fortify them all.' During that year and the next his armies and those of Tilly overran Pomerania, Mecklenburg and Holstein. Wallenstein was created Duke of Mecklenburg and Admiral of the Baltic (*Oceani Baltici Maris Architalassus*). He failed, however, to take Stralsund, the strongest port in Pomerania, to which Gustavus, the King of Sweden, sent help. 'Stralsund must down though it were hung with chains from heaven,' he had boasted but, as the inhabitants jeered when they saw the Imperial standards withdrawing, 'Eagles could not swim.' In spite of the failure at Stralsund, Wallenstein, and through him the Emperor, now towered over north Germany.

It was the peak of both their powers. In 1629 Wallenstein negotiated the Peace of Lübeck with Christian. The Danish King gave up his German claims and withdrew from the war,

and in return his own lands were restored to him. The
political settlement was matched by a religious one. A few
weeks before Lübeck Ferdinand issued the Edict of Restitution.
Essentially, this repeated the two clauses of the Peace of Augsburg that had been infringed. The Protestants were to restore
all Church property taken since 1552, and Lutheranism was
explicitly declared the only alternative to Catholicism. The
Edict affected two archbishoprics – one of them Magdeburg,
the key to north Germany – twelve bishoprics and innumerable
smaller religious houses.

At this moment Ferdinand seemed more powerful than
Charles V had been; but his threat to their lands alarmed the
Lutherans and brought the two Lutheran Electors of Saxony
and Brandenburg a step nearer to the struggle from which they
had so far held aloof.[1] At the same time Ferdinand's display of
independence (it was doubtful if the Edict was quite constitutional) alarmed the Catholic princes of the south and west.
Thirdly, the Emperor's success and the Protestant fears combined to bring Sweden and, indirectly, France into the war.
Richelieu had no intention of allowing the Habsburgs to
control Germany; Gustavus of Sweden, likewise, would not
see them control the Baltic, of which he was determined to be
'Lord'; and nobody wanted a reactionary Emperor with a
successful army and an ambitious general.

The Swedish Period, 1630–35 [2]

In the summer of 1630 the Electors met the Emperor at
Ratisbon. The war of the Mantuan Succession, in which
France was engaged against the Habsburgs,[3] provided Richelieu with an excuse to send representatives. Although he later
disavowed the terms they obtained for France, he must have
been pleased with the result of their efforts to ensure a negative
outcome to the Diet. The Emperor Ferdinand was forced to
recognize the French candidate in Mantua; he was unable to
persuade the Electors to declare his son King of the Romans
(and therefore his successor as Emperor); he was forced to
agree to Wallenstein's dismissal. When the Diet broke up in

---

[1] Even though Saxony was temporarily excluded from the demands of the
Edict of Restitution.

[2] See also Chapter XI.   [3] See Chapter X.

November, Ferdinand's position was thus considerably weaker. Wallenstein retired to his Bohemian estates. He was under no illusions as to the cause of his dismissal: 'I wage more war with a few ministers than all the enemy,' he had said earlier in the year.

A few days before the Diet of Ratisbon had met, Gustavus Adolphus landed in north Germany. There was to be a Swedish army in Germany for the remainder of the war. The King's motives were mixed. The success of Ferdinand's armies in north Germany had alarmed him: 'We must go and find the Emperor at Stralsund, or he will come and find us at Kalmar,' he had told the Swedish assembly. His ambition to make the Baltic a Swedish lake, and the desire to protect the Protestants in the Empire, also played their part. He expected the latter to rush to his support, and boasted that he would 'touch off a rocket of universal rebellion', but he was over-optimistic. He had to compel the Electors of Saxony and Brandenburg to support him, and during the first six months his main triumph was to obtain from Richelieu, by the Treaty of Bärwalde (1631), the promise of an annual subsidy until 1636, provided the Swedes kept an army in the field.

Early in 1631 Magdeburg was taken by Tilly, sacked by his army and fired by one side or the other. Twenty-four thousand inhabitants died in the city, which had been a centre of Lutheranism. The sack had at least the effect of persuading John George of Saxony to support Gustavus a little more actively, and the Swedish army began to move south. In September 1631 Gustavus met and defeated the army of the Catholic League, under Tilly and Pappenheim, at Breitenfeld. After the battle he marched south-west, thus keeping friendly Protestant territory on his right flank and also linking up with the Protestants in the Rhineland, and wintered at Mainz.

In December 1631 the Swedish success compelled Ferdinand to recall Wallenstein, who resumed his command in the following April. The terms on which he returned are unknown. The *Swedish Intelligencer* commented:

> And herein (me thinkes) appeares a strange mixture of spirit in this *Wallenstein*; that being supposed as haughty and ambitious of Command as any man in the world; yet was he so farr foorth master of the greatnesse of his own desires, as that he could with as much moderation now refuse the

Generalship, as he had before resigned it: he would not have authority but with *freedome*, and his own *Conditions*.

Meanwhile the army of the Catholic League had been defeated at the battle of the Lech, Tilly dying later of his wounds, and Gustavus had moved into Bavaria and occupied Munich. Wallenstein, having raised an army and suppressed a rebellion in Bohemia, marched to meet him. Gustavus suffered a check before Nuremberg, and then Wallenstein wheeled away north to threaten the lukewarm John George of Saxony. If Saxony gave way the Swedish lines of communication would be threatened, and Gustavus was therefore forced to follow northwards. In November 1632 the two armies met at Lützen, not far from the earlier battlefield of Breitenfeld. The Swedish forces were victorious, but Gustavus, who always refused to take precautions – 'What is the use of a king in a box?' he would ask – was killed in the early stages of the battle.

Considered from the Swedish point of view, Gustavus was a great king, and his death a disaster. From the standpoint of the Empire, however, it was the Swedish intervention that was disastrous, destroying the power which might have united Germany and ushering in a period during which the foreign armies of Sweden and France marched and counter-marched across the land. There is nothing to suggest that if Gustavus had lived he would have been able to achieve a lasting peace.

Fourteen months after his defeat at Lützen, Wallenstein was assassinated. Proud, inscrutable and contemptuous, he had enemies everywhere. There were good reasons for getting rid of him. He was apparently war-weary: 'When the various lands are laid in ashes we shall be compelled to make peace,' he had said. Ferdinand owed him two million gulden. As an insurance, perhaps, against a second dismissal, he had been in negotiation with Sweden, France, Saxony and the Bohemian rebels. Crippled with gout, and exhibiting a pathological hatred of noise – the very cocks and cats were killed where he lodged – he shut himself off from the world, treacherous and ailing. In January 1634 he was relieved of his command, and a few weeks later he was cut down by his mercenary captains.

Presently [they] drew him out by the heels, his head knocking upon every stair, all bloody, and threw him into a coach and carried him to the castle where the rest lay naked together . . . and there he had the superior place of them, being the right hand file, which they could not do less, being so great a general.[1]

With Wallenstein there perished the Emperor's last opportunity of imposing a settlement on Germany.

In September 1634 one of the few great battles of the war took place at Nördlingen. The Swedish mercenaries and the forces of the German Protestants had been united by the Swedish minister, Oxenstierna, in the League of Heilbronn (1633) under the command of the German Bernard of Saxe-Weimar, who had taken over at Lützen on hearing of Gustavus's death. Against this army there now came the forces of Spain and Austria, acting in unison for the only time in the war. The Imperial troops were commanded by Ferdinand, King of Hungary, the son of the Emperor Ferdinand. The Spanish forces, 15,000 strong, were led by the Cardinal-Infante Ferdinand, the son of Philip III of Spain. They had come north through the vital Valtelline and were on their way to the Netherlands by the traditional Spanish land route. After a seven hours' battle, during which the Swedes charged fifteen times, the armies of the two Ferdinands triumphed completely, Bernard losing 16,000 men killed and prisoners out of a total force of twenty thousand.

Nördlingen seemed decisive, cancelling the defeat at Lützen. Bernard fled northwest to the left bank of the Rhine, the Lower Palatine was re-occupied by Imperial troops and the Elector of Saxony came to terms with the Emperor, leaving only two very minor German states in arms against him. The Cardinal-Infante pursued his way to Brussels, and the Peace of Prague (1635) was signed.

By the Peace Protestants and Catholics were to retain for forty years the lands they had held in 1627 – a partial suspension of the terms of the Edict of Restitution; the *Reichskammergericht* was to contain an equal number of Protestant and Catholic judges; Lutheranism was to be allowed in certain parts of Silesia; the Elector of Saxony was to keep Lusatia; all lands taken since the landing of Gustavus were to be restored to their former owners; and there was to be one Imperial army of about 80,000 men, of which a quarter was to be under the control of the Elector of Saxony.

[1] Wedgwood, p. 360, quoting Poyntz, p. 99.

The Peace of Prague was the third occasion on which the fighting came within an ace of being concluded. Although the terms of the Peace became a dead letter, it is interesting to compare them with the final settlement of Westphalia. They represent a national, *Politique* compromise. Based on this compromise, the Emperor's position seemed strong:

> His armies and those of his allies occupied almost the whole right bank of the Rhine, Württemberg, Swabia and Franconia. . . . The constructive diplomacy of the King of Hungary had placed his father at the head of a coalition which isolated the small Calvinistic minority and forced them into the unpopular position of disturbers of the peace and allies of the foreigner. The exiled Elector Palatine, the Landgrave of Hesse-Cassel and the Duke of Brunswick-Luneberg were left alone against a united Empire.[1]

If the struggle had still been a conflict between two religions, it would have been over, but this was no longer the case. The Pope was opposed to the Emperor, and Catholic France had subsidized Protestant Sweden. When he heard of the Peace Richelieu's reaction was 'Saxony has made his peace, but that will have no effect on us save to make us renew our efforts to keep all in train'.

The French Period, 1635-48 [2]

Since his coming to power in 1624 Richelieu had had a finger in events in Germany. In 1630 he had played his part in the failure of the Diet of Ratisbon, and in the following year France had become the paymaster of the Swedish armies. The Emperor's success at Nördlingen forced him to intervene directly. From now on France was in direct conflict with the Habsburgs.

The remains of the army of Bernard of Saxe-Weimar lay to the west of the Rhine, conveniently to hand; so too did a *casus belli*, for in March 1635 Spanish troops had carried off the Elector of Trier, the head of a state protected by France. Richelieu moved swiftly. A treaty was signed with the Swedes on April 30 in which Oxenstierna promised to support the French demand for the left bank of the Rhine from Breisach to Strasburg, and on May 19 a French herald rode

[1] Wedgwood, pp. 395-6.   [2] See also Chapter X.

into Brussels carrying the French declaration of war on Spain. Although France was not technically at war with Austria until 1638, her active intervention made it certain that the fighting within the Empire would continue.

The war started badly for France, with defeats for her own troops everywhere. Only the forces under the command of Bernard of Saxe-Weimar were relatively successful. Gradually, however, the French gained the ascendancy. Fresh alliances were made with Sweden, Savoy and the United Provinces, while the new ruler of Brandenburg, Frederick William, was persuaded to withdraw from the war. Two brilliant generals were discovered, Condé and Turenne. Spain, already sliding to economic disaster, was further harassed by revolts in Catalonia and Portugal (1640).

In 1638 Bernard had captured Breisach, the key city on the Upper Rhine. He now claimed to hold Alsace not for France, but for himself as her ally. Fortunately for Richelieu, Bernard died in the following year and the French were able to move into Breisach and certain other parts of Alsace. During the succeeding ten years most of the fighting took place along two axes – on the Elbe the Swedes and the Saxons faced the Imperial armies, while from the Upper Rhine through the Black Forest towards the Danube, the French struggled with the Imperial and Bavarian forces. The most decisive battle, though, was fought in neither of these areas, but at Rocroi in the Ardennes, where Condé won a brilliant victory over the Spanish (1643). Of eighteen thousand Spanish infantry, fifteen thousand were killed or captured, and the victory marked both the end of Spanish military power, dominant since Pavia (1525), and also the opening of a great period of French successes, essentially unbroken until Marlborough's victory at Blenheim in 1704.

Soon after Rocroi negotiations for a general peace began in Westphalia, at Münster (one of the centres of the Counter-Reformation, with a Jesuit college and a Catholic university) between the Emperor and France, and at Osnabrück between the Emperor and Sweden. While the lawyers argued over the niceties of precedence and diplomatic protocol, the fighting dragged on for another five weary years. The French were generally successful in the Rhineland, and although Condé was defeated in Spain in 1647, he won a second great victory over the Spanish at Lens (1648) in the Netherlands. Ironically, the Swedes were besieging Prague when peace was finally made, so it could be said that the war ended in the same spot where it had begun thirty years earlier.

The Peace of Westphalia; and the consequences of the war

The collection of treaties signed in 1648 and known collectively as the 'Peace of Westphalia' did more than settle some of the questions which had led to the war. Just as the war had been the first 'European' war, so the Peace was the first of those would-be universal treaties that redraw the boundaries of Europe and thus demonstrate a changed balance of power. It is comparable with such later settlements as those of Utrecht (1713), Vienna (1815) and Versailles (1919).

Four groups of problems had to be solved: those affecting the internal constitution of the Empire (the 'causes' of the war); the question of an amnesty for the rebellious German princes; the question of compensation for other German princes; and, overshadowing all the other questions, that of the 'satisfaction' of Sweden and France. While these were being discussed, the King of Spain signed a private peace treaty with the United Provinces at Münster.

France was confirmed in her possession of Metz, Toul and Verdun, which she had held since 1552. She also got Breisach, and the right to put garrisons in Philippsburg (beyond the Rhine) and Pinerolo in North Italy. Territorially unimportant, these places gave her gateways into Germany and the plain of Lombardy. She obtained, too, the Austrian possessions in Alsace, the Sundgau and ten Imperial towns. Her rights in these areas were – perhaps intentionally – not clear and, during the reign of Louis XIV, 'provided material for future wars more deadly than all the armaments of the seventeenth century'.[1]

Sweden got Western Pomerania, situated on the German side of the Baltic and controlling the mouth of the Oder, together with the bishoprics of Bremen and Verden, which controlled the mouths of the Elbe and Weser, and the port of Wismar in Mecklenburg. These areas carried with them the exercise of three votes in the Imperial Diet, thus enabling Sweden to intervene in the affairs of Germany.

[1] Ogg, p. 178.

The Elector of Brandenburg was given Eastern Pomerania, large but barren; the bishoprics of Minden and Halberstadt; the right of succession in Magdeburg; and confirmation of the acquisition of Cleves, Mark and Ravensburg.

Maximilian of Bavaria received the Upper Palatinate and its Electorate, while an eighth Electorate was created for the Elector Palatine, Charles Louis (his father Frederick had died of plague in 1632), who also recovered the Lower Palatinate. The Elector of Saxony received Lusatia, and certain lesser German princes – the Dukes of Brunswick and Mecklenburg, and the Grand Landgravine of Hesse-Cassel – recovered their old lands or obtained new ones. Switzerland and the United Provinces were recognized as independent states outside the Empire.

With regard to the constitution of the Empire, it was agreed that the individual states should be free to make alliances among themselves or with foreign countries, provided that these were not directed against the Emperor, while the problem of providing a strong central administration was once more shelved. Church lands were to remain in the hands of those who held them in 1624. Calvinism was given the same rights as Lutheranism on the *cuius regio eius religio* principle, and religious minorities were allowed five years' grace in which to move to another state if they wished. Bohemia, since it was now part of the Austrian dominions, naturally was treated as Catholic, so there 'the men who were thrown out of the window triumphed in the end'.

The Treaty registered a change in the relative strengths of the European powers. The Empire now consisted for all practical purposes of 337 independent states (152 under lay rulers, 123 under spiritual ones, and 62 Imperial cities). Henceforth 'the Empire' is simply a convenient way of defining a certain area of central Europe, and 'the Emperor' only a misleading name for the ruler of Austria, whose strength, though more limited, was also more real than formerly. France was poised on the threshold of Germany and of her first great period of aggression. The disregarded protests of the Pope at the religious terms of the settlement advertised the end of the Papacy as an international power – an end that had in fact occurred fifty years earlier, about the time of the death of Sixtus V (1590). (Though Urban VIII (1623–44) had unintentionally affected the course of the war, when by pursuing a policy of support for Richelieu against the Habsburgs he had fatally weakened the Catholic cause in Germany.) The United Provinces were rich and independent. In the north, Sweden had reached the height of her power, and for fifty years dominated the Baltic and complicated the politics of northeast Europe; whilst Brandenburg had taken the first step towards the achievement of her destiny – the replacement of Austria by Prussia as the chief power in Germany.

It is convenient, if not quite accurate, to sum up the struggle which had been ended at Westphalia, as 'the last religious and the first political war'. The wars of the next hundred and fifty years are fought for dynastic, commercial, or colonial ends, and their declared aims are political not theological, until in 1789 the French Revolution ushers in a new era of ideological wars, fought in defence of secular philosophies.

The effect of the war on the economic and social development of the Empire had been disastrous. In the absence of accurate statistics, historians are able to disagree as to the extent of the disaster, but a conservative estimate would be that the population fell by at least a third, from about 21 to about 13 million. This fall was naturally not distributed evenly; some areas, such as Austria, escaped very lightly, while others, such as the Lower Palatinate, probably lost more than two-thirds of their population. These losses were mainly occasioned not by death in battle, but by starvation, when crops failed or were trampled down by soldiers, by the disruption of communications, by the various epidemics known collectively as 'plague', by the sacking, looting, and massacring of armies on the march in summer, of armies in quarters in the winter. The engravings of the Frenchman, Jacques Callot, *Les Grandes Misères de la Guerre* (1633), and the descriptions in *Simplicissimus* (1668), written by a German, Grimmelshausen, illustrate what the people suffered at the hands of the soldiers. Their purpose is satirical, but their fictions are based on facts. Simplicissimus enters a sacked town:

> . . . I found the gates open and partly burnt, yet half barricaded with dung. So I went in, but was aware of no living creature there. Indeed, the streets were strewn here and there with dead, some of whom were stripped to their shirts, some stark naked . . . I learned that the Imperialists

had surprised a few of Weimar's folk there. And hardly had I gone two-stones'-throw into the town when I had seen enough: . . .[1]

Atrocities by the soldiers produced counter-atrocities by the peasants. Simplicissimus followed a file of musketeers: who

. . . came to a cask, which they burst open, and therein found a fellow that had neither nose nor ears, yet still lived. He, when he was somewhat revived, and had recognised some of the troop, told them how on the day before, as some of his regiment were a-foraging, the peasants had caught six of them . . . they had cut off his nose and ears . . . clapped him in the cask here present and buried him alive. . . .[2]

There are innumerable documented stories of horror, from the sack of Magdeburg in the north when twenty-four thousand inhabitants were killed, to Augsburg in the south, when a woman admitted having cooked and eaten a soldier who had died in her house. (There were many other recorded cases of cannibalism: for instance, in Breisach prisoners dismembered and ate a fellow-prisoner when he died.) When Simplicissimus reached Switzerland it seemed

. . . as strange as if I had been in Brazil or China. I saw how the people did trade and traffic in peace, how the stalls were full of cattle and the farmyards crowded with fowls, geese, and ducks, the roads were used in safety by travellers, and the inns were full of people making merry. There was no fear of an enemy, no dread of plundering, and no terror of losing goods and life and limb. . . .[3]

Extracts

1. *The Letter of Majesty, Rudolph II, July 9, 1609:*

. . . Be it known to everybody by this letter to perpetual memory: Whereas all the three estates of our kingdom of Bohemia, that receive the body and blood of Our Lord Jesus Christ in both forms, our leal subjects, have requested us humbly, as King of Bohemia, in the diet held in 1608 . . .:

---

[1] H. J. C. von Grimmelshausen, *Simplicissimus the Vagabond*, trans. A. T. S. Goodrick, Routledge, 1924, p. 40.

[2] Grimmelshausen, pp. 29–30.   [3] Grimmelshausen, pp. 304–5.

That they may be granted all that has been settled in the Confession commonly called Bohemian . . . which was described and handed over to Emperor Maximilian of blessed memory in 1575, together with all other compromises and understandings at which they had arrived in the said diet of 1575, and that they may freely and without hindrance practise their Christian religion *sub utraque* –

. . . .

And whereas it is our entire will that there should be peace and concord in this kingdom among all estates, both those *sub una* and those *sub utraque*, both now and in future, so that each party may freely and without molestation practise the religion from which it hopes to be saved:

Therefore we have . . . provided the estates *sub utraque* with this our letter of Majesty. . . .

That they shall not worry one another, but keep good friends . . . and . . . that all the estates *sub utraque* . . . shall be allowed to practise their religion *sub utraque* and in any place they like, and keep their priests and church-regime according to their own pleasure. . . .

The states *sub utraque* may in any royal town, borough, or village freely erect churches or schools, and nobody has a right to interfere with them.

We likewise forbid any attempt at converting people, either by force or persuasion, to a religion other than the one they profess. We ordain that no existent law, nor any law to be passed in the future, can deprive the present letter of Majesty of its force. (E. Reich, *Select Documents illustrating Mediaeval and Modern History*, King, 1905, pp. 633–4)

2. *Kepler reads Wallenstein's horoscope, 1607:*

. . . of all that man may hope from the heavens, the heavens are but the father, his own soul the mother thereto . . . therefore is it vain to hope for fortune from above, if the individual soul and temper have no bent thither. . . .

Of this gentlemen, I may in truth write that he has a character alert, lively, eager and restless, curious of every kind of novelty, unsuited to the common manner and behaviour of mankind but striving after new, untried or extraordinary ways; moreover he has much more in his head than he allows to be expressed or perceived. For Saturn in the ascendant brings contemplative, melancholy though luminous thoughts, a bent towards alchemy, magic and enchantment, community with sprites, scorn and indifference towards human ordinances and

THE THIRTY YEARS' WAR
1618-48

English Miles

0   50   100   150

Territories of
Austrian Habsburgs

Territories of
Spanish Habsburgs

Boundary of
The Empire

conventions and to all religions, making everything proposed by God or man to be suspected. . . .

. . . he will be unmerciful, without brotherly or nuptial affection, caring for no one, devoted only to himself and his desires, severe upon those placed under him, avid, covetous, deceitful, inequitable in his dealings, usually silent, often violent, contentious also, not to be browbeaten . . . there may also be seen great thirst for honour and a striving after temporal titles and power, whereby he will make for himself many great and injurious enemies both secret and confessed. (Kepler's *Opera omnia*, Vol. III (1870); quoted by F. Watson, *Wallenstein, Soldier under Saturn*, Chatto & Windus, 1938, pp. 52–3)

3. *Wallenstein writes to his agent in Friedland, 1626:*

The following matters I beg you to execute *in continenti*: first pay my cousin Max 24,000 gulden for the Croats; secondly see that Herr Michna (the Imperial General-Commissioner) received the 17,000 sacks of corn soon, so that they can be here this month; thirdly deliver to Herr Michna 2,000 hundred-weight of powder, to be sent here *in continenti* by water, as well as the match-lints that you have, and make up to 3,000 hundredweight of them. Also have 10,000 pairs of shoes made for the infantry, so that later I can divide them out among the regiments. Have them made in my towns and markets and pay a fair price for them in cash. See especially that the shoes are always carefully bound pair by pair, so that one will know which belong together.

At the same time have leather prepared, for I shall shortly order a further few thousand boots to be made. Have cloth ready also, for it may be that clothes will be required. (Wallenstein to Gerhard von Taxis, quoted by Watson, *Wallenstein, Soldier under Saturn*, Chatto & Windus, 1938, pp. 177–8)

FURTHER READING

C. V. Wedgwood, *The Thirty Years War*, Cape, 1938

F. Watson, *Wallenstein, Soldier under Saturn*, Chatto & Windus, 1938

H. J. C. von Grimmelshausen: *Simplicissimus the Vagabond*, translated by A. T. S. Goodrick, Routledge, 1924

X · THE FOUNDERS OF FRENCH GREATNESS;
1589–1661

Henri IV (1589–1610)

THE seventeenth century belongs to France in the same way that the eighteenth century belongs to England. It is for her *le grand siècle*. It is possible to argue that she reached the peak of her power at some point in the second half of the century and that French history from then onwards – in spite of Napoleon – is the tale of a melancholy, if intermittent, decline from that peak. The century falls naturally into two parts, divided at the year 1661 when Louis XIV took the business of government into his own hands. The first part, from 1589 to 1661, is dominated by three statesmen, Henri IV, Cardinal Richelieu and Cardinal Mazarin, who between them laid the foundations upon which Louis XIV's greatness was to rest.

Struggles begun for an ideal have a habit of turning into political wars, fought for limited objectives. The French wars of religion, as we have seen in Chapter VIII, were no exception. The assassination of Henri III in 1589 left the Huguenot Henri of Navarre (1553–1610) as the nearest heir to the throne. Of the other claimants the most powerful was Philip II – and he was a foreigner with a claim disallowed by the French Salic law. The Catholic League was allied with Spain and receiving Spanish subsidies. The Guise family were still regarded as ambitious foreigners. The war had come to be a struggle between the *Politiques*, who put France before religion, and the invader.

Time was on Henri's side. It was fortunate, too, that he was at the late King's headquarters and was thus able to take control of the royal army. A brilliant and inspiring general, he won decisive victories over the forces of the League at Arques (1589) and at Ivry (1590) in northern France, though the approach of Parma's army from the Spanish Netherlands forced him to raise the siege of Paris. He was increasingly popular, '. . . the monarchical tradition, though shaken by

227

the years of disorder, still retained its vitality, and came to the support of a King who showed himself worthy of royalist devotion.' [1]   Only his Huguenot religion stood in his way. Henri, who had become a Catholic once before, in 1572, took '*le saut perilleux*' in 1593 and was converted to Catholicism. It is perhaps apocryphal that he said '*Paris vaut bien une Messe*' (Paris is well worth a Mass).   But the next year he was in Paris.

The war was really over, although it dragged on in a desultory way until 1598.   In that year it was ended by the Peace of Vervins, which for all practical purposes reaffirmed the terms of the Treaty of Cateau-Cambrésis.   The important thing was not the terms of the Treaty, but the fact that the war was over, that Philip's plans had failed, and that Henri had re-established the power of the national monarchy.

A month before the Treaty of Vervins was signed Henri had settled, at least for the duration of his reign, the chief question of internal policy – what was to be the nature of the religious settlement?   The Huguenots were a minority, perhaps a twelfth of the population, but in some areas, for instance the south and the west, they controlled the main towns; for years they had supported Henri, when he was the Calvinist Henri of Navarre.   Now the Edict of Nantes (1598) confirmed the religious privileges they had won during the last ten years. The Huguenots were allowed freedom of worship at two places in each *bailliage* or *sénéchaussée* (administrative divisions), full civil rights and were eligible for all public offices.   The political concessions went further; they were allowed to hold religious synods and political assemblies, and to control about 200 towns, including such key places as La Rochelle (with a population of perhaps 30,000), Montauban and Montpellier.

The religious terms of the Edict were, for the period, generous.   The political terms went far to make the Huguenots a state within a state and contained the seeds of later troubles.   But as a temporary measure the Edict was a success, and the remaining twelve years of the reign are essentially ones of peace and growing prosperity.

There was only one brief war.   In 1600 a long-standing dispute with Savoy for the control of Saluzzo led to fighting in which the French were successful.   In 1601 the Duke of

[1] *C.M.H.*, III, p. 658.

Savoy made peace; France renounced her claims to Saluzzo and received in return Bresse, Bugey, Gex and Valromey. This was a relatively small, but valuable, rectification of the French frontier which was now advanced to the Alps – a move towards those 'natural boundaries' of which Richelieu was to speak so persuasively.

Henri's rule was one of tolerant absolutism, the natural outcome of his cynical, slightly sarcastic character. His power rested on his personality, rather than on custom or institutions. *Equitate non aculeo* (ride without spurs) was one of his mottoes. Temperamentally, he was cheerful, humorous, voluptuous – he is reputed to have had sixty-four affairs – easy in his manner, and accessible. The velvet glove concealed the steel; there is a hint of it in his reply to a recalcitrant provincial governor: 'Your letter is that of a man in a temper, I am not yet in a temper, and I beg you not to put me in one.' Mme. de Stael called him 'the most French king France has ever had'. Later histories echo her judgement:

> In Henry the nation's genius seems to be embodied; gaiety, wit, intrepidity, lucidity, industry and common-sense, are his most distinguishing attributes, and fit him to be the King of a people in whom those qualities are prominently displayed.[1]

In government Henri's rule was absolute, but it was an absolutism tempered by consent, similar in some ways to the rule of Elizabeth I in England. France was tired after thirty years of intermittent civil war. The great French political philosopher, Jean Bodin (1530–96) had written that every state needed a sovereign with unlimited power. Montaigne (1533–92) spoke in his Essais of the need for peace and orderly government under an absolute ruler who had the interests of his people at heart. Henri was such a man; when possible he ruled with the consent and co-operation of the governed.

The nobles were not encouraged to play an active part in politics, but rather to become courtiers. So long as they restricted themselves to this role, Henri left them alone, but when Marshal Biron was discovered to be conspiring against him with the Catholics he was executed (1602), although he had followed Henri in the lean years before he was king. Within

[1] *C.M.H.*, III, p. 695.

the Royal Council the real work of government was carried on, not by the titular councillors, but by twelve administrators, business men of lower rank appointed directly by Henri.

In local government, too, the King quietly extended royal control while weakening the local authorities. The provincial Governors' powers were reduced and Henri sent his own agents to deal with local problems, anticipating the later development of *Intendants*. When the local Estates spoke of their privileges, Henri replied: 'Your most valuable privilege is the favour of the King.'

The *Parlement* of Paris was a closed corporation of lawyers, which often acted as a supreme law court, and which claimed to be able to control the King's legislation by admitting at laws only those edicts which it itself had registered. This claim was not so far-reaching as it sounds, for the King could compel registration by holding a special session technically known as a *lit de justice*. It will be obvious that the *Parlement* did not correspond to the English Parliament in spite of the similarity in names. Nevertheless, the *Parlement* of Paris talked, and sometimes acted, as if it were the representative of at least the propertied classes. It is surprising that Henri did not try to reduce the power of these courts and the privileges of their members. On the contrary, in 1604 a new tax was introduced, the *Paulette* (named after a royal agent, Paulet), which increased their freedom. In return for a yearly payment of a sixtieth of the value of each judicial office, the holder might sell or bequeath it – the office thus became virtually hereditary, and a new middle-class nobility was created, the *noblesse de la robe*. The Crown obtained a valuable income, but the *Parlements* became increasingly independent. Speaking to the *Parlement* of Bordeaux in 1606, Henri said:

> All my parlements are worthless, but you are the worst of all. . . . A man only has to become a councillor and he is rich at once.

The States-General, though cumbersome and with no proper rules, might have held the solution to the problem of French government, but it did not meet once during the reign.

It will be seen from the above outline of Henri's administrative policy that all depended on the character of the King. Henri compared France to a chemist's shop, in which were both poisons and antidotes, and himself to the chemist, compounding from both healing medicines 'by mixing them in the proper proportions'. Flexible, absolute, tolerant, the system suited Henri's character to perfection; but the lack of positive constructive developments could have serious disadvantages in the future.

Henri's economic policy was constructive and far-sighted. Like Walpole he saw the link between internal security and prosperity. In this field his right-hand man from 1596 onwards was a Huguenot, Maximilien de Bethune, baron Rosny and Duke of Sully (1560–1641). The two men made a good team. The economic policy of the country was the King's, the methods by which it was carried out were Sully's. In character the man was very different from his master: vain and humourless (an English observer described how he 'danced all alone, in some sort of extraordinary hat, such as he always wore in his cabinet . . . although he was the most awkward man in the world'); jealous; cautious and economical (he was prepared to pay for the upkeep of the King's mistresses, but not for that of all their relatives!). As Chief Minister and Superintendent of Finance he supervised the restoration of France's finances, agriculture, commerce and – to some extent – industry. He had made a fortune for himself during the Civil Wars, but as Superintendent he was scrupulously honest.

The development of agriculture was encouraged. Henri had said that he hoped that 'every peasant might have a hen in his pot on Sunday'. Sully, more austerely, wrote 'Animal husbandry and arable farming are the two breasts at which France is nourished, the real mines and treasures of Peru'. Attempts were made to give the peasant increased security – for instance, nobles were forbidden to ride over standing corn and the peasants' tools and animals could not be seized for non-payment of taxes. Marshy land was drained and cultivated. Roads were widened and planted with rows of trees known colloquially as 'Rosnys'. Plans were made for the cutting of a series of canals to connect the main rivers of France, though only one was actually started, the Canal de Briare (1605), and work on that ceased with Henri's death and was not resumed till 1638. The encouragement of arable farming was sufficiently successful to produce an exportable surplus, so that the export taxes on corn were reduced, but any great progress was made impossible by the French social system, which remained as a brake on change until the French Revolution swept it away.

Developments in industry owed more to Henri's interest than to that of Sully. The latter believed, like the eighteenth century Physiocrats, that agriculture was the real source of a country's wealth, and that industry could only prosper at its expense. Henri's view was rather that which was to become known as Mercantilism – that the more one could manufacture at home, the less one would have to buy abroad, thus reducing the amount of gold leaving the country. Moreover, by selling to others more than one bought from them, the gold reserves could be increased. With these ends in view, Henri encouraged the expansion of existing industries, such as the manufacture of glass, pottery, linen and iron. In addition, one new industry was successfully created, silk-weaving, which was developed at Lyons, in the neighbourhood of which thousands of mulberry trees were planted. In this last scheme the King was advised by two Huguenots: Bartholomew Laffemas and Oliver de Serres.

Trade was encouraged. Inside France the guild system (which suited Mercantilist ways of thought) was reorganized from the chaos into which it had fallen during the Civil Wars. Trade treaties were signed abroad with England, Holland and Turkey. Champlain was sent off to explore the St. Lawrence and, following Cartier's route of 1535, founded Quebec (1608) and Montreal (1611). In the other hemisphere attempts were made to establish a trading company in India, though this had to be refounded in 1664.

Many of Henri's economic schemes were starved of money by Sully. Rigid economy was needed and Sully exercised it. This was perhaps his greatest service to France. At the beginning of the reign the public debt was enormous, and methods of taxation were so chaotic that only about half the revenue reached the treasury. By a rigid system of accounting, by strictly examining all claims to exemption from taxation, by preventing the provincial governors from raising taxes independently – by methods such as these, Sully made the old system work. The public debt was reduced from 350 to 224 million livres; the income rose from 23 million livres to 39 million; at the end of the reign there was 39 million livres in the treasury. Only one new tax had been introduced, the *Paulette*, already referred to. Sully obtained the best possible results from an out-of-date system.

Henri's plans were cut short by his death in 1610. For the last two or three years of his reign foreign problems had begun to loom large again. The strains and stresses which ultimately produced the Thirty Years' War were becoming apparent. Calvinists and Catholics had formed opposing blocs in Germany. In 1609 the death of the Duke of Cleves-Jülich almost started a European war.

The Duchies of Cleves-Jülich were comparatively rich and strategically most important. They controlled the lower Rhine around and to the north of Cologne, and were thus situated at the crossroads of Europe. Moreover, if it fell into Habsburg hands, Cleves would threaten the Netherlands frontier. The succession was disputed, but the two strongest claims were those of the Protestant states of Neuburg and Brandenburg. Nevertheless the Catholic Habsburg Emperor Rudolph moved troops into the Duchies and put his cousin, the Archduke Leopold, in possession.

Henri could not have ignored these events, even had he wished to do so. In fact they chimed in with his own antagonism to the Habsburg power, which he now felt strong enough to challenge, and with his personal pique (the girl with whom he was currently in love had fled to the Spanish Netherlands, and her husband to Spanish Milan). The King prepared to support the Protestants: he made an alliance with the Calvinist princes of the Rhine, and raised armies which were to march to the Duchies, to Milan by way of Savoy, and perhaps through the Pyrenees. In May 1610, five days before he was due to leave for the front, his carriage was halted by a load of straw in the Rue de la Ferronerie. A fanatical Catholic schoolmaster, Ravaillac, stepped on to the wheel-hub and stabbed him twice in the left side.

Henri was fifty-seven when he died. He might have lived for another ten years, and France would have avoided a long and dangerous minority. On the other hand, had he lived he would have involved the country in an expensive war that would have wasted his treasure and might have reduced his reputation with historians.   In this, as in so much else, Henri's reign is something of an enigma, a reign of uncertain beginnings rather than of completed results.   (A book printed in 1609 shows a peasant kneeling to Henri and saying 'We are beginning to taste the fruits of peace'.)   But it is a reign of foundations; it is difficult to believe that Richelieu and Mazarin, and after them Louis XIV, would have achieved what they did without the cautious, intelligent work of reconstruction carried out by Henri and Sully.   He had been a first-rate soldier, brave, rapid, clear-minded, a good tactician. In religion he had been tolerant, in a political way.   Like Elizabeth of England he did not want to make windows into men's souls.   'Those who honestly follow their conscience are of my religion, and mine is that of all brave and good men,' he said.   In government he was content to make the old system work.   Remembering the later history of France it is tempting to think that he would have been wiser to re-model the administration, but how dangerous and difficult that would have been.   There were more pressing problems to be dealt with first: the Huguenots, the nobles, the economic life of the country.   With these Henri grappled not unsuccessfully.

EXTRACTS

1. *The Ten Wishes of Henri:*

These are mentioned by Sully in the earlier, more reliable, part of his *Economies Royales*.   They are said to date from the War of 1585–9:

1. That God will help me during my life and show mercy at the end of it.

2. That I may never lose my health of body or mind.

3. That God may maintain the religion and party for which I have fought.

4. That God may deliver me from my wife (Margaret of Valois) and give me another more suitable.

5. That I may win the Crown of France and reign long and prosperously.

6. That I may conquer from Spain either Spanish Navarre, or Flanders and Artois.

7. That I may win a battle against the King of Spain; or against the Turk as Don John did.

8. That I may destroy the extremist group of Huguenots.

9. That I may reduce the leaders of the extremist party to submission.

10. That I may accomplish, before I die, my grand designs.

2. *The Edict of Nantes, April 13, 1598:*

I. Firstly, that the memory of everything which has passed between one side and the other, since the first of March, 1585, until our accession to the Throne, and during the earlier troubles, or arising out of them, shall be extinguished and wiped out as though it had never been. . . .

III. We ordain that the Catholic, Apostolic, Roman Religion shall be restored and re-established everywhere in our Kingdom. . . .

VI. And to leave no occasion for trouble or differences among our subjects; we have permitted and we do permit those of the so-called Reformed Religion (*Religion Pretendue Reformée*), to lodge and live in all the towns and districts of our Kingdom . . . without being investigated, vexed, molested, or compelled to do anything, in religious matters, contrary to their conscience. . . . (French text in E. Reich, *Select Documents illustrating Mediaeval and Modern History*, King, 1905, p. 350)

3. *A letter of Henri's to the Comtesse de la Roche-Guyar, 1590:*

My Mistress, I am writing you this word on the day before a battle. The issue is in God's hands. He has already declared what its results must be, and what He knows is expedient for His glory, and for the salvation of my people. If I lose the fight, you will never see me again, for I am not the man to fly, or to retreat. But I tell you this, that, if I die, my last thought but one will be of you, and my last of God, to whom I recommend both you and me. Written this last day of August by the hand of one who kisses yours, and is your humble servant. (Quoted in J. M. Thompson, *Lectures in Foreign History*, Blackwell, 1925, p. 114)

4. *The Queen, Marie de' Medici, hears of Henri's death, 1610:*

As the noise grew I sent Mme. de Montpensier to see what was happening, and I began to fear that something had happened to my son and that he was dead. My fear grew

when I saw Mme. de Montpensier shut the door quickly and come back to me pale with shock, for she had seen the King dead. She . . . only said: 'Your son is not dead.' Wanting to find out for myself the cause of the uproar, I opened the door and as I was leaving my room, I suddenly saw, beyond the crowd, more than two hundred drawn swords, and M. de Praslin, one of the four Captains of the Guards, turning towards me, cried out: 'Oh! Madame, we are lost!' And, at the same moment, I saw the King on a bed. . . .
(J. Boulenger, *Le Grand Siècle*, 1924, p. 1 – author's translation)

Richelieu

With the death of Henri the Cleves-Jülich question lost its urgency. The Protestants temporized, and the German war was postponed till 1618. The new King, Louis XIII (1610–43), was only nine years old. The Regent was Henri's widow, Marie de' Medici, a stupid woman of whose portraits by Rubens Aldous Huxley has written that they 'reveal a large, fleshy, gorgeously bedizened barmaid'.[1] Her husband had called her 'completely obstinate'. Saint-Simon later wrote that she was 'Proud, jealous, excessively dull, always under the sway of the scum of the Court . . .'. Of one thing she was sure; she was a sincere Catholic, and so the reliable Huguenot Sully went into a retirement (as Governor of Poitou) that lasted until his death thirty years later. 'France will fall into strange hands,' he said gloomily. He consoled himself by writing long and unreliable memoirs. The *Economies Royales*, as they are called, are a mixture of recorded fact, deliberate exaggeration and unconscious wish-fulfilment. All these elements are probably present in his description of the 'Grand Design' of Henri's to defeat the Habsburgs and to remodel Europe on a federal basis under the leadership of France.

The events of the next fourteen years must have made Henri turn in his grave as the gains which he had laboriously effected were rapidly dissipated. The complicated sequence of court favourites and palace intrigue is only of importance because it did considerable damage to France's revival, and demonstrated how thin was the crust which had formed over the separatist elements of the preceding century. The Queen-Mother passed under the influence of an Italian favourite,

[1] A. Huxley, *Grey Eminence*, Chatto & Windus, 1942, p. 97.

Concini, who controlled her until his death in 1617.   Henri's army was disbanded, Henri's money was spent in bribes and presents.   Only two isolated events need be recorded.

In 1614 the Princes, including Condé, the first Prince of the Blood, compelled the Queen-Mother to call the States-General.   (In doing this the nobles hid their personal ambitions behind constitutional demands in exactly the same way as they were to do again later, during the Fronde.)   The States-General was a cumbersome body, with no clearly defined rules, consisting of three parts: the nobles; the clergy; and the third estate, essentially the upper middle-class.   These last saw that their only hope against the privileged classes lay in a strong monarchy – there is an interesting parallel here in the attitude of the English middle classes to Tudor 'despotism'.   They declared '. . . That, as the king is sovereign in his kingdom, holding his crown from God alone, there is no power on earth, neither spiritual nor temporal, that has any rights over him . . .'.   But the Estates were unable to work together, being only agreed in their attacks on the Regent, and after six months they were dismissed.   They did not meet again until 1789.

In 1615 an important diplomatic double marriage took place.   Louis XIII married the King of Spain's daughter, Anne 'of Austria', while Louis' sister, Elizabeth, married the King of Spain's eldest son, later Philip IV.   Each wife renounced her rights of succession to her father's throne.   While this was going on fighting broke out again, and the armies of the Huguenots and the Princes marched and counter-marched until peace was patched up once more.

In 1617 Louis XIII and his favourite, Luynes, arranged the assassination of Concini, who was not popular.   After his burial the mob dug him up:

> Everyone would have some part of him: his ears were sold very dear: his entrails were thrown into the river: part of his body was burned before the statue of Henry IV on the Pont-Neuf, and some roasted portions of his flesh in the fire, and gave it to their dogs.

On the wave of this popular feeling Louis and Luynes were able to compel the Queen-Mother to retire to Blois.   With Marie de' Medici went her new adviser, Richelieu.

Armand-Jean Du Plessis de Richelieu (1585–1642) was the third son of one of the lesser nobles of Poitou. He had been brought up as a layman, but entered the Church at the age of seventeen when one of his elder brothers died, in order that he might take over the family bishopric of Luçon. In 1614 he had acted as spokesman for the clergy at the meeting of the States-General, and had been made Foreign Minister by the Queen-Mother in 1616. He now provided a discreet link between Blois and Paris, and when the new favourite Luynes died of a fever in 1621 he returned with the Queen-Mother to Paris. In 1622 Richelieu was made a Cardinal and two years later the King yielded to the pressure of the Queen-Mother (and perhaps of a Capuchin adviser, Père Joseph,) and appointed him to the Royal Council. He was thirty-nine. During the next eighteen years he controlled the course of European history, and he laid down the lines of French development for 150 years.

As he watches us from Philippe de Champagne's painting in the National Gallery, tall and thin, with parchment skin stretched tightly over his cheekbones and cold aristocratic features, Richelieu looks the statesman that he was. His mind was hard as a diamond, infinitely subtle, his thought crystal-clear, his will inflexible. Cavour, the nineteenth century Italian statesman, said: 'What rogues we should be if we did for ourselves what we do for our country!' These are Richelieu's sentiments – though he would not have expressed them so openly. The basis of his policy was 'Machiavellian-ism' in action, the belief that the end justified the means.

There are probably few great characters in modern history regarding whom there is more agreement than Richelieu. He seems to incarnate all the qualities of stratagem, finesse and ruthlessness; his flexibility is that of highly tempered steel; his refined, almost feminine features conceal an iron will; he has none of the coarseness of his contemporaries whom his cruelty sometimes shocked. 'He had the intention of all that he did': never before had a man risen to such political eminence by the exercise of sheer intellectual power. If he had few friends at court, he had nevertheless a fixity of purpose and a rigid con-sistency of intellect infinitely more terrifying than material strength. France under Richelieu had little internal history – the death-rate among the Cardinal's enemies was too high. Some men possess a fund of animal magnetism which seems to radiate strength and confidence among their associates; others, by means equally inscrutable, seem able at will to dry up all the moral and nervous force of those with whom they come into contact, leaving them helpless and impotent. Fortunately the latter is the more rare class, but it is specially powerful because almost always associated with irreproachable morals and even with a suggestion of high idealism. Richelieu is of this type. Much of his power was due to this subtle personal domination unsparingly exercised over men controlled more by their passions than their intellects. [1]

And what were the ends to which this remarkable man worked? To destroy the King's enemies and make him powerful at home; to destroy the Habsburgs and make France great abroad. When he died, Richelieu left behind, in his *Testament Politique*, a compact account of his motives and policy. He wrote:

> When your Majesty decided to take me into your Council and your confidence, I can say with truth that the Huguenots shared the state with you, that the nobles behaved as if they were not subjects, and the most powerful provincial governors as if they were supreme within their provinces. . . .
>
> I promised your Majesty to employ all my energy and all the power it might please you to give me to destroy the Huguenot party, to humble the pride of the nobles, to reduce all your subjects to obedience, and to raise your name among foreign powers to the high place it ought to hold.

All this he accomplished.

The Huguenots had been in a state of sporadic rebellion ever since the death of Henri IV. They had been particularly alarmed by the Spanish marriages of 1615. In 1625 a rebellion broke out, under the Huguenot leader Soubise, while the government was involved in war over the Valtelline (see below). La Rochelle rose, Languedoc was in an uproar. Richelieu was forced to abandon the foreign war, with the help of English and Dutch ships La Rochelle was reduced and peace made again. Richelieu was determined

[1] D. Ogg, *Europe in the Seventeenth Century*, Black, 8th edn., 1960, pp. 187–8.

not to have to deal with two enemies at once in the future:
he wrote to the King

> . . . we must abandon what is to be done abroad until we
> have done what must be done at home.

and again

> So long as the Huguenots in France are a state within a
> state, your Majesty cannot be master in his kingdom, nor
> do great deeds outside it.

Although the King's sister, Henrietta Maria, had married
Charles I of England there was no close alliance between the
two countries.   In 1627 the Duke of Buckingham, partly for
personal reasons, partly because it was thought that a Protestant war would be popular with Parliament, led an expedition to La Rochelle.   The city revolted, but Buckingham was
highly inefficient and Richelieu was able to seal it off on the
seaward side by a gigantic mole nearly a mile in length.
After a siege of fourteen months, during which a third of the
inhabitants died of starvation, the city capitulated.   Fighting went on in the south of France, but in 1629 the English
made peace and in the summer of that year the last Huguenot
stronghold, Montauban, surrendered.

By the Peace of Alais (1629) the Huguenots were confirmed
in their religious freedom, but lost all the political privileges
that they had gained by the Edict of Nantes.

> These gentlemen put forward great claims [said Riche-
> lieu].   They wished to remain as small republics.   They
> were forced to accept peace not on their terms, but as it
> pleased your Majesty to give it to them, not as a treaty,
> but as an act of grace.

The Peace was nevertheless remarkably generous.   The
position of the French Huguenots was much better than, for
instance, that of the Catholics in England.   By his moderation
the Cardinal showed his statesmanship, and it was rewarded.
The Huguenots became loyal and highly industrious citizens,
until they lost their religious freedom when the Edict of
Nantes was revoked in 1685.

Towards the lesser nobility Richelieu pursued a policy of
attrition, gradually curtailing their powers and privileges.   In

1626 the practice of duelling was prohibited, and in the following year Montmorency-Bouteville, who had killed twenty-two men, was executed for breaking this law. (Duelling began again after Richelieu's death; nine hundred and thirty gentlemen were killed in this way during the regency of Anne of Austria.)   In 1626 an edict was passed ordering the destruction of castles, except in frontier regions.   Henry VII had carried out a similar policy in England, 150 years earlier. Richelieu put an end to the custom of appointing nobles to the uncontrolled governorship of provinces.   In 1614 there had been sixteen such Governors, while at the time of the Cardinal's death in 1642 there were only four.

Richelieu was able to clip the wings of the ordinary nobles, but he suffered throughout his rule from the intrigues of the greatest, notably those of the King's brother, Gaston of Orleans, who, until Anne of Austria had a son in 1638, was next in line of succession.   Gaston was involved in plots against the Cardinal in 1626, 1630, 1632 and 1642 (Cinq-Mars).   Of these, the most dangerous occurred in 1630.   Gaston was then supported by the Queen-Mother who had come to hate Richelieu for the religious ambiguities of his foreign policy and for his increasing control over the mind of the King. Richelieu's foreign policy had been only partially successful. The King was seriously ill, and believed to be dying.   Then he began to recover, but the plot went on.   In Paris Marie de' Medici had almost persuaded her son to get rid of Richelieu, when the Cardinal himself appeared in the room. The Queen-Mother stormed at Richelieu, the King apparently promised to dismiss him, and left for Versailles.   Louis was a dull, unintellectual man, fond of such hobbies as hunting, carpentry or working at his private forge; but he could appreciate the relative values of his mother, stupid and emotional, and of Richelieu, calm and intelligent.   He sent for the Cardinal and they talked for four hours that night. Next day Richelieu was back in power.   The Queen-Mother and Gaston retired to Brussels in the Spanish Netherlands. November 10, the day on which so much happened, became known as the 'Day of Dupes'.   Henceforward the King and Richelieu knew and trusted one another absolutely.

The plots continued, but Richelieu's spies exposed them. It was not possible to touch Gaston, but he became more and more discredited as, after each plot, he was persuaded to betray his accomplices. During Richelieu's rule five Dukes, four Counts and a Marshal of France were executed for political crimes. So in this way, too, Richelieu was able to weaken the nobility.

It was in the day-to-day administration of the country that Richelieu's home policy is most open to criticism. As he had promised, he had destroyed the power of the Huguenots, the provincial governors, the nobility; but France needed a great administrator. Richelieu, like Henri IV, was content to rule from above. Too much depended on the centre. That there was no attempt made to use the States-General is perhaps not surprising in view of events across the Channel, where Parliament and Charles I had quarrelled irreparably during the years 1625–9. Fear of local men prevented the growth of country administrators of the type of the English J.P.

Within these limits much was done. The control of every department of state was centralized under Richelieu, 'not often has one man so absorbed every form of government, the social and political life of France was for eighteen years bound up in him'. He developed the use of commissioners, special travelling agents often appointed on an *ad hoc* basis, to deal with local government. These were the *Intendants de justice, police, et finances*. Their origin lay in the preceding century, and it was not till Louis XIV's reign that they became a permanent part of the administration, but it was under Richelieu that their powers were established at the expense of the nobles, the *Parlements*, and the governors.

The same lack of creative statesmanship is apparent in Richelieu's financial policy. The Cardinal's foreign wars necessitated a great increase in expenditure, yet the financial machinery of Henri IV's reign – itself largely that of a century earlier – remained unchanged. The greater part of the revenue came from the three traditional taxes: the *taille* (a sort of income tax); the *gabelle* (salt tax); and the *aides* (excise duties). These taxes varied quite irrationally and unfairly from province to province. Moreover the privileged nobility and clergy, perhaps a quarter of the population, escaped direct taxation. Finally, the indirect taxes were collected by *traitants* (tax farmers), and it has been estimated that the cost of levying the *aides* and *gabelle* absorbed 40 per cent of their total yield. 'The maximum of irritation was combined with a minimum of advantage to the state.' [1]

In order to meet the increased needs of the government, Richelieu relied on the multiplication and sale of offices, and on extensive borrowing. The results of his system – or lack of system – can be read in the following figures:

		million livres
1626	*Revenue*	18
	Expenditure	45
	Interest on debt	2
1640	*Revenue*	43
	Expenditure	116
	Interest on debt	21

A hint of what this policy could lead to was given by peasant rebellions in the provinces. There were four such during the thirties alone, the most dangerous being that of '*Jean Va-Nu-Pieds*' in Normandy in 1639.

Richelieu knew well the need for internal reform, but for several reasons was unable to come to grips with it. For one thing, his genius lay in the direction of government rather than the creation of new institutions. He saw the problem in terms of power politics only – the destruction of the anarchic local rights of Huguenots, nobles and governors. Although he drew up schemes for reform, he was not really interested in finance, or in the condition of the people. Henry IV, with his 'fowl in the pot on Sundays', would never have said, as Richelieu did, '. . . if the people were too comfortable it would be impossible to keep them within the bounds of their duty'. Plans for improvement at home were shelved or sacrificed to the needs of foreign policy.

Where his interest was aroused, however, Richelieu was capable of making innovations. He built up a professional army of 150,000 men. He created a navy, for '. . . strength in arms requires Your Majesty to be strong not only on land, but also at sea'. The whole of the French coastline was brought under the government's control; ship-building yards were developed at Brest and La Rochelle; by 1636 France had a Mediterranean and an Atlantic fleet, totalling eighty-

[1] A. J. Grant, *The French Monarchy, 1483–1789*, C.U.P. 1925, Vol. I, p. 261.

three vessels. The Company of New France was set up in 1627 to develop Canada (though it was starved of government support later). In 1631 the first official newspaper, the *Gazette de France*, was issued. In 1635 Richelieu gave official support to the French Academy, *'les quarantes Immortelles'*, whose aim of purifying and standardizing the language and literature according to upper-class usage was so typical of seventeenth century France.

'I will prove to the world that the age of Spain is passing away and the age of France has come.' Richelieu made good his boast; it is in the area of foreign affairs that the rapier-like flexibility of his Machiavellian intellect won its greatest successes.

In his foreign policy Richelieu was ably assisted by his friend Père Joseph (1577–1638). The latter, born Francois Le Clerc du Tremblay, was a member of the Capuchin order, reformed Friars who, with their rivals the Jesuits, were the spearheads of the Counter-Reformation. His character had two superficially contradictory aspects. On the one hand, he was an austere mystic whose life had been transformed by reading the English work *The Rule of Perfection*, who dressed humbly, walked rather than rode whenever possible, and in general practised considerable austerity. On the other hand, he was *'L'Eminence grise'*, the shadowy amoral diplomat for whom *raison d'état* was God's will, and who saw in the aggrandizement of France and the destruction of the Habsburgs the necessary preliminary to a great Crusade against the Turk. Père Joseph, Richelieu and Pope Urban VIII (1623–44) were at one in their opposition to the Habsburgs.

Richelieu perhaps owed his call to power in 1624 to some extent to Père Joseph. He certainly wrote immediately to the Friar:

> You are the principal agent whom God has employed to lead me to all the honours which I have reached. . . . I beg you speed your voyage and come soon to partake of the management of affairs.[1]

Richelieu, however, was the dominant partner and Père Joseph was only able to practise the good life in the interstices

[1] C. J. Friederich, *The Age of the Baroque*, Harper, 1952, p. 200.

of diplomatic activity. They were on excellent terms. In
1636, when the Cardinal was in despair at the disastrous start
to French intervention in the Thirty Years' War, the Friar
could call him *une poule mouillée* (a wet hen, a molly-coddle)!
Richelieu saw clearly Père Joseph's dual nature, referring to
him sometimes as 'little Ezekiel' and sometimes as 'Tenebroso-
Cavernoso'. When Père Joseph was dying, Richelieu cheered
him, not with the comforts of religion, but with a diplomatic
lie. *'Breisach est à nous'*, though the news of the fall of the
Habsburg fortress did not in fact arrive until the next day.
And when the Friar was dead Richelieu declared *'j'ai perdu
mon appui'* – 'I have lost my main support.'

The chief weakness of the Habsburgs was, as it had been in
the days of Charles V, the scattered nature of their territories
and the weakness of the communications between them. This
was particularly true of the Spanish and Italian territories on
the one hand and the Austrian and Netherlands areas on the
other, for between the two groups lay the Alps. In 1621 the
Spanish seized the Valtelline, the sixty mile valley of the
River Adda which joined Spanish Habsburg Milan to Austrian
Habsburg Tyrol. It would be an invaluable link, for the
passes to the west were controlled by the hostile French and
Swiss, while those to the east were in the hands of the Venetians.
The valley's inhabitants were Catholics, who had been ruled
by neighbouring half-Swiss Protestants, and they had proved
a valuable reservoir of good fighters.

Richelieu attempted to break this vital link, and partially
succeeded. In 1625 the Valtelline was occupied by French
troops, acting in conjunction with the neighbouring Protestants; but the Huguenot rebellion at home forced Richelieu
to come to terms with the Spanish. By the Treaty of Monzon
(1626) the valley was to be virtually independent under joint
Franco-Spanish supervision. Within a year the Spanish were
back in control, Richelieu being involved at La Rochelle. In
the thirties the valley proved its value to the Spanish (the
Battle of Nördlingen was won by Habsburg troops which had
been moved north that way) and in 1635 a French army
under de Rohan seized it. But they were unable to conciliate
the local inhabitants and were driven out in 1637, and in 1639
the Valtelline passed back to their original lords, the Grisons.

Richelieu was also engaged in a second, more successful,

attempt to establish the French as a power in north Italy.   In
1627 the Duke of Mantua and Montferrat died, leaving as his
nearest heir a Frenchman, Charles Duke of Nevers.   The
Duchy of Mantua was strategically situated to the southeast
of Habsburg Milan, the Duchy of Montferrat to the southwest, and the new ruler was prevented from taking over the
Duchies by the Habsburgs and the Duke of Savoy, whose
territory lay between France and Mantua.   At this time
Richelieu was involved at La Rochelle and could not immediately intervene.   As soon as the Huguenots had been
crushed, however, he led an army himself into Savoy, which
was occupied.   The Imperial troops took Mantua, but were
unable to dislodge the French garrison at Casale.   After
negotiations at Ratisbon, fighting began again, but was
ended in 1631 by the Peace of Cherasco, which Mazarin, then
a Papal agent, helped to bring about.   By the Peace the Duke
of Nevers was installed in Mantua, while Savoy became
something of a French puppet and ceded to France the fortress of Pinerolo, which lay on the Italian side of the Alps and
controlled the easiest pass from France into Italy – that of
the Mont Genèvre (1,854 metres).

It was against the Empire that Richelieu achieved his
greatest triumphs, through his exploitation of the Thirty
Years' War (1618–48).   In 1629 the Emperor Ferdinand II
seemed in a stronger position than any Emperor since Charles V
(see Chapter IX).   Within eighteen months the Cardinal
had helped to destroy this position by playing upon the
internal weaknesses of Germany.   The war broke out again
and Richelieu then devoted his energies to keeping the pot
boiling, intervening at first indirectly, later openly, with the
object of weakening the Habsburg power, and advancing
France's frontiers towards their 'natural' limit, the Rhine.
Richelieu had outlined this policy to Louis, in general terms,
as early as 1629.   'We must,' he wrote in his *Advice to the King*,
'think of strengthening our position at Metz, and, if possible,
of advancing to Strasbourg, in order to have a gateway to
Germany.'

At the Diet of Ratisbon in 1630, Père Joseph, 'affable and
persuasive', was able to work on the incipient rift between
the Emperor and the Princes of the Catholic League.   He
was so successful that the Princes refused to recognize the

Emperor's son as King of the Romans (heir to the Holy Roman Empire), and insisted that he dismiss his victorious general, Wallenstein. Ferdinand ruefully remarked that a Capuchin had disarmed him with his rosary, putting in his friar's hood six electoral caps.

While the Emperor's position was thus weakened inside Germany, Richelieu's agents were in touch with the Swedish King, Gustavus Adolphus, helping him to end his war with Poland and encouraging him to move instead into Pomerania, on the northern coasts of the Empire (1630). In the following year France and Sweden signed the Treaty of Bärwalde, by which France was to pay 1,000,000 livres annually until 1636 towards the upkeep of the Swedish army. Gustavus was only too successful. His army cut through Germany, and when it began to occupy the left bank of the Rhine, Richelieu protested. It is said Gustavus replied that

'if His Majesty of France should anger him much, he knew the way to Paris, and he had hungry soldiers would drink wine and eat with as good a will in France as in Germany.' [1]

Perhaps it was fortunate for France that he was killed in the following year at Lützen.

The death of Gustavus compelled Richelieu to take a more active part, while still remaining officially at peace. In 1633 France occupied part of Lorraine, French subsidies were continued to the Swedish army and to Bernard of Saxe-Weimar, leader of the Protestant League of Heilbronn. At the same time Richelieu opened secret negotiations with the leader of the Imperial forces, Wallenstein, with the aim of seducing him from the Emperor's service.

Nevertheless it appeared by 1635 as though the Emperor would end the war on terms favourable to himself. In the preceding year Wallenstein had been assassinated, and the Swedes defeated at Nördlingen. Now peace was made at Prague. There was only one answer: in the same month that the Peace was signed, France formally declared war on Spain and led a coalition constructed by Richelieu which included Sweden, Holland, Savoy and the forces of Bernard of Saxe-Weimar. As a result the War continued for another

---

[1] R. Monro, *His Expedition with the worthy Scots regiment* . . . (1637).

thirteen years, the Emperor's position was destroyed, and so too were large areas of Germany.

Thus, in the long run, Richelieu's policy was a success, but the dividends were not paid until after his death. Indeed the French army was at first remarkably unsuccessful, and for this he was largely to blame; there was no bold attack against one firm objective. Too much was attempted in too many different areas. Then, too, the Cardinal was afraid of his generals, with the result that the command was divided and given to second-rate men. All the same, by the time of his death France had acquired strong positions in Savoy and Alsace, while the Spanish faced revolts fomented by Richelieu in Catalonia and Portugal. And, most important of all, the fighting went on, weakening the Empire. 'His will fanned the flames of war from the Oder to the Ebro.' [1]

Richelieu died in December 1642. The King had sat by his bed, feeding him with beaten-up eggs – as Elizabeth I had fed her dying Cecil with broth. The Cardinal was buried in the Sorbonne. He left behind a country he had made great abroad and a king whom he had made supreme at home. 'Man,' he had said, 'is immortal; his salvation is hereafter; the state has no immortality, its salvation is now or never.' In the pursuit of this aim he had not attempted to solve the problems of French internal administration, or of financial organization. To blame him for not having done so is perhaps to use unfairly the hindsight of the historian, who knows that the French Revolution lies in the future. To contemporaries he appeared perhaps a monster, but a successful monster. A contemporary Englishman wrote:

> The torment and the ornament of his age, France he subdued, Italy he terrified, Germany he shook, Spain he afflicted, Portugal he crowned, Lorraine he took, Catalonia he received, Swethland [Sweden] he fostered, Flanders he mangled, England he troubled, Europe he beguiled. Then shalt thou admire that he is shut up now dead in so small a space, whom, living, the whole earth could not contain.[2]

[1] C. V. Wedgwood, *Richelieu and the French Monarchy*, E.U.P., 1949, p. 191.
[2] Quoted in Wedgwood, p. 191.

Extracts

1. *The Character of Richelieu, as seen by the Cardinal de Retz:*

What he determined was usually right. He was a man of his word, except when some great interest obliged him not to be, and then he did what he could to keep the appearance of good faith. He was not generous, but he gave more than he promised, and seasoned his gifts well. He loved glory more than morality permits; . . . Neither his mind nor his heart were above fear, but they did not sink under it, but one must admit he overcame danger by prudence rather than courage. . . . His power and state eclipsed the King's, but he had such dignity that only those who were above the mob could see in this what was good and what was evil. He could distinguish better than anyone between the bad and the worse, between the good and the better, a great quality in a minister. He was too impatient about those little things that are the prelude to great ones. . . . He had sufficient religion for this world. He did good, either through inclination or through good sense, whenever his interest did not lead him to do evil, in which case he knew quite clearly what he was doing. (de Retz, *Memoirs*, introduction by D. Ogg, Dent, 1917, Vol. I, p. 65)

2. *In what the honesty of Councillors should consist:*

It is one thing to be a good man according to the laws of God, and quite another to be one according to those of men. . . .

The Statesman ought to be faithful to God, to the State, to men and to himself. . . .

The honesty of a public minister does not demand a timid and over-scrupulous conscience, for just as through lack of conscience many injustices and cruelties may occur, so over-scrupulousness can produce many omissions and indulgences harmful to the nation, and it is very certain that those who tremble at certainties through fear of destroying themselves often destroy the state, when they could have saved both. . . .

To sum up, it should be realised that Statesmen must be like the stars, which pay no attention to the snarling of curs, but shine and follow their course . . . their honesty cannot be shaken nor can they be diverted from marching steadily towards the goal which they have selected for the good of the State. (*Testament Politique*, Part I, Chapter VIII, Section 3)

Mazarin

Richelieu had originally intended that Père Joseph should continue his work, at least in the sphere of foreign policy, but the Capuchin died first, in December 1638. In the next year the Cardinal took into his service an Italian diplomat, Giulio Mazarini, whom he intended as his new successor.

Mazarin (1602–61) – to give him the French form of his name – had been born in Sicily, educated by the Jesuits, and employed in the Papal diplomatic service. He had come to Richelieu's notice during the negotiations over Mantua which led to the Peace of Cherasco. When he entered the French service he became a naturalized Frenchman, and in 1641, though only a deacon, he was made a Cardinal. Shortly before Richelieu died, Mazarin became a member of the Royal Council.

Within six months of Richelieu's death, Louis XIII was also dead (1643). Honest, determined, industrious, a good soldier, but of only average intellect, he is obscured by the towering Cardinal. It is a matter of conjecture to what extent he was able to influence Richelieu; it is fairly certain that after the Day of Dupes they trusted one another completely.

The heir to the throne was a boy of four, the future Louis XIV. By the terms of her husband's will Anne of Austria was to be Regent, but her powers were to be strictly limited by a Council of seven which included herself, Gaston of Orleans (who was given the title of Lieutenant-Governor) and Mazarin. None of them was pleased at the prospect of limited power. Anne persuaded Gaston to ask the *Parlement* of Paris to annul the will and they, flattered, did so. Anne immediately appointed Mazarin, who had been carefully absent from the negotiations, as Chief Minister. Henceforward Anne and Mazarin always worked together, and it is not impossible that they were secretly married. Contemporaries certainly thought so.

The new Chief Minister, who was to continue Richelieu's policy unchanged for another eighteen years, was in some ways very different from his predecessor. Where Richelieu had the concealed strength and limited flexibility of a steel spring, Mazarin had rather that of a piece of elastic. He was content to give his enemies infinite scope, believing that in that way they would destroy themselves. His motto was 'Time and I against the world'. He was able, unscrupulous, Machiavellian,

> '. . . compromising and sinuous, courteous and deceitful, vindictive and sarcastic, winning his ends not by frontal attack but by pitting his enemies against each other; able to emerge unashamed from any disgrace, and frankly enriching himself and his relatives at the expense of his adopted country.' [1]

Mazarin was an accessible courtier, almost a cavalier in appearance, easy-going and approachable, always ready to listen – particularly to those whose requests he had no intention of granting. He loved fine women, fine perfumes, fine things in general. He combined this love of luxury and elasticity of policy and method with a steady eye on his ultimate goal, the aggrandizement of France and of Mazarin.

On the surface, Richelieu's death made little difference in French affairs. The war, and the foreign policy on which it was based, continued unchanged. At home the cost of the fighting led to increasing misery for the common people. Gradually, and – at first – quietly, the late Cardinal's enemies returned from retirement or exile; but so long as the war continued the various internal tensions remained controllable. Mazarin's rule falls naturally into three parts: the conclusion of the Thirty Years' War, 1643–8; the internal struggle in France known as the Fronde, 1648–53; the conclusion of the war with Spain, 1653–9. It is convenient to consider the first and third of these parts together, before turning to internal affairs.

In 1643 a brilliant victory at Rocroi, in the Ardennes, made the reputation of the young Condé as a general (he was twenty-two), marked the beginning of the great age of French land victories, and the end of that of the Spanish infantry, which had been generally unbeaten since Pavia (1525). Soon afterwards negotiations opened at Münster and Osnabrück, but the war dragged on for another five years, until the Peace of Westphalia was signed in 1648. Meanwhile, French armies under Turenne and Condé won victories in the

[1] Ogg, p. 206.

Rhineland, and although Condé was defeated in Spain in 1647 he won a last great victory at Lens in the Spanish Netherlands (1648).

The terms of the Peace are discussed in Chapter IX. Here it is only necessary to mention again those that affected France. Her claim to the bishoprics of Metz, Toul and Verdun, which she had held since 1552, was recognized; she acquired the Austrian parts of Alsace, Breisach and the control of Philippsburg (both on the right bank of the Rhine); she kept Pinerolo in Italy. These areas, small in themselves, were important strategically, giving France passages into Germany and the Lombardy plain. Moreover, in Alsace France's rights were not exactly defined, thus providing a pretext for future expansion, and for intervention in the affairs of the Empire – pretexts of which full use was made in the reign of Louis XIV. In the imponderable element of prestige, France became the dominant power in western Europe. Richelieu might have regretted the failure to hold on to Strasbourg, but in general he would have been well satisfied.

The war with Spain went on for another eleven years. Mazarin might have been able to bring it to a conclusion sooner, if France had not been shaken by the internal troubles of the Fronde – troubles of which Spain took full advantage. In 1653, however, internal unity was restored, and the balance of success tipped back again in favour of France. The main events took place on her northeast frontier, where Turenne faced the French general Condé, now leading the Spanish armies. The latter was successful at Valenciennes in 1656, but otherwise Turenne had the best of the struggle.

In 1657 Mazarin concluded the Treaty of Paris with Cromwell, by which he agreed to banish Charles II from France and to cede to England the ports of Mardyke and Dunkirk when they were captured. In return England was to provide an army of 6,000 Ironsides to fight against Spain, the country which Cromwell once called England's 'natural enemy'. The combined Franco-British army, under Turenne, won a decisive victory over Condé and the Spanish at the Battle of the Dunes (1658). Dunkirk and Gravelines, Oudenarde and Ypres fell one after another to the French.

As a result of these events the war was brought to a close by the Peace of the Pyrenees, signed in 1659. In order that neither side might lose face, the representatives met on the Ile des Faisans in the middle of the River Bidassoa which marks the boundary between France and Spain, in specially erected pavilions.   Besides a number of minor frontier adjustments, France's major gains were Artois, from the Spanish Netherlands, and Roussillon and the Cerdagne in the south, which extended her frontier to the 'natural boundary' of the Pyrenees.   (In fact a small enclave of Spanish territory, Llivia, remains to this day on the French side of the frontier.)   France gave back Lorraine, but she obtained rights of passage through the Duchy to Metz and Alsace – rights which made it easy for her to overrun Lorraine whenever she wished.   In return, Condé was allowed to return to France and was restored to the Governorship of Burgundy.

At the same time Spain and France were linked by a diplomatic marriage.   Louis XIV was wedded to the King of Spain's daughter, Maria Theresa, who was to resign her rights to the Spanish throne in return for a dowry of 500,000 crowns.   The marriage took place in 1660, but the dowry was not in fact paid, and the marriage contained within it the seeds of two of Louis's later wars.   (The second of these, the War of the Spanish Succession (1702–13) resulted in one branch of the French royal family acquiring the throne of Spain.   It is interesting to speculate how far Mazarin may have hoped for some such development.)

The terms of the Peace, taken together with those of Westphalia, mark the triumph of France over the Habsburgs and the end of a struggle that had been going on intermittently since 1494.

The middle period of Mazarin's rule, from 1648 to 1653, is dominated by the internal troubles known collectively, if a little mysteriously, as the Fronde.   The causes and consequences of this civil war are of considerable importance, though not the actual confused course of events.

In essence the Fronde was a revolt against the absolutism of Richelieu and Mazarin.   Its underlying causes lay in a financial policy that had consistently sacrificed prosperity at home to success abroad, and future budgets to present expenses. All the ordinary sources of revenue had been exploited, and the government was searching desperately for new expedients.

The privileged classes began to fear that they might have to pay!

To the economic misery of the ordinary people, and the fears of the privileged, was now added a third element, the opposition of the *haute bourgeoisie* of Paris, to some extent organized and vocal in the *Parlement*. In 1644 the government had unearthed an old law forbidding the building of new houses outside the walls of Paris, and they proposed to tax illegal buildings in the suburbs. There was opposition and the government then attempted to impose a forced loan instead. Both taxes were eventually abandoned; they are curiously reminiscent of Charles I's devices during his personal rule in England (1629–40).

The second event that struck at the pockets of the middle-class had been a successful attempt to manipulate the *rentes* by withholding the payment of interest so that their value fell, then buying the stock at its new low value, paying the arrears of interest, and selling again when the price consequently rose. The *rentes*, government stock, had been the only safe investment for the middle-classes. 'It is possible to crush a peasantry so that it cannot rise, but systematic robbery of a prosperous and educated bourgeoisie generally ends in revolution.' [1]

The crisis came in 1648. In that year the *Paulette* was due to be renewed, and the government tried to exact concessions as the price of renewal. This was the one tax that *Parlement* wanted, for obvious reasons, to keep. Under the leadership of Broussel ('moins d'impôts, pas d'impôts') the *Parlement* demanded the removal of Intendants, the regular payment of *rentes*, the reduction of the *taille* by one quarter, trial within twenty-four hours for those imprisoned and no new taxes without the consent of the *Parlement*. The *Parlementaires* were clearly inspired by earlier events in England, especially perhaps by the Petition of Right.

At first Mazarin yielded. Then the news of Condé's victory at Lens encouraged him to arrest the leaders; this step led to a popular explosion in which the desperate elements of the *Parlement*, the mob, and the discontented nobility were temporarily united by the coadjutor to the Archbishop of Paris, Gondi, later Cardinal de Retz. Gondi came of a family

[1] Ogg, p. 209.

of Cardinals and bankers, and was an able, self-seeking conspirator who has left admirable, though biased, Memoirs. Mazarin and the court left Paris, issued from St. Germain a Declaration accepting the *Parlement*'s demands and then used Condé's army to besiege Paris. In April 1649 the first Fronde was ended by the Treaty of Rueil, in which most of the *Parlement*'s demands were accepted. The court returned to Paris.

This marks the end of the constructive period of the Fronde. Condé thought he had discovered that he could make and break governments, and it soon became clear that he was planning to seize power for himself. In 1650 Mazarin felt strong enough to order his arrest, but the action was premature, and precipitated the second Fronde, that of the Princes (1650–3).

The nickname 'Fronde' well describes this second rebellion. *Frondeurs* was the name given to the Paris boys who slung stones and mud at the coaches of the great ones, and then ran away. The nobles now behaved in a similar fashion. The course of events is as complicated as the novels of Dumas (for which indeed it provided several of the plots), as irrational as the scenario of a comic opera. 'All parties came into collision with each other, made treaties, and betrayed each other in turn' (Voltaire). A brief summary of these events is all that is required.

In 1651 Mazarin was forced to leave France, while Turenne led a Spanish army into the northern provinces and Condé negotiated with the Spanish in the south. In 1652 the tide began to turn; Turenne left the Spanish and returned to the court, Mazarin came back from exile. In the summer Turenne defeated Condé, drove him into Paris, and would have taken the city if Gaston d'Orleans' daughter, *la Grande Mademoiselle*, had not persuaded the city to turn the cannon of the Bastille on the royal troops. But the middle-classes were disturbed by the growing disorder and when Mazarin, seeing that hatred of himself was all that held the rebels together, withdrew to Sedan, Condé was driven out of Paris and fled to the Spanish army in the Pyrenees. Early in 1653 Mazarin was able to return to Paris in triumph.

The Fronde had been the last expression of the resentment of the nobility. Fortunately for Mazarin, the *Parlement* of Paris had been alarmed at their allies – the unpredictable, explosive mob; the frivolous and selfish nobility; the foreign armies. For a little de Retz held the various elements together, but 'Turenne and Condé could not agree to betray their country at the same time',[1] and Mazarin's apparently spineless policy allowed the forces of opposition to exhaust and discredit themselves.

The rebellion had important – and unexpected – results out of all proportion to the frivolity and incompetence of its leaders. It delayed the successful conclusion of the war with Spain. It increased the economic misery of the country. In the part played by the city it to some extent foreshadowed the French Revolution. It gave Louis XIV, who had been for a time a virtual prisoner in the Palais Royal, a distaste for Paris with its winding medieval streets that were a deathtrap in times of disorder; we owe the development of Versailles to the Frondeurs. Most important of all, the *haute bourgeoisie*, who had sparked off the original rebellion, had seen the forces of law and order almost destroyed by the irresponsible nobility. Frightened by the sight, they gave their complete support henceforth to the monarchy; the Fronde led to the absolutism of Louis XIV. It revealed at once the strength and weakness of the system built up by the two Cardinals.

Mazarin died in the spring of 1661. It is said that he left to Louis XIV his secretary, Colbert, and the advice to be his own Chief Minister. He also left the King a now unchallenged position as absolute monarch at home, a dominant place abroad over the declining and defeated Habsburgs, and an advanced eastern frontier which might be used as a springboard for further expansion to the Rhine – and perhaps beyond it. But he left too a country exhausted by thirty years of foreign expansion, an empty treasury and a chaotic financial system (in 1661 the net annual deficit was 28 million livres), and a corrupt system of administration.

All this was the legacy of the two great Cardinals. Their work prepared the way for the great age of Louis XIV, but beyond that it implied, unless its dangers were recognized and its weaknesses overcome, the French Revolution. If this qualification is borne in mind, it is difficult to over-estimate

[1] J. M. Thompson, *Lectures in Foreign History, 1499–1789*, Blackwell, 1925.

the importance of Richelieu and Mazarin. They dominated Europe for thirty-eight years, and influenced her politics for another half-century. Their methods were complementary. Mazarin's smooth flexibility might not have been so successful in the stormy days of Richelieu's first six years, but he had in some ways a more difficult situation with which to deal. After 1630 Richelieu had the support of the King, but most of Mazarin's work was done while Louis XIV was a minor, his main support the Queen-Mother, who was a foreign Habsburg, while he himself was an Italian, who never learnt to speak French without a foreign accent. Where Richelieu compelled, Mazarin had sometimes to persuade.

During the half-century covered by this chapter much that we connect with the great age of Louis XIV was already flowering, and it would be a mistake to remember solely the economic misery of the country. Only to list the great names is to show that France's cultural golden age had already begun. In painting the brothers Le Nain (1588–1648), Poussin (1594–1665), Claude (1600–82), and de la Tour (1593–1652) had, as their dates indicate, completed the bulk of their work before the death of Mazarin.

In literature the first Salons date from 1616; Corneille (1606–84) was writing steadily from 1636; the first plays of Molière (1622–73) had been acted – Les Précieuses Ridicules in 1659. Pascal (1623–62) had composed Les Lettres Provinciales and Les Pensées (though the latter were not printed till 1670). In philosophy and mathematics Pascal, Descartes (1596–1650) and Fermat (1601–65) were all advancing the frontiers of human thought. The great French accomplishments both at home and abroad of the second half of the century must always be related to the first half, when the foundations were laid by Henri IV, Richelieu and Mazarin.

EXTRACTS

1. *The Character of Mazarin, as seen by the Cardinal de Retz:*

On the steps of the throne from which the hard and terrible Richelieu had destroyed rather than governed men, there was a gentle kind successor, who wished for nothing, who was so very sorry that his cardinal's dignity prevented him from humiliating himself so much as he would have wished to everybody, who drove through the streets with only two little footmen behind his carriage. . . .

His strength was to listen, to raise peoples' hopes; to give hints, to take them back again; to make clear, to confuse. He set himself up as a Richelieu, but he did not have the impudence to imitate him. He was neither so kind nor so cruel, because he remembered neither favours nor injuries. He had brains, an insinuating manner, cheerfulness, style, but his shabby mind spoilt it all. He had plenty of brains but no soul. . . .

But he did so well that he was ahead of everyone while they thought he was still by their side. (de Retz, *Memoirs*, introd. by D. Ogg, Dent, 1917, Vol. I, p. 68)

2. *The Barricades in Paris, 1648:*

. . . the common people won over by the factionists crying 'To arms!' were breaking the windows of the more well-to-do citizens and merchants in order to force them to come out and join them. Which they did not dare to do yet without an order from the town, being content to shut their shops so that at two o'clock in the afternoon it seemed as if it were a feast-day, everything being shut. There were no artisans, not even the most petty, who had not left their work, except in the rue du Montmartre, where I live, which still respected the royal authority. During this time some companies of the guards marched through the streets, which were up in arms, with tinder alight and bullet in mouth to try to make the rioters retire. But they were so insolent that they laughed at them and at their march. The grand Master was struck twice by stones before escaping from these rogues. Thus the uproar continued till night. (W. F. Reddaway, *Select Documents of European History*, Vol. II, 1492–1715, Methuen, 1930, p. 136)

3. *Origin of the name of the Fronde:*

One day Bachaumont happened to compare jestingly the *Parlement* to the school-boys who used to fling stones with a sling in the ditches round Paris, who run away the moment they spy some town-officers coming towards them, and who return to their sport as soon as those officers disappear. . . . These words were revived, and were chiefly made use of and applied after the peace was made between the king and the *Parlement* to the private faction of those who came to no accommodation with the court. We took care to keep them in vogue, for we had observed that party-names are of some help for inflaming people, and we resolved all of us to wear hatbands made in some sort like a sling, or Fronde. . . . Everything was made *a la mode de la Fronde*; bread, hats, gloves, handkerchiefs, fans, trimmings: and our party became even more in fashion by means of this trifle, than by anything else of greater moment. (de Retz, *Memoirs*, Dent, Vol. I, pp. 262–3)

FURTHER READING

C. V. Wedgwood, *Richelieu and the French Monarchy*, E.U.P., 1949

G. P. Gooch, *Courts and Cabinets*, Longmans, Green, 1944, Chaps. I–IV (Mazarin and the Fronde)

A. Huxley, *Grey Eminence* (Père Joseph), Chatto & Windus, 1941

J. Lough, *An Introduction to Seventeenth Century France*, Longmans, Green, 1954

de Retz, *Memoirs*, introd. by D. Ogg, Dent, 1917

Richelieu, *Testament Politique*, ed. L. André, Robert Laffont, 1947, Paris

XI · THE MARCHLANDS OF WESTERN EUROPE

THE northern and western boundaries of Europe are unmistakable – the Atlantic and Arctic Oceans – but for both the historian and the geographer it is less easy to fix satisfactory boundaries to the east and south. This is particularly so when one is dealing primarily with the history of western Europe. England, France, Spain and Portugal, the Italian peninsula, the Empire – these are areas obviously involved with one another, but beyond them lies a zone of transition, of countries the history of which has been only intermittently linked with that of the west and which have their own connections with areas farther east. This transitional zone is that of the marchlands of western Europe.[1]

During the sixteenth and seventeenth centuries there are four important political developments in the marchlands. In the north, Sweden rose during the seventeenth century to the temporary status of a great power, dominating the Baltic, and intimately involved in the affairs of Germany. On the eastern frontier of the Empire, ruling lands partly within and partly outside it, the Hohenzollerns of Brandenburg were laying the foundations of Prussian greatness, although Prussia did not emerge as a great power until the eighteenth century. Farther east, Russia under Ivan III and Ivan IV began the process of expansion both east and west that was, in the eighteenth century, to make of her a great colonial and European power. Finally, in the southeast the Turks had overrun the Balkans and throughout the sixteenth and seventeenth centuries were threatening to advance into central Europe by way of the Danube valley, and also to win control of the western Mediterranean.

Since the history of these four countries is only partly bound up with that of the west, it is not surprising that 1660 is for none of them a particularly significant date: the great age of

---

[1] See O. Halecki; *The Limits and Divisions of European History*, Sheed & Ward, 1950, for an interesting, if biased, discussion of where 'to draw the line'.

Sweden runs from the accession of Gustavus Adolphus in 1611 to the death of Charles XII in 1718; the foundations of Prussian greatness were laid between 1608 and 1688; Russian history enters a new chapter with the accession of Peter the Great in 1682; the Turkish pressure on central Europe was exerted from the first siege of Vienna in 1529 to the siege in 1683.

A history of the marchlands that ends about the year 1660 can therefore be only in the nature of an interim report. At that time Sweden was the most respected of the four powers, while the Turks were opening new offensives in the Mediterranean and in Transylvania – only the historian who reads the history of the next fifty years can discover that the future lay, not with Sweden and Turkey, but with Russia and Prussia, still relatively disregarded in 1660.

Sweden, 1523–1660

Untouched by Roman civilization, cut off by physical barriers, with its roots in its own Viking culture, Scandinavia remained largely isolated from the main line of European development until the sixteenth century. She lay at the end of the trade routes, on the edge of Europe.

In 1397 the whole of Scandinavia had been united under Denmark by the Union of Kalmar. Sweden was never wholly reconciled to the Union and in 1520 a noble, Gustavus Vasa, put himself at the head of a popular revolt. In 1523 the *Riksdag* (Diet) elected him King Gustavus I (1523–60). In 1527 the Church lands were confiscated and a state-controlled Church created, very similar to the one Henry VIII was to set up in England. The Church had owned 21·3 per cent of the Swedish homesteads and these lands met the ruler's need for money and the nobles' demand for territory. Wittenberg-trained preachers were already in Sweden and in 1536 the state Church became Lutheran. As in other Protestant countries a Swedish translation of the Bible (1541) helped to fix the form of the national language.

In 1537 a war with the Hanseatic League freed Sweden from the commercial control of Lübeck, while in 1544 a national army was created and the monarchy, hitherto elective, was declared hereditary. Trade was encouraged, the King – like Henry VII and Louis XI – participating himself. German miners arrived and developed the working of copper at Falun, silver at Sala and bar-iron at several centres. Gustavus had created a strong national monarchy, with two-thirds of Sweden controlled by the Treasury, a national Protestant Church, and an administrative organization – an autocracy by consent reminiscent of the other 'new monarchies' of western Europe.

Eric XIV (1560–69) introduced military reforms, and experimented with ship-building; but he suffered from wild extremes of enthusiasm and melancholy, and in 1569 he was deposed. The most important event of his reign was the acquisition of Estonia in 1561, which gave Sweden control of the Gulf of Finland.

Eric's successor, John III (1569–92), flirted with Catholicism and his son was brought up as a Catholic. John was involved in wars with Denmark and Russia, and acquired Narva from the latter in 1581. In 1587 his son was elected King of Poland and in 1592 succeeded his father as Sigismund III (1592–1604). He attempted to make Sweden Catholic again, and was suspected of being willing to sacrifice her to her rival Poland. In 1599 he was deposed by the *Riksdag* which declared him a 'Papist, oathbreaker, and enemy of the realm', and was succeeded by his uncle, Charles of Sodermanland, who was elected Charles IX (1604–11). During his short reign Charles was menaced by Denmark, which wanted to recover Sweden, and Poland, which now claimed through Sigismund the Swedish throne. More important than Charles's foreign entanglements – he intervened with some success in Russian affairs, where the state of Ivan the Terrible was dissolving in the civil war known as 'the Time of Troubles' – were his development of the army, to which each province now had to send a number of men, his encouragement of commerce and manufacture, and his foundation of the new port of Göteborg. Indeed Denmark was so alarmed by this last development that she declared war on Sweden in 1611, a few months before Charles died.

The new king, Gustavus Adolphus (1611–32), was seventeen. He had been trained by his father to rule: when he was nine he had attended meetings of the *Råd* (Council, roughly equivalent to the Tudor Privy Council); by the time he was thirteen he was receiving ambassadors; at fifteen he had been created

Duke of Västmanland and became for all practical purposes co-ruler with his father.

Gustavus had been given a good education. While not a scholar, he was full of curiosity, and an excellent linguist. As well as Swedish he spoke German (which he had learnt from his mother) like a native; Latin, Dutch, French and Italian 'as if born to them'; and understood something of Spanish, English, Polish and Russian! He had studied history, law, rhetoric, arithmetic, geometry – and the new methods of fighting which were being developed by his idol, Maurice of Nassau. Like his father he was a sincere Calvinist in a mainly Lutheran country. He was a huge man, with broad shoulders, golden hair and tawny beard – in later life his Italian mercenaries called him *il re d'oro* or 'the golden lion'.

Gustavus began his reign by securing peace at home and abroad. In 1612 he accepted the Charter by which he undertook to give the nobles their share of the great offices of state, and to consult the *Råd* and the *Riksdag* on all matters of lawmaking and of foreign affairs – a guarantee against royal misgovernment which it was not necessary to enforce. In 1613 he brought the recently-begun Danish war to an end by the Treaty of Knäred. Each country gave up its conquests; the Swedes were promised free passage through the Sound; the Danes were guaranteed freedom of trade with Courland and Livonia in the eastern Baltic. They were also left in control of the west coast of Sweden as security for the payment of an indemnity of one million *dalers* by the Swedes.

In thus buying off the nobles and the Danes Gustavus had secured his western flank, and was able to concentrate on securing concessions from Russia. That country was torn by civil war, and both Sweden and Poland, led by the rival branches of the house of Vasa, hoped to profit from the breakdown of the power which had seemed so menacing under Ivan the Terrible. Gustavus's policy proved successful. In 1617 the new Tsar, Michael Romanoff, acknowledged Sweden's rule in Karelia and Ingria by the Treaty of Stolbova. Sweden thus controlled both coasts of the Gulf of Finland, and Gustavus burst out: 'I trust to God it shall hereafter be hard for the Russians to cross or leap over that stream.' [1]

From 1617 to 1629 Gustavus was intermittently at war

[1] I. Andersson, *A History of Sweden*, Weidenfeld & Nicolson, 1956, p. 162.

with the second of his adversaries, Poland. The war is episodic and confusing, but the causes are clear enough. The struggle can be regarded as in many ways a northern extension of the Thirty Years' War. Poland was Catholic, Sigismund was connected by marriage with the Austrian Habsburgs, the country was a centre of the militant Counter-Reformation and was encouraged by the Jesuits to go crusading against schismatic Russia and heretic Scandinavia. Both countries were ambitious to control the north German Baltic coast, but until the power of Denmark had been completely destroyed (as it was by Wallenstein in 1628) Gustavus dare not commit himself to full-scale intervention in Germany, for fear of a 'stab in the heel', but was eager for a limited war. 'What have we to expect of King Sigismund,' he declared to the *Riksdag*, 'who is not only evil himself, but allows himself to be governed by that Devil's party the Jesuits, the authors of the grievous tyranny in Spain, France, and elsewhere.' [1]

Meanwhile, with an army of 19,000 men and a fleet of about 160 ships, Gustavus landed in Livonia and captured Riga in 1621. He was unable to over-run the country though, and next year signed a three-years' truce with the Poles. When the truce expired in 1625 Gustavus renewed the war, and in January 1626 won a great victory at Wallhof against odds of five to one. It marked Sweden's rise to the rank of a great military power – a rank that they held until 1709. Gustavus left Livonia, and later in the year occupied Prussia and the coast as far south and west as Danzig. This was a critical step. He was moving towards Germany.

Richelieu, who knew of Gustavus's plans to start an offensive war against the Emperor and who was himself alarmed at the latter's success, encouraged the Poles and Swedes to reach an agreement, in order that the Swedish King might have his hands free to intervene in Germany. As a result, peace was made in 1629 (the Truce of Altmark), by which Sweden obtained Livonia and ports on the Prussian coast, together with customs dues – 500,000 *dalers* in 1629 – which would help to finance a German campaign.

Gustavus was now poised for the invasion of Germany. What, meanwhile, had he achieved at home in constitutional

[1] Andersson, p. 165.

and economic matters? He developed and used both the *Råd* and *Riksdag*. From the former he chose a small committee the members of which were appointed for life and, instructed by Gustavus, governed while the King was abroad. In 1626 the nobility was limited to those who then held the title and they were expected to work for the good of the kingdom, a hall being built in Stockholm in which they could meet.

Between 1614 and 1634 the central administration was organized in five *Collegia* (departments) headed by five ministers of state; the Steward (justice, 1614), the Treasurer and the Chancellor (1618), the Marshal and the Admiral (1634). Of these, the Chancery rapidly became the most important organ of government, thanks to the activities of the Chancellor, Axel Oxenstierna, who worked in all things with Gustavus and carried on his plans unchanged for sixteen years after the King's death.

> His retentive memory, his astonishing mastery of detail, were matched by an ability to select what was important . . . He turned from war to administration, from administration to diplomacy, with sovereign unconcern; unhurried, untiring, precise, acute, copious in Latin and German and a Swedish grievously bespattered with both.[1]

Eleven years older than the king, Oxenstierna was calmer and perhaps more civilized. When Gustavus once remarked 'If we were all as cold as you, we should freeze,' the Chancellor replied, 'And if we were all as hot as Your Majesty we should burn.' The combination of phlegm and choler made a good partnership.

The main legislative organ, the *Riksdag*, although still not further developed than the English parliament in the fourteenth century, was used by Gustavus to get popular opinion, particularly that of the free peasants, on his side, and was encouraged to discuss, in a secret committee, foreign affairs (1627). It consisted of four Estates, the numbers attending (as distinct from the numbers entitled to attend) being approximately as follows:

Nobility	200
Clergy	70
Burgers	60
Peasants	200[2]

[1] M. Roberts, *Gustavus Adolphus, 1611–32*, Longmans, Green, 1953, Vol. I, p. 272.

[2] Roberts, p. 301.

An attempt to give the Church a more centralized organization in 1623 was rejected by the clergy themselves. The following year local government was reformed, in a manner
reminiscent of the Tudors. The country was divided into
twenty-three districts, with a representative of the king in
each – 'viceroys' Oxenstierna called them – who was intended
to act as a link between central and local government.

Peace at home and war abroad, both demanded an active
enlightened economic policy, for Sweden was under-populated
even by seventeenth century standards, with less than one and
a half million people, and no towns of any size. Fifteen new
towns were started by Gustavus, a system of free schools
(*gymnasia*) begun and great endowments made to the existing
university at Uppsala. Göteborg, situated at the one point
where Sweden's territory touched the North Sea coast, was
enlarged in 1619. The country's economic strength lay in
its mineral resources and, after the conquest of the south
Baltic coast, in tolls and profits from the Baltic sea trade.
The early seventeenth century was a time of metal starvation.
Copper, of which Sweden had a virtual monopoly, was in
great demand; Spain had adopted a copper coinage in 1596,
and the metal was essential for the development of cannon –
as was iron, with which Sweden was also well-supplied. Copper
exports increased from 100 tons in 1548 to 2,600 tons in 1650,
iron exports during the same period rose from 1,600 tons to
20,000 tons. When Gustavus visited the copper mines at Falun
he exclaimed: 'What potentate has a palace like to that in
which we now stand?' [1] And a modern economic historian
has commented, 'Without copper, presumably, Sweden's part
in the Thirty Years' War would not have been feasible.' [2]

The aim of all seventeenth century governments was to
control trade and manufactures in the interests of the state,
and Sweden was no exception. Oxenstierna said, 'The
King's Majesty controls and steers mines, commerce, manufactures, and customs just as a steersman steers his ship.' [3]
Gustavus was particularly anxious to make industry and commerce equip and pay for the new army he was creating and

[1] Roberts, II, p. 89.
[2] E. Heckscher, quoted in *Econ. Hist. Rev., Second Series*, Vol. IX, No. 1, p. 132.
[3] *C.M.H.*, IV, p. 187.

the ships he was building. Regulation made taxation easier; trade with foreigners was confined to thirteen towns, and internal trade to market towns. Industrial standards were supervised by reorganized guilds. Chartered companies were given a monopoly of foreign trade in copper, iron, corn and salt. Dutch and French traders and technicians – notably Louis de Geer, a Liègeois Calvinist from Amsterdam – were responsible for most of the progress made and for a time the Dutch really controlled the economic life of the country.

These measures were so successful that when Gustavus left to take part in the Thirty Years' War in 1630 the army he took with him had been completely fitted out from Swedish sources. On the other hand, he was no more able to balance his budget in time of war than any other statesman. The main sources of revenue available to Gustavus were the traditional taxes such as market and mill tolls and excise; the alienation of crown lands; tax-farming; the establishment of monopolies; and tolls from the conquered Baltic ports. The last provided at least 10 per cent of his income. Mercenaries however were expensive, and though the revenue trebled (1623: 2,550,000 *dalers*; 1632: 6,500,000 *dalers*) the King's debt in 1629 was 7,000,000 *dalers*.

Gustavus's army consisted of about 70,000 men, of which 40,000 were active troops while the remainder were used on garrison duty and to guard the rather vulnerable lines of communication. In general, the cavalry and artillery were Swedish (there was conscription from fifteen to fifty), while the bulk of the infantry were mercenaries, including many Scots and some English who were able later to apply in the English Civil War the lessons they had learnt under Gustavus. For the King taught the seventeenth century how to fight.

Military ideas were in a state of flux, and Gustavus adopted or adapted all the most valuable innovations, especially those of Maurice of Nassau. The object of his changes was to make the army flexible and mobile. Much attention was paid to artillery; the guns were made lighter, and the King introduced a light regimental gun, a three-pounder that could be moved by three men or one horse. Instead of a great block of pikemen, surrounded by an unwieldy collection of musketeers, Gustavus organized his army in two or three lines, each line not more than six deep. The lines were broken into a

'chessboard' formation of small alternate blocks of pikemen
and musketeers, with gaps between through which the cavalry
could operate.   Musketeers were also attached to the cavalry,
who were ordered to advance slowly, gallop the last fifty
yards, and then use their swords.   The musketeers were armed
with matchlocks in place of arquebuses and were arranged in
ranks so that while one rank was firing the rest were preparing
to fire or reloading.   In this way a relatively continuous rate
of fire could be kept up;   alternatively, the ranks could fire a
salvo simultaneously.   All this demanded strict training, good
discipline and reliable equipment.

The list of lesser innovations is endless: field-chaplains;
some attempt at uniform (blue and yellow, or blue with red
facings); charge wired to the shot; and so on.   In the second
half of the century the Swedish methods – linear order, training, combination of arms, light regimental artillery – were
adopted all over Europe, and their immediate influence on
Turenne and Cromwell was great.

While Sweden had been fighting Poland in the eastern
Baltic, the Imperial general Wallenstein had gained control
of the western shores from Denmark to Stralsund.   By 1628
Denmark was decisively defeated, and the Catholic Habsburg
power faced Sweden across the Baltic Sea.   It was no coincidence that Sweden's first direct intervention in the Thirty Years'
War was to raise the siege of Stralsund in 1628.   'We must go
and find the Emperor at Stralsund, or he will come and find
us at Kalmar,' said Gustavus, speaking to the *Riksdag*, '. . .
Pomerania and the Baltic coast are the outworks of Sweden.'

War was declared in October 1629, and in June 1630
Gustavus began to disembark his troops at Peenemünde.
Although he styled himself *Restitutor Germaniae* and wrote to
Oxenstierna that he hoped '. . . to touch off a rocket of
universal rebellion throughout Germany', he got little help
at first from the Germans and none at all from the Protestant
Electors of Saxony and Brandenburg.   The invasion pro-
ceeded slowly therefore, and by January 1631 the Swedes had
occupied only the Baltic coastal states of Pomerania and
Mecklenburg.   Then Sweden and France concluded the
Treaty of Bärwalde, by which Gustavus was to keep an army of
36,000 in the field until 1636, for which Richelieu would pay

an annual subsidy of 400,000 *dalers*. The sack of Magdeburg and the pressure of Gustavus at last persuaded the Protestant Electors to support him, and he began to move south.

On September 17 one of the few great battles of the war took place at Breitenfeld, a few miles north of Leipzig. Gustavus had about 17,000 foot, 7,500 horse and 60 guns, together with a Saxon army of 18,000 under the Elector. The army of the League and the Emperor, under Tilly, consisted of 23,000 foot, 12,000 horse and 30 guns. When the battle had been going on for two hours the Saxons, on the left wing, broke and fled; but Gustavus's flexible formation enabled the Swedes not only to turn and face an encircling movement on their own right wing, but also to check the Imperial forces on their broken left. Late in the afternoon, the wind and the sun having moved round behind him, Gustavus in his turn launched his attack, cutting off the Imperial cavalry from their own infantry, recapturing the Saxon guns and finally driving the broken army back along the Leipzig road. The Swedes lost 2,100 men, the Imperial losses were 7,600 dead on the field and 6,000 prisoners. The battle was a triumph for the King, and for the new style of fighting.

Gustavus now had a choice of plans: he could drive southeast to Vienna, or turn southwest through Franconia to the middle Rhineland. To seize imperial Vienna would be spectacular, but it would not be a safe base and the long lines of communication would be exposed to Catholic states, to the doubtful Elector of Saxony, to hostile Poland. Gustavus marched southwest instead. In this direction the land to the north was in friendly hands, he was able to link up with the Protestant Rhineland and to be in close touch with France – too close for Richelieu, who protested when the Swedes occupied territory on the left bank of the Rhine. Gustavus set up his winter quarters at Mainz.

In 1632 Tilly was wounded to death and the army of the Catholic League defeated at the battle of the Lech, and Gustavus, marching through Bavaria towards Vienna, occupied Munich in May. The Emperor had meanwhile recalled Wallenstein, and Gustavus failed to drive him from Nuremberg, where the Imperial forces lay encamped. Then word came that Wallenstein was moving north to Saxony, to conquer, or perhaps to negotiate with, the lukewarm Elector.

Gustavus, his communications seriously threatened, moved north also. On November 16 the two armies met at Lützen, very close to the earlier battlefield of Breitenfeld. After a fierce struggle the Swedes were victorious. But Gustavus had been killed early in the battle, cut off in an isolated cavalry movement by the November mist and hanging battle-smoke. He was thirty-seven.

If Gustavus had lived, would he have been able to end the war? The answer would seem to be: probably not.

> Gustavus was one of those born conquerors to whom peace is an ideal state, always for excellent reasons unattainable. He had never in his life made any conclusion to a war that was more than an armistice and it was hardly likely that he had changed his character in the course of his last year on earth. . . . History has too many records of aged warriors, for the mellowing of Gustavus to seem an altogether probable theory.[1]

For sixteen years Gustavus in a way ruled Sweden from his grave. He left behind a girl of six, Christina, and Oxenstierna was able to carry on his policy unchanged, so that the Peace of Westphalia is the logical conclusion of Gustavus's work. The Chancellor united Sweden and the Protestant princes of western and central Germany in the League of Heilbronn, under the command of Bernard of Saxe-Weimar, who had taken charge at Lützen when Gustavus was killed. At first the League was successful, but in 1634 Spain entered the war, large bodies of troops were moved north through the Valtelline, and the Swedes were decisively defeated at Nördlingen. As a result Richelieu was forced to intervene directly, and Sweden ceased to play an important part in the war. At the Peace of Westphalia Gustavus obtained his posthumous reward: Western Pomerania; Bremen and Verden; and the port of Wismar in Mecklenburg; territories which gave Sweden the right to be represented in the German Diet. The Swedes now held all the important north German ports except Hamburg and Danzig.

Gustavus is the greatest King of Sweden, though it is difficult to assess the relative importance of the different

[1] C. V. Wedgwood, *The Thirty Years' War*, Cape, 1938, p. 331.

aspects of his greatness. Is it as the essential creator of a powerful, though short-lived, Swedish empire based on the Baltic – the *dominium maris Baltici* – that one should praise him? Perhaps he achieved too much:

> The conclusion seems thus inescapable, that Gustav Adolf committed Sweden to a position which in the long run (though not immediately) she could not hope to sustain; . . . But it is not easy to point to a flaw in the chain of political logic which led him step by step to the landing at Peenemünde.[1]

Are the less spectacular, but more lasting successes at home, in the spheres of economic progress and constitutional development, his true title to fame? What of his effect on military progress? Even isolated England was interested, and bought the *Swedish Intelligencer*:

> Wherein, out of the Truest and choysest Information, are the famous Actions of that War-like Prince Historically led along; from the Norimberg Leaguer, unto the day of his death, at the Victory of Lutzen. . . . The times and places of every Action, being so sufficiently observed and described; that the Reader may finde both Truth and Reason in it. . . .

What part did religion play in his actions? Gustavus was a sincere Calvinist; 'He thinks the ship cannot sink that carries him,' observed a contemporary, and nineteenth century historians tended to see him as the blond Lion of the North [2] roaring to the defence of his fellow Protestants:

> there dwelt and reigned a certain King in Sweden; . . . there was a Gustav Adolf overseas, an Oliver Cromwell overseas; and 'a company of poor men' were found capable of taking Lucifer by the beard

wrote Carlyle. It is certainly true that with his death the religious element in the Thirty Years' War died too, but today historians notice also that when Sweden entered the war in 1629, Gustavus, addressing the *Riksdag*, declared:

> The Papists are on the Baltic, their whole aim is to destroy Swedish commerce, and soon to plant a foot on the

---

[1] Roberts, Vol. II, p. 779.
[2] In 1546 a prophecy attributed to Paracelsus declared that a golden lion would come out of the north and destroy the Eagle. See *Isaiah* xli, v. 25.

southern shores of our Fatherland. Sweden is in danger
from the power of the Habsburg; that is all, but it is enough;
that power must be met, swiftly and strongly.[1]

The emphasis is on politics rather than religion. It is only
in 1630, when Gustavus is appealing to the people of Brandenburg to support him, that the crusading motive is stressed:

> . . . the Emperor and his friends are resolved to go on
> until the Evangelical religion in the Empire is completely
> rooted out, . . . God is fighting with the devil. If the
> Elector [of Brandenburg] will hold to God, let him join me;
> if the devil, he will have me to contend with; no third
> course will be allowed.[2]

After Gustavus's death, Oxenstierna persuaded the Estates
to accept the Form of Government, which he claimed that
Gustavus had approved. This document completed the reform of the administration, and gave increased powers to the
Råd at the expense of the *Riksdag*. In 1644 there was a brief
war with Denmark, ended by the Treaty of Brömsebro, in
which Sweden secured Halland and freedom from all tolls in
the Sound. In that year Gustavus's daughter Christina came
of age; an intelligent, masculine type of woman, who read
Thucydides and talked with the French philosopher Descartes
at five o'clock in the morning. She announced that she had
no intention of getting married. She ceased to consult Oxenstierna and persuaded the *Riksdag* to acknowledge her cousin
Charles as her successor. As early as 1649 she was speaking
of abdication. Meanwhile the Crown lands were rapidly
being alienated, and during her reign the numbers of the
nobility were doubled. After ten years' rule she abdicated
(1654), became a Catholic, and left Sweden. She died in
Rome in 1689.

Charles X (1654–60) immediately recalled Oxenstierna and
when the old man died a month later made his son, Eric,
Chancellor. Then, by the 'Reduction', he took back a large
part of the alienated Crown lands – an essential step if the work
of ruling was to be carried on. In 1656 the first Swedish

[1] W. F. Reddaway, *Select Documents of European History*, Vol. II, 1492–1715,
Methuen, 1930, p. 124.
[2] Reddaway, p. 125.

bank was set up, and the iron and steel works at Ekilstuna founded.

The greater part of the reign was devoted to a war with Poland, which soon led to the intervention of Russia, Denmark and, ultimately, Brandenburg. The uneasy truce between Sweden and Poland had expired in 1651, and in 1654 the Polish Vasa ruler, John Casimir, protested at the transference of the Swedish crown from Christina to Charles. (The elder branch of the Vasa family, ruling in Poland, had always felt that they ought to rule in Sweden also.) In these circumstances it is not surprising that Charles X decided to get his blow in first and by doing so to acquire Poland's Baltic coastline.

Charles declared war in 1655 and was at first very successful, routing the Poles and occupying Warsaw, but his success brought the usual alliance of all Sweden's enemies against her. The details of the subsequent fighting are complex, but one may say that Sweden had the best of it. Charles died in 1660 of a fever, at the age of thirty-seven, and the Council of Regency which ruled for his infant son made peace, encouraged by Mazarin's envoys. The two treaties of Oliva and Copenhagen (1660) are usually known collectively as the Treaty of Oliva. By then the Polish branch of the Vasa family gave up all claim to the Swedish throne, and recognized the Great Elector as independent ruler of East Prussia, while Sweden acquired the province of Scania in south Sweden, hitherto held by Denmark.

Together with the Peace of Westphalia and the Treaty of the Pyrenees, the Treaty of Oliva makes the mid-seventeenth century a convenient terminal point, with France supreme in the west and Sweden in the north. 'For the first time in the seventeenth century, Sweden was at peace with all the world.' But the Treaty of Oliva was only a 'half-time' treaty. Sweden, Denmark, Poland, Brandenburg and Russia renewed their struggles in the second half of the century, and in the end it was Brandenburg and Russia which triumphed at the expense of the others. This must be taken into account when assessing the success of the Swedish rulers in the first half of the century. By great efforts they had made of Sweden a first-class power, and had turned the Baltic into a Swedish lake, but the very extent of those efforts, when prolonged for a further half century, ruined the country and the Swedish dominion passed away. It is arguable that the more permanent achievements of settled government and economic development are those upon which their claim to greatness should be based.

EXTRACTS

1. *Gustavus's Character, as seen by the English envoy, Sir Henry Vane, 1632:*

. . . he hath often told me, . . . That he would give all he had to be Master of his Passions; but that when he begins to be moved, he hath something rises in his Brain, that makes him forget what he saith or doth; that this he finds in himself, and the Inconveniences that grow thereof, as soon as he is posed again; but yet he cannot get it mastered, though he hath often designed the same; and therefore he hopes God and all the World will forgive him. (Quoted by M. Roberts, *Gustavus Adolphus 1611–1632*, Longmans, Green, 1953, Vol. I, p. 786)

2. *Gustavus's Character, as seen by a Scottish mercenary:*

For though he had bin no King, he was a brave warriour, and which is more, a good man, magnificent, wise, just, meeke, indued with learning, and the gift of tongues, and as he had strength of body, and a manlike stature, he had also the ornaments of the minde, fitting a brave commander.

O would to GOD I had once such a leader againe to fight such another day; in this old quarrel! and though I died standing, I should be persuaded I died well. (R. Monro, *His Expedition with the worthy Scots Regiment . . .*, 1637)

FURTHER READING

M. Roberts, *Gustavus Adolphus, 1611–1632*, Longmans, Green, Vol. I, 1953, Vol. II, 1958
I. Andersson, *A History of Sweden*, Weidenfeld & Nicolson, 1956
C. V. Wedgwood, *The Thirty Years' War*, Cape, 1938, Chapter VII
Trevor-Roper, *Historical Essays*, Macmillan, 1957

The Rise of Brandenburg, 1415–1660

In 1415 the Emperor Sigismund gave to Frederick Hohenzollern of Nuremberg the Electorate of Brandenburg. During the next 450 years this relatively obscure Franconian family swallowed up the rest of Germany and became themselves Emperors, ruling until 1918.

The success of Brandenburg, poor in soil, poor in men, lacking defensible frontiers, is largely a tribute to the Hohenzollern rulers, whose political testaments show with what hard-headed ability they weighed their opportunities. For two hundred years they cautiously and unobtrusively extended their frontiers:

> The Hohenzollern Electors were not great captains nor great gamblers. . . . They seem to have taken the measure of their own capacity. They nibbled and they negotiated. They also married or gave in marriage, with prudence and foresight, and they won the reward of nibbling, negotiating, and marrying in the right way.[1]

German states were liable to be partitioned among the sons of the ruler and gradually break up into ridiculous fragments. Brandenburg avoided this danger when the Elector Albert Achilles (1471–86) made his *Dispositio Achillea* in 1473. This laid down that Brandenburg should never be partitioned, but should pass undivided to the eldest son. The northern lands grew to be more important than the original homeland of the Hohenzollerns. (The principle of the *Dispositio* was reaffirmed at Gera in 1603.)

During the first half of the sixteenth century the inhabitants of Brandenburg began to turn Lutheran, partly as a result of the influence of Lutheran Saxony to the south. The Elector Joachim II (1535–71) adopted at first an ambiguous attitude to the Reformation; at last, after the Peace of Augsburg, he secularized the three sees of Lebus, Havelberg and Brandenburg, and the official religion became a strict if cautious Lutheranism.

Under the Elector John Sigismund (1608–19) three important developments took place. In 1613 the Elector became a Calvinist. Since his people were Lutheran, as were those of the surrounding states of Saxony, Pomerania and Prussia, religious toleration (at least for the adherents of the two main branches of German Protestantism) seemed the best solution.

---

[1] J. A. R. Marriott and C. G. Robertson, *The Evolution of Prussia*, O.U.P. 1937, p. 55.

Then the Electorate gained an interest in the Rhineland when the Treaty of Xanten (1614) settled the Cleves-Jülich crisis by assigning Cleves, Mark and Ravensburg to John Sigismund. Thirdly, the Duchy of East Prussia was acquired by Brandenburg. Prussia had been converted and colonized during the Middle Ages by the Crusading Order of the Teutonic Knights. In 1511 the Order, now weak and seeking protection, had elected as High Master a member of the Hohenzollern family, Albert. In 1525 he became a Lutheran and secularized East Prussia, which he now held as a vassal of the Polish King. John Sigismund had married his descendant, Anne of Prussia, in 1594 and on the death of her father Prussia passed, unwillingly but permanently, into the hands of Brandenburg. Thus to the west on the Rhine, and to the east on the Baltic coast, the lines of the Electorate's expansion were marked out.

It was very nearly disastrous for Brandenburg that the Thirty Years' War coincided with the rule of probably the most inept of the Hohenzollerns, George William (1619–40),

> . . . a pleasant, pious, well-intentioned young man, with a Teutonic appetite for meat and drink, a third-rate brain, and fourth-rate moral power.[1]

He was unable to support either side efficiently, armies occupied his lands and towards the end of his reign he retired miserably to East Prussia.

Frederick William, the Great Elector (1640–88), succeeded to a country which seemed to be on the verge of partition among its envious neighbours:

> Pomerania is lost, Jülich is lost, we hold Prussia like an eel by the tail, and we must mortgage the Mark.[2]

He immediately ended his father's policy of half-hearted support for the Emperor. In 1641 he concluded a truce with Sweden, and five years later he married the eldest daughter of the ruler of the United Provinces, Frederick Henry. In these ways the Great Elector established Brandenburg on the winning side. At the Peace of Westphalia she obtained the secularized bishoprics of Halberstadt and Minden, and the

---

[1] Marriott and Robertson, p. 73.   [2] Wedgwood, p. 439.

right of succession in Magdeburg; a confirmation of her right
to Cleves, Mark and Ravensburg; and the eastern, poorer
half of Pomerania. Brandenburg had emerged, against all
probability, as after all the strongest Protestant state in the
Empire; her territories were scattered, but they controlled
the main lines of communication from north to south, lying
across the Rhine, the Weser, the Elbe and the Oder.

The Great Elector pursued a tortuous foreign policy,
changing sides as and when it pleased him, with the dual aims
of freeing East Prussia from Polish overlordship and obtaining
Western Pomerania, to which he had a good claim on paper,
from the Swedes. In the second of these he was unsuccessful –
it was not till 1653 that he was even able to get Sweden out
of Eastern Pomerania, where she had remained illegally after
Westphalia. In the war between Sweden and Poland (1655–
60) he at first supported Sweden, and then sold the help of his
army of 27,000 men to John Casimir of Poland, who in return
gave up all claim over East Prussia. This was confirmed in
the Treaty of Oliva in 1660. (During the years 1672–88,
Frederick pursued a similarly variable policy towards France.)
Foreigners watched with admiration. The Venetian ambassador wrote:

> The Elector has many states, little money, good soldiers,
> great ambitions and is devoted solely to his interests.

More succinctly, a French observer called him 'the most
accomplished fox in Europe'.

Diplomatic success depended on the possession of a strong
army; this could only be built up by efficient taxation, and
that in turn depended on a centralized, organized government. Development along these lines began before 1660,
though the most important changes took place after that date.
The following summary therefore includes some changes
which took place in the second half of the century.

In all his territories the Great Elector pursued a policy of
increasing the rights of the nobles, particularly over their
peasants, while taking away their political power, and of
obtaining for the central government powers of taxation
which made it independent of the local Estates. This was
achieved in Brandenburg in 1653, in Cleves by the enactments

of 1660 and 1661 and in Prussia in 1663. Generalizing, one
may say that this policy was most acceptable in Prussia, and
met with the greatest opposition in the Rhineland. Ultimately in each province there was a Governor, with full power
under the Elector, served by regularly-paid officials who were
responsible to the central government, while in local matters
there was a working understanding between the Elector and
the gentry.

In Berlin there was a Central Council of State, with sub-
divisions dealing with foreign policy (the Chancery), Finance,
War and Justice. From 1658 onwards the Great Elector's
chief minister and right-hand man was Otto von Schwerin.
Their main object was to work towards the fusion of the
three groups of states which made up Brandenburg–Prussia –
as one means to this end a unified postal system was introduced – and to make the state prosperous. A prosperous
state could bear taxation, taxation was needed to build an
efficient, relatively large army, a large army was needed to
defend the state and to gain Western Pomerania: such is a
crude, but essentially accurate blueprint of the Great Elector's
policy, though his coins might carry the words *Pro Deo et
Populo*.

To make the state prosperous, agriculture was encouraged
and foreign immigrants were welcomed. Potato-growing
and dairy-farming were developed, mulberry trees introduced
and the ubiquitous Dutch given every encouragement. A
canal was cut to link the Spree and the Oder; perhaps echoing
Colbert, Frederick William declared that commerce and
navigation were the two chief props of the state. The population of Berlin rose during the reign from 6,000 to 30,000.
Contemporaries marvelled that a letter could get from Königs-
berg to Berlin in four days.

Besides the powers of taxation that Frederick William had
obtained from the nobles, new taxes were introduced – for
instance, an excise on beer and a land tax. The money was
spent on the official and the '*miles perpetuus*' – the creation of
a bureaucracy and a standing army. The army grew during
the reign from 4,000 to 27,000, the total population (excluding
Prussia) being about 400,000. Austria had fifteen times as
many people, but her army was less than four times as large.

Most of the Great Elector's work was done after 1660, but

the lines along which it was to develop had been indicated by that year. On these developments his successors built a powerful state. Carlyle wrote:

> There hardly ever came to sovereign power a young man of twenty under more distressing, hopeless-looking circumstances. . . . He found Brandenburg annihilated, and he left Brandenburg sound and flourishing; a great country, or already on the way towards greatness . . . he was essentially an Industrial man; great in organising, regulating, in constraining chaotic heaps to become cosmic for him. He drains bogs, settles colonies in the waste-places of his Dominions, cuts canals; unweariedly encourages trade and work.
>
> [In youth he was] A thickset stalwart figure; with brisk eyes, and high strong irregularly-Roman nose . . . [in old age] a sedate, ponderous, wrinkly old man, eyes slightly puckered (eyes *busier* than mouth); a face well-ploughed by Time, and not found unfruitful; one of the largest, most laborious, potent faces (in an ocean of circumambient periwig) to be met with in that Century.

In the eighteenth century Frederick the Great had the Great Elector's coffin opened and, putting his hand on the corpse's, said to the bystanders:

Messieurs, celui-ci a fait de grandes choses.

Extracts

1. *The Great Elector on Toleration, 1652:*

We believe that no Lutheran Elector or prince in the whole Roman Empire can be found who would act towards the Calvinists with our impartiality. . . . If peace-loving theologians could be found (a great rarity to-day) who would restrain their untimely and needlessly bitter zeal so as to refrain from unchristian reviling, slander and condemnation in school and pulpit, we should not hesitate to give them places in the theological faculty also. But the Lutheran Estates cannot seriously suppose that we should commit the young men who will serve in church and state to teachers who revile, slander and condemn our religion and thereby make us hated by our subjects. Thereby we should burden our conscience. (W. F. Reddaway, *Select Documents of European History*, Vol. II, Methuen, 1930, pp. 188–9)

2. *Frederick the Great on the Great Elector, 1751:*

He had all the qualities which make great men, and Providence furnished him with occasions to display them. He was prudent when youth is usually sowing its wild oats. He fought only to defend his country and succour his allies. He was cautious and wise, which made him a great statesman; laborious and humane, which made him a great prince. Insensible to the seductions of love, his only weakness was for his wife. If he loved wine and company, he set limits to his indulgence. His warm temper sometimes led to a loss of self-control; but if he failed to repress the first emotion, he always mastered the second, and his heart fully repaired the mistakes of his hot blood. Prosperity could not intoxicate him nor misfortunate break his spirit. Magnanimous, polite, generous, humane, he never belied his character. He became the restorer and defender of his country, the founder of the power of Brandenburg, the arbiter of his equals, the honour of his nation. In a word, his life is his eulogy. (Quoted in G. P. Gooch, *Frederick the Great*, Longmans, Green, 1947, p. 301)

FURTHER READING

J. A. R. Marriott and C. G. Robertson, *The Evolution of Prussia*, O.U.P., 1915
F. Schevill, *The Great Elector*, C.U.P., 1947

Russia, 1462–1667

The original Russian state, based on the steppes of the Ukraine and with its capital at Kiev, had been destroyed during the Mongol invasion of Europe in the thirteenth century. The shattered fragments survived as duchies in the forested areas to the north. Moscow, though well-situated at the intersection of a number of water-routes, was then only an isolated military settlement, paying tribute to its Mongol overlords. When the Mongol empire began to disintegrate in the fifteenth century, however, the duchy of Moscow became the nucleus of the second Russian state.

This new Russia was isolated from western Europe in almost every way. Its religion was Orthodox, its people therefore schismatics in the eyes of the Catholic world; its alphabet, based on that of the Greeks, was an obstacle to communication; the forests and frosts to the north, the Turks and Tartars to the south, were each in their different ways formidable barriers. In the sixteenth century Russia's Western neighbours attempted to maintain this isolation:

> . . . it was the deliberate policy of the intermediate states, which were continually at war with Moscow and jeopardised by her ambition, to keep the Russians at as low a level of civilisation as possible, to hinder them from improving their army in accordance with West European ideas, to prevent them from competing in industries; and they did what they could to shut Russia away and check intercourse with the West.[1]

Russia's attempt to westernize herself provides one of the two constant themes in her history.

To Russians, it was the West which had lost the tradition of the Roman Empire; it was the Catholics who were the schismatics in religion; Constantine had moved the capital of the Roman Empire from Rome to Constantinople, and the Empire had survived there till the city fell in 1453. Now her mantle had descended on Moscow, which had been converted and civilized from Byzantium. At Pskov a monk wrote:

> Two Romes have fallen, but the third is standing, and there shall be no fourth.

The other constant theme in Russian history has been her expansion into, and development of, the empty lands to the east, the steppes and forests of Asia. It is a theme in some ways similar to the movement of the American frontier, in others like the acquisition of a colonial empire.

In their struggles with the Tartars the Russians had developed a specialized type of fighting frontiersman, the Cossack, organized in semi-autonomous 'hosts' under an elected chief, which were named after the region in which they operated – the host of the Don against the Turks; that of the Dnieper against the Poles; that of the Urals against the Tartars. In this last area expansion was rapid in search of open pasture and of trade, especially in furs. When Cossacks settled, their place on the frontier was taken by others, who moved on. 'We serve for grass and water, not for lands and estates,' declared

[1] *C.M.H.*, V, p. 512.

these prototypes of the cowboy. Progress was astoundingly rapid. They would go, it was said, 'with crucifix, axe and boots to the end of the world'. The Urals were crossed in 1581, and by 1639 there was a Cossack settlement at Okhotsk on the Pacific coast, 7,000 miles from Moscow. Twenty years later there were about 70,000 Russians in Siberia; compare this figure with the 3,000 French in Canada at about the same date. The expansion of Russia into Asia is of greater historical significance than her confused internal history during this period.

Ivan III (1462–1505), the Great, known to the Russians as 'the collector of lands', created a viable Russian state. He defeated the Mongolian Tartars in 1481 and again in 1487, and added vastly to his territory in the north and west, absorbing especially the great municipal trading republic of Novgorod. He was conscious of his Imperial role: he married Zoë, the niece of the last Byzantine Emperor, Constantine Palaeologus, and adopted the Byzantine two-headed eagle as his emblem, thus underlining the claim of Moscow to be the 'Third Rome'.[1] When the Emperor Frederick offered him the title of king, he replied – with some justification, one feels: 'We have desired it from no one, and do not desire it now.' His son, Vasily III (1505–33), continued his father's work, annexing Pskov and Ryazan, and taking Smolensk from Poland.

Under Ivan IV (1533–84), the Terrible, Russia's expansion continued. The Cossacks, as we have seen, entered Siberia; the Tartars were defeated at Kazan, and Astrakhan on the Caspian Sea was annexed (1554). (The Tartar menace was not quite destroyed, for in 1571 the Crimean Tartars sacked Moscow.) Livonia was occupied from 1561 to 1582, but by the latter year the combined attacks of Poland and Sweden had forced Ivan to give back the province to the former and to cede to the latter all the Russian coastline of the Gulf of Finland, except for a narrow strip at the mouth of the River Neva.

New contacts had been made between western Europe and

---

[1] Ivan employed Western architects to rebuild parts of the Kremlin, notably Fioraventi, who had worked at Bologna and Milan and had built a bridge for the King of Hungary, before moving on to Russia in 1475.

Russia. In 1533 an English expedition under Chancellor, while searching for the North-East Passage, had discovered the White Sea and had reached Moscow. In 1555 the English Muscovy Company was set up to trade with Russia and an English ambassador was soon established in the capital. Later in the century Ivan made an unsuccessful offer of marriage to Elizabeth I.

The internal history of Ivan's reign falls into three distinct parts. From 1533 to 1547, during his minority, there was chaos as the *boyars* (feudal nobles) fought and intrigued among themselves for power. When he was seventeen Ivan was crowned (with the title of 'Tsar', that is, Caesar) and took control. From 1547 to 1564 he ruled largely through a Council of advisers, and reforms were initiated which strengthened the central government while the local administration was taken out of the hands of arbitrary governors and placed in those of elected local officials. But between 1560 and 1563 the Council gradually lost its powers; in 1564 Ivan left Moscow and retired to a monastery some fifty miles away. From there he wrote to the merchants of Moscow, accusing the nobles and clergy of treachery and announcing his intention of abdicating. The city begged him to come back, on his own terms.

The remainder of Ivan's reign, from 1564 to 1584, is full of wild, unbalanced actions. His mania for cruelty was directed against the nobility, against corrupt officials, against all whom he suspected of betraying him, but to the ordinary person he represented a safeguard against civil war and foreign invasion. (Perhaps there is a parallel here in the twentieth century?) The most interesting development was the creation of a special court (*oprichnina*) of chosen officials, who were granted territory in, and control of, about half Russia – a great strip of land running from north to south, while the *boyars* were left in control of the outer less productive areas. The central part thus became, as it were, the Tsar's 'crown lands', and through it rode *Oprichniks* in black robes, a symbolic broom hanging at their saddlebow, cleansing the land of treachery and feudalism – but often torturing and plundering also. Historians are divided as to whether the *oprichnina* was 'a monstrous police force built up and trained to satisfy the bloodthirsty appetites and lusts of a paranoiac?

Or . . . a social revolution intended to achieve what the Tsar realized was unachievable under normal circumstances, namely the creation of a new government, a new class of service gentry, reliable and free from the ties of tradition?' [1]

The death of Ivan was followed by new internal conflicts, which culminated in the 'Time of Troubles' (1610–13). From 1584 till his death in 1605 the dominant figure and *de facto* ruler was Boris Godunov, the new Tsar's brother-in-law. While he was in control two significant developments occurred: in 1590 the Orthodox Church in Russia became autonomous, with its own Patriarch, the equal of those at Constantinople, Antioch, Jerusalem and Alexandria; the second development occurred in 1597 when the peasants were attached to the land, becoming for all practical purposes serfs.

The death of Boris was followed by civil war during which Russia was afflicted with puppet pretenders, foreign invasion – the Poles occupied Moscow and the Swedes seized Novgorod – and internal risings of the reactionary *boyars* on the one hand, and the revolutionary serfs and Cossacks on the other. Alarmed at the approaching disintegration of the state, the middle classes chose a distant relative of Ivan the Terrible as Tsar, Michael Romanoff (1613–45). During his reign and that of his son Alexis (1645–76) Russia gradually recovered.

In 1617 the war with Sweden was ended by the Peace of Stolbova; Russia regained Novgorod but gave up Ingria and Karelia to Gustavus Adolphus. A successful Cossack rising in the Ukraine against Poland (1648) led to a war (1654–67) which was ended by the Peace of Andrusov; Russia regained Smolensk and acquired the Ukraine as far west as the River Dnieper. The Peace marks the end of the Polish danger.

The Patriarch Nikon initiated a series of Church reforms in 1653, designed to bring the Moscow liturgy into line with that of Kiev – they dealt with such points as whether the sign of the Cross should be made with two fingers or with three. These changes evoked violent opposition from the old ritualists who were alarmed at any change in Russia. They had attacked the presence at Court of scientists: 'How dare you keep at your Court men who have the hardihood to measure with a yard-rule the tails of the stars?' and again: 'Abhorred of God is any who loves geometry; it is a spiritual sin.' [2] The

[1] *N.C.M.H.*, II, p. 555.   [2] B. Pares, *A History of Russia*, Cape, p. 179.

dispute over westernization has been perennial. In this case the conservatives refused to conform – it is said that about 20,000 burnt themselves to death to avoid contamination – and became schismatics (*raskolniki*).

In 1667 Russia had survived astonishing internal and external dangers, but – except for the fact of that survival – there was no hint yet of the extraordinary increase in power that was to come during the next fifty years, largely as a result of the efforts of Peter the Great.

EXTRACTS

1. *Dinner with Ivan the Terrible, as seen by the English Ambassador, Anthony Jenkinson; 1557:*

When dinner time approached, we were brought againe into the Emperour's dining chamber, where we were set on one side of a table that stoode over against the Emperour's table, to the end that he might wel behold us al: . . . the tables aforesayde were covered onely with salt and bread, and after that we had sitten a while, the Emperour sent unto every one of us a piece of bread, which were given and delivered unto every man severally by these words: The Emperour and great Duke giveth the bread this day, and in like manner three or foure times before dinner was ended, he sent unto every man drinke, which was given by these words. The Emperour and great Duke giveth thee to drinke. All the tables aforesayd were served in vessels of pure and fine golde, . . . As for costly meates I have many times seene better: but for change of wines, and divers sorts of meads, it was wonderfull: for there was not left at any time so much void roome on the table, that one cuppe more might have bin set, and as far as I could perceive, all the rest were in like manner served.

In the dinner time there came in sixe singers which stood in the midst of the chamber, and their faces towards the Emperour, who sang there before dinner was ended three severall times, whose songs or voices delighted our eares little or nothing.

The Emperour never putteth morsell of meate in his mouth, but he first blesseth it himselfe, & in like manner as often as he drinketh: for after his maner he is very religious, & he esteemth his religious men above his noble men.

The dinner continued about the space of five houres. . .
(*Hakluyt's Voyages*, Dent, 1907, Vol. I, pp. 420–1)

2. *The Tartars, described by the English Ambassador, Giles Fletcher, 1588:*

For person and complexion they have broade and flatte visages, of a tanned colour into yellowe and blacke; fierce and cruell lookes, thinne haired upon the upper lippe, and pitte of the chinne, light and nimble bodied, with short legges, as if they were made naturally for horsemen: whereto they practise themselves from their childhood, seldome going afoot about anie businesse. Their speech is verie sudden and loude, speaking as it were out of a deepe hollow throate. When they sing you would thinke a kowe lowed, or some great bandogge howled. (*Hakluyt's Voyages*, Dent, 1907, Vol. II, pp. 321–2)

FURTHER READING

B. Pares, *A History of Russia*, Cape, 1937
R. Charques, *A Short History of Russia*, Phoenix House, 1956
B. H. Sumner, *A Survey of Russian History*, Duckworth, 1944

The Southern March: the Ottoman Empire, 1451–1656

The Mongol invasions of the thirteenth century, besides destroying the first Russian state, had set in motion lesser tribes throughout the steppes. One of these moved westward until it reached northwestern Asia Minor. There it was established by 1280 and from this base these Ottoman Turks expanded their lands, at first at the expense of the disintegrating Seljuk Turkish Empire which had been established two hundred years earlier, and then at that of the decaying Byzantine Empire, from which they acquired in the next century their first European possessions (1358). Soon the Ottomans were ruling in Thrace – the first Asiatics to do so since the days of Xerxes and Darius. By 1450 the greater part of the Balkans had been conquered, and in 1453 Constantinople fell after a siege of five weeks, the last Byzantine Emperor, Constantine Palaeologus, being killed in the final assault. The Sultan Mohammed II (1451–81) was now able to expand his Empire in every direction; southeast Asia Minor was added as early as 1473, the remainder of the Balkans over-run by 1483, and the north coast of the Black Sea occupied by 1484.

It would be wrong to regard the conquest of the Balkans as the triumph of barbarism over civilization. The Ottomans represented an alien civilization, but a civilization none the less. Nor were they concerned to root out the westerner. The infidel was taxed but not persecuted. Mohammed himself could read Greek, he encouraged Greeks to remain in the Phanar quarter of Constantinople, and sat to the Venetian Bellini for his portrait.

On his death at the age of fifty-one, the succession was disputed by two of Mohammed's sons; one, Jem, fled to the west where he remained a puppet prisoner until he died; the other, Bayezid II (1481–1512), was a mild and inefficient Sultan, during whose reign Europe enjoyed a temporary respite from Turkish pressure. Machiavelli wrote that two Sultans of his type would have led to the collapse of the Ottoman Empire. Under his successor Selim I (1512–20), 'the Grim', the work of conquest was renewed. Persia was defeated, Syria and Egypt conquered. The latter area had a twofold importance. It turned the flank of such western outposts as Cyprus, Rhodes and Crete. It also led to the acquisition by the Sultan of the faded title of Caliph. (One of the basic rules of Islam is that all Muslims must be ruled by one Caliph.) Much more important was the fact that at the same time the Sherif of Mecca recognized Selim as the protector of the holy cities of Mecca and Medina. These spiritual claims helped the Ottomans to extend their temporal power wherever there were Muslims – for instance, along the north African coast.

Selim was succeeded by Suleiman I (1520–66), 'the Magnificent'. An unknown quantity at his accession, he immediately showed that he was bent on adding to the Ottoman lands, especially at the expense of the west. In 1521 he captured Belgrade, the key to the Danube, and in 1522 the island of Rhodes, the key to the eastern Mediterranean. The two bastions of the west had fallen, as Pope Adrian VI recognized, writing '. . . the passages to Hungary, Sicily and Italy lie open to him'.

In 1526 Suleiman moved north with a large army (100,000 men and 300 cannon) and destroyed the power of Hungary at the battle of Mohacz on the Danube, a hundred miles south of the capital. The Turks entered, but did not hold, Buda.

Three years later Suleiman led north a second army, captured
Buda, and laid siege to Vienna.   The city survived a siege of
seventeen days and Suleiman was forced to retreat; the distances had proved too great.   The effective campaigning
season lasted from April to October, and it was 800 miles as
the crow flies from Constantinople to Vienna.   Suleiman had
set out on May 10 and had not reached Vienna until September 27, too late in the year.   Nevertheless the danger
had been acute.   Western observers believed that, had the
city fallen, the Turks would have been able to winter there
and push on into Germany the following season.   Vienna lies
almost exactly halfway between Constantinople and London
and so far, although the Ottoman advance had often halted,
it had never ended.   Suleiman tried again to take Vienna in
1532, and again failed,[1] but the Turks remained within about
eighty miles of the city for over 150 years, and it was again
besieged in 1683.   This constant pressure against the back
door of western Europe is a factor that can never be disregarded when considering the history of France and the
Empire during this period.

There were other consequences of the appearance of the
Turks in Europe.   The power of the Archdukes of Austria
and the birth of the Habsburg state from the Holy Roman
Empire were partly the result of Turkish pressure and the
need for an adequate bulwark against it.   The Turkish and
Habsburg Empires declined and fell together.   The Protestant
cause in Germany owed part of its success to the distraction
of Charles V's attention by 'the Frenchman and the Turk'.
After the battle of Pavia, when the King of France was Charles
V's prisoner in Madrid, Francis had got in touch with the
Sultan, and in 1536 semi-official contacts were replaced by a
formal treaty.   At the sight of 'the Most Christian King' and the
infidel in alliance the rest of Europe professed itself shocked.
In 1543 the Ottoman fleet wintered at Toulon, and helped the
French to take the town of Nice from the Imperialist forces.

At about the same time (1536–71) a struggle was in progress for naval supremacy in the Mediterranean; broadly
speaking, the Turks won control of the eastern part, but in
spite of the French alliance failed to dominate the western.
In 1540 Venice surrendered, by treaty, her control of the

[1] Thanks to the heroic resistance of the town of Güns, August 7–28.

Aegean. In various naval encounters the Genoese Admiral, Andrea Doria, was in general outfought by the Muslim Khair ad-Din Barbarossa. In 1536 Charles V captured the Muslim corsair stronghold of Tunis and, though he failed to repeat this success in a later attack on Algiers, Tunis was in Christian hands until the Ottomans recaptured it in 1574. In 1571 the Turks occupied Cyprus and the west was scared into a 'Holy League' which for once was successful. Spain, Venice and the Papacy got together a fleet, under Don John of Austria. The Ottomans met it at Lepanto, off the Gulf of Corinth. The two forces were numerically well-balanced though the Christian one was technically superior. Don John won a decisive victory and, though Venice ceded Cyprus (1573) and the Turks rebuilt their fleet within three years, Lepanto had in fact saved the western Mediterranean. The Pope, Pius V, preached a sermon of thanksgiving on the text: *There was a man sent from God, whose name was John.*

At the time of Lepanto Suleiman had been succeeded by Selim II (1574–86), whose reign forms a pendant to that of his father. With the death of Selim and of his Grand Vizier a few years later the Ottoman period entered upon a period of decline. The Sultans were weak, incompetent or mad, and their Grand Viziers not much better. Only Murad IV (1623–40) showed any ability. In the second half of the seventeenth century, the Ottoman power revived under the Vizier Kuprili (1656).

The greatest of the Ottoman rulers is Suleiman the Magnificent, called in the east 'the Lawgiver'. Contemporary observers agree that wisdom, ruthlessness, justice and self-control were the essence of his character. During his reign and that of his father the area of the Ottoman Empire had been trebled, and he spent much of his revenue on the defence of the new extended frontiers and the reconstruction of fortresses at Buda, Belgrade and Rhodes. His claim to greatness rests not only on foreign conquest, but also on the efficiency with which he administered the Empire. The new conquests had made his Empire more Muslim in character and by his orders a new code of law was drawn up some time before 1549, which was the basis of Ottoman Law until the nineteenth century.

The Empire over which Suleiman ruled was a civilized

one, but its civilization was very different from that of western Europe. The Ottoman state and the Muslim law both stemmed from the Muslim religion – any division between them is to some extent artificial. There were four religious bases: the *Koran*; the *Sunnas*, rules resting on tradition and deduction from the Prophet's life; the explanations and decisions of the Prophet's disciples; and the *Kiyas* – the canonical conclusions of the four great *Imams* of the seventh and eighth centuries. From the interpretation of these sources by judges one could appeal to the *Mufti*, an interpreter of the law, whose authority was morally binding, though it could only be enforced by the *Caliph*, who could depose the *Mufti*.

The Sultan was in effect a spiritual, military and political dictator, everything depended on his strength and capacity. The Grand Vizier was his representative, his regent, his chief executive officer. But he was also the Sultan's personal slave who could be deposed and strangled at a moment's notice. Usually he was not an Ottoman – of the forty-eight Grand Viziers between 1453 and 1623 only five were Turks, the great majority coming from the Balkans.

Financially, the Ottoman Empire was stronger than its Christian opponents. During Suleiman's reign his income doubled, and by 1550 it was about 10,000,000 ducats. Sixty per cent of this was derived from a head tax on unbelievers. (At this time the revenue of the Emperor Charles V was not more than 6,700,000 ducats.)

Next to the power of the Sultan, the most important reason for the success of the Turks lay in the organization of their army. This consisted essentially of two parts. There were about 100,000 *Sipahis* – feudal levies who held their land as a reward for past services and a pledge for future ones. They were essentially a summer fighting force, and they differed from the western feudal knight in the important particular that their fiefs were not necessarily hereditary. The *Janissaries* ('new soldiers') numbered about 12,000 and were the first regular standing army to operate in Europe since Roman times. Christian children were acquired by seizure, purchase or most usually by tribute every four or five years. They were educated in Islam and trained, according to their abilities, as slaves, administrative officers or soldiers. These last were recruited at the age of twenty-five:

The fundamental laws which regulated their discipline were absolute obedience to the commanders, abstinence from luxury, modest attire, fulfilment of the duties of Islam. They were unable to marry or exercise any trade, or leave their camp. It is clear that the existence of such a body of warriors was in itself a constant incentive or even compulsion to warlike enterprises; . . . Without any bonds of family or country, they were the creatures of the Sultan, in turn imposing their yoke on him.[1]

The extraordinary success of the Ottomans was partly the result of their own strength and partly due to the weakness of their adversaries. The west was hopelessly divided; there were bad relations between the Empire and the rulers of Hungary; the Catholic and Orthodox Churches were at loggerheads; western traders were jealous of Venice, and hoped to see her lose her grip on the eastern Mediterranean; Charles V was hampered by Francis I and the German Protestants; in the Balkans the Bogomil heretics found the Turk more tolerant than the Christian. These antagonisms rendered impotent the natural opponents of the Ottoman advance.

The Ottomans met western dissension with unity. In a centralized autocracy the genius of the individual ruler – Mohammed II, Selim I, Suleiman I – counted for everything. As virtual head of church and state such Sultans found expansion easy over lands already Muslim and speaking Arabic – since the Koran was never translated, a universal language. The peasant was better off under Ottoman rule; his rights were limited, but at least they were guaranteed. While the Empire was efficient, the Balkans were well-governed. An efficient army, a single religion, a large and rising income were advantages that Charles V never enjoyed.

If the Ottoman Empire possessed such striking advantages, why did its power decline after 1566? It had the Achilles' heel of all dictatorships – everything depended on the character of the ruler, a weak Sultan meant a weak Empire. When the Empire was weak, misgovernment followed, and the subject peoples began to resent a minority rule that was inefficient. The Ottomans, too, had certain strategic weaknesses: they were always relatively incompetent at sea; in the east they were exposed to pressures from Persia and from

[1] *C.M.H.*, I, p. 100.

the new Portuguese empire. Military discipline became corrupted, especially when the superb fighting force of the Janissaries ceased to be a culled élite and became a corps open to ambitious Muslims. (Between 1574 and 1595 it was opened to all Muslims except Negroes, and grew in numbers to 100,000.) One can see that the Ottoman power had in fact reached its peak when Suleiman died in 1566, but this was of course not understood by contemporaries. For over a hundred years the fear remained: northern litanies appealed for deliverance 'from the cunning of the Pope and the terror of the Turk', and regarded the Ottoman Empire, in the words of the Elizabethan Richard Knolles, as '. . . the present terror of the world'.

EXTRACT

A Fleming describes the Ottoman system, 1555:

In Turkey every man has it in his power to make what he will of the position into which he is born and of his fortune in life. Those who hold the highest posts under the Sultan are very often the sons of shepherds and herdsmen, and, so far from being ashamed of their birth, they make it a subject of boasting, and the less they owe to their forefathers and to the accident of birth the greater is the pride which they feel. . . . Just as they consider that an aptitude for the arts, such as music or mathematics or geometry, is not transmitted to a son and heir, so they hold that character is not hereditary, and that a son does not necessarily resemble his father, but his qualities are divinely infused into his bodily frame. Thus, among the Turks, dignities, offices, and administrative posts are the rewards of ability and merit; those who are dishonest, lazy and slothful never attain to distinction, but remain in obscurity and contempt. This is why the Turks succeed in all that they attempt and are a dominating race and daily extend the bounds of their rule. Our method is very different; there is no room for merit, but everything depends on birth, considerations of which alone open the way to high official position. (E. S. Forster, *The Turkish letters of Ogier Ghiselin de Busbecq*, O.U.P., 1927, pp. 59–60)

FURTHER READING

A. H. Lybyer, *The Government of the Empire in the Time of Suleiman the Magnificent*, O.U.P., 1914

XII · SPAIN AND HOLLAND IN THE EARLY SEVENTEENTH CENTURY

The Decline of Spain, 1598–1665

ALTHOUGH there were signs at the end of the sixteenth century that the glory of Spain rested on insecure foundations, the reigns of Charles V and Philip II had made it 'a golden century'. When Philip died, it might still have been possible for a powerful, far-sighted ruler to halt the unseen decline which had already begun. Unfortunately for Spain, his successors Philip III (1598–1621) and Philip IV (1621–65) lacked both the desire and the ability to govern. An absolute, bureaucratic monarchy of the sort that had been created in the sixteenth century depends entirely on the character of the ruler, or of the men to whom he deputes his power. Philip had worked immensely hard at the trade of kingship, just as did those spiritual descendants of his, Louis XIV and Frederick the Great – his Spain was a prototype of the absolute monarchies of the later seventeenth and early eighteenth centuries; but his successors would neither govern themselves nor entrust power to those fitted to do so. Consequently Spain was controlled only by the forces making for her decline and fall.

Philip II, when dying, is supposed to have lamented: 'God who has given me so many kingdoms has not granted me a son fit to govern them.' To that son he said,

I should have wished to save you this trial; but I want you to see how the monarchies of this earth end. Behold! God has stripped me of all the glory and majesty of sovereignty that they may pass to you. In a few hours I shall be covered only with a poor shroud, and girded with a coarse rope. The kingly crown is already falling from my brows, and death will soon set it upon yours. Two things I especially commend to you: one is that you always keep faithful to the Holy Catholic Church, and the other is that you treat your subjects justly. The crown will one day fall from your head, as it now falls from mine. You are young, as I too have been. My day draws to a close;

the tale of yours God alone can see; but it must end like mine.[1]

Philip III exhibited a mechanical and intermittent piety, but otherwise disregarded his father's advice. He played no real part in the business of ruling, being content to leave that to his favourite, the Duke of Lerma. The latter removed the old courtiers and packed the key positions with his own relations, and the atmosphere at court changed from one of grim austerity to wasteful extravagance. In 1562 the ordinary court expenses had been 415,000 ducats a year, during Philip III's reign they averaged 1,300,000 ducats. Every event was celebrated in the most lavish fashion.

When Philip III went to San Sebastian in 1615 to attend the double wedding which was to bind together the houses of Austria and Bourbon, he was accompanied by a train of 74 carriages, 174 litters, 190 state coaches, 2750 saddle mules, 374 beasts of burden (of which 128 had coverings embroidered with the royal coat of arms), 1750 mules with silver bells, and 6500 persons, besides an escort of 4000 Guipuzcoans.[2]

By 1617 the expenditure was eight million ducats and the revenue less than five and a half million. Some misplaced attempts were made to remedy this situation, notably the removal of the capital from Madrid, where it had been since 1561, to Valladolid. The court remained there from 1601 to 1606, Valladolid paid for the privilege, and Madrid paid for the restoration of its old status, but thousands of Madrileños were ruined in the process. Another short-sighted measure was the continual debasement of the coinage, which had the usual consequence of raising prices and driving good money out of circulation. One of the odder results was a complaint in 1624 that 'a great number of individuals fail to gain papal indulgence and the dead do not enjoy suffrage because there is no silver money to pay for the bulls'.[3]

The economic situation was made slightly less disastrous than it would otherwise have been by the fact that Spain was at peace from 1609 to 1620. The need for a period of rest

[1] C.M.H., III, p. 525.
[2] C. E. Chapman, A History of Spain, Macmillan, 1918, p. 284.
[3] R. T. Davies, The Golden Century of Spain, Macmillan, 1937, p. 267.

had combined with shortage of money and the changing political situation to bring to an end the three wars in which Spain was currently engaged. That against France was concluded by the Treaty of Vervins, signed in 1598 a few months before Philip II's death. The war with England continued until 1604. An expedition to Ireland in 1601 which suffered the usual fate of such Spanish exploits, and the accession of James I, made it easier for the two countries to come to terms. Meanwhile the war with the Dutch dragged on. This was partly a matter of prestige, the United Provinces were not, after all, a foreign country with which one might negotiate as between equals, but a rebellious part of the Spanish empire. Moreover, Spinola was winning victories for the Spanish and carrying the war into the rebel territory beyond the Rhine: but he was handicapped by shortage of men and money, and at last, in 1609, a Twelve Years' Truce was signed.

Within Spain, the most striking event of the reign was the expulsion of the *Moriscos* from the remaining Spanish provinces between 1609 (Valencia) and 1614 (Murcia). Their conversion was barely skin-deep, and now this last section of the former Arab conquerors was deported. To Spaniards it was the logical final act in the series of struggles against the 'paynim' that went back to the days of Charlemagne. There was recent evidence that the *Moriscos* had encouraged and aided Muslim raids from Africa, and that they had been negotiating with Elizabeth of England; but the real reason for their unpopularity seems to have been envy at their prosperity, obtained by that hard work which was becoming so unwelcome in the rest of Spain. They were called 'the sponges that suck up all the wealth of Spain', and the usually tolerant Cervantes wrote:

> Their one and only aim is to coin money . . . so that, ever getting and never spending, they gain the greater part of all the money in Spain. . . . They gather up everything. Consider that they are many, and that every day they conceal little or much, and that a slow fever consumes life just as surely as a violent one. . . . They all of them marry, they all multiply. . . . They rob us easily and, with the fruits of an inheritance which they resell to us, they grow rich. . . .[1]

[1] Davies, p. 279, quoting from the *Coloquio de los Perros*.

Estimates of the number expelled range from 150,000 to
500,000.   Lerma received 250,000 ducats as his share of their
wealth.   On the economic life of the country the effect of
the expulsion was to intensify the already serious depression;
trade, finance, weaving, metal-working and agriculture were
all pursuits in which the *Moriscos* had been skilled.

In 1618 the Duke of Lerma fell from power, only to be
succeeded by his equally unscrupulous son.   Three years later
Philip III died at the age of forty-three, leaving

> an exhausted, depopulated country, swarming with beggars
> and hangers-on of the court, of the nobles and of the monas-
> teries; and holding in precarious subjection states in Europe
> and beyond it that hated the name of Spain.[1]

The reign of Philip IV completes the story of Spain's decline
and fall, for now there was added to decadence at home
military defeat abroad.   The new king was sixteen years old,
and passed naturally into the hands of a favourite, the Count-
Duke of Olivarez.   Olivarez was himself a great improvement
on the Duke of Lerma, but he was not able to deal with the
disastrous situation which had developed within Spain.   His
attempts to reduce local liberties led eventually to a series of
rebellions, while in foreign affairs he was unfortunate in finding himself matched against the great Richelieu.

> He was energetic, intelligent, and well educated, but was
> stubborn, proud, irascible, boastful, and insulting.   He was
> able to make plans on a gigantic scale, and had real discern-
> ment as to the strength of Spain's enemies, but lacked the
> practical capacity to handle the details.[2]

The character of his master, Philip IV, is not so easy to
define.   Easy-going, not unintelligent, with well-developed
aesthetic interests, he was at the same time lazy, self-indulgent
and religious.   In the sphere of government he became
almost literally 'a rubber-stamp', using a die which read
Yo el Rey to sign state documents.   He was a patron of Velas-
quez, and he fathered at least thirty-two illegitimate children.
In general his behaviour alternated between degraded dissipa-
tion and degrading acts of contrition.

Philip was aware of the state of Spain.   In 1626 he described

[1] Davies, p. 260.   [2] Chapman, p. 261.

to his Council the condition of the country when he came to the throne:

> The finances were so utterly exhausted – in addition to the terrible debts incurred by Philip II – that every resource was anticipated for several years to come. My patrimony was so distressed that in my father's time alone grants and voluntary gifts had swallowed up 96,000,000 ducats, without calculating what had been given in four or five of the principal Spanish kingdoms, from which returns have not yet been made. The currency had been raised to three times its face value: a thing never seen in any nation before, which threatened us with utter isolation, but for God's help. . . . The State itself was so degraded that the King, my father, had been forced to negotiate with the Hollanders as if they had been an independent sovereign State, over which he had no claims; . . . Portugal was discontented with the Viceroy, and the rest of the monarchy was ill-ruled or not ruled at all. Roman affairs were totally ruined: we were in a state of war with Venice; and the realm of Naples was bordering upon a popular revolt, with the coinage completely debased. This was the sad condition in which I found my country on my accession, from no fault of the King my father, or of his predecessors, as all the world knows, but because God Almighty decreed that it should be so; and I myself experience this every day: for no matter how adequate may be the remedies I adopt, our sins suffice to condemn all our affairs to the most miserable state imaginable.[1]

Economies had been introduced by Olivarez, but these were short-lived and Spain's foreign policy soon led to increased taxation and renewed bankruptcy. The government repudiated its debts with mechanical regularity in 1607, 1627 and 1647. In 1626 an effort to get more money from the *Cortes* of Aragon, Valencia and Catalonia, almost led to revolt in the last-named province, which refused to vote anything until an earlier loan to the Crown had been repaid. This was, as it were, a dress-rehearsal for the full-scale rebellion that was to come later in the reign.

The main interest of the reigns of Philip III and Philip IV lies in foreign affairs. In the early seventeenth century the uneasy

[1] *C.M.H.*, IV, pp. 638–9.

peace within the Empire was coming to an end, as the internal contradictions of the peace of Augsburg developed. The peace had lasted for almost sixty years, but it no longer represented the balance of forces within the Empire. At the same time France, which owing to internal conflict had been unable to exert much influence in international matters in the second half of the sixteenth century, was now, thanks to the work of Henri IV, once more a great power. Spain, linked so closely with the other branch of the Habsburgs ruling the Empire, and with her traditional enmity to France, was drawn inevitably into a series of wars that did not really concern her and which she might very well have avoided. What follows is a summary of the part played by Spain in these wars, a fuller account of them will be found in Chapters IX and X.

In 1610 it had appeared possible that war might come over the question of the Cleves–Jülich succession, but the danger was averted by the death of Henri IV and by the later Treaty of Xanten. In 1615 the double marriage of Louis XIII to Philip's daughter Anne and of the future Philip IV to Louis' sister Elizabeth marked an abortive attempt to establish better relations with France, which was temporarily pursuing a policy of friendship towards Spain. The decade witnessed a series of minor explosions. From 1614 to 1617 Spain was involved in a successful war with Savoy for control of the strategically important Duchy of Montferrat; in 1617 there was an obscure scuffle with Venice (which had supported Savoy); and in 1620 the Spaniards took steps to seize the vital Valtelline, linking Habsburg Tyrol and Habsburg Milan.

This last move was due to the fact that the long-expected European war had broken out in 1618; Spain had sent troops to aid the Emperor Ferdinand in 1619 and 1620, and it was important to safeguard this weak link in the line of communications. Spain had in fact entered, almost light-heartedly, into a series of wars which were to last for thirty-nine years and from which her old rival, France, was to emerge as the dominant force in Europe while Spain herself became only a second-class power. This period of warfare really consists of three closely linked struggles: the Thirty Years' War itself, in which Spain was involved from 1620 to 1648; war with the United Provinces, where the Twelve Years' Truce had now expired, from 1621 to 1648; and war with France which began in 1635 and continued after the conclusion of the Thirty Years' War until 1659, when the whole inter-connected series of conflicts was brought to an end by the Treaty of the Pyrenees. (There was also a brief struggle with England, where the failure of long negotiations for a marriage between Charles, Prince of Wales, and the Infanta Maria led to a half-hearted conflict from 1625 to 1630.)

At first the Spanish forces, though handicapped by being involved in so many theatres of war, exercised considerable influence. They were still in many ways the best in Europe and the fighting in the Netherlands had led them to adopt new military techniques and aids such as the telescope, the hand grenade and the use of winter quarters. In 1620 the movement of 20,000 troops under the great Spinola from the Spanish Netherlands made certain the defeat of the Elector Frederick, and the Spanish occupied the Lower Palatinate. In 1625 Spinola captured Breda in the Netherlands – (the surrender shown in Velazquez's painting 'The Lances'). During the twenties the Spanish also clashed with Richelieu over the question of the control of the Valtelline, and the succession to the Duchies of Mantua and Montferrat, with partial success in the first area and failure in the second. In 1634 the Spanish army won its last great victory when, in conjunction with the Imperial forces, it defeated the hitherto successful Swedes at Nördlingen (1634), a battle that ensured the retention of southern Germany by the Catholic forces. The effect of Nördlingen was also, however, to bring France directly into the war. At first the Spanish successes continued, and in 1636 they invaded northern France, captured Corbie and were on the road to Paris.

The years from 1620 to 1636 had thus been years of success for Spain. Now the strains of the war coupled with internal revolts at home demonstrated her essential weakness. In 1639 the Spanish fleet was defeated by the French and Dutch. On May 19, 1643, the cream of the Spanish army was routed at Rocroi by the French under Condé. The battle marked the end of the supremacy of the Spanish infantry – a supremacy that had lasted since Pavia (1525).

In 1648, by the Treaty of Münster, the Spanish recognized the United Provinces as an independent country, and agreed to the closure of the Scheldt, which cut Antwerp off from the

sea. The war with France went on. There Spain gained
some respite since her enemy was engaged from 1648 to 1653
in that complex of civil struggles known as the Fronde. In
1653, as a consequence of the civil war, Condé deserted to the
Spanish, where he won one last victory for them at Valenciennes in 1656; but in 1658 the Spanish were again defeated
by the French (supported by Cromwell's Ironsides) at the
Battle of the Dunes, and in the following year the Peace of the
Pyrenees was signed.

France kept Artois, taken from the Spanish Netherlands,
and Roussillon and Cerdagne to the northeast of the Pyrenees.
In the following year the Peace was confirmed by the marriage
of Louis XIV to Philip IV's daughter Maria Theresa and,
surprisingly, the two countries remained allies for a hundred
and fifty years.

The defeat of Spain had been accomplished partly by a
series of revolts within her own territories. These expressions
of separatist feeling had been caused by Olivarez's attempt to
suppress local liberties. As the Venetian ambassador wrote,
Olivarez 'hated the constitutions'. As a result of his high-
handed behaviour, coupled with the heavy war taxation,
Spain was faced with risings in Catalonia, Portugal and Naples.
The Catalan revolt lasted from 1640 to 1659 and was in some
ways the most dangerous, for it opened the door to the French,
who invaded Spain and garrisoned the Catalan towns. The
Portuguese had never been really reconciled to the union with
Spain, and in 1640 the Duke of Braganza, a distant descendant
of John I (1383–1433), was proclaimed King. The revolt
lasted until 1668 and then Portugal became once more an
independent country. The rising in Naples was brief (1647–8).
but alarming, for the Spanish power had seemed secure there.
The revolts of Catalonia and Portugal were followed by the
fall from power of Olivarez in 1643, the year of Rocroi.

Spanish culture continued to flourish during the reigns of
Philip III and Philip IV, reaching then perhaps its greatest
heights. This is a not uncommon feature of the decline and
fall of empires, like the galvanic twitchings of an already dead
frog's leg. In literature the great names are those of Lope
de Vega (1562–1635) and Cervantes (1547–1616). The

former was a fantastically prolific playwright. He is said to have written 1,800 comedies – 470 of them have survived. In these circumstances, it is not surprising that his plots are condemned as being too facile! His natural dialogue, the division of the play into three acts, and the prominent roles given to women, were all features of his work. Cervantes is better known to foreigners. His life was mainly lived under Philip II, and his work influenced by sixteenth century Spanish writers, such as the anonymous author of Lazarillo de Tormes (1554) – (one of the hundred European claimants to the title of 'the first novel') – but the work by which he is remembered, *Don Quixote*, appeared between 1605 and 1611 and looks forward to the seventeenth century, rather than backwards to the sixteenth.

In painting a whole series of masters emerged: the Cretan, El Greco (?1545–1625); Ribera (1588–1656); Zurbaran (1598–1663); Murillo (1618–82); and one of the greatest of all European painters, Velazquez (1599–1660). In architecture the classical style of Herrera continued to be fashionable in the reign of Philip III, but under Philip IV architecture (and also clothes, and indeed all applied decoration) became exuberant and extravagant. (A style known as Churriguer-esque, from the architect Churriguera.)

During the later part of Philip II's reign, that of Philip III, and the earlier part of Philip IV's, Spain was the arbiter of fashion in Europe, her influence making itself felt mainly by way of Italy. But by 1660, as in so much else, Spain had been supplanted by France. When the King of Spain's daughter married Louis

Velvets, brocades, cloth of bullion, and cunning gold-smiths' work, gloves, perfumes and laces, such as only Spain could produce, burdened seventy-five sumpter mules, for the use of the future Queen of France; but when . . . Philip and his host of courtiers wended their way home-ward, their dark doublets and stiff *golillas* [ruffs] had grown old-fashioned in their eyes, and the lank hair clear of their projecting collars seemed antiquated and uncouth, by the side of the frizzled curls and piled periwigs of the French nobles and the elegance of their wide-skirted coats of embroidered brocade and their dainty lace cravats.[1]

[1] *C.M.H.*, IV p. 661.

Extract

Cervantes suggests some rules for better government, 1615:

. . . Sancho passed that afternoon in making several regulations, for the better establishment of that which he imagined to be an island. He published an order against the higglers and forestallers of the markets; and another to encourage the bringing in of wines from any part whatever, provided the owners declared of what growth they were, that they might be rated according to their value and goodness; and that they who should adulterate wine with water, or give it a wrong name, should be punished with death. He lowered the price of all kinds of apparel, and particularly that of shoes, as thinking it exorbitant. He regulated servants' wages, that were unlimited before, and proportioned them to the merit of their service. He laid severe penalties upon all those that should sing or vend lewd and immoral songs and ballads, either in the open day, or in the dusk of the evening; and also forbid all blind people singing about miracles in rhymes, unless they produced authentic testimonies of their truth; for it appeared to him, that most of those that were sung in such manner were false, and a disparagement to the true.

He appointed a particular officer to inspect the poor, not to persecute, but to examine them, and know whether they were truly such; for under pretence of counterfeit lameness, and artificial sores, many canting vagabonds impudently rob the true poor of charity, to spend it in riot and drunkenness.

In short, he made so many wholesome ordinances, that, to this day they are observed in that place, and called, 'The Constitutions of the great Governor Sancho Pança.' (M. de Cervantes, *The Life and Achievements of Don Quixote de la Mancha*, Part II, Dent, 1947, Vol. II, p. 337)

The United Provinces, 1609–53

The first half of the seventeenth century is the Golden Age of the United Provinces, a brief period sandwiched between the years dominated in turn by their two great antagonists, Spain, with whom they had fought from 1572 to 1609, and France, who was to threaten them intermittently from 1672 to 1713. The decline of the Dutch was gradual: politically they remained powerful until 1713; economically they were significant until well on into the eighteenth century; but from

1609 to 1672 they had been 'the country of herrings, artists and philosophers', later only the herrings remained.

Three threads of development must be followed: the complex religious and constitutional struggle for control of the new state; the rapid economic and colonial expansion; and, finally, the artistic, philosophical and scientific achievements which that economic expansion made possible.

During this half century the United Provinces were controlled in turn by Maurice of Nassau (1584–1625); his half-brother, Frederick Henry (1625–47); Frederick Henry's son, William II (1647–50); and by John de Witt (1653–72), the Grand Pensionary of Holland. This last surprising shift in power provides a clue to the nature of the earlier constitutional struggle.

At the conclusion of the Twelve Years' Truce with Spain in 1609 the United Provinces were faced by the problem of how to govern the new state that had emerged – a problem which had been masked by the earlier fight for very existence. The situation was in some ways very similar to that in which the American colonists found themselves in 1783 at the conclusion of the War of Independence, when old rivalries re-emerged and they were confronted with the question of the relation between the parts and the whole, between the states and the central government. It took both the United Provinces and the U.S.A. seventy or eighty years to find a final answer to that question.

The United Provinces consisted of seven states. There were two organs of central government, the Council of State, formed in 1584 and consisting of twelve deputies, and the States-General, 'really an assembly of ambassadors from sovereign states', elected for three or six years, and called by the Council of State. Each state had also an elected Stadtholder. The army was paid by the states in proportion to their quota, and the Stadtholders were responsible for the army, for keeping order, supporting the reformed religion and administering justice. In 1609 Maurice was Stadtholder in six of the seven states. Finally, the state of Holland had in its Advocate, or Grand Pensionary, an official of great practical power.

There were many differences, which had been concealed by the unity imposed by the struggle for existence. Over half, and perhaps as many as two-thirds, of the population were still Catholics, ruled by Calvinists who since 1602 were themselves split into two bitterly-opposed factions. Power within the separate provinces was not even in the hands of all the Calvinists, but was confined to the narrow oligarchies of the town corporations. Each province was jealous of its neighbours, and they were all jealous of Holland, which contained a third of the population and was as rich as all the rest of the country put together. In the years after 1609 these differences and jealousies were embodied in two personalities, those of the Stadtholder Maurice and of the Grand Pensionary of Holland, Oldenbarneveldt (1547–1619).

The ostensible cause of the struggle was religious. Calvinism had developed two factions: the strict, or 'Reformed', Calvinists (who appear in English Jacobean literature as 'precisians'); and the more liberal, or 'Libertine' Calvinists, who said, 'You turn God into a tyrant and an executioner,' [1] Article 13 of the Union of Utrecht had given independence to the Provincial Churches and even a measure of freedom to each congregation, and this local autonomy had been confirmed by later ordinances.

After 1602 the two religious groups found spokesmen in rival professors at the university of Leyden, Gomarus the strict Calvinist and Arminius the 'Libertine'. Arminius himself died in 1609, but in the following year forty-four of his followers drew up a Remonstrance at Gouda, appealing from the national Church to the local states and linking the religious to the constitutional quarrel. An Arminian thus became considered as one who supported the State's power over the Church. Meanwhile, the Gomarists had retaliated with a Counter-Remonstrance, asserting the extreme Calvinist position, and referring the matter to a National Synod.

As the religious dispute became involved with the political issue, two sides emerged: Maurice of Nassau, together with four of the provinces, supported the extreme Calvinists, in opposition to Oldenbarneveldt, with three provinces (Utrecht, Overyssel and Holland but not the city of Amsterdam) which supported the Arminians. In 1616 Holland began to raise a force of 4,000 local militia to defend its independence. In 1617 Maurice seized a church at the Hague for the use of the

[1] P. Geyl, *The Netherlands Divided (1609–48)*, Williams & Norgate, 1936, p. 45.

extremists. Oldenbarneveldt replied by persuading the Estates of Holland to pass the 'Sharp Resolution'. This reasserted the independence of the separate provinces in matters of religion, and the duty of the leader of the army (Maurice) to carry out the province's wishes. As Stadtholder of Holland Maurice was bound to support the Sharp Resolution, as Captain of the Union it was his duty to carry out the orders of the States-General, which had decided to call the National Synod demanded by the extreme Calvinists. Faced with this conflict of loyalties, Maurice naturally supported his own party and in 1618 staged a *coup d'état*. The province of Utrecht was occupied, the leading Arminians, including Oldenbarneveldt and the scholar Grotius, were arrested, and an international Synod met at Dort.

In May 1619, Oldenbarneveldt, who had adopted a *Politique* philosophy,[1] was executed, Grotius and others were imprisoned, and the Synod of Dort asserted the unity of the Dutch Established Church. The supporters of that Church were provided with a 'Confession' clearly defining their beliefs, while the Arminians were reduced to the same legal position as Catholics, tolerated but barred from holding office and with no legal rights of worship.

Considering the events described above, one may feel that Maurice had acted in an unscrupulous way, that the execution of Oldenbarneveldt was poor recompense for his services to the state, that the imposition of narrow orthodoxy was a retrograde step, and that the whole business is a confused, rather parochial, quarrel. Its consequences, though, were momentous. There was a great danger in 1618 that the state would split up into its several provinces. Maurice's actions ensured the survival of the United Provinces, and the dominance of the central government and of the Orange family for the next thirty years. The successes of the Dutch during those years rest on the *coup d'état* of 1618.

The unity of the state was the more important since the period between 1609 and 1648 was dominated by the preparations for, and course of, the Thirty Years' War. The Cleves–Jülich question had brought the United Provinces to the

---

[1] '. . . among papists, too, there are numbered many loyal upholders of the fatherland.'

threshold of war with Spain, but this was avoided in 1614 by
the partition agreed to in the treaty of Xanten. Four years
later the Thirty Years' War began, and in 1621, when the
Twelve Years' Truce with Spain came to an end, Maurice
once more faced his old enemy Spinola. The latter won a
decisive victory at Breda in 1624 and the town was forced to
surrender soon afterwards. In the following spring Maurice
died.

> He was perhaps the most accomplished soldier of his
> time, but as a politician weak, hesitating, and easily led,
> and he passed away under a cloud, for the splendour of his
> great achievements was overshadowed by the dark memory
> of the catastrophe of 1619.[1]

His young half-brother Frederick Henry succeeded Maurice
as Captain-General, and as Stadtholder in five provinces, at a
time when the United Provinces were seriously threatened by
the Spanish Imperial forces. Although, like his father William
of Orange, he was perhaps greater as a diplomat than as a
soldier, he was successful as both. Unofficial toleration helped
to unite the population of the country, while in 1631 the
States-General passed the *Acte de Survivance*, declaring Frederick's
son – five years old at the time – the future Captain-General,
and Stadtholder in Holland, Zeeland and Guelderland. This
greatly strengthened the power and prestige of the Orange
family, and went near to turning a republic into a monarchy.
Frederick further improved his position by the marriages of
his children. William married Mary the daughter of Charles I
and later became the father of the future William III of
England, while Louisa married the Great Elector of Brandenburg.

At the same time that Frederick was moving into the club
of European ruling families, he was also winning a series of
victories, insignificant when placed on the immense canvas of
the European war, but of considerable importance to his own
country. The capture of 's Hertogenbosch (1629) and the recapture of Breda (1637) strengthened his position to the south
of the Rhine, while the capture of Maestricht (1632) defended
the eastern flank. In 1639, at the Battle of the Downs, the
Dutch admiral Tromp destroyed the Spanish fleet and with it

[1] *C.M.H.*, III, p. 656.

the naval power of Spain. Six years later the Dutch navy sailed into the Baltic and, without firing a shot, forced Christian of Denmark to alter the shipping dues of the Sound in favour of the Dutch.

When the French had entered the war in 1635 the Dutch had signed a formal alliance with them, and the closing years of the war were largely taken up with a scheme of Frederick's to partition the Spanish Netherlands with France '. . . the provinces in which the French tongue is generally spoken should be assigned to the Crown of France, those remaining should and ought to be left to the United Provinces'. Besides the obvious attractions of this plan, there was a more subtle point – the acquisition of Antwerp would enable the Orange family to dispose of a commercial rival to the overmighty port of Amsterdam.

In 1647 Frederick Henry died and was succeeded, in accordance with the *Acte de Survivance*, by his son William II, then aged twenty-one. By the Peace of Münster, Spain at last recognized 'that the Lords States-General of the United Provinces and the respective Provinces thereof, with all their associated territories, towns and dependent lands, are free and sovereign States', and all points at issue were settled in their favour. The Dutch conquests south of the Rhine were recognized; the Scheldt was closed, thus sealing off Antwerp from the sea; and the Dutch were allowed to trade freely with the West and East Indies and to keep those areas which they had captured from the Portuguese.

In 1652 there was a brief tussle with England. The triumph of a republican form of government had led to an offer by Parliament to unite the two countries, but both were highly developed mercantile communities, and everywhere their interests clashed. There was a perpetual quarrel over the rights of fishing off Greenland; the Dutch had massacred English traders trespassing in Java; the English demanded that Dutch ships should acknowledge English control of the Channel by saluting the flag. More important were the Dutch treaty with Denmark (the latter had promised not to reduce the Sound Dues for any other power) and the English Navigation Act (which struck at the Dutch carrying trade), both concluded in 1651. As a result, instead of an alliance being concluded, a naval war broke out, which was brought to an end in 1653 by the Treaty of Westminster. The Dutch agreed to salute the flag, to pay compensation for the massacre in the East Indies and for fishing rights in English waters, and the Grand Pensionary agreed also to a secret clause by which the House of Orange was to be excluded from the posts of Stadt-holder and Captain-General.

The Grand Pensionary was now the effectual ruler. During the life of Frederick Henry the constitutional struggle had been in abeyance, but with the accession of his son, William II, and the conclusion of the Thirty Years' War, it flared up again, just as it had done after the conclusion of the Twelve Years' Truce. There are close parallels between the situation in 1618–19 and that in 1648–50, with this difference, that in the earlier period the ostensible cause of disagreement was religious, while in the later one it was military. William had tried to prevent the conclusion of a treaty with Spain, just as Maurice had opposed the Twelve Years' Truce. The Estates of Holland then demanded a greater reduction in the size of the army than William desired. In spite of protests by the States-General and an appeal by William, the Estates of Holland went ahead with their reductions. Behind the scenes, Spain supported them, while France (still at war with Spain) encouraged William. All the old differences were remembered. In general, one may say that those who approved of the action of the Estates of Holland were republican, separatist, mercantile, in favour of peace, tolerant in matters of religion, and afraid of the French, while William's supporters represented the opposite principles and saw in Spain the great enemy.

In the summer of 1650 William staged a *coup d'état* just as Maurice had formerly done. Six deputies from Holland were arrested, and preparations for the siege of Amsterdam were begun. Remembering the fate of Oldenbarneveldt and fearing to share it, the opposition collapsed, and William found himself supreme. But within six months he was dead of small-pox, leaving as his heir a posthumous son, the future William III of England. In the circumstances, power was rapidly recovered by the Estates of Holland. At their suggestion a 'Great Assembly' was convened in 1651, at which the offices of Captain-General and Stadtholder were abolished by several of the provinces, and in 1653 the Grand Pensionary of Holland, the same John de Witt who had negotiated the Treaty of Westminster with England, became in effect the ruler of the country. A rising young lawyer, he was destined to hold power until 1672, when a foreign war – this time against France – once more brought the Orange family back into power.

Although the years from 1600 to 1650 may seem from the above account to be essentially ones of fluctuating constitutional struggles at home and rather undramatic battles abroad, yet they were in fact a period of great stability, based on economic progress and prosperity. Between 1572 and 1621 the population of the country doubled, reaching in the latter year a figure of about 2,500,000. Concentrated into a small area, this represented a considerable density (40 per sq. km.; compare France, 34; and Spain, 17) but as an absolute total, it was ridiculously small compared with that of France (16,000,000) or Spain (8,000,000). Yet during these years the economic power of the Dutch was out of all proportion to their numbers.

This power was concentrated in the province of Holland, with a population of 600,000, of which 100,000 lived in the city of Amsterdam, where about a quarter of all the wealth of the Netherlands was to be found. There the new techniques were developed that had once made Antwerp the economic metropolis of northwest Europe. In 1609 the Bank of Amsterdam was established. It was not a bank of issue, but a bank of deposit. Merchants might deposit money of any type and fineness and were then credited with the real value of their deposit in 'bank money', which 'as it represented money according to the standard of the mint was always of the same real value, and intrinsically worth more than current money', as Adam Smith wrote in admiration, over a century and a half later. The value of the deposits rose from 1,000,000 florins in 1610 to 8,000,000 in 1640, and the bank was able to lend money at from 3 to 6 per cent, a low rate of interest for the times. Coupled with the Bank was the Exchange, a meeting-place for business men where they might conclude bargains and also a stock exchange where they might speculate in the stock of the trading companies.

The commercial strength of the United Provinces was founded upon the sea, upon the North Sea herring fisheries and the Baltic (in the seventeenth century over 60 per cent of all ships passing through the Sound came from the Netherlands), and the great trading companies. The Dutch had always been sailors; during the war with Spain this side of their economy had developed rapidly and when Lisbon was closed by the Spanish to Dutch shipping they began to send expeditions direct to the East. At first these were relatively unsuccessful. The turning-point came with the foundation of the Dutch East India Company in 1602, an amalgamation of local companies, which mirrored the distribution of mercantile strength in the country. The business was conducted by six local chambers, based on Amsterdam, Delft, Zeeland, Rotterdam, Hoorn and Enkhuizen, while the central organization was managed by a board of seventeen directors, of which Amsterdam chose eight, and Zeeland four. The cost of sending out a fleet was borne by the areas concerned in proportion to the number of these directors. Shareholders subscribed 6,450,000 florins, but the real control of the Company was in the hands of the directors.

The Company was immensely successful. It lasted for almost two centuries, during which it paid an average dividend of 18 per cent per annum (1605–48; 22 per cent). Under Coen (Governor-General 1617–23 and 1627–9) and van Diemen (1636–45) it drove the Portuguese from their empire in the East, obtaining control of the strategic ports and trading centres from Persia to Japan. The most important individual acquisitions were the capture of Batavia in 1619 and Malacca in 1640. It was a powerful instrument for war as well as trade, sapping the Spanish strength. Secret instructions in 1608 ran:

> The ships, which cannot be of use to you, you shall burn; and in no way release them for money, not even persons of distinction, if they cannot be exchanged for some prisoners of the Company.[1]

The Company was responsible for the first importation of tea (1610) and coffee (1616) to Europe. The emphasis was always on trade rather than settlement. Australia, sighted by the Portuguese in 1542, was visited in 1605 and later years, but no attempt was made to explore the coast. The only

[1] *C.M.H.*, IV, p. 729.

Dutch colony in new lands was that established at Table Bay in South Africa by van Riebeek in 1651 to serve as a stepping-stone to the markets of Asia.

The Company was so successful that in 1621 an attempt was made to repeat its triumph by the foundation of a West India Company. The organization was similar in structure to that of the earlier company, with five local chambers (Amsterdam, Zeeland, Rotterdam, Hoorn and Friesland, and Groningen), and a central committee of nineteen members, eight of whom were chosen by Amsterdam, which also held four-ninths of the stock. There the similarity ends. The West India Company was much more of a political venture, which aimed 'by bearding the King of Spain in his treasure-house to cut the sinews by which he sustained his wars in Europe'.[1] It achieved this aim, notably in 1628 when the entire Spanish silver fleet was captured off Cuba by Piet Hein, who brought back loot valued at 11,509,524 florins. Significant was the arrival in 1619 at the English colony of Virginia of 'a Dutch man of warre that sold us twenty negars', and the establishment of a Dutch settlement at Manhattan in 1623. Between 1630 and 1654 the Company was almost successful in driving the Portuguese out of Brazil; but the Company had not the resources to carry on a full-scale war and after its defeat there it declined, and came to an end in 1674.

The Bank, the Exchange, the fleets and the trading companies all combined to create Dutch economic power. Louis de Geer (d. 1652) was typical of the Dutch capitalists. He used his fortune to equip the Protestant forces in the Thirty Years' War with artillery, to raise two fleets to fight the Danes (1644) and to make loans to Gustavus Adolphus from whom in return he obtained control of the Swedish iron and copper mines. The success of the United Provinces rested on such men, and on the identity for them of politics and economics, of the merchant and the state. In 1629 the merchants of Amsterdam announced:

> During the Truce, through our economic management and exertions we have sailed all nations off the seas, drawn almost all trade from other lands hither, and served the whole of Europe with our ships.

[1] *C.M.H.*, IV, p. 703.

EUROPE
ABOUT 1660
English Miles
0   100   200   300

NORWAY

SCOTLAND

IRELAND

ENGLAND

DENMARK

Bremen

Brandenbur

UNITED PROVINCES

Spanish Netherlands

THE EMPIRE

Verdun

Metz

Toul

Bavaria

Aust

FRANCE

SWITZERLAND

SAVOY

Milan

VENICE

PORTUGAL

SPAIN

PAPAL STATES

TUSCANY

Naples

Corsica

Minorca

Majorca

Sardinia

Sicily

Algiers

Tunis

Twenty years later, the Seventeen Directors of the East India Company were writing

> . . . we must work heart and soul to remain masters of the profit-yielding Molucca spices of nutmeg, nuts and mace, to the exclusion of all other nations.[1]

The economic and political identity was complete:

> . . . loans were subscribed direct by the original lender to the states; the states and other public borrowing bodies were corporations responsible for payment; the republic was a trade-state; the lender-class was identical with the regent-class, the ruling oligarchy. They were not passive *rentiers* but active business men whose business was dealing in loans to the states. Both as lenders and as borrowers they were on the spot and dealing with men they knew. They were the members of a thoroughly business-like community.
>
> That was really the most important point of all. Sound public finance is not likely to exist except on a basis of sound private finance; and sound private finance comes into existence when there is a healthy business community to give it employment and keep it straight.[2]

The wealth of Holland was the basis on which her cultural achievements rested. Other factors played their part: the influx of refugees, the relative freedom of the press, and the breaking down of social barriers. The university of Leyden continued to be the intellectual power-house of the state, supported by five provincial universities. The Arminian, Hugo Grotius (1583-1645), historian, theologian, poet and lawyer, opened up new ground with his writings on international law – a topic very relevant to the international nature of Dutch commerce. In 1609 he produced his *Mare Liberum*, a plea for the freedom of the seas (answered by England, now becoming the commercial rival of the Dutch, in John Selden's *Mare Clausum* (1635)). In 1625 he published his greatest work, a study of international law, *De jure Belli ac Pacis*. Grotius was now living in France; having been imprisoned during Maurice's *coup d'état*, he had escaped concealed in a trunk-load of Arminian books and dirty washing!

---

[1] Quoted by Geyl, p. 184.
[2] G. N. Clark, *The Seventeenth Century*, O.U.P., 1929, p. 45.

The French philosopher, Descartes (1596–1650) had moved to Holland in 1629 and remained there until 1649, publishing his *Discours de la Méthode* there in 1637. His disciple, Spinoza (1632–76), was born in Amsterdam, and spent his life in the United Provinces. Dutch scientists of international reputation included the microscopist, Leeuwenhoek (1632–1723) and Christian Huyghens (1629–93), astronomer, mathematician and inventor.

The solid prosperity of the Dutch encouraged sound craftsmanship and comfortable, well-designed houses and furniture. It encouraged, too, the production of paintings to hang in those houses. Two artists stand head and shoulders above the mass of competent Dutch painters: Rembrandt (1607–69); and Vermeer (1632–75).[1]

EXTRACT

John Evelyn visits the United Provinces, 1641:

13th August. We arrived late at Rotterdam, where was their annual mart or fair, so furnished with pictures, especially landscapes and drolleries (as they call those clownish representations), that I was amazed. Some of these I bought and sent into England. The reason of this store of pictures, and their cheapness, proceeds from their want of land to employ their stock, so that it is an ordinary thing to find a common farmer lay out two or three thousand pounds in this commodity. Their houses are full of them, and they vend them at their fairs to very great gains.

19th. We returned to the Hague, and went to visit the Hoff, or Prince's Court, with the adjoining gardens full of ornament, close walks, statues, marbles, grots, fountains, and artificial music. There is to this palace a stately hall, not much inferior to ours of Westminster, hung round with colours and other trophies taken from the Spaniards; and the sides below are furnished with shops. . . .

It was on a Sunday morning that I went to the Bourse, or Exchange, [in Amsterdam] after their sermons were ended, to see the Dog-market, which lasts till two in the afternoon in this place of convention of merchants from all parts of the world. The building is not comparable to that of London,

[1] See Chapter XIV.

built by that worthy citizen, Sir Thomas Gresham, yet in one respect exceeding it, that vessels of considerable burthen may ride at the very quay contiguous to it; and indeed it is by extraordinary industry that this city, as well generally all the towns of Holland, are so accommodated with graffs, cuts, sluices, moles, and rivers, made by hand, that nothing is more frequent than to see a whole navy, belonging to this mercantile people, riding at anchor before their very doors: and yet their streets even, straight, and well paved, the houses so uniform and planted with lime trees, as nothing can be more beautiful. . . .

This part of Amsterdam is built and gained upon the main sea, supported by piles at an immense charge, and fitted for the most busy concourse of traffickers and people of commerce beyond any place, or mart, in the world. (*The Diary of John Evelyn*, Dent, rev. ed. 1952, Vol. I, pp. 21–3, 24–5)

FURTHER READING

R. T. Davies, *The Golden Century of Spain, 1501–1621*, Macmillan, 1937

R. T. Davies, *Spain in Decline, 1621–1700*, Macmillan, London, 1955

P. Geyl, *The Netherlands in the Seventeenth Century*, Part I, 1609–1648, Benn, 1961

XIII · THE MAIN LINES OF ECONOMIC DEVELOPMENT

Introduction

THE next two chapters indicate some of the main developments in economics, political thought, the arts and science. History is the account of all man's activities, but no historian has yet discovered a satisfactory technique which will enable him to weave them all into one account. The simplest narrative thread in the sixteenth and seventeenth centuries is that of political development; but it is important to realize that if other aspects of the period are removed from the main narrative and described separately this does not mean they have been relegated to a sort of lumber-room, where they can be disregarded. They can none of them be divorced from the main narrative, nor it from them – indeed, some historians would make economic change and technological discoveries the foundation of all other historical processes. The broad generalizations which follow should be continuously related to the more detailed political chapters.

In economic matters the period covered by this book saw the emergence of commercial capitalism, and the partial control of economic affairs by the state through a series of empirical decisions, later known collectively as Mercantilism. The rate of economic change, though faster than in earlier times, was still sufficiently slow for these changes to have neither a beginning nor an end in our period. In Chapters I and II the point was made that many of the new financial techniques and commercial practices of the fifteenth century had their origin in the cities of the later Middle Ages. There is, however, a change of tempo in the middle of that century. The preceding hundred years or more had been a period of economic contraction and depression. In the second half of the century economic expansion becomes once more general. This renewed activity does not have a natural terminus in 1660.

317

The line of development runs unbroken to at least the middle of the eighteenth century.

Within our period the most remarkable features are the use of surplus capital to finance trade and to create larger economic units in both agriculture and industry; the development of a limited number of new industrial processes; the appearance of international financiers and cities of international exchange; the state control of economic development (Mercantilism); and the first wave of European expansion overseas; all driven forward and at the same time overshadowed by the great price rise which was one consequence of the voyages of exploration.

The Expansion of Europe

For four hundred years the expansion of Europe was the most important series of events in the history of the world, affecting as it did not only Europe, but also the other continents that were discovered, exploited and colonized. It is now clear that this phase in world history came to an end about 1900. The first partition of Africa at the Berlin Congress of 1885, and the arrival at the South Pole of Amundsen in 1911, may be taken as symbolic of the end of the era. Then there was virtually nothing left to discover, nothing left to annex, and already some of the original colonies had grown into independent states.

The later Crusades were one of the first symptoms of the European search for markets and sources of supply, enabling Venice and Genoa to obtain a trading foothold in the eastern Mediterranean. The obstacles, physical and political, to expansion eastwards limited this development.

The movement outwards from Europe acquired a new dimension with the voyages of the Portuguese in the fifteenth century. The half-English Prince Henry the Navigator (1394–1460) organized a methodical series of expeditions down the west coast of Africa and out into the Atlantic to the Azores. The first voyage took place in 1418. The idea was not new; the Genoese had tried to sail round Africa in 1291. What was fresh was the careful way in which the information brought back was systematically studied at a base at Sagres in southwest Portugal, and the lessons learnt there used to improve the technique of each succeeding expedition. An ocean-going ship, the caravel, was developed and instruments of navigation were improved.

The motives behind these voyages were not simple, for religious zeal mingled with commercial cupidity, curiosity with national pride. On the one hand Henry, a pious man, hoped to convert the heathen, turn the flank of the Muslim world and link up with the mythical Christian kingdom of Prester John, imagined as being somewhere in the neighbourhood of modern Ethiopia. On the other hand, a new route to Asia would be financially profitable and would enable whoever controlled it to escape from the commercial stranglehold that Venice, Genoa and the Ottoman Turks exercised over the spice trade.

At the time of Henry's death the Portuguese were almost half-way across the Atlantic, and had mapped about 2,500 miles of the African coastline. This work bore fruit in the next two generations. In 1471 the Equator was crossed and in 1488 an expedition led by Bartholomew Diaz rounded the Cape of Good Hope. Ten years later Vasco da Gama reached India, and successfully completed the round trip, reaching Portugal again in 1499. He had sailed 24,000 miles, half his men had died, and the profit on the voyage was 6,000 per cent. Once what one might call the 'Africa-barrier' had been broken the Portuguese rapidly sketched in the outlines of an Asiatic empire, in the form of a collection of trading centres based on Goa. This was largely the work of one man, Alfonso de Albuquerque (d. 1515).

Meanwhile the Spanish had successfully accomplished the Atlantic crossing and were engaged in colonizing Central America and the Pacific coast of South America.   Columbus, sailing west in search of an alternative route to Asia, had reached the West Indies in 1492, and two years later he set up the first permanent settlement in the New World, on the island of Haiti. From Cuba and Panama the Spanish *Conquistadores* conquered Mexico (Cortez, 1519–22) and Peru (Pizarro, 1530–41). Soon the ubiquitous German bankers, the Fuggers, were financing settlements in South America. The first printing press in the new continent was set up in Mexico in 1539 and by 1575 there were about 175,000 Spanish settlers in America. Mexico and Peru had become parts of Europe overseas.

Spain and Portugal naturally discouraged interlopers, and

tried to divide the world between themselves into spheres of influence. In 1493 the Spanish Pope Alexander VI had granted Spain a monopoly of all lands more than 100 leagues west of Cape Verde Islands, but the Portuguese objected, and in the following year by the Treaty of Tordesillas the dividing line was fixed 370 leagues to the west of the islands. (This gave the Portuguese Brazil, reached by Cabral in 1500.) Between 1519 and 1522 the world was circumnavigated for the first time by a Spanish expedition led by the Portuguese Magellan. He was killed *en route* and only eighteen Europeans survived the voyage. It raised the question of a line of demarcation on the far side of the globe, and in 1529 Spain and Portugal, by the Treaty of Saragossa, agreed to fix it 15° east of the Moluccas.

The other Atlantic peoples, the French and English, and later the Dutch, made attempts to break the Spanish–Portuguese monopoly. The first two powers concentrated on efforts to find a northern route to Asia – the North-East and North-West Passages. These were in fact not technically possible, but the attempt to find them led unintentionally to important discoveries. The French acquired an interest in Canada; in 1535–6 Cartier sailed up the St. Lawrence, and in the early seventeenth century Champlain carried on the work of exploration, founding Quebec in 1608 and Montreal in 1611. Yet in spite of government encouragement there were only about 3,000 French settlers in the region by the middle of the century.

In the same area the English King Henry VII had encouraged the Cabots in a series of expeditions beginning in 1497, when John Cabot reached Newfoundland. In the sixteenth century an expedition to look for the North-East Passage (Chancellor and Willoughby, 1553) resulted instead in the setting-up of the Muscovy Company to trade with Russia. Later in the century one of the Company's officials, Anthony Jenkinson, travelled overland from Moscow to the Caspian, Bokhara and Persia. (He brought back a yak's tail – 'a white cow's tail from Cathay' – as a present for the Tsar!) The Russians themselves were exploring and colonizing by land across the Asiatic steppes, and reached the Sea of Okhotsk, on the eastern coast of Asia, in 1639.

The Dutch and English colonial empires were created in the first half of the seventeenth century. The Dutch took over a great part of the Portuguese settlements in Asia between the years 1594 and 1658, so that in the latter year the Portuguese held only Goa, and Macao off the south China coast. Meanwhile the English had been setting up a string of colonies of settlement along the east coast of North America (1607–67), from French Canada to South Carolina, with a total population of perhaps 200,000.

The consequences of this expansion were numerous. Most obvious were the rapid technical improvements in the design of ships, and in the construction of instruments for determining latitude. These, in their turn, stimulated progress in astronomy and the compilation of astronomical tables. The new geographical information led to the appearance of modern maps; the first modern atlas was produced at Antwerp by Ortelius in 1570. The shift in the trade routes helped to bring about a decline in the wealth of Mediterranean trading states such as Genoa and Venice. The last voyage of the famous Venetian galleys to Flanders took place in 1532. There was a corresponding rise in the trade and importance of the Atlantic seaboard states of Portugal, Spain, France, England and the United Provinces. Luxury goods from Asia such as china, tea, coffee and cottons became available; and the New World provided many products hitherto unknown in the west, including tobacco, potatoes, chocolate and maize. The natives suffered. Columbus had hunted the West Indians with dogs to make them give up the gold they had not got; in 1512 the Laws of Burgos, which were the first European colonial code, declared that the natives were free men, but must be made to work. Five years later a Spaniard, Las Casas, was writing of 'The Ruined Indian'.

The Price Rise

For Europe the most immediate consequence of the discoveries was the introduction by the Spanish of large quantities of gold and silver from America. These imports of precious metal were the most important cause of the great sixteenth century price-rise. (Other factors were perhaps the rise in urban population; increased government expenditure, mainly on war; the development of credit facilities such as bills of exchange; and financial speculation.)

During the Middle Ages the amount of treasure in Europe had remained more or less constant. A certain amount of silver was mined in central Europe, and a certain amount flowed out to Asia. The second half of the fifteenth century saw an increase in European production, but this was soon dwarfed by the Spanish imports of gold and silver from Mexico and Peru. From 1564 onwards a treasure fleet sailed yearly to the Indies and back to the *Casa de Contratación* (House of Trade) at Seville. From there the golden tide spread through western Europe by way of Italy and Antwerp. Between 1503 and 1660 the Spanish in this way brought into Europe about 18,600 tons of silver and 200 tons of gold. The impact of these imports was greatest between 1550 and 1600, the actual volume of imports reaching a peak in the last ten years of the century. They provided anything up to 25 per cent of the Spanish revenue and their effect was to treble the amount of bullion in Europe.

Incomprehensible to the vast majority of men in the sixteenth century was the fact that this increase in bullion (aided by the other factors mentioned above) produced a corresponding rise in prices. Why, they asked, is everything getting dearer? The answer, crudely, was that the more there is of anything, the less each unit of that commodity will be worth. An increase in the available stocks of gold and silver reduces the value of those metals, just as surely as if they were apples. Therefore prices, which are measured in terms of bullion, rise. At the same time people can afford to pay the higher prices, since there is more gold and silver available.

Men accustomed to a stable economy could not believe that the price-rise was nobody's fault, and went round looking for a scapegoat. A debate in English on the subject, in which each class blames the others, is the *Discourse of the Common Weal* (1549). (The price-rise in England had been started, before the American treasure could make itself felt, by Henry VIII's debasement of the coinage.) In Spain the connection between the treasure and the price rise was mentioned 'almost casually' by a Spanish priest, Francisco de Gomara, some time before 1558. But the explanation seems to have passed unnoticed, and it had to be rediscovered in 1568 by the French writer Jean Bodin.

'I find,' he wrote, 'that the scarcity we are witnessing springs from three causes. The chief and almost the only one (which no one has yet touched on) is the abundance of gold and silver, which in this kingdom today is greater than at any time in the last four centuries.' [1]

In general, prices trebled between 1500 and 1660. The rise occurred at different dates in different countries, Spain and Portugal being naturally affected first, and trading countries experiencing the rise before less developed ones. When prices rise, the merchant and trader normally benefit, since the price of goods or raw materials is likely to rise between the time they buy and the time at which they sell. On the other hand, the person with a relatively fixed income suffers, since each year he finds that the same income will buy fewer goods. Incomes fixed by custom, or by law, will tend to lag behind prices. Classes affected in this way are likely to be the Crown, the landlord, the wage-labourer and, to some extent, the peasant. The Crown sought new sources of income, finding that it could no longer 'live of its own', or borrowed from the financiers and then failed to honour its debts; landlords had to wait till leases fell in, when they could relet the land at higher rents, or enclose it. Failing that, they might sell their land to *nouveaux riches* anxious to become gentlemen. The wage-earner found it hardest to increase his income, and although his wages did rise, they tended to lag a long way behind prices. The following figures illustrate this:

SPANISH PRICES [2]

Years	Goods	Wages
1501–1510	100	100
1591–1600	303	277

ENGLISH PRICES

Years	Goods	Wages
1501–1510	100	100
1593–1602	256	130

[1] *A Discourse of the Common Weal of this Realm of England*, ed. E. Lamond, C.U.P., 1929. For Gomara, see R. T. Davies, *The Golden Century of Spain*, Macmillan, 1937, p. 283. Bodin's book was called *Response au Paradoxe du Sieur de Malestroit touchant l'encherissement de toutes Choses*.

[2] S. B. Clough and C. W. Cole, *Economic History of Europe*, Harrap, 1946, pp. 128–9.

Finance and Trade

An economic development which played its part in aggra-
vating the price rise, but was also of importance on its own
account, was the increased use of credit instruments. These
made easier the business of trade and the use of capital. Bills
of exchange, originating in the Middle Ages, were now widely
used, as were promissory notes. The latter – 'I promise to
pay the bearer the sum of . . .' – were issued by traders and
bankers, and from them, later in the seventeenth century, the
'bank note' developed.

All credit instruments encouraged, and were in their turn
encouraged by, the development of public banking and public
exchanges in the great commercial cities. There were city
banks in Italy in the Middle Ages at such places as Siena
(1233). The first public bank appears to have been that of
Barcelona (1401). In 1587 Venice opened the deposit bank
of the Rialto, a public bank which accepted deposits of money
in any currency, and would carry out transfers, but was forbidden to make loans. This naturally made for much greater
stability. The first great deposit bank north of the Alps was
that of Amsterdam (1609).[1]

Closely connected with the bank, was the Exchange, which
at first was rather like a medieval fair that never closed. There
was an exchange at Bruges in the fourteenth century, at Antwerp about 1460, and at Lyons shortly afterwards. 'Merchants
can no more be without exchanges than ships at sea without
water,' wrote Sir Richard Gresham in 1538, and his son, Sir
Thomas, built the London Exchange, modelled on that at
Antwerp, and named by Queen Elizabeth I 'the Royal
Exchange' in 1571. The exchange at Amsterdam was opened
in 1611, and there merchants dealt in over 300 commodities.
At these exchanges merchants also bought and sold the stocks
of companies, and gambled on the possible future prices of
commodities. By 1660 the exchanges had come to perform
in a primitive way all the functions of the modern Stock
Exchange.

The history of Antwerp is a conveniently self-contained
example of the life of these new commercial cities, since its

[1] See Chapter XII.

rise and fall occupied a comparatively short time. The estuary of the Rhine, Waal, Maas and Scheldt lay at the junction of three trade routes; that from the Hanseatic towns in the east, that down the Rhine valley from Italy, and the sea-route up the Channel and from England. In addition, Flanders had early developed its own manufacturing industries. At first the centre of all this economic activity had been at Bruges, but during the fifteenth century its place had been taken by Antwerp. There were three reasons for this, geographical, political, economic. The Scheldt, on which Antwerp stood, was a better waterway than the Zwin, which served Bruges and was tending to silt up. When the Netherlands passed into the hands of the Dukes of Burgundy, they encouraged Brabant and its capital, Antwerp, to expand at the expense of Flanders and Bruges: in 1488 a charter of Maximilian's specifically called for a transfer of foreign trade from Bruges to Antwerp. Finally, the town council of Antwerp pursued a liberal economic policy, making it easy for merchants to trade there, and adopting a 'modern' approach to the needs of business men. Antwerp rose and Bruges declined.

The signs of Antwerp's economic convenience and the guarantees of its prosperity were the establishment there of the Portuguese spice market (1499), and of the English cloth-trade, which had moved from Bruges in Edward IV's reign. Of the other 'nations' which traded there, the most important were the merchants of the Hanseatic League, dealing in Baltic goods; the South Germans from Nuremberg, Augsburg and Frankfurt, handling copper and silver; and the Italians, bankers and financial *entrepreneurs*, who introduced the practice of double-entry book-keeping.

The city's great age lasted from about 1500 to about 1560, with its peak in the period 1530–45. At this time her trade was three times as great as that of London. Guicciardini analysed the value of Antwerp's imports about the year 1560, when she was handling 85 per cent of the Netherlands' trade, as follows: English cloth (31 per cent); Italian wares, including fine cloth (18 per cent); Baltic wheat (10 per cent); German wines (9 per cent); French wines (6 per cent); and Portuguese spices (6 per cent). The secretary of the Merchant Adventurers, commenting on the fact that other countries took the risks and Antwerp made the profit, wrote:

First, for the Portingall, we know, that like a good simple man, he sayled everie yeare full hungerly (God wot) about 3 parts of the earth almost for spices, & when he had brought them home, the great rich purses of the Antwerpians, subjects of the King of Spain, ingrossed them all into their own hands. . . .[1]

Besides its position as an *entrepôt*, Antwerp had a highly-developed manufacturing life of its own, in which the most important single item was the dyeing and finishing of English cloth.   Then there were the money-markets, the Antwerp–Augsburg one mainly controlled by Germans, and the Antwerp–Lyons–Genoa one in the hands of the Italians. These various activities supported a population of 100,000, making Antwerp the seventh largest city in Europe.

The second half of the century witnessed the decline of Antwerp from a position of international to one of only national importance.   The pillars of her prosperity were shaken.   She ceased to be the centre of the Portuguese spice trade in 1549; the Merchant Adventurers began to look for a new centre in the sixties, and eventually settled at Middleburg in the United Provinces (1598).   Spain and France went bankrupt in 1557 and Portugal in 1560 – serious blows for the international financiers who had lent them money.   Then, political disorders played their part;   the iconoclastic riots of 1566, the sacking of Antwerp in the Spanish Fury of 1576, the French Fury of 1583, the expulsion or flight of the Protestants when the Spanish captured the city in 1585, and finally the closure by the Dutch of Antwerp's route to the sea, the Scheldt, a closure made permanent in 1648.

Trading companies, like the other economic phenomena discussed, had their origins in medieval practice, but were extended and improved in the sixteenth and seventeenth centuries.   Two main types came into existence, the regulated and the joint stock company.   In the regulated company the merchant traded on his own, using his own capital, taking his own profits and sustaining his own losses: '. . . every man tradeth apart and particularlie with his own stocke . . .' as John Wheeler wrote.   Yet each member was at the same time one of a chartered company, the governors of which decided

[1] Quoted in *N.C.M.H.*, I, p. 449.

general policy, provided protection, administered foreign depots, laid down the rules and controlled the conditions of entry. The company was thus not unlike a medieval guild of merchants, but on an international scale. The Merchant Adventurers of England were a typical example of such a company.

The joint-stock company, on the other hand, was a combine of money rather than of merchants. Each member invested money in the joint stock. The size of his investment would determine how much of the profits he received, and his voice carried weight according to the number of shares he held, even though he might do no trading himself. The money was not withdrawn at the end of each venture, but remained at the disposal of the officials until the investor sold out. In all this, one can see the pattern of the modern company. Joint-stock enterprises had existed in Italy and Germany in the Middle Ages, but there is no physical continuity between them and the companies set up in the sixteenth and seventeenth centuries. The first English Company to be organized on a joint-stock basis was the Muscovy Company in 1555, and forty-nine others were founded between that date and 1680. They included the Mines Royal Company (1568), which was not a trading company, but was started to promote copper and silver mining in England, and the great East India Company, which floated its 'First Joint Stock' in 1613.

The new techniques supported new men, who lived by the manipulation of money. Reaping where they had not sowed, they faced the charge of being usurers. An English financier robustly retorted: 'Tush, tush, Scripture is Scripture, but for all Scripture, a man must live by his own, and I tell you my money is my plough.' International financiers appeared, as great as princes. The most powerful in the fifteenth century were the Medici (c. 1430–80) who ruled Florence, owned a banking establishment and three cloth-works in the city and had eight branches abroad strung across Europe from London to Rome.[1] The first half of the sixteenth century was

. . . the last age before the nineteenth century during which the machinations of great international financiers

[1] See also Chapter I.

independent of territorial governments played a major part in affairs: the age of the Fuggers has much in common with the age of the Rothschilds, but little with what came between.[1]

Hans Fugger was a weaver who moved to Augsburg about 1380. There he made and sold fustians (coarse cloth woven from a mixture of linen and cotton) and died a rich man worth 3,000 gulden. His son Jacob (d. 1469) continued to make money along the same lines, but the third generation. Ulrich, George and especially Jacob II (1459–1525) branched out in three directions. They extended the business to include rich materials, such as velvet, silk and damasks, and other luxury goods, spices and jewels. Augsburg was ideally situated as a centre from which to establish commercial links in these products between Italy and the north, and soon there was a string of Fugger agents across Europe. Secondly, the Fuggers used this commercial network and their growing profits to develop the financial side of the business, banking, lending money and handling bills of exchange. The scale of operations grew. They dealt with the transfer of Papal revenue from Scandinavia to Rome; they helped to supply the funds that secured the election of two popes and an Emperor, Charles V. They made themselves invaluable to the Habsburgs. These royal and ducal clients led to the third development. Everywhere they obtained the right to mine the minerals which Europe was beginning to demand so fiercely – silver in the Tirol, copper in Hungary, iron in central Europe, quicksilver in Spain. They made a price agreement with their main rivals in the copper market, the Hochstetter, by which the latter were to supply Italy, while the Fuggers supplied the Netherlands. They also worked and refined the raw materials which they controlled.

When Jacob II died, the firm's capital was estimated at 2,000,000 gulden. Under his nephew, Anton, it rose to 5,000,000 gulden in 1546, and in 1552 he lent 400,000 ducats to the Emperor Charles V to enable him to carry on the war against the French and the Protestants after he had been driven south by Maurice of Saxony. Thereafter the Fuggers's fortunes declined, until the firm went bankrupt in 1627. Lending to kings and princes had brought great rewards, but it had one

[1] *N.C.M.H.*, II, p. 16.

drawback – no one can make a government honour its debts. The national bankruptcies of 1557, 1607 and 1627 proved disastrous.

Industry and Agriculture

It is harder to generalize about developments in industry and agriculture, where the pattern varied greatly from country to country. The main fifteenth century industrial changes included the appearance of two new crafts, printing and cannon-founding, and an increasing scale of operations in the manufacture of cloth and in mining. The annual output of silver increased 500 per cent between 1460 and 1530, reaching a level of 3,000,000 ounces a year, and the output of copper increased at least as fast. In Styria the output of iron quadrupled during the same period, and reached a figure of over 8,000 tons a year. Charles V estimated that metal-working in one form or another provided employment for one hundred thousand people in the Empire. The most highly developed coal-mines were at Liège, where the adits which drained the mines were cunningly planned to provide the city's water-supply. In less fortunate areas, the increased demand for minerals led to improved pumps which in their turn stimulated research into the pressure of the atmosphere.[1]

In the sixteenth century English cloth exports were greater in quantity than those of any other European country. They were mainly in the form of undyed cloth of two main types, old-fashioned woollens and the 'New Drapery' of the worsted type copied from Flanders. Methods of production varied, but the most general was that known as 'the putting-out system'. Capitalist clothiers supplied wool to be spun into yarn in cottages, the yarn was then distributed to weavers, working at looms in their own cottages, and the woven cloth collected from them and taken to the markets. One of the advantages of the system was that the new industries were able to establish themselves in the countryside, away from the restrictions of town control.

The 'putting-out system' required capital and great skill in

[1] For the details given in this paragraph, see *The Cambridge Economic History of Europe*, C.U.P., Vol. II, 1952, pp. 470–3.

organization, but the growth of the English cloth-trade did not depend on any technical inventions. (The only new machine, the water-powered fulling mill, had appeared sometime in the thirteenth century.) In this the English cloth-trade is typical of the Industrial Revolution of the sixteenth century. The changes are everywhere the result of a plentiful supply of capital, and of the organization, by one method or another, of labour and machinery into comparatively large units capable of increased output. It is thus essentially an administrative revolution. The technological innovations do not in general appear until after 1660.

The vast majority of the people of Europe still lived on the land, and changes in agriculture took place more slowly than in any other sphere of life. It is very hard to generalize as to exactly what those changes were. In England the most obvious change was the enclosure of land, in Flanders and Holland it was the development of improved agricultural techniques. In western Europe the agricultural decline of the fifteenth century gave place to *une fièvre agricole*, inspired by a rise in the demand for land which took the form of more intensified agriculture, and also brought into cultivation marginal lands – marshes, waste and so forth. In general, where the peasant's status was not firmly protected by medieval law or custom, his position grew worse. This is most obvious in central and eastern Europe on the great demesne farms of Germany and Poland.

Mercantilism

The economic ferment coincided with a growth in the power of the state, and the latter attempted to bring the former under control. Its ad hoc, largely unorganized, decisions were later tidied up into the theory of Mercantilism. It is important not to regard the word as a fact. The historian who has made the most complete study of Mercantilism concludes that it is only '. . . a convenient term for a phase of economic policy and economic ideas'.[1] With this qualification, one may say that by 1660 most states attempted to control economic

---

[1] E. Heckscher, *Economic History Review*, Nov., 1936.

change in accordance with the following principles: that to be powerful, a state should collect as much gold and silver as possible (bullionism); that the best way to achieve this was to have a favourable balance of trade, '. . . to sell more to strangers yearly than we consume of theirs in value' as Thomas Mun put it about 1630; a country should therefore be as far as possible self-sufficient, in agriculture so that she might not be dependent on the foreigner for her food, in industry so that she might have a surplus of manufactured goods to export; commerce must be protected and developed in every way, and to this end it is obviously desirable to have a large merchant navy, a state navy to protect the merchants, and plenty of colonies. The final objects of Mercantilism are prosperity and political power. In France political power was seen as the chief aim, and prosperity as a means to that end, while in the United Provinces, on the other hand, the order of importance was perhaps reversed. In general, Mercantilism is a convenient shorthand term 'which may be applied to those theories, policies and practices, arising from the conditions of the time, by which the national state, acting in the economic sphere, sought to increase its own power, wealth and prosperity'. [1] Francis Bacon, in his *Essay of Seditions and Troubles* (1625), plainly regards economic policy as serving political ends:

> The first remedy or prevention is to remove by all means possible that material cause of sedition whereof we spake; which is want and poverty in the estate. To which purpose serveth the opening and well-balancing of trade; the cherishing of manufactures; the banishing of idleness; the repressing of waste and excess by sumptuary laws; the improvement and husbanding of the soil: the regulating of prices of things vendible; the moderating of taxes and tributes; and the like. . . .
> It is likewise to be remembered that, forasmuch as the increase of any estate must be upon the foreigner (for whatsoever is somewhere gotten is somewhere lost), there be but three things which one nation selleth unto another: the commodity as nature yieldeth it; the manufacture; and the vecture or carriage. So that if these three wheels go, wealth will flow as in a spring tide.

[1] *N.C.M.H.*, I, p. 446.

Economic change brought with it social change. The population of Europe increased a little:

	1497	*1600*	*1600*
		(population per sq. km.)	
The Empire	15	20	28
France	15	16	34
England	3	5·5	30
Spain and Portugal	8	10	17
Italy	no figures	13	44
United Provinces	available	2·5	40

At least 90 per cent still lived in the countryside, but there was almost everywhere a movement to the towns. In the early seventeenth century the great cities were Paris, London, Madrid, Vienna, Amsterdam and Lyons, with populations ranging downwards from 300,000 to 100,000. Of the great cities of a century earlier, Antwerp, Lisbon, Milan, Rome and Venice had all declined. Constantinople remained the biggest city in eastern Europe.

The price rise and the increasing commitments of the state, particularly when waging war which was now a very expensive business, had led to a desperate search for new sources of revenue. *Nervus belli est pecunia.* Crown lands were developed, or sold. Much mercantilist legislation was aimed at increasing the Crown's revenue. Taxes on imports and exports proved relatively easy to collect, while within the state one country after another imposed an excise – a sort of purchase tax. As has already been seen, governments borrowed money and, when they could not pay their debts, declared themselves bankrupt. 'The one state which throughout the [seventeenth] century was always solvent was the Dutch republic.' [1] It is impossible to compare revenues, but here are some figures for the sixteenth century, based on the purchasing power of the £ today:

	£
The Sultan	9,600,000
Charles V	6,600,000
Francis I	4,800,000
Henry VIII	950,000

The old personal relationship between master and apprentice, landlord and peasant, lay and cleric, was giving place,

[1] G. N. Clark, *The Seventeenth Century*, O.U.P., 1929, p. 44.

slowly and steadily, to an impersonal division between rich
and poor. The anonymous townsman makes his appearance
in this significant comment of Descartes, living abroad in
Amsterdam:

> In this great town, where apart from myself there dwells
> no one who is not engaged in trade, everyone is so much out
> for his own advantage that I should be able to live my
> whole life here without ever meeting a living soul.[1]

The growing fluidity of class structure received a satirical
comment in Rabelais:

> I think many are at this day Emperours, Kings, Dukes,
> Princes, and Popes on the earth, whose extraction is some
> porter, and pardon-pedlars . . .

and a more philosophical one in Ulysses's speech in *Troilus and
Cressida*:

> Take but degree away, untune that string,
> And, hark, what discord follows! each thing meets
> In mere oppugnancy; the bounded waters
> Should lift their bosoms higher than the shores,
> And make a sop of all this solid globe:
> Strength should be lord of imbecility,
> And the rude son should strike his father dead:
> Force should be right; or rather, right and wrong,
> Between whose endless jar justice resides,
> Should lose their names, and so should justice too.
> Then every thing includes itself in power,
> Power into will, will into appetite;
> And appetite, an universal wolf,
> So doubly seconded with will and power,
> Must make perforce an universal prey,
> And last eat up himself.

EXTRACT

*John Wheeler defends foreign trade, and the Merchant Adventurers,
1601:*

And who knoweth not that we have no small need of many
things, whereof foreign Countries have great store, and that
we may well spare many things, whereof the said Countries
have also need? Now to vent the superfluities of our Country,

[1] Quoted by P. Geyl, *The Netherlands Divided*, Williams & Norgate, 1936, p. 248.

and bring in the Commodities of others, there is no readier or
better means than by merchandise; and seeing we have no
way to increase our treasure by mines of gold and silver at
home, and can have nothing from abroad without money or
wares, it followeth necessarily that the abovesaid good council
of Cato to be sellers and not buyers is to be followed; yet so,
that we carry not out more in value over the seas than we bring
home from thence, or transport things hurtful to the State, for
this were no good husbandry, but tendeth to the subversion of
the land and diminishing of the treasure thereof; whereas by
the other we shall greatly increase it, the trade being carried
and managed under a convenient Government and orders,
and not in a dispersed, loose, and straggling manner; the
practice whereof we may see in this Realm almost these 400
years together: First in the Staple and Wool trade, and next
in that of the M.M. Adventurers and Cloth trade. . . . (*A
Treatise of Commerce* . . ., by John Wheeler, 1601. Spelling
modernized. Text in R. H. Tawney and E. Power, *Tudor
Economic Documents*, Longmans, Green, 1924, Vol. III, pp. 280–1)

FURTHER READING

H. Heaton, *Economic History of Europe*, Harper, 1936

S. B. Clough and C. W. Cole, *Economic History of Europe*, Harrap, 1946

M. Postan and E. Rich, *The Cambridge Economic History of Europe*, Vol. II,
    C.U.P., 1952

New Cambridge Modern History, C.U.P., Vol. I, 1957, Chap. II.   The Face
    of Europe on the Eve of the Great Discoveries;   Chap. XV.   The New
    World;   Chap. XVI.   Expansion as a Concern of all Europe
        Vol. II, 1958, Chap. II, Economic Change

J. N. L. Baker, *History of Geographical Discovery and Exploration*, Harrap, 1931

R. H. Tawney, *Religion and the Rise of Capitalism*, Murray, 1937

G. N. Clark, *The Seventeenth Century*, O.U.P., 1929

XIV · DEVELOPMENTS IN THE ARTS, POLITICAL THOUGHT, AND SCIENCE

The Arts

In the later sixteenth and early seventeenth centuries the arts did not colour their age to the same extent that the Renaissance had done a hundred years earlier.   Yet they gave their name to the whole of seventeenth century civilization, the Age of the Baroque.

The life of Michelangelo (1475–1564) spans the period between the consummation of the High Renaissance and the first works of the Baroque.   The change can be seen in his own paintings in one room, the Sistine Chapel in Rome.   Those on the ceiling (1508–12) are just within the Renaissance idiom.   That of the Last Judgement on the wall above the altar (1541) foreshadows the Baroque style.   However, the Baroque did not develop directly from the work of Michelangelo.   In Tuscany painters were content to imitate his exaggerations, his foreshortening, his emphasis on movement and on shadow, without adding anything to them.   They produced a dead, tortured style, called 'Mannerist', perhaps from Vasari's comment that they painted 'in the manner of Michelangelo'.

Outside Tuscany, in the work of the Venetian Tintoretto (1518–94) and – in a special way – of the Cretan, El Greco, (1545–1625) the line of development continued away from classical perfection, from 'emotion recollected in tranquillity' towards a romantic expression of the artist's personal vision. In the work of these two artists, and of Caravaggio (1569–1609), a lesser painter but a more perfect example of the style, one can study what Baroque means in the world of painting.   Where the Renaissance emphasized line, the Baroque emphasized surface areas of colour; instead of the picture being planned as a series of planes more or less parallel to the spectator and built round a central axis, it now tended to recede in a series of serpentine diagonals; the composition was what artists call 'open' instead of being 'closed'; a pellucid clarity gave place to a deliberate contrast between bright light and heavy shadow.

In a Baroque painting, therefore, the figures are caught in movement as by a camera, their faces express strong emotions, and the scene is made dramatically intense by violent fore-shortening, by spiral movements in the composition and by strong contrasts of light and shade (*chiaroscuro*). Such a picture will depend for its effect on the total impact it makes on the spectator. For that reason, one cannot isolate details in a Baroque work of art. Thus isolated, they will usually appear comic, or vulgar.

The greatest painters in the Baroque tradition stood, as geniuses always do, just outside the conventional definition of their art. In their work one finds not only Baroque character-istics, but also a pinch of the Renaissance classical tradition, these two elements being fused and having added to them the painter's own individual vision. The very great Baroque painters are a Fleming, Rubens (1577–1640); a Spaniard, Velazquez (1599–1660); and a Dutchman, Rembrandt (1606–69). To see the range of which they were capable, look at one of the set-pieces of Rubens, the *Rape of the Daughters of Leucippus*, and then at the portrait of his wife's sister Susanne Fourmont, *Le Chapeau de Paille*; at Velazquez' painting of the Infanta of Spain's maids of honour, *Las Meninas*, and then at his portrait of Innocent X; at Rembrandt's painting of the Amsterdam Civil Guard, *The Night Watch*, and then at any of his self-portraits in old age.

Though the Baroque style continued throughout the seven-teenth century, by the end of our period a classical calm is falling on the swirling draperies, the chequer-board of light and shade. The mathematically constructed compositions of Poussin (1594–1665) and Vermeer (1632–1675), point the way towards a new phase of classicism. In fact, from the seven-teenth century to the present day the classical and romantic styles have existed side by side. Nevertheless, there seems to be an oscillation between the personal and the impersonal, between Rubens and Piero della Francesca, and the historian must at least wonder why this might be so. There is, of course, no agreed answer. Two explanations are often put forward to explain the change in the sixteenth century. One is that the Renaissance artists had pushed to the limit, for the time being, the possibilities of the classical style, and that later artists, unless they were prepared to resign themselves to being slavish imitators, were compelled to introduce into their paintings those elements that the Renaissance had disregarded. The other explanation is that the painters reflected the changed times in which they worked. The Counter-Reformation and the nation-state both demanded an active emotional style which would exalt temporal power or spiritual glory. The time was one of violent alteration in society, and the new work in science and mathematics was also concerned with problems of movement and change. Was it possible that the needs of the patrons combined with an appreciation, conscious or unconscious, of the unstable earth and the vortices of Descartes to produce paintings in which the characters are all caught in arrested movement, and did this appreciation send the robes of saints billowing and swirling upwards?

It is impossible to show that painting was, or was not, affected by the political and intellectual currents of the day. It is possible, however, to demonstrate a partial connection in architecture, particularly church architecture. The great architect of the later Renaissance had been Palladio (1518–80), building villas in which respect for the classical rules of proportion was combined with originality in fitting the 'bits' together. Now the process of rearranging the classical style was taken a stage further.

The church of *Il Gesù* in Rome was begun for the Jesuits in 1568, and it has as good a claim as any to be called the first Baroque building. Today it appears restrained, but compared with the churches of the High Renaissance it was a startling creation. Although the façade is composed of classical elements, the proportion and balance of those elements no longer adheres to classical standards. It was this which shocked or delighted contemporaries. The details are not just applied ornament, without them the west end of the building would have no shape or form; they are the building. The double columns and pilasters are like steel girders, and above them the great curves (volutes) on either side of the upper storey complete its pattern. The inside of the church was as revolutionary as its exterior. Renaissance churches had usually been symmetrical, based on the plan of an equal-armed cross, with a cupola over the junction of the arms. The new church returned to the earlier oblong form, with a series of chapels down either side.   The attention of the congregation was thus concentrated on the high altar.

Il Gesù was only the beginning.   To appreciate what is meant by the High Baroque style in architecture, one should look at its descendants, the churches built by Borromini (1599–1667) and decorated by Bernini (1598–1680).   Applied ornament, gilding and marble, great sunbursts and clouds of floating cherubs, surround the altars above which saints swoon in ecstasy or ascend in triumph amidst a hurricane of draperies. The interiors have become theatres in which the drama of the Mass is played.   In the greatest examples genius achieves the apparently impossible and creates a masterpiece.   Lesser examples are often artistically rather unpleasant.

In secular architecture, similar developments took place and palaces were built to emphasize the power and the glory of earthly kings.   The main examples occur after 1660; one must look to the reigns of Louis XIV and his contemporaries to find a parallel to church Baroque.   Moreover, as in painting, so too in architecture, classical simplicity continued to exist alongside the Baroque complexities.

Music acquired a similar dramatic quality.   Once again the stimulus came originally largely from the Jesuits.   Harmonic music was developed, in which solo voices were set against a rich accompaniment.   The resulting oratorios were known at the time as 'in the Jesuit style'.   There was also an increased emphasis on instrumental music – that of the organ or the violin, for instance – as music in its own right, not requiring the addition of voices.   The oratorio in its turn affected secular music, and led to the appearance of the opera.   The first public opera-house was probably that opened in Venice in 1637.

Political Thought

The outstanding political facts of the period are the emergence of the nation-state and the triumph of religious nonconformity.   From the struggle of these two with one another, and of both of them with the dominant Catholic Church, there emerged new political and religious structures, Church-States and State-Churches, and new political theories to justify – and sometimes to fight for – their existence.   These theories drew some of their material from earlier medieval and classical thought and some from the brute facts of the contemporary conflicts.

Medieval political thought had based its theories primarily on the Bible, and to a lesser extent on the classical writers, especially Aristotle. From Aristotle was taken the idea that the state exists to make possible the good life, from classical thought, the idea that there exists a natural (moral) law outside and above man-made law, and from the Bible specific indications as to what this natural law was. The medieval ruler was thus always a limited ruler. St. Augustine wrote, *Remota justitia, quid regna nisi magna latrocinia*, government without justice is highway robbery; and St. Thomas Aquinas said that when a man-made law conflicts with the law of nature 'it at once ceases to be a law'.

Much of this had come under fire from anti-Papal writers, supporters of the Emperor, in the later Middle Ages. In the sixteenth century the rival arguments occupy the whole stage, and engage in one long debate on the terms of political obedience. The practical creators of the new state and of the breach with Rome – men like Louis XI, Thomas Cromwell, Luther, and even Calvin – are in their political attitudes, still partly medieval. After all, they are empiricists, dealing with day-to-day facts. The problems which are raised by them are on the whole answered – or not answered – in the second half of the century or in the succeeding hundred years.

During that time there is a great spate of pamphlets and political theorizing. The theories still spring from the old premises, but they take the arguments to new conclusions in their attempts to make them fit the new political facts of life. For, as an Englishman wrote towards the end of the next century, '. . . whosoever sets himself to study Politicks, must do it by reading History'. And the history of the times was full of new political phenomena. The United Provinces, for example, could not be fitted easily into Aristotle's classification of constitutions, nor could religious toleration be easily accepted by those who had read St. Augustine's views on the treatment of heretics – 'compel them to come in'. Two linked problems posed themselves inescapably: by what right could the state claim the absolute obedience of its subjects; and, if the state's power was not absolute, in what circumstances were its subjects entitled to withhold their obedience? These were not academic questions but, then as now, matters of life and death.

Those who supported the absolute state and those who claimed a conditional right to revolt based their arguments on certain assumptions common to both of them. There was the old one that the state existed for the good of the community, and there was a new one, that the relationship between governor and governed was as if there had been a legal agreement or contract between the two parties. (It is important to remember that theorists did not usually suppose that such a contract had ever actually existed.)

The theory of a social contract dominated political thinking from the sixteenth to the end of the eighteenth century. A general statement of the theory would run something like this: since man was imperfect (as all Christians knew), and could not live a full or even a safe life by himself (as Aristotle had observed), it was necessary for men to put themselves under some sort of control, each giving up a little of their liberty in order that they might enjoy more fully that which remained.

Consider these two statements from English political theorizing. Richard Hooker, concerned to justify the Elizabethan Church, wrote in his *Laws of Ecclesiastical Polity* (1594–7):

> . . . the cause of men's uniting themselves at first in politic Societies [is] . . . to supply those defects which are in us being single and solely by our selves.

Then at the end of our period Thomas Hobbes, generally considered to be an atheist, started from much the same jumping-off point in his *Leviathan* (1651). Without society, he writes, the life of man is 'solitary, poore, nasty, brutish, and short'. He then continues:

> The finall Cause, End, or Designe of men, (who naturally love Liberty, and Dominion over others,) in the introduction of that restraint upon themselves, (in which wee see them live in Common-wealths,) is the foresight of their own preservation, and of a more contented life thereby; . . .

So much was common ground, but beyond this point in the argument the paths divided. Was this agreement perpetual?

Hobbes was in general a supporter of the absolute power of the state, yet he thought that there were circumstances in which the contract might be dissolved.   He said:

The Obligation of Subjects to the Soveraign, is understood to last as long, and no longer, than the power lasteth, by which he is able to protect them.

Not everyone agreed with Hobbes.   The supporters of the absolute power of the state claimed that, once entered into, the contract could never be broken by the governed; others claimed that if the ruler broke his side of the contract the subject had not only a right, but even a duty, to rebel.   Catholic and Protestant extremists sometimes went even further, under persecution, and claimed that tyrannicide was a moral obligation.   There was plenty of room for disagreement; since the social contract had never actually occurred, each theorist was at liberty to draw up his own terms.

As the years went by there grew up a body of theory devoted to justifying the power of the absolute ruler and emancipating him from the medieval view that all political power is a trust and that his law-making powers are limited by natural law. This view had the support not only of extremists but also of many middle-of-the-way men who felt that a strong central government was essential in a time of change and stress.   On the other hand there developed also a rival body of theory concerned to lay emphasis on the idea of natural law restraining and controlling the ruler's actions – the medieval view which still survived, concealed within the new doctrine of the social contract.

These two bodies of theory did not coincide with the religious divisions of Europe.   Minorities which, when persecuted, asserted the right of the subject to rebel, naturally became – if they achieved power – convinced supporters of the absolute power of the state subject only to religious qualifications. Catholics and Protestants could be found in both camps.

The theory of absolute monarchy was perhaps the more orthodox of the two views of sovereignty.   From Ferdinand of Spain and Louis XI of France to Richelieu and Gustavus Adolphus, the period is one of rulers with great and growing powers.   They provide protection for the ordinary man

against the demands of the great noble or the Church.   Here is
an English expression of this point of view:

> Yea, and it is better to have a tyrant unto thy king than a
> shadow: a passive king that doth naught himself but suffreth
> other to do with him what they will and to lead him whither
> they list.   For a tyrant, though he do wrong unto the good,
> yet he punisheth evil, and maketh all men obey, neither
> suffreth any men to poll [rob] but himself.   A king that is
> soft as silk . . . shall be much more grievous unto the realm
> than a right tyrant.   Read the chronicles and thou shalt find
> it ever so . . .[1]

Until an alternative form of secure government could be
clearly seen this was a natural point of view, and it received
added support later in the century from all those who, tired of
religious persecution or civil war, took refuge in political or
religious scepticism.   Montaigne, wearily observing the French
scene, commented:

> How many men and women have we not seen who have
> patiently endured to be burnt and roasted for misunder-
> stood and vain opinions which they have borrowed of others.

The most extreme claims for the absolute power of the
national ruler were made by Jean Bodin (1530–96) in his *Six
Livres de la Republique*, published in 1576.   Bodin was a *Politique*,
anxious to strengthen the power of the prince at the expense of
both groups of extremists – the Huguenots and the Catholic
Leaguers.   For Bodin the state was composed of two parts, the
subjects and the sovereign power.   Sovereignty consisted in
the exercise of supreme power over subjects, and in every state
there was – or ought to be – a sovereign with a right always to
do anything.   'The main characteristic of absolute sovereignty,'
he wrote, 'lies in making laws for his subjects without their
consent.'   Law is thus the embodied will of the sovereign –
Quod principi placuit legis habet vigorem, what pleases the prince
has the force of law, as the Roman legal tag phrased it.   (In
practice Bodin was prepared to qualify these powers, but the
stark statements remained, for the use of later rulers.)

Bodin also took God out of politics.   Sovereignty was, for
him, the creation of men, because it was needed to make
civilized life possible, and was not produced by a special act of

[1] William Tyndale, *The Obedience of a Christen Man*, 1528.

God. For many other political thinkers, however, absolute monarchy continued to rest upon Divine Right. Kings were appointed by God and accountable only to Him. In the Church of England Order for Morning Prayer God was referred to as . . . *the only Ruler of princes* . . . and in 1610 James I summarized the theory for the benefit of his English Parliament:

> The state of Monarchy is the supremest thing upon earth; for kings are not only God's lieutenants upon earth and sit upon God's throne, but even by God they are called gods. . . . And though no Christian man ought to allow any rebellion of people against their Prince, yet doth God never leave kings unpunished when they transgress these limits . . . it is sedition in subjects to dispute what a king may do in the height of his power; but just kings will ever be willing to declare what they will do, if they will not incur the curse of God.

The current was running strongly in favour of absolute monarchy, whether divinely ordained or humanly constructed, and only a religious motive was strong enough to enable men to stand against it. Catholicism had always placed at least theological limits on the power of the ruler, but at first Protestants had tended to preach a doctrine of non-resistance to authority. Luther had declared

> I would rather suffer a prince doing wrong than a people doing right.

Calvin had preached passive obedience to even the worst of rulers, who must be regarded as a punishment imposed on the people for their sins:

> The most wicked kings are placed on their thrones by the same law which has established the authority of all kings.

Under the stress of persecution both Lutherans and Calvinists soon developed a theory of conditional, active resistance. The Lutherans of Magdeburg were the first to state the theory in 1550 when the Emperor Charles V, apparently all-powerful after the battle of Mühlberg, was attempting to impose his religious peace on the Empire.[1] Although sovereignty is given

---

[1] See Chapter V.

by God it is not therefore unlimited.   When the ruler behaves
unjustly he may be resisted, since God has invested him with
authority for the sake of justice.   Therefore if he threatens the
life, liberty or property of his subjects unjustly he may be
resisted, though the subject has not a positive duty to do so.
If he threatens the true religion, then resistance becomes a
duty.

Calvinists, not Lutherans, suffered in the second half of the
sixteenth century, and they quickly adopted the political
philosophy outlined in the Declaration of Magdeburg.   In
Scotland John Knox thundered:

> It is blasphemy to say that God hath commanded kings
> to be obeyed when they command impiety.

In France the anonymous author of the *Vindiciae contra
Tyrannos* (1578) writes of kings as God's viceroys, but viceroys
who are entitled to obedience only so long as they serve the
purposes for which they were called into existence.   The
author describes sovereignty as created by a pact between the
ruler and the people – the contractual theory in fact.   The
ruler has a duty to maintain the true religion; to enforce the
existing laws and not to alter them except with the agreement of
the people, and to rule so as to promote the natural (moral)
law.   If the ruler fails in any of these duties, the community
has itself a duty to remove him.   This must not be done by
private individuals, but by the 'magistrates'.

This doctrine passes over from theory to practice in 1581
in the political Act of Abjuration of the States-General of the
United Provinces:

> When, therefore, the prince does not fulfill his duty as
> protector;   when he oppresses his subjects, destroyes their
> ancient liberties, and treats them as slaves, he is to be con-
> sidered not a prince, but a tyrant.   As such, the estates of
> the land may lawfully and reasonably depose him, and elect
> another in his room.

In practice, Calvinism became increasingly linked with
attacks on the power of the absolute monarch, since Calvinism
had always implied that the Church was independent of, and
superior to, the state.   It was this aspect that James I had in
mind when he burst out at the Hampton Court Conference of
1604:

. . . a Scottish presbytery . . . as well agreeth with a monarchy as God and the Devil. Then Jack and Tom and Will and Dick shall meet, and at their pleasures censure me and my Counsil and all our proceedings . . . I know what would become of my Supremacy, for *No Bishop, No King*.

From the other side of the religious fence, too, came attacks on the doctrine of absolute sovereignty. These were made largely by Jesuit writers, their object being to assert the right of Catholics to rebel and even in some cases to depose heretic rulers, and to remind monarchs that their temporal powers were limited by the spiritual overlordship of the Pope. With such aims writers like Mariana (*De rege et regis institutionae*, 1589), Bellarmine and Suarez reached positions indistinguishable from those occupied by extreme Calvinists. Once more James I summed up the situation, saying pithily: 'Jesuits are nothing but Puritan-papists.'

And so it came about that, while the efforts of *Politique* statesmen (who believed in the absolute power of the state) led to a measure of religious toleration, the efforts of religious extremists (who believed in the absolute power of the church) led to a measure of political freedom!

Science

The scientific beliefs of the later Middle Ages and the picture of the universe which followed from those beliefs rested, in general, on the writings of Aristotle (384–322 B.C.), modified, so far as the system of the universe was concerned, by the amendments of later Greeks embodied in the *Almagest* of Ptolemy (second century A.D.). Some of Aristotle had been available in the west from the sixth century, but his scientific works reached the west through the Arabs, largely by way of Toledo, in the twelfth century. Viewed at first with suspicion, the greater part of Aristotle's theories were made acceptable to the Catholic world by St. Thomas Aquinas (1225–74) in his works of synthesis, the *Summa Theologica* and the *Summa contra Gentiles*. By the fourteenth century Aristotle had come to be accepted as 'The Philosopher'; in the words of Dante, 'the master of those who know'.

There were both advantages and disadvantages in the uncritical acceptance of everything in Aristotle which did not directly conflict with Christian teaching. His object had been to describe the qualities of things in a universe that did not change. The virtues of this approach were that the resulting description was complete, self-contained, neat and logical. The disadvantages were that it took no account of quantity or of development, and disregarded the possibility of a mathematical description of the world. For Aristotle things are as they are because that is their nature. There is no room for questions of causation – the problem of why things behave as they do. For him there was no problem: things behave as they do because that is part of their nature.

Aristotle's explanation of motion, and his description of the universe, were the two parts of his scientific thought that were most affected by the new developments of the sixteenth and seventeenth centuries and they were eventually seen to be two aspects of the same problem. These developments were themselves the most important aspects of the scientific revolution which began then.

Take first the question of motion. A stone, Aristotle would have said, falls to the ground because to fall downwards is one of the properties inherent in being a stone. This obviously closes the door to further inquiry. The Aristotelian explanation ran as follows. The 'natural motion of a heavy body was towards the centre of the universe, located for Aristotle at the centre of the earth'. Motion in any other direction was 'violent' – that is, unnatural – motion. It was 'natural' for a body to come to rest as soon as possible, and it was therefore always motion which had to be accounted for. Like so much of Aristotle's teaching, this is a common-sense explanation: it fits the observed facts of everyday life, for things do come to rest when we stop pushing them.

The Aristotelian view of the construction of the universe was that, fixed at the centre, was the earth together with its surrounding envelopes containing the other three 'elements' of water, fire and air. Outside this complex were eight transparent spheres in each of which was embedded, counting outwards from the earth, one of the following 'planets': the Moon, Mercury, Venus, the Sun, Mars, Jupiter, Saturn and the fixed stars. Beyond was the *primum mobile* which kept these spheres in motion round the earth.

Unfortunately, the planets do not appear to move in circles, as this explanation required them to do, but wander about the sky in a most erratic way. (The word 'planet' comes from the Greek for 'wanderer'). To deal with this difficulty Greek astronomers were compelled to modify Aristotle's model almost at once. They suggested that the planets revolved in small circles around a centre which itself revolved around the earth (*epicycles*) or around a centre close to the earth. By introducing modifications of this sort, the observed movements of the planets could always be explained, but the explanation itself began to involve a great deal of complicated celestial machinery. This modified system, described by Ptolemy, was the one accepted by the Catholic Church, with the addition of Heaven, which was placed beyond the *primum mobile*, outside both space and time.

Aquinas had hardly made Aristotle respectable before the latter's views on motion came under attack from a number of thinkers who adopted just that experimental or mathematical approach to their investigations that had been disregarded by him.

It is important to realize that a scientific attitude was not unknown in the later Middle Ages. The thirteenth century has been called 'a century tormented by doubt', and some of this intellectual questioning took the form of experiments (Albertus Magnus, besides more orthodox inquiries, tested experimentally the apparently unlikely story that ostriches could eat metal objects). The fourteenth century saw the beginnings of a mathematical analysis of the nature of things. Much of this work was carried out by Franciscans working at Oxford or Paris – men such as William of Occam (*c.* 1300–49), Jean Buridan (d. *c.* 1359), and Nicholas Oresme (d. 1382). It was William of Occam who laid down the general philosophical principle that the simplest hypothesis that fits all the facts should be preferred to any more complicated one. This, the basis of modern scientific reasoning, became known as 'Occam's razor'. His own words were: 'It is pointless to do with more what can be done with less.'

Buridan investigated two forms of motion; the behaviour of projectiles, and of falling bodies. (This was the century in which cannon first made their appearance.) According to Aristotle the potentiality for movement was contained in an object, but could only be made active by contact with a motive force – for instance, a hand throwing a stone. To explain why the stone continued to move after it had left the hand, Aristotle assumed that the hand passed on the power of being a mover to the air touching it, this air passed it on to the next layer of air and so on, until the power gradually decayed. In a vacuum a stone would be unable to behave as a projectile. With regard to falling bodies, Aristotle taught that heavier bodies fell faster than lighter bodies of the same shape and size. Acceleration he explained as due to the increasing joy a body experienced as it got nearer and nearer to its natural resting place. In a vacuum a stone would fall with an infinite velocity. All these explanations were wrong.

Buridan introduced the idea of *impetus*, which proved to be the clue to the right answers. Thus a projectile was given impetus by the motive force, and this would carry it forward with a uniform velocity but for the fact that this *impetus* was gradually destroyed by the resistance of the air and by a tendency to fall to earth:

> The *impetus* would last indefinitely if it were not diminished by a resisting contrary, or by an inclination to a contrary motion; and in celestial motion there is no resisting contrary. . . .[1]

Projectiles in the heavens and upon earth were thus made to obey the same laws, which affected both the stars in their courses and the paths of cannon-balls.

In the case of a falling body Buridan held that the velocity increased as gravity provided successive additions of *impetus*, and concluded by saying:

> One can, I think, accept this explanation because the other explanations do not appear to be true whereas all the phenomena accord with this one.[2]

Nevertheless, it was three centuries before the argument was developed to its mathematical conclusion. The next step was not taken until the middle of the sixteenth century. There was a general pause in the progress of scientific reasoning. The causes of this are obscure, but certainly the fourteenth century lacked both an intellectual and a technical stimulus. The

[1] A. C. Crombie, *Augustine to Galileo*, Falcon Press, 1952, p. 253.
[2] Crombie, p. 251.

world-picture provided by the Church gave no encouragement to abstract speculation, while the absence of technical change resulted in a lack of any incentive to consider new practical problems.   The work done so far had been carried out by men 'playing on the margin', in Professor Butterfield's illuminating phrase, of the Aristotelian system.

In the next century the Renaissance, in its intellectual aspect, was concerned with words and authorities rather than with physics or engineering; Italian humanism was the last of the scholastic philosophies.   The texts recovered by the scholars certainly played their part in later scientific developments – there is a connection between the renewed reverence for Plato and the work of Copernicus, for instance – and the critical attitude to authorities helped to weaken the foundations of the Aristotelian system.   In general, though, the Italian Renaissance was characterized by the growth of superstition, and by an interest in astrology rather than astronomy.   There were scientific thinkers, men like Leonardo, and Nicholas of Cusa (1401–64) (who, among other matters, described an experiment by which men might 'attain to know the weight of air'), but they were men brooding in isolation.

So far as the problems connected with motion were concerned, the next important step was taken by a Polish canon, Copernicus (1473–1543).   He was interested in producing a simpler model of the universe than the modified Aristotle one. He developed the first outline of his hypothesis between 1506 and 1512, but it was not till 1543 that his work on the *Revolution of the Heavenly Spheres* was published.   He seems to have been restrained by fear of ridicule, rather than of persecution, from making his views known earlier.   In his dedication to Pope Paul III he wrote:

> And though the idea appeared absurd, yet I knew that others before me had been allowed freedom to imagine what circles they pleased in order to represent the phenomena of the heavenly bodies. I, therefore, deemed that it would readily be granted to me also to try whether, by assuming the Earth to have a certain motion, representations more valid than those of others could be found for the revolution of the heavenly spheres.
>
> And so, having assumed those motions which I attribute

to the Earth . . . the order of succession and the dimensions of the planets, and of all the spheres, and the heaven itself, would be so bound together that in no part could anything be transposed without the disordering of the other parts and of the entire Universe.[1]

Two words are significant 'order' and 'spheres'. Copernicus's aim was not to replace the Aristotelian system, but to make the explanation of it more orderly. He kept the spheres, but placed at the centre of the universe a stationary sun, around which he allowed the Aristotelian system to revolve. The earth now moved in that sphere formerly occupied by the sun, and the moon moved round the earth, so that the order was as follows: fixed Sun, Mercury, Venus, Earth and Moon, Mars, Jupiter, Saturn, fixed stars.

Copernicus's work was thus one of adaptation rather than creation. The paths of the planets were simpler if looked at from the sun instead of from the earth, and he was able to reduce the number of circles required to describe these paths from eighty to thirty-four. That was the extent of 'the Copernican revolution'. His outlook was medieval, except in this desire for mathematical simplicity and economy; and even in that he had been anticipated by William of Occam.

Yet it was a revolution. Copernicus had displaced the earth from the centre of the universe and he had destroyed the Aristotelian system. If one accepted his model, other consequences followed. The most startling referred to the position of the fixed stars. If the earth moved in a great circle round the sun, as Copernicus said it did, then the position of the stars should differ if viewed from opposite sides of this circle (annual parallax). No difference could be found. This meant either that Copernicus was wrong, or that the stars were immensely far away. Most people naturally accepted the first explanation. Luther and Calvin both rejected his hypothesis. The former called him '. . . an ass who wants to overturn the whole art of astronomy and deny what is said in the book of Joshua'. In the next century Francis Bacon, who had in many ways a most advanced scientific outlook, admired the economy of Copernicus's theory, but rejected it as false all the same.

[1] A. Armstrong, *Copernicus and the Reformation of Astronomy* (Historical Association Pamphlet, G. 15, 1950, p. 14).

The universe had begun to expand, but it was not for another ninety years, until Aristotelian physics had been destroyed and the Copernican system modified, that men were forced to choose between the scientific and theological descriptions of it.

The next step was taken by the Danish astronomer, Tycho Brahe (1546–1601). He was no theorist (his planetary hypothesis was much further from the mark than that of Copernicus), but he was a painstaking, systematic observer, using more accurate instruments – that is, larger ones, his quadrant had a radius of nineteen feet! A body of exact observational data was exactly what was needed. Two astronomical events helped to weaken the Aristotelian system. In 1572 a new star blazed out in the sky, shone for about eighteen months, and then disappeared. Brahe's observations showed that it must be farther away than the moon – but Aristotle had said that beyond the moon the universe was unchanging. Then, in 1577, a comet was observed, the track of which lay beyond the sun. How did it manage to pass through Aristotle's crystal spheres?

Brahe's assistant, Johann Kepler (1571–1630), inherited his colleague's records. They showed that the Copernican system might be right in essentials, but required modification in detail. Kepler was an odd mixture. He believed in the magic of numbers and the music of the spheres, yet he saw through astrology ('Astrology', he wrote, 'is the foolish daughter of a wise mother, and this wise mother could not have survived the last hundred years without the aid of her foolish daughter') and made an important mathematical contribution to the new view of the universe. This was contained in his three laws of planetary motion, worked out between 1609 and 1619. The first law stated that the planets moved in ellipses, with the sun at one focus. This was the last nail in the coffin of the idea that heavenly bodies must move in 'perfect' circles. The second law stated that a line joining the planet to the sun would sweep over equal areas in equal intervals of time. This implied that the planet's velocity varied, being greatest, naturally, when the planet was nearest to the sun. The third law compared the movements of the planets one with another; it stated that the square of the time taken by a planet to revolve around the sun is directly proportional to the cube of its average distance from the sun. It was with the help of this third law that Newton was able to show that his theory of gravitation applied to the solar system. The music of the spheres had become the mathematics of the universe.

It was Galileo, born in 1564, the year of Michelangelo's death, and dying in 1642, the year when Newton was born, who completed the destruction of the Aristotelian system – and he did it by means of mathematics. He was able to marry mechanics to astronomy and to interpret both in terms of mathematics. The understanding of nature through mathematics was the hallmark of the followers of Plato. The Aristotelian view was put by Galileo into the mouth of Simplicio in his *Dialogue on the Two Principal World Systems* (1632):

> The mathematical subtleties are true in the abstract, but they do not hold good when applied to the physical matter of our senses. The mathematicians may prove well enough, for instance, that a sphere touches a plane in a point. But when one comes to the matter, things turn out quite another way.

Galileo's own view (and it is the mathematical, the Platonist view) was:

> Philosophy is written in this grand book the universe, which stands continually open to our gaze. But the book cannot be understood unless one first learns to understand the language and to know the letters in which it is written. . . . It is written in the language of mathematics, and the letters are triangles, circles, and other geometrical figures, without which it is humanly impossible to understand a single word.

These sentences echo Leonardo da Vinci's earlier statement of faith:

> No human investigation can be called true science without passing through mathematical tests. . . .

Galileo's mathematics is not pure mathematics, but an instrument to be used to explain the physical world:

> Any one [he writes] may invent an arbitrary type of motion . . . but I have decided to consider the phenomena of bodies falling with an acceleration such as occurs in nature.

Galileo was born in Pisa and early in his life lectured at the university there.　In 1592 he moved to the university at Padua, then part of the republic of Venice.　In 1610 he left Padua and came to Florence, where he lived under the patronage of the Grand Duke of Tuscany.　His reasons for moving are interesting:

It is impossible to obtain from a Republic, however splendid and generous, a stipend without duties attached to it; for to have anything from the public one must work for the public. . . . I have no hope of enjoying such ease and leisure as are necessary to me, except in the service of an absolute prince.

Galileo's work on mechanics is contained in his *Dialogues Concerning Two New Sciences*, which was published at Leyden in 1638, but was based on work done much earlier.　The *Dialogues* were concerned with dynamics – the behaviour of pendulums, projectiles and falling bodies.　His conclusions are based on a series of carefully controlled experiments, often repeated and accurately observed.　In the case of falling bodies they took the form of rolling 'a hard, smooth, and very round bronze ball' down a smooth wooden trough twelve cubits long. Incidentally, to measure accurately the time taken for the ball to reach the end of the trough from different points along its length and at different elevations, Galileo was still forced to use a waterclock.

Galileo's conclusions in the *Dialogues* were revolutionary. With regard to motion in general he held that all moving terrestrial bodies would continue to move in a straight line with uniform velocity, unless their velocity or direction was altered by the action of some external force (in the case of a rolling ball, friction, air resistance and the downward pull of gravity).　This was the exact converse of the Aristotelian view.　With regard to falling bodies, he established the law that when a body falls its velocity increases at a constant rate, and thus the acceleration is the same for all bodies.　(In actual practice their rate of fall will depend on the extent of the air resistance which they encounter, but in a vacuum the acceleration will always be thirty-two feet per second per second.)　With regard to projectiles, Galileo showed that their path would be that of a parabola, a compound movement which was the resultant of a constant horizontal movement forwards and a vertical acceleration downwards.

These conclusions destroyed Aristotelian dynamics. More dramatic, though less fundamentally important, was Galileo's astronomical work. In 1609 he heard that the Dutch had developed a telescope. He worked out the principles on which it must be constructed and within a year he had made one 'which enabled me to see objects almost a thousand times as large and only one-thirtieth of the distance in comparison with their appearance to the naked eye'. This he demonstrated to the Venetian government:

> Many gentlemen and senators, even the oldest, have ascended at various times the highest bell-towers in Venice, to spy out ships at sea making sail for the mouth of a harbour, and have seen them clearly, though without my telescope they would have been invisible for more than two hours. . . .

It was soon after this that Galileo moved to Florence. From his observatory there he saw the moons of Jupiter (he called them the 'Medicean satellites' in honour of his patron), the craters of the moon, sunspots and the phases of Venus. At every point these observations supported the modified Copernican model of the universe. The Professor of Philosophy at Padua tried, as Galileo said, 'to charm the new planets out of the sky' by logical arguments to show that they could not possibly be there. The Roman Inquisition took action against the Copernican theory, condemning it as 'foolish and absurd philosophically, and formally heretical, since it expressly contradicts the doctrines of Holy Scripture in many places' (1616).

In 1632 Galileo published his *Dialogue on the Two Principal World Systems*. In it he showed the experimental, and therefore logical, weaknesses in the Aristotelian system. In the following year he was called before the Inquisition and, under threat of torture, recanted. He was ordered to recite the seven penitential psalms every week for three years and, after several months' detention, was allowed to live in seclusion near Florence. The Catholic Church was not alone in condemning him. For example, in 1634 the new Dutch university at Utrecht, rejected his argument 'as contrary to Scripture and Reason'. Nothing could now prevent the victory of the new astronomy, however, and in the second half of the century the line of thought that we have traced was completed in the synthesis of Newton (1642–1747).

The great discoveries in the other branches of science occurred a little later than the advances in physics, and belong to the history of the later seventeenth century. Meanwhile two writers profoundly affected the climate of scientific thought: Francis Bacon (1561–1626), who emphasized the importance of collecting and analysing evidence, and René Descartes (1596–1650), who was more concerned with methods of interpreting that evidence.

Bacon was a many-sided man, a lawyer who became Lord Chancellor, and hence an amateur in science. (William Harvey said that he always wrote on science like a Lord Chancellor.)   He was worried by the divorce between theory and experiment.   Philosophers, he felt, were like spiders, spinning theories out of their own private worlds, scientists were too often like ants, merely collecting and arranging material.   We must, he said, be like bees, which both collect and arrange.   Nothing must be taken on trust, we must avoid the worship of what he called 'Idols' – prejudices.   There are the 'idols of the tribe', prejudices common to all human nature; 'idols of the cave', prejudices peculiar to the individual investigator; 'idols of the marketplace', prejudices due to the inaccurate use of words; and 'idols of the theatre', prejudices due to the uncritical adoption of specific philosophies.   Bacon wanted to see scientific knowledge and research organized, and in the *New Atlantis* (1627) he described an imaginary institution, which he called 'Solomon's House', designed for this purpose. Bacon had his blind spots: he did not accept the Copernican theory, and he underestimated the part that could be played by mathematics in the interpretation of science; but he understood that the scientist must accept the world he is investigating – 'Nature to be commanded must be obeyed.'   Besides the *New Atlantis* his chief scientific writings were the *Advancement of Learning* (1605), and the *Novum Organum* (1620).

Descartes was a very different sort of person.   He was not, like Bacon, a man of the world.   (It has been said that he 'did most of his scientific work in bed'.)   He felt that the key to the universe lay in mathematics; he was 'converted' to this view in the same kind of way that Calvin was 'converted', by a sudden flash of insight, after which the world could never look the same. Descartes recorded the date, November 10 (1619), which he always kept as a sort of saint's day. He fled from France to Holland in 1629 and lived in the latter state for twenty years. Then, at the invitation of Queen Christina, he went to Sweden, and that indefatigable woman hastened his death by insisting on discussing philosophy with him at five o'clock in the morning. Descartes' key work is contained in his *Discourse on Method* (*Discours de la Méthode*), 1637.

Looking for a basis for philosophy, Descartes was determined to doubt everything that it was possible to doubt. This does not leave very much, but it does leave the doubt. To doubt is to think, to think implies a thinker. *Cogito ergo sum;* I think therefore I am. 'I judged,' wrote Descartes, 'that I could receive it as the first principle of the philosophy that I sought.' From this point he was able to move on to knowledge, and ultimately to a proof of the existence of God.

Included as an appendix to the *Discourse* was Descartes' other great contribution to seventeenth century thought, the severely practical invention of co-ordinate geometry; the algebraic treatment of geometrical ideas. Its importance lies in the fact that it is an instrument for solving problems connected with times and velocities – just those problems that, as we have seen, were central to the new physics.

In the seventeenth century the flood of scientific discoveries began to affect all branches of experimental knowledge. There is no room here to do more than indicate some of the pioneers: in chemistry van Helmont (1579–1644), and Boyle (1627–91), whose *Sceptical Chymist* was published in 1661; in biology and medicine, Vesalius (1514–64), Harvey (1578–1657), and Leeuwenhoek (1632–1723); in magnetism, Gilbert (*c.* 1540–1603). In their various ways these men were helped by, and helped to develop, new scientific techniques. In mathematics one may notice the first comprehensive printed algebra (1494); the development of decimals by Stevin (1585), and of logarithms by Napier (1614). The prototypes of many of the basic scientific instruments were constructed – the microscope (Holland, *c.* 1590); the telescope (Holland, 1608); the air thermometer (Italy, *c.* 1590); the barometer (Italy, *c.* 1640); the air-pump (Germany, *c.* 1650); the pendulum clock (Holland, *c.* 1650).

As scientific knowledge accumulated, scientific societies, where scientists and their patrons met to discuss the new discoveries, were set up. One of the earliest of these, and by far the most important, was the Royal Society. This had originated in weekly private meetings in London about 1645, and received its charter from Charles II in 1662. In the following year the President of the Royal Society, Robert Hooke, wrote:

> . . . this society will not own any hypothesis, system or doctrine of the principles of natural philosophy, proposed or mentioned by any philosopher ancient or modern, nor the explication of any phenomena whose recourse must be had to original causes (as not being explicable by heat, cold, weight, figure and the like as effects produced thereby); nor dogmatically define nor fix axioms of scientificall things, but will question and canvass all opinions, adopting nor adhering to none, till by mature debate and clear argument, chiefly such as are deduced from legitimate experiments, the truth of such experiments be demonstrated invincibly.

This emphasis on 'legitimate experiments' on which the 'axioms of scientificall things' shall be based, combined with a critical reading of 'any philosopher ancient or modern' – these were the legitimate standards of scientific inquiry which Galileo, Bacon and Descartes had, in their different ways, helped to establish.

The consequences of this scientific revolution were that the closed, fixed, harmonious order of medieval and early Renaissance thought was replaced by an open field for man's warfare against nature, in which the emphasis was on change and development. The spiritual world was sharply separated from the physical. The new outlook marks an important division in the history of Europe. Writing of the years around 1660, Professor Butterfield says:

> We may take the line that here, for practical purposes, our modern civilisation is coming out in a perceptible manner into the daylight. . . .

We know now that what was emerging towards the end of the seventeenth century was a civilisation exhilaratingly new perhaps, but strange as Nineveh and Babylon. That is why, since the rise of Christianity, there is no landmark in history that is worthy to be compared with this.[1]

For the scientific revolution was not all gain. Man learnt more about the universe and, paradoxically, the more he learnt, the stranger it became, and the more foreign to his experience:

> And new Philosophy calls all in doubt,
> The element of fire is quite put out;
> The Sun is lost, and th'earth, and no man's wit
> Can well direct him where to look for it.
> And freely men confess that this world's spent,
> When in the Planets, and the Firmament
> They seek so many new; then see that this
> Is crumbled out again to his Atomies.
> 'Tis all in pieces, all coherence gone;
> All just supply, and all Relation:
> Prince, Subject, Father, Son, are things forgot,
> For every man alone thinks he hath got
> To be a Phoenix, and that then can be
> None of that kind, of which he is, but he.

> (John Donne, *An Anatomy of the World*, 1610.)

EXTRACTS

1. *The author of the* Vindiciae contra Tyrannos *discusses limitations of the sovereign's power* (*1579*) :

. . . there are many princes in these days, calling themselves Christians, which arrogantly assume an unlimited power, over which God himself hath no command, and . . . they have no want of flatterers, which adore them as gods upon earth, many others also, which for fear, or by constraint, either seem, or else do believe, that princes ought to be obeyed in all things, and by all men. . . .

We have shewed before that it is God that does appoint kings, who chooses them, who gives the kingdom to them: now we say that the people establish kings, puts the sceptre into their hands, and who with their suffrages, approves the election. . . .

---

[1] H. Butterfield; *The Origins of Modern Science*, Bell, new edn. 1957, pp. 180 and 190.

Now, seeing that the people choose and establish their kings, it follows that the whole body of the people is above the king. . . .

Seeing then that kings are ordained by God, and established by the people, to procure and provide for the good of those who are committed unto them, and that this good or profit be principally expressed in two things, to wit, in the administration of justice to their subjects, and in the management of armies for repulsing their enemies: certainly, we must infer and conclude from this, that the prince who applied himself to nothing but his peculiar profits and pleasures . . . may truly and really be called a tyrant, and that those who in this manner govern their kingdoms, be they of never so large an extent, are more properly unjust pillagers and free-booters, than lawful governors. (*A Defence of Liberty Against Tyrants*, with an historical introduction by H. J. Laski, Bell, 1924, pp. 65, 118, 124, 143)

2. *Galileo recants before the Inquisition, 1633 :*

I bend my knee before the honourable Inquisitor-General, I touch the holy Gospel and give assurance that I believe, and always will believe, what the Church recognizes and teaches as true. I had been ordered by the holy Inquisition not to believe nor to teach the false theory of the motion of the Earth and the stationariness of the Sun because it is contrary to Holy Scripture. Nevertheless I wrote and published a book in which I expound this theory and advance strong grounds in its favour. I have consequently been pronounced suspect of heresy. Now, in order to remove every Catholic Christian's just suspicion of me, I abjure and curse the stated errors and heresies, and every other error and every opinion that is contrary to the teaching of the Church. I also swear that in future I will never, whether by written or spoken word, utter anything that may bring me again under suspicion. And I will immediately inform the holy tribunal if I see or suspect anything heretical anywhere. (Quoted by A. Wolf, *A History of Science, Technology and Philosophy in the Sixteenth and Seventeenth Centuries*, Allen & Unwin, 1935, p. 37)

3. *Galileo describes the experiment designed to measure the acceleration of falling bodies, 1636 :*

A piece of wooden moulding or scantling, about 12 cubits long, half a cubit wide, and three finger-breadths thick, was taken; on its edge was cut a channel a little more than one finger in breadth; having made this groove very straight, smooth, and polished, and having lined it with parchment, also as smooth and polished as possible, we rolled along it a hard, smooth, and very round bronze ball. Having placed this board in a sloping position, by lifting one end some one or two cubits above the other, we rolled the ball, as I was just saying, along the channel, noting, in a manner presently to be described, the time required to make the descent. We repeated this experiment more than once in order to measure the time with an accuracy such that the deviation between two observations never exceeded one-tenth of a pulse-beat. Having performed this operation and having assured ourselves of its reliability, we now rolled the ball only one-quarter the length of the channel; and, having measured the time of its descent, we found it precisely one-half of the former. Next we tried other distances . . . in such experiments, repeated a full hundred times, we always found that the spaces traversed were to each other as the squares of the times, and this was true for all inclinations of the plane. . . .

For the measurement of time, we employed a large vessel of water placed in an elevated position; to the bottom of this vessel was soldered a pipe of small diameter giving a thin jet of water, which we collected in a small glass during the time of each descent, whether for the whole length of the channel or for a part of its length; the water thus collected was weighed after each descent, on a very accurate balance; the differences and ratios of these weights gave us the differences and ratios of the times. . . . (*Dialogues Concerning Two New Sciences*, trans. H. Crew and A. de Salvio, Macmillan, 1914)

FURTHER READING

G. N. Clark, *The Seventeenth Century*, O.U.P., 1947

B. Willey, *The Seventeenth Century Background*, Chatto & Windus, 1934

E. Newton, *European Painting and Sculpture*, Penguin, 1941

N. Pevsner, *An Outline of European Architecture*, Penguin, 1950

G. H. Sabine, *A History of Political Theory*, Harrap, 1951, (Chapters XVII to XXIII)

J. Bowle, *Western Political Thought*, Cape, 1947, (Book Three, Chapters I to IV)

J. W. Allen, *A History of Political Thought in the Sixteenth Century*, Methuen, 1960

R. H. Tawney, *Religion and the Rise of Capitalism*, Murray, 1937

B. Russell, *A History of Western Philosophy*, Allen & Unwin, 1946

J. Lindsay, ed., *The History of Science*, London, 1951

J. Bronowski, *The Common-Sense of Science*, Heinemann, 1951

A. Hall, *The Scientific Revolution, 1500–1800*, Longmans, Green, 1954

H. Butterfield, *The Origins of Modern Science*, Bell, new edn., 1957

A. Wolf, *A History of Science, Technology and Philosophy in the Sixteenth and Seventeenth Centuries*, Allen & Unwin, 1935

A. C. Crombie, *Augustine to Galileo*, Falcon Press, 1952

A. Armitage, *Copernicus and the Reformation of Astronomy*, Historical Association, G.15, London, 1950

INDEX